W9-BXZ-627

Mike Meyers' CompTIA A+® Guide to Managing and Troubleshooting PCs Lab Manual

Third Edition

(Exams 220-701 & 220-702)

About the Authors

Mike Meyers, lovingly called the "AlphaGeek" by those who know him, is the industry's leading authority on CompTIA A+ certification. He is the president and co-founder of Total Seminars, LLC, a provider of PC and network repair seminars, books, videos, and courseware for thousands of organizations throughout the world. Mike has been involved in the computer and network repair industry since 1977 as a technician, instructor, author, consultant, and speaker. Author of numerous popular PC books and videos, Mike is also the series editor for the highly successful Mike Meyers' Certification Passport series, the Mike Meyers' Computer Skills series, and the Mike Meyers' Guide To series, all published by McGraw-Hill.

Debby Hallcom is an educator and lover of technology who has taught CompTIA A+ certification courses for the past six years while working to improve the IT curriculum and how it is taught. Exposure to the world of technology in the 1980s led her to a life of teaching today. A believer in "customized training," she has developed courses and other materials to help teachers integrate technology into their classrooms. Debby has chaired CompTIA's E2C (Education to Careers) Secondary Advisory Council and currently teaches Computer Systems Technology at Highland Springs Technical Center, helping students learn to use technology as an essential part of their lives.

About the Technical Editor

Christopher A. Crayton (MCSE, MCP+I, CompTIA A+, CompTIA Network+) is an author, technical editor, technical consultant, security consultant, and trainer. Formerly a computer and networking instructor at Keiser College (2001 Teacher of the Year), Chris has also worked as network administrator for Protocol and at Eastman Kodak Headquarters as a computer and network specialist. Chris has authored several print and online books on topics ranging from CompTIA A+ and CompTIA Security+ to Microsoft Windows Vista. Chris has provided technical edits and reviews for many publishers, including McGraw-Hill, Pearson Education, Charles River Media, Cengage Learning, Wiley, O'Reilly, Syngress, and Apress.

Mike Meyers' CompTIA A+® Guide to Managing and Troubleshooting PCs Lab Manual

Third Edition

(Exams 220-701 & 220-702)

Mike Meyers
Debby Hallcom

New York Chicago San Francisco
Lisbon London Madrid Mexico City
Milan New Delhi San Juan
Seoul Singapore Sydney Toronto

The McGraw·Hill Companies

Library of Congress Cataloging-in-Publication Data

Meyers, Michael, 1961-

Mike Meyers' CompTIA A+ guide to managing and troubleshooting PCs lab manual
(exams 220-701 & 220-702) / Mike Meyers, Debby Hallcom. — 3rd ed.
        p.   cm.
Includes index.
ISBN 978-0-07-170299-7 (alk. paper)
1. Microcomputers—Maintenance and repair—Examinations—Study guides. I. Hallcom, Debby. II. Title.
III. Title: A+ guide to managing and troubleshooting PCs lab manual.
TK7887.M46   2010
621.39'160288—dc22   2010012159

McGraw-Hill books are available at special quantity discounts to use as premiums and sales promotions, or for use in corporate training programs. To contact a representative, please e-mail us at bulksales@mcgraw-hill.com.

**Mike Meyers' CompTIA A+® Guide to Managing and Troubleshooting PCs Lab Manual,
Third Edition (Exams 220-701 & 220-702)**

Copyright © 2010 by The McGraw-Hill Companies. All rights reserved. Printed in the United States of America. Except as permitted under the Copyright Act of 1976, no part of this publication may be reproduced or distributed in any form or by any means, or stored in a database or retrieval system, without the prior written permission of publisher, with the exception that the program listings may be entered, stored, and executed in a computer system, but they may not be reproduced for publication.

All trademarks or copyrights mentioned herein are the possession of their respective owners and McGraw-Hill makes no claim of ownership by the mention of products that contain these marks.

23456789 WDQ WDQ 1543210

ISBN   978-0-07-170299-7
MHID   0-07-170299-7

Sponsoring Editor Timothy Green	**Technical Editor** Christopher Crayton	**Production Supervisor** George Anderson
Editorial Supervisor Janet Walden	**Copy Editor** William McManus	**Composition** Glyph International
Project Manager Harleen Chopra, Glyph International	**Proofreader** Claire Splan	**Illustration** Glyph International
Acquisitions Coordinator Meghan Riley	**Indexer** Claire Splan	**Art Director, Cover** Jeff Weeks

Information has been obtained by McGraw-Hill from sources believed to be reliable. However, because of the possibility of human or mechanical error by our sources, McGraw-Hill, or others, McGraw-Hill does not guarantee the accuracy, adequacy, or completeness of any information and is not responsible for any errors or omissions or the results obtained from the use of such information.

McGraw-Hill is an independent entity from CompTIA. This publication may be used in assisting students to prepare for the CompTIA A+ Exams. Neither CompTIA nor McGraw-Hill warrants that use of this publication will ensure passing any exam. CompTIA is a registered trademark of CompTIA in the United States and/or other countries.

*This book is dedicated to students young and old,
and to Debby's students in particular.*

　　—Mike Meyers

*I dedicate this book to my current and future students
that choose to keep up with the hustle and bustle of
the CompTIA A+ curriculum while striving to make
their dreams come true. I say every year that I never
know when I'll be teaching the next Bill Gates and
hope one day that I will see many of your names
highlighted for technology accomplishments and
whatever it is the future holds.*

*I could not have completed this book without divine
intervention; the direct support of my awesome
principal, Johnnie Collie, and co-teacher, B.J. Crowder;
and of course the love and understanding of my
number one supporter and fan, my best friend and
husband, David Hallcom.*

　　—Debby Hallcom

Contents at a Glance

Contents

Acknowledgments

Many great people worked together to make this book happen.

As our sponsoring editor at McGraw-Hill, Tim Green did a great job keeping us focused on task with words of encouragement. Thanks, Tim!

Our Editor in Chief at Total Seminars, Scott Jernigan, performed his usual magic, especially in the early stages of the writing. Aaron Verber came in and did an outstanding job editing and proofing as well.

Also at Total Seminars, Dudley Lehmer took off his CEO hat and put on his managing editor hat while Mike and Scott went off to teach in the middle of the project, keeping the process going. Michael Smyer provided excellent photographs, and Ford Pierson lent his able hands to the editing and illustrating tasks.

On the McGraw-Hill side, our editorial supervisor, Janet Walden, managed our global team with grace and style. Meghan Riley, our acquisitions coordinator, did an outstanding job as usual with pieces and people.

Our project manager, Harleen Chopra, and her team at Glyph International, handled both copyediting and layout and excelled at both tasks. To the copy editor, proofreader, and the compositors—Bill McManus, Claire Splan, and the folks at Glyph—thank you!

Additional Resources for Teachers

The answer keys to the lab manual activities in this book are provided along with the resources for teachers using *Mike Meyers' CompTIA A+® Guide to Managing and Troubleshooting PCs, Third Edition (Exams 220-701 & 220-702)*. The answer keys are provided via an Online Learning Center that follows the organization of the textbook and the lab manual.

For instructor and student resources, check out www.mhaplusolc.com. Students using *Mike Meyers' CompTIA A+® Guide to Managing and Troubleshooting PCs, Third Edition (Exams 220-701 & 220-702)* will find chapter quizzes that will help you learn more about troubleshooting and fixing networks, and teachers can access support materials.

Chapter 1
The Path of the PC Tech

Lab Exercises

Well, now you've really done it. The fact that you hold this lab manual in your hands says one thing loud and clear—you're deadly serious about getting that CompTIA A+ certification! Good. Even though the CompTIA A+ certification exams are considered entry-level, you still need to take them seriously if you want to pass.

Because you're serious, I'm going to let you in on a secret: The key to passing these exams is preparation. When I say "preparation," I'm not talking about studying—although of course studying is important! I'm talking about *preparing to study*. You need to know exactly how to study for these exams, and you need to have the right tools to get that studying done. Sure, you have a textbook and a lab manual, but you're not yet ready to hit the books.

In this chapter, you'll go through the steps you need to take to start studying for the CompTIA A+ exams. First, you'll organize what you need to study. Second, you'll learn how the CompTIA A+ certification helps move you toward more advanced certifications. Finally, you'll get some ideas on how to gather equipment so that you can reinforce what you read with real hardware and software. So stay serious, roll up your sleeves, and start preparing to study for the CompTIA A+ exams!

 60 MINUTES

Lab Exercise 1.01: Preparing to Study

If you're a child of the TV age—and who isn't these days?—then you might have heard of a TV show called *The A-Team* starring George Peppard and Mr. T. Okay, so maybe it wasn't the greatest TV show, but I always remember one line from this show: "I love it when a plan comes together!" That's how you should feel as you get ready to become CompTIA A+ certified. In fact, just for fun, let's call ourselves the "A+ Team" as we put a plan together to knock that test right into next week's episode!

Learning Objectives

This lab helps you lay out a logical path for your studies. To do this, you need to deal with three issues: determining your weak points, checking your study habits, and scheduling the exam.

At the end of this lab, you'll be able to

- Identify the CompTIA A+ topics you need to learn
- Develop a good study plan
- Understand how to schedule the CompTIA A+ exams

Lab Materials and Setup

The materials you need for this lab are

- A PC with Internet access
- A telephone

Getting Down to Business

Total Seminars has been teaching CompTIA A+ certification for years, and we've developed a handy template to help you determine what you need to study and how much time you need to devote to preparing for the CompTIA A+ exams. This is the same table shown in the *Mike Meyers' CompTIA A+ Guide to Managing and Troubleshooting PCs* textbook, but with an extra step added to help you determine the topics you need to study.

Step 1   For each skill listed in the table that follows, circle the number that corresponds to the amount of experience you have: None, Once or Twice, Every Now and Then, or Quite a Bit. You'll use that number to calculate the total number of hours you have to study for the exams.

Technical Task	Amount of Experience			
	None	**Once or Twice**	**Every Now and Then**	**Quite a Bit**
Installing an adapter card	12	10	8	4
Installing and configuring hard drives	12	10	8	2
Installing modems and network interface cards (NICs)	8	6	6	3
Connecting a computer to the Internet	8	6	4	2
Installing printers and scanners	4	3	2	1
Installing random access memory (RAM)	8	6	4	2
Installing central processing units (CPUs)	8	7	5	3

Technical Task	Amount of Experience			
	None	Once or Twice	Every Now and Then	Quite a Bit
Fixing printers	6	5	4	3
Fixing boot problems	8	7	7	5
Fixing portable computers	8	6	4	2
Building complete systems	12	10	8	6
Using the command line	8	8	6	4
Installing/optimizing Windows	10	8	6	4
Using Windows 2000/XP	6	6	4	2
Using Windows Vista	10	8	4	2
Configuring NTFS permissions	6	4	3	2
Configuring a wireless network	6	5	3	2
Configuring a software firewall	6	4	2	1
Installing a sound card	2	2	1	0
Removing malware	4	3	2	0
Using operating system diagnostic tools	8	8	6	4
Using a Volt-Ohm Meter (VOM)	4	3	2	1

Great! You now have a good feel for the topics you need to study. Now you need to determine the total study time. First, add up the numbers you've circled. Then add the result to the number from the following table that corresponds to your experience. The grand total is the number of hours you should study to be ready for the exams.

If you have this much direct, professional experience . . .	Add this number of hours to your study time
0	50
Up to 6 months	30
6 to 12 months	10
More than 12 months	0

A total neophyte usually needs around 200 hours of study time. An experienced technician shouldn't need more than 40 hours.

The total number of hours for you to study is _____.

Step 2   Go to the Computing Technology Industry Association (CompTIA) Web site and download a copy of the exam objectives for both the CompTIA A+ Essentials (exam code 220-701) and the CompTIA A+ Practical Application (exam code 220-702) exams. As of this writing, you can find them here:

www.comptia.org/certifications/testprep/examobjectives.aspx

You have to fill out a short form (requiring your name, e-mail address, country of residence, and how soon you'll be testing) before you can view the objectives. Bear in mind, however, that CompTIA changes its Web site more often than TV networks invent new reality shows, so be prepared to poke around if necessary! Compare the circled areas on the preceding form to the CompTIA A+ exam objectives. Note that any single topic on the form covers more than one objective on the CompTIA A+ exams. Circle the objectives that you think parallel the weak areas you circled on the form, and don't be afraid to add or remove circles after you've seen the CompTIA A+ exam objectives in detail.

Step 3   Now that you know what topics are most important to you and how much time you need to devote to studying them, you need to develop your study plan. Take the amount of time you've set aside and determine how many days you have to prepare. Consider work, holidays, weekends, and anything else that will affect your study time. If you're in an instructor-led course, then this part is easy—just use the end of the course! Then break down your textbook into manageable chunks. Again, if you're in a course, then your instructor will already have done this for you. You now have your deadline—the day you'll say, "I'm ready to take the exams!"

Step 4   Go online and schedule your exams with either Prometric (www.prometric.com) or Pearson VUE (www.vue.com). You'll almost certainly need to make a phone call to do this. Make sure you have both a method of payment (credit cards are preferred) and some form of identification when you call. In the United States you need your Social Security number to schedule CompTIA exams. It's very important that you schedule your exams *now*—setting a test date early in the process will help motivate you to study, and keep you from procrastinating!

✔ **Cross-Reference**

For details about taking the CompTIA A+ exams, go to the CompTIA Web site (www.comptia.org).

60 MINUTES

Lab Exercise 1.02: Considering Other Certifications

CompTIA A+ certification may be your first certification, but it certainly should not be your last! The information technology (IT) industry considers obtaining certifications an ongoing process, one that continues as long as you're working in the IT field. You need to appreciate how the CompTIA A+ certification leads into other certifications.

Learning Objectives

This lab helps you learn about the various IT certifications that are available, and how they fit with both your skills and aptitude.

At the end of this lab, you'll be able to

- Understand some of the more common certifications that follow the CompTIA A+ certification

- Plan in what order you might attain those certifications

Lab Materials and Setup

The materials you need for this lab are

- A PC with Internet access

Getting Down to Business

It's time to jump onto the Internet and do a little research! You'll tour some of the more popular IT certifications and see how CompTIA A+ helps you gain these more advanced certifications.

✔ **Cross-Reference**

To review the exam objectives of each CompTIA A+ exam, refer to "The Basic Exam Structure" in Chapter 1 of *Mike Meyers' CompTIA A+ Guide to Managing and Troubleshooting PCs.*

Step 1   Fire up a Web browser and go to the CompTIA Web site (www.comptia.org). CompTIA offers many other certifications related to the IT field, so take some time to research their certification offerings, such as:

- CompTIA Network+ (www.comptia.org/certifications/listed/network.aspx)

- CompTIA Server+ (www.comptia.org/certifications/listed/server.aspx)

- CompTIA Security+ (www.comptia.org/certifications/listed/security.aspx)

CompTIA strongly recommend CompTIA A+ and then CompTIA Network+ as a clear pathway to certification. Why do you think they do that? Would you take CompTIA Security+ before or after CompTIA Network+?

Step 2   Head over to the Microsoft Certifications site and explore the FAQs section:

www.microsoft.com/learning/en/us/certification/cert-get-started.aspx

Then go here:

www.microsoft.com/learning/en/us/certification/cert-overview.aspx

Hover your mouse pointer over the various tabs available, such as By Product/Technology or By Name, and examine the many Microsoft tracks available. In your opinion, would it make sense to take these certifications before getting your CompTIA A+ certification?

Step 3   Go to the Cisco Web site (www.cisco.com); click on the Career Certifications and Paths button under the Training & Events dropdown menu; and research the Cisco Certified Network Associate (CCNA), Cisco Certified Network Professional (CCNP), and Cisco Certified Internetwork Expert (CCIE) certifications. Compare the CCNA to the CompTIA Network+. How are they different?

Step 4   Now that you've seen the more common certifications that follow the CompTIA A+, chart out your next three certifications and explain why you chose them.

 TIMES WILL VARY

Lab Exercise 1.03: Gathering Equipment

Although it's theoretically possible to obtain your CompTIA A+ certification by doing nothing but reading books, you'll be far better prepared for the real world if you get your hands on some real equipment so that you can practice. You also need some tools so you can take things apart—and put them back together. Finally, you need some operating system software, in particular Windows 2000, Windows XP, and Windows Vista. If you're taking a course, all of this equipment should be provided to you. If not, you could find yourself facing some fairly serious cash outlay trying to buy everything you need!

Learning Objectives

In this lab, you'll discover some rather interesting ways to get inexpensive or free hardware and software. None of these ideas will work every time, but with a little patience you'll be amazed how much you can get for very little!

At the end of this lab, you'll be able to

- Acquire inexpensive or free hardware and software

- Acquire a standard PC technician toolkit

Lab Materials and Setup

The materials you need for this lab are

- A telephone

- Transportation

- A PC with Internet access

Getting Down to Business

Most of the objectives on the CompTIA A+ exams don't require state-of-the-art hardware. If you're willing to use systems that are a few years old, you can get plenty of good hands-on practice with the techniques you need to know to pass the CompTIA A+.

Step 1   Go on a scavenger hunt. Get a list of the smaller "mom and pop" PC repair companies and small PC parts suppliers in your town. Drive to these companies (don't call them) and ask them, "What do you guys do with your broken or obsolete parts?" The vast majority of these stores simply throw the parts away! Ask when they toss stuff and if you can have what they throw away. Most of these companies pay to get rid of equipment and will be glad to give it to you. Oh, and you can forget the big chain stores—they almost never let folks have equipment.

Step 2   Shop the sale bins at the local computer parts stores. You'll always find one or two pieces of equipment at outrageously low prices. Granted, you may end up using a bright pink Barbie keyboard, but if it only costs $3, who cares? Don't forget about rebates—you can often get parts for free after rebate! Really!

Step 3   Tell everyone you know that you're looking for PC hardware. Almost every organization will have occasional in-house sales where they sell older (but still good) PCs, printers, and so on to employees. If you can get in on some of these, you'll have some amazing deals come your way!

✔ Hint

You'll often find that older machines still have the Windows 98 or Windows Me operating system software installed. If you come across one of these systems, see if you can work with the seller or donor to get the licensed disc. Working with an older operating system (even DOS) will introduce you to the installation and configuration process. Having an operating system installed will also enable you to verify that the hardware is working.

Step 4   Take one weekend to check out local garage sales. People often sell older PCs at a tiny fraction of their original cost. If you're not afraid to barter a bit, you'll get incredible deals—just watch out for equipment that's simply too old to be worthwhile.

✔ **Hint**

I avoid PC flea markets. The problem is that these folks know the value of their computer equipment, so it's often hard to find excellent deals.

Step 5   Locate the local PC user groups in your town—almost every town has at least one. Explain your situation to them; you'll usually find someone who's willing to give you a part or two, and you may also find others who are studying for the CompTIA A+ exams. You may even be able to start or join a study group!

Step 6   Check out the Craigslist page for your area (www.craigslist.com) and look in the For Sale/Computer category. Craigslist is like a big online garage sale, and you can almost always find someone trying to get rid of old PC equipment for next to nothing. Failing that, you can check out their forums, or even place an ad yourself saying that you're looking for old PC parts.

Step 7   Speaking of study groups, try teaming up with as many fellow students as you can to pool cash for parts and to work as a study group. If you're in a course, this is easy—your fellow students are your study group! Have everyone go equipment hunting, using the different methods described to get equipment, and pool the items you find for everyone to use. You might even hold a drawing after you all get certified, to choose who gets to keep the equipment.

Chapter 2
Operational Procedures

Lab Exercises

Achieving CompTIA A+ certification is a great way to demonstrate to prospective employers that you have the appropriate technical skills to make you a worthy candidate for their workplace. But you have to demonstrate more than just technical skills to get hired by and succeed in an organization. You also need to demonstrate that you have the appropriate interpersonal skills to interact effectively with fellow employees and with clients. CompTIA recognizes the importance of interpersonal skills in the workplace and thus includes related questions on its A+ certification exams to make sure you are prepared to show that you have the people skills to work well with others. Face it, you're great at fixing computers and extremely interested in the latest gadgets, but do you have the people skills to land a job, keep a job, and climb the ladder of success? I've seen many talented young individuals who can fix just about anything struggle in the area of how to communicate professionally with others; their impressive résumé allows them to walk in the front door to a promising future...only to slink out the back door in disappointment after failing due to lack of people skills.

Whether you like it or not, people evaluate you based on how they perceive you. Developing and maintaining personal and professional workplace habits ensures that people perceive you as the IT professional that you are. This set of labs applies the information you learned in Chapter 2 of *Mike Meyers' CompTIA A+ Guide to Managing and Troubleshooting PCs*, with a focus on communicating properly, presenting yourself professionally at all times, and demonstrating your technical knowledge regarding safety. These labs will help you not only to pass the CompTIA A+ exam, but also to develop skills that will serve you well throughout your career, whether in IT or another field.

The CompTIA objectives challenge you to conduct yourself in a professional manner while on the job. Objective 6.2 (exam 220-701) goes into detail to clarify how you should act on the job. Let's review some of the major points:

6.2 GIVEN A SCENARIO, DEMONSTRATE THE APPROPRIATE USE OF COMMUNICATION SKILLS AND PROFESSIONALISM IN THE WORKPLACE

- Use proper language—avoid jargon, acronyms, slang.
- Maintain a positive attitude.
- Listen and do not interrupt a customer.
- Be culturally sensitive.
- Be on time.
    - If late, contact the customer.
- Avoid distractions:
    - Personal calls
    - Talking to co-workers while interacting with customers
    - Personal interruptions

Many of the following labs will require you to have a partner, and your instructor will actually lead the classroom through a few of them, so buddy up.

 30 MINUTES

Lab Exercise 2.01: The Rude Computer Technician

Everyone is familiar with the stereotype of the rude technician so wrapped up in technology that he is unable to relate to the people around him. Sneering technobabble, a condescending attitude, and rude remarks have become traits that people expect to find in techs, and, all too often, the techs don't disappoint. In this exercise, you'll work with a partner first to roleplay the part of the stereotypical rude tech and then to roleplay a professional, well-behaved tech. In this way, you'll learn how you should and should not behave as a technician.

Learning Objectives

The plan is to have a classmate play the role of the client, and you play the role of the PC tech. Work through the scenario in a live person-to-person role playing of the situation, just as if it were real.

At the end of this lab, you'll be able to

- Demonstrate proper communication skills
- Avoid distractions in the workplace

Lab Materials and Setup

The materials you need for this lab are

- Blank drawing paper and pencil

- A clock with a second hand, or a timer

- A space to place chairs so that you can face your partner

- The *Mike Meyers' CompTIA A+ Guide to Managing and Troubleshooting PCs* textbook, for reference

- A PC with Internet access

Getting Down to Business

In this exercise, one person will act as the PC technician while the other acts as a customer sitting in a cubicle. As the PC technician, you will first try to emulate as many bad communication habits as possible while your partner, the customer, identifies and writes down those bad habits. Then, repeat the process, this time using proper communication skills. You will then trade roles and repeat the scenario.

Step 1   Create a scenario in which a customer would ask for technical support. For example, try "My computer is running slowly and all these Web pages keep popping up!"—a classic case of malware infection. The person playing the customer should act as if he or she is not technically savvy and is unable to answer any technical questions or understand any terms outside of what might be considered "common." What is considered "common" is up to the person playing the customer, so have fun!

Step 2   Between 1999 and 2001, the popular television show *Saturday Night Live* put on a series of comedy sketches called "Nick Burns, Your Company's Computer Guy." Many of these sketches are available online. Do a search for and watch a few of these humorous sketches to see actor Jimmy Fallon portray how insensitive a technician can be in his personal communications. Why are these sketches so funny? What does their popularity tell you about how techs are perceived by our society? Use these videos to get an idea of how to behave during the next step, and how never, ever to behave in real life.

Step 3   It's now time for the technician to do his thing in a timed scenario. Pretend the customer is sitting in a cubicle. Every computer has an "asset tag number," and the tech must confirm that number to make sure he is working on the right computer. After that, it's up to the tech! Be as rude as possible (but not so rude that a person normally would get fired), concentrating on the issues listed in step 1 of this lab. Your goal is to try to get started working on the PC within three minutes.

As the customer, your job is to describe the problem and answer the tech's questions to the best of your ability. You want your computer fixed, but you won't get up until you have confidence in the tech. As the tech talks, jot down how he is rude or inconsiderate to you.

The scenario ends when either the tech is sitting at the customer's computer or three minutes have elapsed, whichever happens first.

Step 4   Discuss the issues that the customer wrote down. After a quick discussion, repeat the process, this time using good communication techniques. In most cases, the customer will quickly relinquish her seat and let you get to work.

The scenario ends when the tech is sitting at the customer's computer or three minutes have elapsed, whichever happens first.

Step 5   Repeat the entire process, this time trading roles. The person now playing the tech should attempt to come up with different ways to be inappropriate, within reason.

 45 MINUTES

Lab Exercise 2.02: Communicating Effectively

So, you want to be a successful IT technician but you have trouble communicating? One of the keys to professional communication is being able to listen well as duties are being assigned to you, so that you can produce the results expected.

Learning Objectives

At the end of this lab, you'll be able to

- Communicate more effectively

- Help discern when it's best to talk and when it's best to listen

Lab Materials and Setup

The materials you need for this lab are

- Blank drawing paper and pencil

- A clock with a second hand, or a timer

- A sufficient number of folding chairs for all the students involved in the exercise

- The *Mike Meyers' CompTIA A+ Guide to Managing and Troubleshooting PCs* textbook, for reference

For the setup, arrange the chairs back to back in pairs around the room, with about five feet between each set of chairs.

Getting Down to Business

In this exercise, you'll listen as your partner speaks to you and you'll write down whatever he or she tells you under a tight timeline. The goal is to help you work under pressure while remaining professional at all times.

Step 1 Students should pair up. Each pair of students should designate one person to be the PC tech and the other to be the customer and then write their respective titles on the top of their papers.

Step 2 The instructor should start the timer and ask the designated customers to say the first five technology-related problems that come to mind; they have 20 seconds to do this. As the customers speak, their respective partner techs should write down what they say, in the order stated. *An example might be system fails to boot, no wireless connection, printer not printing properly, no picture on the monitor, etc.*

Stop the timer at 20 seconds.

Step 3 The PC techs write a brief solution to the five words or phrases just spoken by the customers. They have three minutes to complete this and must address them in the order received.

Stop the timer at three minutes.

Step 4 The PC tech and customer groups face each other for one minute and share their information. Then, each pair presents their problems and solutions to the class, in turn. They have two minutes to present their solutions. The other groups should sit quietly and listen. After all groups finish, the instructor will give feedback to each group as to how they could communicate better. Students should be allowed to participate in the feedback as well.

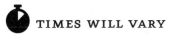 TIMES WILL VARY

Lab Exercise 2.03: Preparing for the Technical Interview

Sitting for an interview and selling yourself to complete strangers is the stuff of many a PC tech's nightmares. Trust me! You might think it sounds easy, but once you're in the hot seat and actually doing it, everything changes. So buckle down and pay attention during this lab because it could make or break your chance of landing that $30,000–$40,000+ job!

Before we get started in earnest, here are some tips to keep in mind when interviewing for a job.

- No chewing gum.

- Turn your cell phone off and keep it out of sight. No texting!

- Comb your hair and keep it out of your eyes (if you have to swing your hair to the side every minute, get a haircut). Messy hair looks very unprofessional and reflects poor self-image.

- Brush your teeth.

- Males—Tuck in your shirt, pull up your pants, and wear a belt.

- Females—No miniskirts or low tops, and keep your stomach covered.

- Shake hands firmly.

- Maintain good eye contact at all times.

- No sneakers allowed!

- Do not offer information that is not pertinent to the interview. Think before speaking and always tell the truth.

For more tips on job interviewing, see "10 Killer Job Interview Questions and Answers," by Carole Martin, available at www.bspcn.com/2007/08/24/10-killer-job-interview-questions-and-answers/.

Learning Objectives

In this lab exercise, you will practice role modeling as an interviewee (if no interviewers are present, you may also have to roleplay as an interviewer). You will be critiqued as you are probed to say and do the right thing at all times. So get ready for some fun in preparing for the interview process.

At the end of this lab, you'll be able to

- Speak clearly, professionally, and technically

- Describe how IT affects the workplace

- Effectively communicate what you know

- Know what to bring and wear to the interview

Lab Materials and Setup

The materials you need for this lab are

- An updated résumé that lists all your skills; technology courses that you're currently taking or have completed; and reliable references, other than family—preferably customers or people that know your skill level and character, and have worked with you for a period of a minimum of six months.

- A digital portfolio (a CD) that includes an updated copy of your résumé; pictures or short video clips of you working on computers, possibly building a computer; any presentations or technology-related projects you've been involved in implementing; a log of customers you've supported; and any Web sites you've created that demonstrate your skills. Not MySpace or Facebook! By the way, this is a CD you will leave with your interviewer, so make it good.

Instructors: For the setup, enlist or bring in at least four volunteers from the technology industry, such as local PC repair shop managers, Geek Squad reps, and so forth, to help you interview your students. Use people from the business world as much as possible, but if you're under tight timelines, just ask your school's principal, guidance personnel, media specialists, or other teachers to assist you. They make great interviewers because your students most likely do not know them as well as they know you and thus will take this exercise more seriously.

Getting Down to Business

This is a work-in-progress lab that will be beneficial to you for life. Once you've started the process of learning to present yourself effectively, you will be surprised at how many opportunities you'll get to use these skills.

Step 1   Write your résumé and save it to multiple places. Have your instructor guide you as to what to include and what not to include. Run a spell check! Print and proof it yourself first and then allow your instructor to critique it.

> ✔ **Hint**
>
> The Web offers many places for the serious job seeker to post a completed résumé electronically, such as www.monster.com, but it is wise to have properly formatted paper copies as well, to turn in with your application.

Step 2   Type a list of personal and professional references on a separate document and contact the people you are listing to make them aware they may get a call about your potential interview.

Step 3   Have a room set up with at least four tables/stations, one for each volunteer interviewer, with at least three chairs at each station. Have students "dress for success" on the day of the interview and let them know that evaluation of their appearance comprises 50 percent of their grade.

Step 4   Enter the interview area quietly. Make sure to have your printed résumé, references, and digital portfolio ready to turn in. Interviews should last no more than ten minutes. Ideally, the interviewers will ask everyone the same questions, but you never know what you'll be asked.

Step 5   Once you have been interviewed, the interviewers will compare their thoughts and choose two or three top students to be interviewed by the entire group of interviewers. This is called a panel interview and is the type of interview students will most likely encounter when being interviewed for various jobs.

30 MINUTES

Lab Exercise 2.04: Integrating Safety into the Workplace

Demonstrating safety precautions at all times is one of the most important things you can do to protect yourself and your customers...and impress your employer. This mostly involves using common sense, but you should also make sure to carefully read and put into practice the safety guidelines provided in Chapter 2 of *Mike Meyers' CompTIA A+ Guide to Managing and Troubleshooting PCs*.

Many techs go into the field with the mindset that safety is not that important, but it can save your life and the lives of others. The U.S. Department of Labor Occupational Safety and Health Administration has a Web site at www.osha.gov that is loaded with information for employers and employees to help them understand the importance of safety. It offers guidelines for electronics and computers/peripherals that we'll explore in this lab exercise.

Learning Objectives

In this lab, you will identify the safety hazards in the workplace and become more aware of guidelines that are useful in a PC environment.

At the end of this lab, you will be able to

- Explain ESD

- Explain MSDS and various hazards

- Explain proper equipment disposal procedures

Lab Materials and Setup

The materials you need for this lab are

- A PC with Internet access

- A notepad

- Presentation software, if possible, to present your findings

Getting Down to Business

In Chapter 2 of *Mike Meyers' CompTIA A+ Guide to Managing and Troubleshooting PCs*, you read that electrostatic discharge (ESD) can cause permanent damage to some components and erase data on some storage devices. If you take this to heart and practice ESD safety measures as a PC tech early on, you will gain respect in the workplace and demonstrate that you care about your employer's investment.

Step 1 Research ESD, material safety data sheets (MSDSs), and how to dispose of old computer equipment properly, while typing results. You can use the Internet, magazines, tech articles, manuals, and so forth, but make sure you properly document where you find your information.

Step 2 Compile the data into a presentation type document. Include the following:

- Pages that describe and define ESD, MSDSs, and proper disposal
- Pictures of
  - Various anti-static devices
  - Samples of MSDSs
  - Disposing of old, outdated computer devices
- A short video clip of either
  - A student wearing an anti-static wrist strap and installing components into a PC
  - How to fill out an MSDS
  - How to properly dispose of computer components
- A bibliography page

Step 3 (If Time Permits) Students take turns presenting their report to the class to demonstrate their knowledge.

 30 MINUTES

Lab Exercise 2.05: Safeguarding Your IT Future—Becoming a Professional

To safeguard your IT future, it is extremely important that you know how to carry yourself as a professional and keep your customers satisfied. As discussed in *Mike Meyers' CompTIA A+ Guide to Managing and Troubleshooting PCs*, good techs always protect themselves and the systems they work on from electrical damage, properly use tools to safeguard the components of the system unit against ESD damage, and demonstrate professionalism in the workplace at all times.

Learning Objectives

In this lab you will learn the proper way to dress and present yourself in the workplace.

After completing this lab, you'll be able to

- Properly dress and present yourself on the job
- Understand the do's and don'ts about cell phone usage on the job

Lab Materials and Setup

The materials you need for this lab are

- A PC with Internet access

Getting Down to Business

Choosing the proper way to dress and present yourself is extremely important in securing and maintaining a good job. Did you know that within the first 15 seconds of meeting someone, they form opinions of you based entirely on your appearance—your body language, your demeanor, your mannerisms, and how you are dressed? Once you have made that first impression, it is virtually irreversible, so you must be aware at all times how you are being perceived and maintain a positive and clean self-image.

Step 1 Read the following descriptions and choose which person you would want to work on your computer. After you've made your decision, write a short statement supporting your decision and why.

- Sloppily-dressed technician
- Well-dressed technician
- Technician properly using technology (tech using a laptop, sitting straight up, not slouching)
- Technician misusing technology (tech talking on cell phone or texting while on the job)
- Technician with clean, well-kept hair
- Technician with not-so-nice hair

Step 2 Go to www.mindtools.com/CommSkll/FirstImpressions.htm and read the article "Making a Great First Impression!" Are there any points that you would add to this list? Write a short essay explaining why or why not.

Step 3 Read the article "Top 6 Rules for Using Cell Phones at Work," by Dawn Rosenberg McKay, at http://careerplanning.about.com/od/workplacesurvival/tp/cell_phone.htm. Then, read the following scenarios and choose the appropriate response:

1. Your boss has specifically stated that you cannot use your cell phone on the job unless you are on break (away from your work space) or at lunch. You found out before you left for work that your father will be having out-patient surgery today, and you want to be informed right way about his status. What should you do?

    A. Keep your phone on vibrate and out of sight, wait for a phone call, and discreetly leave the work area so you can take the call.

    B. Inform your boss that you're dealing with a family situation and may need to be excused at an unexpected time to find out the status of your father's condition.

2. You're on the phone with a client, attempting to walk her through various troubleshooting steps so that you don't have to travel to the client's location to fix the problem. Your cell phone suddenly rings (because you forgot to turn it off) and you can see on the caller ID that it's an old friend you have not talked to in a while. What should you do?

    A. Quickly turn off your cell phone and put it away.

    B. Place your client on hold and take the call.

3. Your boss just came in the office from a meeting with his boss and is extremely frustrated about issues that do not involve you. He speaks to you rather harshly and then abruptly leaves. The moment he leaves, you receive a phone call from a client who demands that you return his PC to him today and a text message you've been waiting for about a part for the client's computer that's due in. What should you do?

    A. Place the client on hold, read the text, and then give him an up-to-the-minute update.

    B. Speak harshly back to him and place him on hold while you regain your composure.

Lab Analysis Test

1. Your coworker Sara constantly takes personal calls on her cell phone even though she knows your employer has a rule banning personal use of the cell phone while in the workplace. Whenever she's on her cell phone, she does not answer her regular work phone, thus adding more work for you and others. How do you think you should handle this situation?

2. You just got a phone call from a PC repair company that wants to interview you today. It is dress-down day at your workplace, so you're wearing jeans and a T-shirt. Should you accept the offer to interview today or decline? Explain your answer.

3. You're the lead PC technician for a company and have been put in charge of two inexperienced technicians who know nothing about ESD and MSDSs. What steps will you take to educate them to ensure they use anti-static devices and dispose of hazardous materials properly?

4. What is EMI and which components are particularly susceptible to it?

5. What is RFI? Write down three examples of RFI.

Key Term Quiz

Use the following terms to complete the following sentences. Not all terms will be used.

cell phones

electromagnetic interference (EMI)

electrostatic discharge (ESD)

honesty

integrity

professional

radio frequency interference (RFI)

responsibility

1. A(n) _____ technician is one who not only possesses great technical expertise, but also has good communication and people skills.

2. Interference produced by microwaves and cell phones is an example of _____.

3. Anti-static wrist straps prevent _____.

4. When on the job, it is your _____ to follow the rules and guidelines set by the company regarding the use of _____.

5. _____ can disrupt wireless network communication.

Chapter 3
The Visible PC

Lab Exercises

Every competent tech knows the PC inside and out. Nothing destroys your credibility in the eyes of a client as quickly as not knowing the basics, like the difference between a graceful shutdown and a forced power down. The word "Oops!" doesn't always go over well in the real world! This set of labs applies the information you learned in Chapter 3 of *Mike Meyers' CompTIA A+ Guide to Managing and Troubleshooting PCs*, so you'll be poking and prodding a PC. You'll begin by exploring the functions of a PC, and then you'll examine the typical user-accessible components, as well as the external connectors found on most PCs. After taking a moment to protect both yourself and the PC components from electrical damage, you'll open up the system unit's case and take a tour inside. Finally, you'll finish up with a complete disassembly of the system.

 30 MINUTES

Lab Exercise 3.01: Exploring the Functions and Components of a PC

Everything a computer does falls into one of four categories: input, processing, output, and storage. You need a good understanding of these four processes, and the components that are involved with each one, to troubleshoot PC problems successfully.

Learning Objectives

At the end of this lab, you'll be able to

- Define the four functions of computer systems

- Detail common components involved in each of these four functions

Lab Materials and Setup

The materials you need for this lab are

- A notepad and pencil, to draw a four-column table

- Optional: Access to a working computer with a word processing or spreadsheet application installed, to aid in drawing the table

- The *Mike Meyers' CompTIA A+ Guide to Managing and Troubleshooting PCs* textbook, for reference

---

✔ **Hint**

Get used to taking notes and drawing pictures. Even after many years of repairing computers, from mainframes to PCs, I still use a notepad to keep track of what I see and what I change. I recommend that you save your drawings and notes, as you'll find them useful in subsequent labs.

Getting Down to Business

In this exercise, you'll review, list, and define the various components involved in the PC's vital functions.

Step 1 Reread the "How the PC Works" section in Chapter 3 of *Mike Meyers' CompTIA A+ Guide to Managing and Troubleshooting PCs*, paying particular attention to the sections on input, processing, output, and storage.

Step 2 For each of the following functions of a computer system, write a definition and give a brief example:

Input:

_____

_____

Processing:

_____

_____

Output:

_____

_____

Storage:

_____

_____

Step 3 Using the following table, list the components that operate in each of the four functional categories. Try to include as many components as you can; you might take a peek at some of the later chapters in the textbook to see if you can add any other components. Think about how each of the components contributes to the overall workings of the PC, and include as much detail about the component as possible.

Input	Processing	Output	Storage

Step 4 If you completed the table right here in the lab book, you'll have it handy throughout the rest of the lessons. If you made a table in your notebook, or created an electronic version, make sure you can get to it easily. As you work on later chapters, you'll want to update the table with additional components and further detail on the components. The information in the table (and in your head) will expand as you develop a better understanding of how the components relate to the PC's "big picture."

 30 MINUTES

Lab Exercise 3.02: Examining User-Accessible Components

It's been one of those days. You walked into what should have been a simple job interview, only to meet a very frantic IT manager who was dealing with a crisis of epic proportions. She doesn't even bother to interview you—instead she shuttles you out of her office, points down the hall, and says, "Go check Jane's PC, fourth cubicle on the left. She says the PC has locked up on her, and she can't even turn it off! Don't change anything or open it up. Right now I simply need to know if it will shut down, boot properly, and access the drives." Then the IT manager is off to deal with her crisis, and you're on the spot.

This exercise looks at the many PC components that you can access without removing the case. You can use a quick scan to determine whether a PC is functioning properly at the most basic level. Take your time, and jot down notes where you feel the need. Practice each step until you're confident you can do it on the job as a PC tech.

Learning Objectives

In this lab exercise you will locate and describe the various user controls and built-in user-accessible devices of a PC system. You *will not* be opening the system case during this lab.

At the end of this lab, you'll be able to

- Recognize and manipulate user controls

- Describe the use of built-in user-accessible devices

Lab Materials and Setup

The materials you need for this lab are

- One fully functioning desktop computer system unit, with monitor

- A working *optical drive* (any drive that reads or records CD, DVD, or Blu-ray discs)

- One readable data CD with files

- One keyboard

- One mouse

- A notepad on which to take notes and make sketches of the computer and components

- Optionally, a digital camera to take photos of the computer and components (can be a standalone camera or part of another device, such as a mobile phone)

✔ **Hint**

In Lab Exercise 3.01, I recommended that you get used to taking notes and drawing pictures. Thanks to the wide popularity and availability of digital cameras, you have another excellent way to record the configuration of computer systems and the steps taken during disassembly, repair, and assembly. A digital camera can be a handy tool for supplementing your trusty pencil and paper.

Getting Down to Business

As a technician, you need to know how everything works on a PC. The best place to begin is with the externally accessible devices.

Step 1 Before you can do much work with a PC, you need a functioning output device, such as a monitor. Check the monitor to see if it has power. The small *light-emitting diode (LED)* on or near the monitor's power button should be lit: orange if the system is turned off or asleep, or green if the system is fully on. If you determine that the monitor is not plugged into a wall outlet, plug it in now.

Step 2 Look at the front of your system unit. Locate the power button. Compare your button to the one in Figure 3-1.

FIGURE 3-1 Recognizing the power button on the front of a PC

Once you have located the power button on your system, make a note of its appearance. Is it in plain sight, or hidden behind a door or lid? Is it round, square, or some odd shape? Pressing the power button to start a PC when the electricity is off is known as a *cold boot* or sometimes a *hard boot*.

Describe your power button here:

_____

Sometimes software will lock up your system and the only way to shut the system down is to force a *power down*. This requires that you press and hold the power button for four to six seconds.

Notice the two LEDs on the front panel near the power button. One generally lights up green to indicate that the power is on, and the other flashes when the internal hard drive is active.

✔ **Hint**

On older systems, the power button or switch may be located on the back of the system. Many newer systems have a power switch located on the back of the case that controls the flow of electricity to the power supply, and a power button on the front that boots and shuts down the PC. Most systems also have a reset button, which you can use to restart the PC if it becomes unstable or locked up because of some software glitch.

Step 3 Locate the floppy drive. You can recognize it by the 3½-inch horizontal slot. Do you see the eject button below the slot on the right side of the drive? Below the slot on the left side is an LED that lights up when the drive is actively reading or writing information on a floppy diskette.

✔ **Hint**

Because floppy diskettes can store only a relatively tiny amount of data, floppy drives are disappearing from PCs. In fact, most new computer systems ship without floppy drives. If your system doesn't have a floppy drive, you may want to explore an older machine to see one in action. As a computer tech, you will most likely still have to deal with floppy drives for at least a few more years.

On the front of your system, you should also see the external face of your system's optical drive. You'll see either the front edge of the tray that opens to accept an optical disc, or a small door that protects the tray when it's retracted. Once you've located this drive, notice that it too has a button in the lower-right corner. When the system is on, you can press that button to open the tray door (if there is one) and slide the tray out to receive your disc (see Figure 3-2). Pressing the button while the tray is out retracts the tray so that the drive can read the disc.

Don't be tempted to force the disc tray to close. Always press the button on the front of the drive to close the tray or to eject a disc. Forcing the tray to close can cause the gears inside to become misaligned, so that the tray no longer closes properly.

FIGURE 3-2 Can you locate the floppy drive and optical drive on this system unit?

✔ **Hint**

If you forget to remove an optical disc before turning off the system power, you can straighten a strong paper clip and insert one end into the tiny hole on the front of the drive. Pressing directly inward with the paper clip will cause the tray to open.

Your system may have other devices installed, such as a *USB flash drive* (a solid-state device that plugs into a USB port but acts like a hard drive), a tape drive, a Blu-ray Disc drive, or various media card readers, such as those for CompactFlash or Memory Stick cards. Each of these uses removable media; take care when inserting or removing the media.

➜ **Note**

With USB flash drives—or *thumb drives*, as they're often called—the drive *is* the removable media.

Step 4 Now it's time to prepare your system for the scenario outlined in the opening text:

a. Turn on your system and log on in a normal fashion so that you are viewing the operating system desktop.

b. Press the eject button on the front of the optical drive. When the tray opens, carefully insert a disc. Press the eject button again to close the tray. If you haven't done this a lot, practice inserting and removing a disc until you feel comfortable with the process. Does the LED on the front of the optical drive flash or stay on continuously at any point?

✖ **Warning**

Don't start any applications yet! Close any open applications or open windows before performing Step 5. You're going to force a "power down," and you do not want to damage any of the software applications.

Step 5 Now you're going to simulate a PC that has become nonresponsive and "locked up." Perform a forced power down as follows:

a. Press *and hold the* power button.

b. While continuing to hold the power button in, count out loud (one–one thousand, two–one thousand, three–one thousand . . .) until the system powers down and the screen goes blank.

According to your count, how many seconds did it take for the screen to go blank?

_____

Step 6 After the system has been powered down for approximately one minute, do the following:

    a.   Press the power button and allow the system to boot.

        Did the system boot properly? _____

    b.   Log on in a normal fashion so that you are viewing the operating system desktop.

        Were you able to log on as normal? _____

    c.   Select Start | My Computer or Computer and double-click the icon that represents the optical drive. This should enable you to view the contents of the disc that was inserted prior to the forced power down.

        List some of the contents of the disc: _____

        _____

    d.   Select Start | Shut Down. If you're using Windows Vista, it goes straight to a shutdown routine. Windows 2000/XP opens the Shut Down Windows dialog box, in which you select Shut down from the drop-down list. This performs a graceful shutdown of the system.

✔ **Hint**

If all the actions in Step 6 were successful, the system likely is stable and you can report to the IT manager that Jane's machine is back up and running. If any of the actions failed, you should select Start | Restart in Windows Vista or Start | Shut Down in Windows 2000/XP. In the Shut Down Windows dialog box, select Restart from the drop-down list. After the system reboots, you may complete actions b, c, and d once more. Sometimes the forced power down leaves some of the files in a state of flux; restarting shuts the computer down "gracefully," properly closing all open files before powering down. This should clear everything up and enable the computer to function properly.

Step 7 While the computer is turned off, pretend you lost power and must remove the disc from the optical drive without power. Use a paper clip to remove the disc, as noted earlier in the Lab Hint under Step 3.

Step 8 As a technician, you need to understand the keyboard, because it is still one of the most important human interfaces connected to a PC. Look at the way your keyboard is laid out: it basically has three main sections, with some extra keys thrown in for good measure (see Figure 3-3).

FIGURE 3-3 Exploring the QWERTY keyboard

The largest area of the keyboard is the standard *QWERTY* (pronounced "kwerty") letter key layout, which is familiar to touch typists everywhere. If you never took a typing or keyboarding class, you may be wondering what I mean by QWERTY; it's simply the standard keyboard used in the U.S. and most English-speaking countries, so named for the first six letters in the top row of letter keys.

To the right of the letter keys you'll usually see a square numeric keypad similar to those found on old adding machines. This feature is popular with people like accountants and merchants, because it makes entering numbers quicker and easier.

Above the letter keys, you'll find a special row of keys called *function keys*, normally labeled F1 through F12. What these keys do depends on the software you're using when you press them; pressing the F1 key, for example, generally calls up a program's help feature. Function keys are used for various tasks, including accessing basic system settings at startup. You'll use the function keys a lot when troubleshooting a downed system.

→ **Note**

Many modern keyboards include a switch to toggle the purpose of the function keys from performing the standard F1 through F12 functions to being some sort of multimedia controls, such as volume up or down or go to the next song. Others offer helpful functions, such as back and next keys for controlling a Web browser. If the function key doesn't behave as a standard key, look for the function key toggle.

In the keyboard's upper-left corner, next to the function keys, you'll see the Escape key, labeled ESC. In many programs, particularly older ones, pressing this key backs you out of what you're doing, sometimes even causing your current program to close down. In more modern software, pressing ESC is a way to make a program let go of some text or graphic you've selected, or to close the current dialog box without implementing any changes.

To the right of the function keys are the PRINT SCREEN, SCROLL LOCK, and PAUSE/BREAK keys; depending on your keyboard, any or all of these key names may be abbreviated. These specialized keys aren't heavily used these days, although some programs (such as Windows Clipboard) use the PRINT SCREEN key to capture snapshots of the monitor display (known as a *screen shot*). Screen shots can come in handy when you're troubleshooting program or application problems and need to show someone else what you're seeing (see Figure 3-4).

Along the bottom row of the keyboard, on either side of the SPACEBAR, you'll find the special keys labeled CTRL (for Control) and ALT (for Alternate). On keyboards designed for use with Windows operating systems, you'll also find a key with the Windows logo (which opens the Windows Start menu), and possibly one with a menu symbol as well (which opens a context menu without using the mouse). For the most part, the CTRL and ALT keys don't do anything by themselves, but they are incredibly useful when combined with other keys. In many word processing programs, for example, holding down the CTRL key while pressing the S key has the same effect as selecting File | Save using the mouse—only faster and easier. Techs use these types of key combinations a lot; in this manual you'll see them represented with a hyphen between the keys, for example CTRL-S.

```
C:\WINDOWS\system32\cmd.exe                                    _ □ ×

C:\>ipconfig /all

Windows IP Configuration

        Host Name . . . . . . . . . . . : AndyXP
        Primary Dns Suffix  . . . . . . : totalhome
        Node Type . . . . . . . . . . . : Hybrid
        IP Routing Enabled. . . . . . . : No
        WINS Proxy Enabled. . . . . . . : No
        DNS Suffix Search List. . . . . : total

Ethernet adapter Local Area Connection 2:

        Connection-specific DNS Suffix  . :
        Description . . . . . . . . . . : Realtek RTL8139 Family PCI Fast Ethe
rnet NIC
        Physical Address. . . . . . . . : 00-40-F4-3A-E6-D0
        Dhcp Enabled. . . . . . . . . . : Yes
        Autoconfiguration Enabled . . . : Yes
        IP Address. . . . . . . . . . . : 192.165.4.25
        Subnet Mask . . . . . . . . . . : 255.255.255.0
        Default Gateway . . . . . . . . : 192.165.4.1
        DHCP Server . . . . . . . . . . : 192.165.4.11
        DNS Servers . . . . . . . . . . : 192.165.4.11
        Primary WINS Server . . . . . . : 192.165.4.11
        Lease Obtained. . . . . . . . . : Tuesday, September 19, 2006 11:57:53
 AM
        Lease Expires . . . . . . . . . : Wednesday, September 27, 2006 11:57:
53 AM

C:\>_
```

FIGURE 3-4 A screen shot showing important information for a networked PC

30 MINUTES

Lab Exercise 3.03: Recognizing External Connections

Just as you finish working with Jane's PC, her intercom buzzes. It's the head of IT, and she has a new assignment for you: The new satellite office in Albuquerque has received a delivery of new PCs, but the machines are all in boxes and not one of the salespeople there knows a mouse from a monkey wrench. Your job is to call them up and walk them through the process of connecting a PC, describing each cable and connector, and explaining how they connect to the PC.

Learning Objectives

In this lab, you will identify, describe, and explain the function of the external connections on a standard PC.

At the end of this lab, you will be able to

- Identify the external connectors on a PC and the related cables

- Explain the function of each external connection

Lab Materials and Setup

The materials you need for this lab are

- At least one fully functioning PC that's less than two years old (two or more systems is ideal, with one older than and one newer than two years old)

- A notepad on which to take notes and make sketches of the computer, connections, and connectors

- Optionally, a digital camera to record the connections and connectors instead of sketching

    In addition, a lab partner would be useful.

✔ **Cross-Reference**

Before you begin this lab, read the sections "External Connections" and "Devices and Their Connectors" in Chapter 3 of *Mike Meyers' CompTIA A+ Guide to Managing and Troubleshooting PCs.*

Getting Down to Business

Now it's time to learn about all the external things that can be attached to a PC. This lab exercise steps you through identifying and understanding the function of the various connectors. If you have access to the same computer that you used in the previous lab, consult your drawings, notes, and any photos you may have taken to assist you in the completion of the exercise.

✖ Warning

Shut off the power to your system and *unplug your PC* from the wall socket before you start the following exercise.

Step 1 Look at all those wires coming from the back of your PC! There's a power cable, a telephone or network cable, probably a printer cable, a keyboard cable, a mouse cable, and maybe a few others, depending on your system. Looking at the back of my current system (the one I'm using to write this manual), I count 15 cables directly connected to it. Yowza!

The great thing about PCs is that it's difficult to connect the cables incorrectly. Each one has a unique connector; some are male (connectors with pins), and some are female (connectors with holes). Each connector has a particular shape and a specific number of pins or holes that match those of a specific device connected to the system unit.

Get your notepad ready to take notes and draw pictures.

✔ Hint

Cables have conductors. A *conductor* is a wire that can carry electrical signals. You may see a cable described by the number of conductors it has; for example, a telephone cable can be a two- or four-conductor cable. A power cable is a three-conductor cable. A network cable is an eight-conductor cable.

Step 2 Unplug each of your PC's cables one at a time and practice plugging it back in until you get a feel for how it fits. You should not have to force any of the cables, though they may be firm. How is each cable held in place and prevented from coming loose? Is there a screw, clip, or some other fastener that holds the cable connector tight to the system? Is the connector keyed? What does it connect to? What is the shape of the connector on each end? Is it round, rectangular, D-shaped? How many pins or holes does it have? How many rows of pins or holes are there?

Step 3 Is it possible to plug any cable into the wrong connector? If so, which one(s)? What do you think would happen if you plugged something into the wrong connector?

_____

_____

Step 4 Remove or disconnect any of the following cables from your system and describe its connector. Follow this example:

- Data cable from the monitor to the PC

    Type of connector: End 1 (PC) __D-sub__   End 2 __D-sub__

    Male or Female: End 1 (PC) __F__   End 2 __M__

    Number of pins/holes/conductors: __15__

✔ **Hint**

Your PC may not have all of these cables; just document the ones you do have.

Now it's your turn!

- Data cable from the printer to the PC (both ends)

    Type of connector: End 1 (PC) _____   End 2 (printer) _____

    Male or Female: End 1 (PC) _____   End 2 (printer) _____

    Number of pins/holes/conductors: End 1 (PC) _____   End 2 (printer) _____

- Data cable from the keyboard to the PC

    Type of connector: _____

    Male or Female: _____

    Number of pins/holes/conductors: _____

- Data cable from the mouse to the PC

    Type of connector: _____

    Male or Female: _____

    Number of pins/holes/conductors: _____

- Data cable from the network (cable modem/DSL modem) to the PC (both ends)

    Type of connector: _____

    Male or Female: _____

    Number of pins/holes/conductors: _____

- Data cable (telephone wire) from the internal modem to the telephone jack (both ends)

    Type of connector: _____

    Male or Female: _____

    Number of pins/holes/conductors: _____

Step 5 If you're working with someone else, play "Flash Cords." Have your partner hold up various cables, and try to guess what they connect to by the connectors on the ends. Then switch roles and quiz your partner. Another really good way to learn the connector names is to have your partner sit behind the computer, while you reach around from the front, feel the various ports with your fingers, and call them out by name. Switch back and forth with each other until you both can easily identify all the ports by touch.

Step 6 Properly reconnect all the cables that you removed and prepare to turn on the system. If you have an On/Off button on the back of the system, be sure it is set to the on position. Make sure the monitor is turned on as well.

Step 7 Examine other computers to see if they have different connectors from the ones you've already documented. See if you can identify the peripherals that connect to those sockets and plugs.

Step 8 The two system units in Figure 3-5 look different, but they have many connectors in common. Try to find the following connectors on each system unit:

- Power
- Monitor
- Mouse
- Keyboard
- Printer
- Network

FIGURE 3-5 Can you match the connectors on these two system units?

Step 9 Describe the connector that matches each type of cable in the list. Use Chapter 3 of *Mike Meyers'
CompTIA A+ Guide to Managing and Troubleshooting PCs* or your notes (photos) for reference.

Cable Type	Connector Type(s)
Keyboard cable	
Mouse cable	
Speaker cable	
Monitor data cable	
Printer data cable (printer end)	
Printer data cable (PC end)	
Network data cable	
Modem/telephone wire	

Step 10 Identify the connectors pictured next. What is the name of each connector and what does it
connect to?

A. _____   B. _____   C. _____

D. _____   E. _____   F. _____

G. _____   H. _____   I. _____

30 MINUTES

Lab Exercise 3.04: Safeguarding Against Damage from Electrostatic Discharge (ESD)

So far, everything that you've explored has been accessible without removing the cover of the PC. In the next few labs, you'll be opening up the case to explore the components inside. As discussed in *Mike Meyers' CompTIA A+ Guide to Managing and Troubleshooting PCs*, good techs always protect themselves and the systems they work on from damage caused by electricity and *electrostatic discharge* (ESD), the movement of a static charge from you to something you touch that can cause damage to sensitive electronic components. Protecting yourself is fairly easy at this point: unplug the power cord from the electrical outlet and from the power supply on the PC (see Figure 3-6).

To protect the system unit's sensitive components, you can use the following tools:

- Anti-static wrist strap

- Anti-static mat or anti-static wrist strap and mat combination

- Anti-static bag

Proper use of these tools will help safeguard the components of the system unit against ESD damage— just as removing the power cord from the PC and the wall will help ensure that you are around to work on PCs for many years to come!

Learning Objectives

In this lab you will learn the techniques to protect both yourself and the sensitive components of the computer system from damage caused by electricity and ESD.

FIGURE 3-6 Unplug the power cords to protect yourself.

After completing this lab, you'll be able to

- Disconnect the power cord from the PC and the wall outlet, protecting yourself from electrocution
- Properly connect an anti-static wrist strap or anti-static wrist strap/mat combination
- Properly store unused components in an anti-static bag

Lab Materials and Setup

The materials you need for this lab are

- At least one PC that isn't vital to your (or anyone else's) home or business, not necessarily in working order but preferably less than a few years old
- An anti-static wrist strap
- Optional: anti-static mat
- Twelve anti-static bags of various sizes
- A clean, well-lit workspace of about 3' × 4' (a kitchen table with some newspaper spread about usually makes a fairly decent ad hoc lab bench)

In addition, a lab partner would be useful.

Getting Down to Business

The key to working on PCs without damaging their delicate components is caution. In this exercise, you'll prepare for a cautious (and if done properly, harmless) exploration of the system's internal organs.

> ✖ **Warning**
>
> *Shut off* the power to your system and *unplug* the power cord from your PC and from the wall socket before you do the following exercise.

Step 1 Disconnect all the external cables (monitor, keyboard, mouse, printer, etc.) from the PC you are going to use and place it on a flat, stable surface (preferably on an anti-static mat) near which you can sit or stand comfortably to inspect the insides.

Step 2 Using whichever method applies to your case (thumbscrews, Phillips-head screws, locking tabs, or Torx screws), remove the cover of your system unit. Don't get frustrated if the cover-removal method isn't obvious at first. Even seasoned techs can have a hard time figuring out how an unfamiliar case opens.

Step 3 Locate a place on the chassis (the metal frame inside the case) to which you can attach the alligator clip of the anti-static wrist strap or anti-static mat (whichever one you decided to purchase). Be prepared to wear the anti-static wrist strap in later labs (see Figure 3-7).

FIGURE 3-7 Proper use of an anti-static wrist strap

Step 4 Locate and place the anti-static bags on your workspace. These will be used in later labs to store components safely after removal. This machine may be disassembled for a few days, so you'll need to protect the components from any ESD exposure during that time. Anti-static bags do a great job of preventing ESD.

 60 MINUTES

Lab Exercise 3.05: Disassembling the System Unit and Identifying Internal Components and Connections

As promised, it's finally time to go under the hood!

You're now going to walk through the complete disassembly of the system unit. You should try to do this in the sequence presented in this lab exercise, but, depending on the configuration of the machine you are disassembling, you may have to perform one or two of the steps out of sequence. For example, you may have to remove an optical drive before you can gain access to remove the power supply.

When you're on the job, you'll encounter different models of personal computers manufactured by different companies. Along with learning the slightly different methods of component removal and installation, you should also learn how to identify the major internal parts of the PC system, regardless of the manufacturer. This lab exercise will help you practice doing that.

Learning Objectives

In this lab exercise you will locate, remove, and describe the various internal components and connectors of a standard PC system.

At the end of this lab, you'll be able to

- Remove all major components of a PC
- Recognize all major components inside a PC
- Describe the function of each component
- Define the relationship of internal components to external connections

Lab Materials and Setup

The materials you need for this lab are

- At least one PC that isn't vital to your (or anyone else's) home or business, not necessarily in working order but preferably less than a few years old
- An anti-static wrist strap
- Optional: an anti-static mat
- Twelve anti-static bags of various sizes
- A simple technician's toolkit
- A plastic cup or box to organize the various screws, nuts, and bolts that you'll remove
- A clean, well-lit workspace of about 3' × 4' (a kitchen table with some newspaper spread about usually makes a fairly decent ad hoc lab bench)
- A notepad on which to take notes and make sketches of the computer and components
- Optionally, a digital camera to record the placement, configuration, connections, and connectors associated with the components you'll be removing from the system unit

In addition, a lab partner would be useful.

Getting Down to Business

This lab exercise might remind you of the biology labs in which students dissect animal specimens. You'll be going inside to examine and remove various parts—but unlike in those biology labs, your specimen has a good chance of leading a perfectly normal life afterward!

✖ Warning

Shut off the power to your system and *unplug* the power cord from your PC and from the wall socket before you do the following exercise.

Step 1 Disconnect all the external cables (monitor, keyboard, mouse, printer, etc.) from the PC you are going to use and place it on a flat, stable surface (preferably on an anti-static mat) near which you can sit or stand comfortably to inspect the insides.

Step 2 Use proper anti-static procedures while opening the case and during this entire exercise (see Lab Exercise 3.04). Using whichever method applies to your case (thumbscrews, Phillips-head screws, locking tabs, or Torx screws), remove the cover of your system unit and then lay the system down so that the open side faces the ceiling.

✔ **Cross-Reference**

Review Chapter 3 of *Mike Meyers' CompTIA A+ Guide to Managing and Troubleshooting PCs* to confirm your understanding of proper ESD procedures, and how to open a PC system case.

Look inside your system case. What do you see? To begin with, you'll see lots of cables and wires. Some appear to be single-colored wires, while others seem to be multiple gray-colored wires in the shape of wide ribbons. Most colored wires originate at the power supply and end at the various devices to supply the needed direct current (DC) power to run the PC. The wide *ribbon cables* attach at various points and are used to transfer data. These are sometimes referred to as *logic cables* or *data cables*.

See if you can locate in your system case the major components labeled in Figure 3-8. You may have to move some of the fan shrouds, wires, and cables in order to find them, especially components on the motherboard—but remember your anti-static procedures and be gentle. Sometimes the slightest bump is enough to unseat a connection.

Step 3 Now it's time to take some notes, draw some sketches, or take a few pictures. Before you start disassembling this machine, document where the components belong and what wires and cables are connected to the different components. Be prepared to take a few notes on how you actually removed the component. Include as much detail as possible; it will help you tremendously when you're putting the system unit back together.

FIGURE 3-8 Inside a typical PC

Step 4 To start, you'll need to clear the way—a bit like peeling an onion, layer by layer—by removing the easily accessible components and cables first.

Look inside the PC and find the expansion slots. How many total expansion cards can be plugged into your system? _____

Some of the expansion slots may have cards in them. These may be modem cards, sound cards, network cards, or video cards. Since expansion cards are designed to "expand" the capability of the computer system, they are designed to be installed after the system unit is assembled. For this reason, the expansion cards are a great place to begin your disassembly.

Look at the expansion cards installed in your PC, and then look at the external connectors on each. Can you match the cable to the expansion card?

Remove all installed expansion cards from your system unit. Place each card into an anti-static bag to protect it from ESD damage.

Step 5 If the machine you are disassembling is only a few years old, it will probably have multiple fan shrouds to make sure the airflow is getting to the main components to keep them cool.

Remove any fan shrouds from your system unit and place them out of the way on your work space.

✔ Hint

After you remove each item, especially the bulky items such as fan shrouds, wiring, and cables, it would be good to take a few more notes or pictures. Now that you have a better view of the components underneath, you will be able to consult these notes or pictures during reassembly.

You can complete the next three steps in the order written, or out of order if that works best for your system unit. You'll be removing the power supply wires, the power supply, and the data cables from the components and motherboard. If one of the data cables is in the way of one of the wires, it's okay to remove the data cable first. Please remember to keep good records (notes or photos) of your configuration.

Step 6 Locate the power supply, which is a large silver or black box in one corner of the system unit case. Trace the colored wires leading out of it. Remember to be gentle!

Find the power plug(s) for the motherboard. If you have a newer PC, it will probably look like the one shown in Figure 3-9.

Find the power connectors for the floppy drive, optical drive, and hard drives. Do they look like one of the connectors shown in Figure 3-10? They should!

Remove all the power connectors from the motherboard and all data drives. Place them to the side as best as you can until you remove the power supply itself.

FIGURE 3-9 Power plug for the motherboard

Step 7 If possible, remove the power supply at this point. If there are still many cables and components in the way, you can perform this step later in the lab.

Step 8 Look at the floppy drive, which should be attached to a flat ribbon cable. (Don't worry if your system doesn't have a floppy drive—just move on and explore your other data drives.) Trace the ribbon cable to the motherboard. Do the same for all your other data drives, both hard drives, and optical drives.

These ribbon cables are about 1.5 inches wide, and they are normally gray with a colored stripe on one side. The stripe—usually red—orients the cable properly to the connections on the motherboard and the drive.

FIGURE 3-10 Power connectors

The cable to the floppy drive has 34 wires (conductors) and in most cases has a twist in the center. Its position relative to this seven-wire twist determines whether a floppy drive is the primary or A: drive for the system (attached to the connector at the end of the cable past the twist), or the secondary B: drive on the system (attached to the center connector).

✔ Hint

It's rare to find one floppy drive in a newer system, let alone two. Systems without a floppy drive will also be without a floppy drive cable, though you may still have a 34-pin connector on the motherboard. Systems with only one floppy drive may have a shorter floppy drive cable with no twist and no second drive connector.

Current systems use small, seven-wire data cables for serial ATA (SATA) hard drives and optical drives; these cables have connectors keyed like the letter L. Older systems use wider, 40- or 80-wire flat ribbon cables. Both of these wider cable types still have a colored edge on one side for orientation.

Step 9 After noting the current state of the data cables, disconnect and reconnect each device's cable in turn. Practice this a few times. Can you plug a cable in backwards? Try it. Plug the cable into the device the wrong way if you can. Older types of cables can be plugged in incorrectly, but newer cables and connectors have built-in keying to prevent this from happening. Make sure that the cables are properly connected when you've finished.

Now look at where the ribbon cables connect to the motherboard. Make note of the proper cable orientation. Practice disconnecting and reconnecting the cables at the motherboard. Is it difficult (or possible) to plug these cables in backwards?

When you feel you have practiced enough, remove the cables and place them safely away from the computer on your work surface. Now would be a great time to make a drawing or take a photograph of the de-cluttered system unit interior.

Step 10 Most modern systems have a set of small wire and cable runs connecting front panel indicator lights (primarily the power-on and hard drive activity LEDs) and front panel universal serial bus (USB) ports to the motherboard (see Figure 3-11). Look for these individual wire connections (often collectively called *case wires*), which are usually grouped together near one corner of the motherboard. Make careful note of where each tiny connector plugs in—a photo would be incredibly helpful here—and then disconnect them all and tuck the wires out of the way.

Step 11 Now that all the wires and cables are removed, you should have plenty of room to finish up the disassembly. You're now going to remove all the drives. Drives are usually the most cumbersome to remove because of the drive cages or frames in which they're mounted. Figure 3-12 shows an older system. Depending on the mounting the manufacturer has used, removing a drive may be as simple as pulling out a sliding mechanism, or as complicated as opening up the other side of the system case, removing all the decorative plastic facing, and removing a handful of screws.

FIGURE 3-11 Various case wires connected to a motherboard

Remove the floppy drive, all optical drives that are present, and the hard drive(s), and set them on your work surface.

Step 12 Look in your PC and find the random access memory (RAM) modules. RAM comes in thin, wafer-like modules, about three to five inches long by one inch wide. A row of metal contacts running along one of the long edges plugs into a matching socket, three to five inches in length, located on the motherboard. Look for a long wafer standing on its edge; often you'll find two or more RAM modules lined up in a row.

FIGURE 3-12 Typical drive configuration in a PC tower system case; note the cages or frames used for mounting the various drives

How many RAM modules do you have? _____

Do you have dual inline memory modules (DIMMs) or single inline memory modules (SIMMs)?

_____

Making sure to follow proper anti-static procedures, remove the SIMMs or DIMMs from their slots and place them in an anti-static bag for safekeeping.

Step 13 Look in your PC and see if you can locate the central processing unit (CPU). Running CPUs generate a fair amount of heat, so they need their own dedicated cooling mechanisms. Because of this, when you search the motherboard to try to find the CPU, you'll generally find it hidden under a fan/ heat sink unit.

Carefully remove the fan/heat sink unit from the CPU.

✖ Warning

Make sure you fully understand how to remove your particular model of CPU fan before you try it!

If you were able to remove the fan, make a note of the type of CPU chip you have:

_____

If you're in a computer lab with multiple systems, examine a number of different CPU chips. Note where each CPU is located on the motherboard.

Making sure to follow proper anti-static procedures, lift the lever of the zero insertion force (ZIF) socket, remove the CPU, and place it in an anti-static bag for safekeeping.

Step 14 See if you can locate any jumpers or switches on your motherboard. Resist the temptation to play with them at this point—just make a note of what you find. In particular, look for the identifying labels on the motherboard.

Step 15 Making sure to follow proper anti-static procedures, remove the screws that secure the motherboard to the chassis or frame of the system case. Place the motherboard in a properly sized anti-static bag and put it aside.

Congratulations! You have just successfully disassembled your first PC! If you have used an area where you can leave the components, wires, cabling, and hardware for a while, you can leave the PC disassembled for later labs. If you really need to clean up the area for now, you can either follow your notes (and lab steps) in reverse order to reassemble the system, or find a large box in which to store the disassembled machine until your next lab session.

Don't worry about the ESD-sensitive components; as long as they are in their anti-static bags, they should be fine.

Step 16 You have explored and removed nearly all the components of a typical PC system unit. To finish this lab exercise, see if you can correctly match the components in the following list to the items indicated in Figure 3-13.

Hard drive	_____	Optical drive	_____
Chipset	_____	RAM	_____
CPU/Heatsink	_____	PCI Express slot	_____
PCI slot	_____	SATA cable	_____
Power supply	_____	IDE cable	_____
Video card	_____		

FIGURE 3-13 Do you recognize these components inside your PC?

Lab Analysis Test

1. Joe has just moved his PC to his new office. After hooking up all the cables, he turns on the system, and when it asks for his password, the keyboard will not respond. What could possibly be wrong?

2. Theresa has just finished the production of a PowerPoint presentation detailing the design of a new office building. She has included some cool 3-D animations in the presentation to show off the design. When she attempts to save the presentation to a floppy diskette, an error occurs. What might have caused the error? Do you have any suggestions that may solve the problem?

3. Cal has purchased a new set of speakers for his PC. The old ones worked just fine, but he wanted more power and a subwoofer. When he plugged in the new speakers, they would not work. Power is on to the speakers. What is the first thing you would check?

4. John had a new modem installed in his computer at a local computer shop, where he watched as the system successfully connected to his AOL account. When he got home and tried, however, he couldn't get a dial tone. He calls you to ask for help. What should you suggest that he check first?

5. Audrey removed the case of her PC to check the type of RAM she has installed. When she put the case back on and tried to start the PC, she got a message that there's a problem with her hard drive. What is a good reason this might have happened?

Key Term Quiz

Use the following terms to complete the following sentences. Not all of the terms will be used.

ALT key

anti-static bag

anti-static mat

anti-static wrist strap

case wires

cold boot

CTRL key

data cable

electrostatic discharge (ESD)

ESC key

female connector

FireWire

function keys

hard boot

light-emitting diode (LED)

male connector

optical drive

power cable

power down

QWERTY

random access memory (RAM)

ribbon cable

thumb drive

USB flash drive

1. A standard keyboard is referred to as a(n) _____ keyboard.

2. The _____ are used for various tasks depending on the software you're using when you press them.

3. The movement of a static charge from you to something you touch is called _____ and can damage sensitive electronic components.

4. A solid-state device commonly used to store data is called a _____.

5. A Blu-ray Disc drive is a type of _____.

Chapter 4
Understanding Windows

Lab Exercises

Every good PC technician should know the Windows environment inside and out. This is vital to any troubleshooting scenario, and it won't happen automatically—it takes some practice and discovery on the technician's part. You need to be fluent in navigating the PC from a user's perspective. If there's anything magical about Windows, it's that there's almost always more than one way to get a desired result, and your preferred way might not be the same as your client's. As a good customer-oriented tech, you need to be flexible in your thinking, and this comes only through practice and more practice. As you study and work through these labs, always look for more than one way to access the files or programs you need. Many of the shortcuts and hot keys you'll discover can be invaluable aids for a busy tech!

✔ Hint

Windows enables right-click menus for most of its buttons, icons, and other screen elements. Be sure to right-click everything you see in Windows to explore the many shortcut menus and options.

In the field, the PC tech is perceived as the Master (or Mistress) of All Things Technical. This might not be a fair assessment—for example, why should a PC hardware technician need to know how to open and close the user's programs?—but that's the way it is. You need to be comfortable and confident with the Windows interface, or you'll lose all credibility as a PC technician. If you show up to service a PC and have trouble moving or resizing a window or locating the information you seek, it won't instill a lot of confidence in your client. There's nothing more embarrassing to a tech than having to ask the user how to find or use a Windows feature!

The creators of the CompTIA A+ Certification exams understand this, so they test you on Windows user-level information, such as using power saving settings, changing the appearance of the interface, manipulating files and folders, locating information stored on drives, and using Windows' built-in OS tools. You must also know how to navigate to the basic Windows features—the CompTIA A+ exams are big on identifying paths to features. Although you may already know much of the information about to be covered, the labs in this chapter will help you review and perhaps catch a few bits and pieces you might have missed along the way.

🕐 30 MINUTES

Lab Exercise 4.01: The Windows Interface

Most new PC systems sold as of this writing have Windows Vista or later installed, but keep in mind that the A+ exams cover Windows 2000 and Windows XP as well, so you'll need to be versed in all three. Most Windows operating systems come in several editions; for example, Windows XP editions include Professional, Home Edition, and Media Center Edition, as well as 64-bit editions. Microsoft targets XP Home Edition and Media Center Edition at consumers, while business and power users tend to use XP Professional. Windows Vista has various options as well, such as Vista Home Basic and Home Premium for consumers, and Vista Business and Ultimate for businesses and power users. Vista editions come in 32- and 64-bit variations. Windows 2000 comes in only a single version: Windows 2000 Professional.

→ **Note**

Windows 7, though similar in many ways to Windows Vista, is not covered on the exams.

At its most basic level, XP Home Edition is a subset or truncated version of XP Professional. According to a Microsoft VP, "Everything you can do in Home Edition, you can do in Pro." Media Center Edition is essentially Home Edition with some added functionality to simplify access to music, video, and photos. The major advantages of XP Professional include remote access, tighter security, and the ability to network in domains. If possible, try going through these lab exercises with different versions or editions of Windows so you can see what changes and what stays the same.

Learning Objectives

The main objective of this exercise is to familiarize you with the different "looks" of Windows. Although there are several similarities between each version, especially in appearance, paths to and locations of many tools and features differ considerably, so it's important to understand both.

At the end of this lab, you'll be able to

- Switch the system appearance between the default interface and the Windows Classic style
- Switch between the default Start menu mode and the Classic Start menu mode
- Switch the view of the Control Panel between the default view and Classic View

Lab Materials and Setup

The materials you need for this lab are

- A fully functioning PC with Windows XP or Vista installed

Getting Down to Business

Windows has a look that's aligned with a task-oriented Web view. You'll notice this right away when you open a window and look at the title bar and window contents. The newer versions are filled with bright colors, round edges, and big icons. Some feel that this look is a great improvement over previous versions of Windows, while others don't really like it. Happily, though, if you don't like Windows XP or Vista's native look, you can choose to use the Windows *Classic* look instead, which more closely resembles Windows 2000.

→ **Note**

Since this lab is about making newer versions of Windows look like Windows 2000, you won't be able to complete it on a Windows 2000 machine—it's set to "classic" permanently!

Step 1   To set the system theme to Classic mode, follow these steps:

   a.   Right-click the desktop.

   b.   Select Properties in Windows XP, and Personalize in Windows Vista.

   c.   In Windows XP, the Themes tab is the default view; to get the same result in Vista, click *Theme*.

   d.   Under Theme, use the drop-down menu to select Windows Classic (see Figure 4-1).

   e.   Click Apply and then click OK.

FIGURE 4-1 Changing the theme to Windows Classic in Windows XP

Switch back and forth between the default and classic interfaces. Each time, open other windows to observe the different looks.

✔ **Hint**

To give your windows and buttons the Windows Classic look without changing personalized settings such as your wallpaper, you can select the Appearance tab instead of Themes; click the *Windows and buttons* drop-down list and select *Windows Classic style*. Vista has separated all these options into menus of their own, so I encourage you to explore them all and change various settings to get the look you desire.

Step 2 Changing the theme of your Windows XP interface doesn't change the way the Start menu works, which is significantly different from earlier versions of Windows. The Start menu has the same functionality as in previous Windows versions, but it was restyled for XP. As it does for the overall screen look, Windows XP enables you to change the Start menu to Classic mode, if you prefer it that way. Before you can explore the XP style of Start menu, though, you need to know which style you're working with. The following steps will ensure that your Windows XP system is using the Windows XP Start menu style:

   a.   Right-click the Start button and select Properties to display the Taskbar and Start Menu Properties dialog box.

   b.   Select the Start Menu tab.

   c.   Select the *Start menu* radio button.

   d.   Click OK.

➔ **Note**

Vista has eliminated the word "Start" from the Start menu button and replaced it with a button that displays the Vista logo.

Click Start to open the Start menu. Notice that the left side of the Start menu shows your recently used applications. You can adjust the number of applications that Windows displays there. The top two applications are the default Web browser and e-mail client, which you can also modify. Follow these steps:

   a.   Right-click the Start button and select Properties.

   b.   Select the Start Menu tab.

c.   Be sure the *Start menu* radio button is selected, and click Customize.

d.   Under the General tab (see Figure 4-2), change any of the following settings if you like:

- The number of programs on the Start menu

- Whether to show the icons for your preferred Internet and e-mail programs

You'll notice in Vista that you also have access to the Notification and Toolbars menu as well.

The Start menu's All Programs menu shows a list of all programs installed on the system; it works like the Programs menu in Windows Vista.

Step 3   Earlier versions of Windows included icons for My Computer and My Documents on the desktop by default, but Windows XP and Vista only show the Recycle Bin. These other icons are now in the Start menu, but you can add them to the desktop, too:

a.   Click the Start button.

b.   Right-click My Computer in the menu. Vista eliminates the word "My," so right-click Computer.

c.   Select Show on Desktop.

d.   Repeat steps a through c for My Documents. Again, Vista eliminates the word "My," so right-click Documents.

FIGURE 4-2 The General tab on the Customize Start Menu dialog box

Step 4   For greatest compatibility with the lab exercises in upcoming chapters, you should now put your Start menu in the Classic Start menu mode.

To set the Start menu to Classic mode, follow these steps:

a.   Right-click the Start button.

b.   Select Properties.

c.   Choose *Classic Start menu*.

d.   Click OK.

✖ **Warning**

Most of the following lab exercises will assume you have a Windows XP or Vista system in the Classic mode.

Step 5   Another change that came with the advent of Windows XP (and continued with Vista) is the way you view the Control Panel. The Control Panel icon now opens by default in Category View (see Figure 4-3).

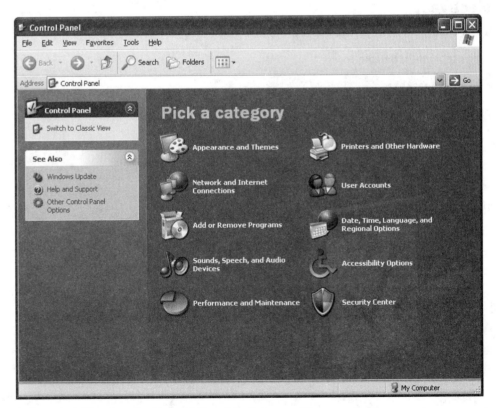

FIGURE 4-3 Viewing the Control Panel in Category View

Follow these steps to switch the Control Panel view between Category View (default) and Classic View:

a.   On the Classic Start menu, select Start | Settings | Control Panel.

b.   Depending on how it was configured when you turned on the system, you'll see either the Category View (default) or Classic View of the Control Panel.

c.   An option on the top-left sidebar in the Control Panel enables you to switch between the two views.

d.   Set your Control Panel to Classic View for the rest of the exercises.

 30 MINUTES

Lab Exercise 4.02: The Windows Desktop

The Windows desktop is the starting point for all operations. It doesn't matter whether you have a new Vista installation or an existing installation of Windows 2000 from years ago; there's a desktop graphical user interface (GUI) that you can use as a home base. The purpose of this lab exercise is to ensure that you're familiar with the desktop.

Learning Objectives

In this lab, you'll work with certain features of the Windows desktop.

At the end of this lab, you'll be able to

- Use the Windows taskbar

- Run a program from the Start menu

- Change settings for the Recycle Bin

- Change the appearance of the desktop

Lab Materials and Setup

The materials you need for this lab are

- A working computer running Windows 2000, Windows XP, or Windows Vista

➜ **Note**

Though outlining every step for each Windows operating system is beyond the scope of this book, these labs are designed to be as Windows-generic as possible. You should develop and practice the ability to navigate through the interface, achieving the end result, even if you are working with a version of Windows 2000 or the latest version of Windows 7 Ultimate. If the lab exercise doesn't produce the expected results, it may be because you're using a different operating system than the one used to write and illustrate the exercise. I've tried to show you a variety of examples. Be flexible and look on your system for the same results via a different method.

Getting Down to Business

For most users, the Windows desktop is the interface to computer applications and folders that they use every day. Even though you may already be comfortable with the desktop, you should walk through the steps to validate and refresh your skills. Everything you see has a purpose, with the possible exception of the background wallpaper—but even that has amusement value! You most likely have icons that start a variety of programs, such as My Computer/Computer, Internet Explorer, and Outlook Express, and you have the taskbar with all of its built-in features. Make sure you know where everything is, and what everything does!

Oh, and don't forget that with the proper video card installed, Windows Vista allows you to enable the Aero interface, which adds visual stimulation to the desktop by the use of transparencies and the Windows Flip 3D screen. If Aero is disabled and you want to enable it, right-click your desktop, select Personalize, select Window Color and Appearance, and click the text that reads *Open classic appearance properties for more color options*. Next, choose Windows Aero in the Color Scheme window and click OK. Now test the fun feature of Aero by pressing the WINDOWS and TAB keys and flipping through windows. By adding the CTRL key to that sequence, you can keep Flip 3D open and cycle through various windows as needed with just the TAB key.

✔ **Cross-Reference**

To refresh your memory on the various parts of the Windows interface, refer to the "User Interface" section in Chapter 4 of *Mike Meyers' CompTIA A+ Guide to Managing and Troubleshooting PCs*.

Figure 4-4 The Windows XP taskbar

Step 1   The taskbar, by default, runs along the bottom of the Windows desktop (although you can move it to any side: top, bottom, left, or right). The taskbar handles a number of critical jobs. Most important, it displays the Start button, probably the most frequently clicked button on all Windows systems. To find the Start button, look at the far left end of the taskbar (see Figure 4-4). Next to it is the Quick Launch toolbar, if it's currently turned on (see the accompanying Hint). At the right end of the taskbar is the notification area—often referred to as the *system tray*—which displays the time and any number of small icons for system programs currently stored in RAM. In the middle of the taskbar are buttons representing the user-started programs that are currently running.

✔ Hint

If you don't see the Quick Launch toolbar, point to an unused area of the taskbar, right-click, and select Properties. Check the Show Quick Launch box and click OK. You can now drag program icons or even folder shortcuts from the desktop onto the Quick Launch toolbar for quick access any time.

Step 2   Microsoft says, "Everything starts with Start." Clicking the Start button opens the Start menu, where you'll find the programs available on the system, the system settings via the Control Panel, and various system tools such as Search and Help. Another useful feature is the ability to review your recent documents. The Start button is also where you'll find the Shut Down command, as odd as that may seem.

Click the Start button. Look closely at the icons on the Start menu. Some icons have a small arrow pointing to the right on the edge of the menu bar. When you see an arrow, it means there's another menu beyond the one you're observing. To access the next menu, slide your mouse pointer across the highlighted Start menu icon area toward the arrow and into the next menu. This concept applies throughout Windows (see Figure 4-5). If you don't choose to click an option, you'll need to click somewhere else on the desktop to tell Windows, "Never mind—close the Start menu." Work through the following navigation steps using Notepad to explore many of the methods, menus, settings, and options that are provided to you through the Windows desktop.

a.   Open Notepad by clicking Start | All Programs | Accessories | Notepad.

 •   Type the following sentence and save the file in the My Documents (or Documents, in Vista) folder as Command Line Test.txt (see Figure 4-6):

 This is a small sentence of text created in Notepad that I will visit again in the Lab Exercises in Chapter 15.

 •   Close Notepad.

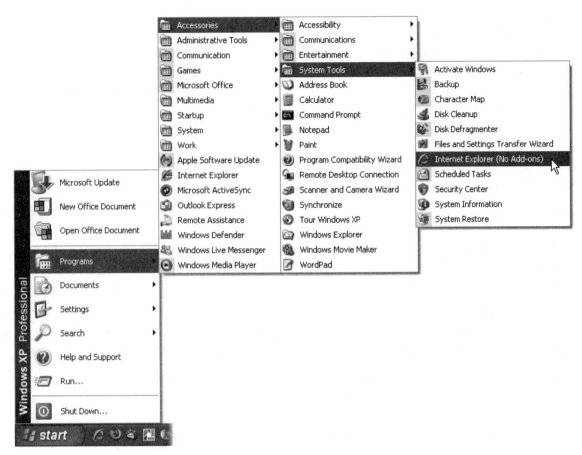

FIGURE 4-5 Exploring cascading menus

b. Open Notepad by clicking Start | Run, typing **notepad** in the dialog box, and clicking OK.

- Open Command Line Test.txt by clicking File | Open, navigating to the My Documents/ Documents folder, and selecting the appropriate file.

- Close Notepad.

c. Open Notepad from the Start menu's recent documents/items list.

- Click Start | Documents/Recent Items | Command Line Test.txt.

- Close Notepad.

FIGURE 4-6 Using Notepad

✔ **Hint**

Each time you open Notepad, you should be able to open and edit the text file Command Line Test.txt. You should also see a corresponding button appear in the taskbar. The button, space permitting, includes an icon for the application, the filename, and the application name. Folders also appear in the taskbar with an icon and folder name, but no associated application.

Step 3 Now look all the way on the right side of the taskbar. This is officially called the *notification area*, but as I noted earlier, it's often called the *system tray*. In spite of Microsoft's official terminology, most techs call it the system tray, so I'll call it that for the sake of this exercise as well.

At the far right end of the system tray, you should see a display of the current time; on most Windows systems, you'll also see a number of small icons in this area of the taskbar. These icons represent programs running in the background.

You often see icons in the system tray for network status, volume controls, and virus programs, and laptops may have additional icons for battery state and PC Card status. What you see in the system tray depends on your version of Windows, what hardware you use, and what programs you have loaded.

Click the various icons in your system tray to see what they do. Depending on the icon, you may need to click, double-click, or right-click and select from a menu.

Step 4 Now you'll look at customizing your environment. (Once again, the Start menu should be in the Classic mode.)

Right-click on the taskbar and select Properties. This opens the Taskbar and Start Menu Properties dialog box, which you brought up before by right-clicking the Start button and selecting Properties.

Each version of Windows has a slightly different look, but you'll find the following three items listed in some manner on the leftmost tab of the Taskbar and Start Menu (or equivalent) dialog box in all Windows versions:

- **Show the clock** controls the time display in the right side of the taskbar.

  Turn off the *Show the clock* option and click Apply. Did the time disappear from the taskbar?

  _____

  Select the *Show the clock* option again and click Apply. Does the time now show up in the taskbar?

  _____

- **Auto-hide the taskbar** makes the taskbar disappear until you point the mouse at the edge of the screen where the taskbar resides (generally the bottom edge), or press the Windows Start key on the keyboard. Why would you want to hide the taskbar? For certain programs, you need all the display area you can get. The auto-hide feature minimizes the taskbar to allow more room on the screen.

Select *Auto-hide the taskbar* and click Apply. Did the taskbar disappear? _____

Move your mouse pointer toward the bottom of the screen. Does the taskbar pop up when you reach the bottom? _____

Turn the auto-hide feature off again. Is the taskbar now visible on your screen? _____

- **Keep the taskbar on top of other windows** prevents programs from covering up the taskbar. If you observe a program using the entire screen, you know this feature is turned off, and you can't access the taskbar until you resize the program window or press the Windows Start button on your keyboard.

Step 5 As you know, a file isn't actually erased from your hard drive when you delete it. When you delete a file in Windows, a shortcut to the deleted file is saved in the Recycle Bin. It stays there until you empty the Recycle Bin, until you restore the folder or file, or until the Recycle Bin grows larger than a preset size. Once you empty it, the files are permanently deleted, so make sure you're certain before you do this.

✔ **Hint**

Remember that most everything in Windows has Properties settings, which you can generally access by right-clicking the object and selecting Properties. You can also access Properties by highlighting the object and pressing ALT-ENTER.

To change the Recycle Bin's properties, access the Recycle Bin settings by right-clicking the Recycle Bin icon on the desktop and selecting Properties. Your Recycle Bin Properties dialog box may look different because of the version of Windows you have, because you have multiple hard drives, or because of some other factor, but all versions basically work the same way (see Figure 4-7).

FIGURE 4-7 Setting properties for the Recycle Bin in Windows XP

FIGURE 4-8 Setting properties for the Recycle
Bin in Windows Vista

Note that 10% is the default amount of drive space to use for the Recycle Bin. Change this to 5% and close the Recycle Bin Properties dialog box. Vista adds some interesting new features beyond what Windows' other versions offer. In particular, Vista lets you set the Recycle Bin size in bytes instead of percentage of drive size (see Figure 4-8).

✔ Hint

If a hard drive starts to run low on space, emptying the Recycle Bin is a quick way to try freeing up some space.

Step 6   Microsoft gives you many ways to change the look of your desktop to suit your personal preferences, from the color of the background to the size of the fonts. There are too many possible combinations to cover them all, so you'll look at only the most popular one, the background graphic. Follow these steps:

   a.   Right-click in an unused area of the desktop and select Properties. Again, Personalize is the choice for Vista users.

   b.   Select the Desktop tab. (It's the Background tab in Windows 2000, and Desktop Background in Vista.)

   c.   Choose a background of your choice and click Apply.

✔ **Hint**

When you become more familiar with Windows, you can use the Browse button to locate your own photo to use for the background.

Step 7 One other thing to look at while you have the Display Properties dialog box open, which you should also remember for the CompTIA A+ exams, is where to locate the Power Savings settings.

    a. Click the Screen Saver tab in the Display Properties dialog box.

    b. At the bottom of the dialog box, you should see the Energy Star icon. Click the Power button next to this icon. In Vista, click the Change Power Settings menu option.

    c. Look at all the different settings here, and note exactly what you clicked to help you remember where to find them in the future.

 30 MINUTES

Lab Exercise 4.03: Windows Explorer

Windows Explorer is a program that enables you to see all the program and data files on a given storage device. Explorer works with hard drives and removable media such as optical media, USB flash drives, and floppy diskettes. Everyday users and technicians alike use this program more than any other when they need to locate and manipulate files and folders.

Learning Objectives

In this lab, you'll explore the Windows file structure.

    At the end of this lab, you'll be able to

- Use Windows Explorer
- Understand and use the contents of the Windows and Program Files folders

Lab Materials and Setup

The materials you need for this lab are

- A working computer running Windows 2000, Windows XP, or Windows Vista

✔ **Hint**

You can perform these steps on any Windows system, but some of them may involve functionality that's available only in Windows XP.

Getting Down to Business

When you click (or double-click) a folder icon to view what's inside, you're seeing Windows Explorer in action. It's really just a great graphical interface that enables you to see and manipulate files, folders, and their organizational structures quickly and easily, without memorizing a bunch of commands. Becoming familiar with its ins and outs is vital to becoming an effective PC technician.

Step 1 Begin by looking at the internal directory structure of Windows. Start Windows Explorer by selecting Start | All Programs | Accessories | Windows Explorer.

Look at the top of the list on the left pane of the Windows Explorer window; you'll notice an icon called Desktop. Anything you put directly under this folder will appear on the desktop itself, as well as in a "Desktop" folder on your C: drive. Remember that C: is your root directory (on a standard Windows system), and no file stored on the hard drive is "outside" that. The first place to go exploring in the Windows directory structure is the root directory:

a. Locate the My Computer/Computer icon in the left pane of Windows Explorer and click the plus sign (+). If it already has a minus sign (−) to the left, leave it there and continue.

b. Locate the C: drive icon, and click it once to highlight it. You should not need to click the plus sign, as clicking the drive's icon automatically expands its contents. The right pane now displays the contents of the root directory of your C: drive (see Figure 4-9). Now, check out Vista's look using the similar path indicated in Step a.

Figure 4-9 Viewing C:\ in Windows Explorer on Windows XP

✔ **Hint**

You can choose from several different views, or ways of displaying folder contents. The view shown in Figure 4-9 is called Icons view; other views include Thumbnails, Tiles, List, and Details. When you open the View menu, the current view is marked with a large black dot. You can switch views as often as you like, simply by selecting another view from the list. For the same result in Vista, just click the Views menu and rotate through the various screens available.

c. Find the folders named WINDOWS (sometimes named WINNT in Windows 2000) and Program Files. These two folders contain the majority of your operating system and program files.

d. Click the WINDOWS (or WINNT) folder icon. Look at Figure 4-10 for a sample of what you should see at this point if you're running Windows XP.

FIGURE 4-10 Exploring the WINDOWS folder

✖ Warning

Some system administrators may have changed the names of these folders, but in general this is not the best practice. If you need to contact Microsoft for assistance, they always start by directing you to the default folder names, so changing them can increase your troubleshooting time.

Step 2 In the next few substeps, you'll configure your folder options to provide the maximum information about your files and folders. Techs usually find that the more information they have about a component, the easier it is to troubleshoot or configure. Take a moment and explore the different folders and files in the WINDOWS folder. A typical WINDOWS folder will have more than 15,000 files in more than 1000 folders (see Figure 4-11). To view the number of files and folders in your WINDOWS folder, click the WINDOWS folder and then right-click somewhere in the blank area of the right pane and select Properties from the drop-down menu.

    a.   Maximize your Windows Explorer window (if it isn't already) by clicking the small box icon next to the × icon in the upper-right corner of the window. Then click the Views icon in the toolbar at the top left of the screen, and select Details.

    b.   Notice the column headings across the right pane, as shown in Figure 4-12. Click each of these headings to sort by that value. Click any heading again to sort in reverse order.

    c.   In Windows XP, select Tools | Folder Options. In Vista, select Organize | Folder and Search Options.

FIGURE 4-11 Viewing the WINDOWS folder's properties

Figure 4-12 Windows Explorer column headings in Details view

d. Select the View tab.

e. In the Advanced settings area, click the radio button *Show hidden files and folders*. This displays all files and folders, even those for which the Hidden attribute has been set.

f. Remove the check mark next to *Hide extensions for known file types*. This directs Windows Explorer to display the filename extensions in all views. This is useful for a tech, and these days it also helps users with things like identifying e-mail viruses hiding as (for instance) FILE.MP3.SCR.

g. Remove the check mark next to *Hide protected operating system files (Recommended)*. This will enable you to examine critical system files (for example C:\boot.ini or C:\bootmgr) when troubleshooting problems.

h. Click Apply to commit these changes to the folder view.

i. Before closing the folder options, click Apply to All Folders in the Folder views section. This will apply the Details view to every folder on the system, and enable you to see file extensions, hidden files, and system files in all folders as well.

j. Sort the folders and files by Type (click the Type column heading), and see if you can locate the files with these extensions:

- **.INI** These are initialization files used to install and configure the system.

- **.BMP** These are Windows bitmap graphics.

- **.EXE** These are executable files (in other words, programs).

- **.TXT** These are text files containing only ASCII text and symbols, readable across a wide range of systems.

k. Sort the list by Name, and locate these files:

- **EXPLORER.EXE** This is the Windows Explorer application you're using for these exercises.

- **DESKTOP.INI** This contains the configuration data for your desktop.

- **WIN.INI** This contains configuration settings for the boot process.

✖ **Warning**

Do not alter these files in *any* way! You won't like the results.

Step 3   Although MS-DOS is no longer used as an operating system, some of the original MS-DOS applications (commands) are still very much alive. These are now launched from the command-line interface in Windows as well as when you need to invoke the Recovery Console. As a PC technician, you're likely to need one or more of these command-line tools, so you'll work with some of them in Chapter 15; for now, you should just learn where to find them.

    a.   While still in Windows Explorer, find the C:\WINDOWS\System32 folder and open it. This folder stores all the command-line applications.

    b.   Sort the details list by Type, scroll down to the MS-DOS applications, and locate these files (see Figure 4-13):

        •   **FORMAT.COM**   This is used to prepare hard drives and floppy diskettes for storing data.

        •   **EDIT.COM**   This text editor program can create and modify configuration files in the command-line mode. The Windows equivalent is Notepad.

If you're using Vista, you may have to add the Type column. Right-click the column bar as shown in Figure 4-14 and check Type.

Step 4   When working with modern-day Windows, it's important to know the key system files involved in the boot process and fundamental core files. Use the *Search for files and folders* tool to locate and record the absolute path of the following system files. For a list of all command-line commands, open the Command Prompt and type **help**.

✔ Cross-Reference

For additional information on the files used to boot the Windows operating system, review the "The Boot Process" section in Chapter 4 of *Mike Meyers' CompTIA A+ Guide to Managing and Troubleshooting PCs.*

FIGURE 4-13 Locating command-line applications in Windows XP

FIGURE 4-14 Adding the Type column in Windows Vista

a. Click Start | Search | For Files or Folders, then click *All files and folders*, and finally click *More advanced options*.

b. Select the following check boxes (Figure 4-15):

- Search system folders

- Search hidden files and folders

- Search subfolders

c. If you're running Windows 2000 or XP, look in the local hard drive (on most systems this will be the C: drive) where your operating system is located and search for the following files. Make notes of their absolute paths:

- **NTLDR**   The filename is an abbreviation for NT Loader. This file is the "master of ceremonies," responsible for beginning the boot process and launching the other system files.

- **BOOT.INI**   This text file lists all operating systems available to the NTLDR. Double-click BOOT.INI in the Search Results window and examine the contents of the file. This is an important, editable file, especially on a multiboot system where you may need to change the boot order of the operating systems.

- **NTDETECT.COM**   This file detects installed hardware on systems that boot Windows 2000 or XP.

- **HAL.DLL**   This file loads many of the Hardware Abstraction Layer drivers.

- **NTOSKRNL.EXE**   The filename is an abbreviation for the NT Operating System Kernel. This file completes the loading of the Windows Registry, initiates all device drivers, and starts WINLOGON.EXE to display the Windows logon screen.

FIGURE 4-15 The Search utility in Windows XP

d. If you're running Vista, you have a different group of critical boot files. All of the 2000/XP boot files are now consolidated in one BOOTMGR file. Using the same method described, see if you can find BOOTMGR. It's almost always on the C: drive.

Step 5 Some of the other important folders and their contents are listed here. Look at each one to gain more experience using Windows Explorer. Remember, the location may be slightly different across the Windows family of operating systems. For instance, Windows 2000 uses WINNT as the default Windows folder. These are the folders you'll find:

- **WINDOWS\CURSORS** Windows stores the many different cursors you can use here.

- **WINDOWS\FONTS** Windows stores all its fonts in this folder. Note that fonts usually have one of two extensions, .FON or .TTF. The .FON files are the old-style screen fonts, and the .TTF files are modern TrueType fonts. You can double-click a font icon to see what the font looks like. Some users even print their favorite fonts and keep them in a three-ring binder for later reference.

- **WINDOWS\HELP**   This folder is the default location for all .HLP and .CHM (help) files. Open one to see what program uses it.

- **WINDOWS\MEDIA**   This folder is the default location for sounds and audio clips. Double-click a file with a .WAV or .MID extension to hear sounds.

- **WINDOWS\SYSTEM32**   This folder is the heart of Windows. Here you can see the core operating system files: HAL.DLL and NTOSKRNL.EXE. This folder also stores almost all of the .DLL files used by Windows.

Step 6   Collapse the WINDOWS folder, and expand the Program Files folder (see Figure 4-16). Microsoft doesn't like people messing around in these folders, so you may have to look to the left and click Show Files to see the folders. This is the default location for applications installed on your system. (Remember to scroll down if you can't see the end of the list.)

FIGURE 4-16 Exploring C:\Program Files in Windows Explorer

Follow these steps:

a.   Open the Windows Media Player subfolder, and find the application. Remember to look for the .EXE extension.

b.   Click the .EXE file icon to start the program.

c.   Close the program you just opened.

d.   Exit Windows Explorer.

 30 MINUTES

Lab Exercise 4.04: The Windows Control Panel

The Windows Control Panel is the technician's toolbox. It contains the tools you need to do everything from changing the mouse settings to installing new device drivers. This lab exercise won't attempt to examine every tool in the Control Panel, but it will help you become familiar with many of them. Some Control Panel programs—known as *applets*—are specific to particular hardware, while others are used for software configuration. Windows initially sets up defaults that work for most installations, but as a technician, you may need to tweak some of the settings. Also, not all Windows features are enabled in a normal installation, so you may need to enable or disable features according to the needs of a particular user.

✔ **Cross-Reference**

For a refresher on the Windows Control Panel, refer to the "Control Panel" section in Chapter 4 of *Mike Meyers' CompTIA A+ Guide to Managing and Troubleshooting PCs.*

Learning Objectives

In this lab, you'll practice accessing the Control Panel and making configuration adjustments.

At the end of this lab, you'll be able to

- Navigate to the Control Panel

- Explain the use of some common Control Panel applets

Lab Materials and Setup

The materials you need for this lab are

- A working computer running Windows 2000, XP, or Vista

Getting Down to Business

The Control Panel is the toolbox, and one of the key tools in the Control Panel is the Device Manager. The Device Manager lists all your system hardware. From it you can load drivers, set resources, and configure other aspects of your hardware devices. You'll now get familiar with both.

Step 1   As a technician, you'll access the Control Panel and the Device Manager often. You really do need to know the path to these important tools in each versions of Windows. The CompTIA A+ exams have numerous questions about paths to these tools.

✔ **Hint**

Throughout the rest of this manual, when a lab involves changing settings located in the Control Panel or the Device Manager, the directions will assume you know how to get that far, and the steps will begin with the Control Panel or Device Manager already open. Refer back to this exercise if you need a refresher on opening the Control Panel.

a.   To open the Control Panel, click on the Start button. In Windows 2000 and the Classic view of other versions, select Settings, then Control Panel. In Windows XP and Vista, select Control Panel directly from the Start menu. The Control Panel dialog box opens, as shown in Figures 4-17 and 4-18.

FIGURE 4-17 The Control Panel (Classic View) in Windows XP

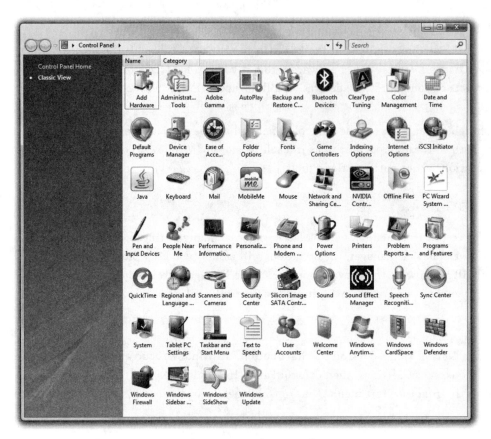

FIGURE 4-18 The Control Panel (Classic View) in Windows Vista

b. Start with the System applet. The System applet is the gateway to many important tools and utilities you will use as a PC technician. You'll explore some of these utilities in other labs throughout the manual; for now, just take a high-level view of the following:

   • **Device Manager**   In Windows 2000 and XP, select the Hardware tab and click the Device Manager button to see a list of hardware installed in your system. In Vista, you open the Device Manager directly, but it can also be found in the System applet. Expand various items to see the list of devices in each area. Highlighting any device, right-clicking, and selecting Properties will give you configuration information for that device. You'll return here later in the lab manual to configure these devices.

   • **Driver Signing**   In Windows 2000 and XP, close Device Manager, and while still on the Hardware tab, click the Driver Signing button. This is where you tell Windows how to handle device drivers that have not been tested and approved by Microsoft. The three settings are Ignore, Warn, and Block. In Vista's Control Panel, open the System applet. Click Remote Settings, Continue, the Hardware tab, and then Windows Update Driver Settings. Once there, observe the radio button choices, and then click Cancel.

- **Startup and Recovery** Select the Advanced tab and click the Settings button under the Startup and Recovery box. Examine the settings for the Startup options. Now, click Environment Variables and choose the Edit button for both User and System variables. Do you recognize the file that is displayed?

c. Close Notepad and the Startup and Recovery and System Properties dialog boxes, all without saving changes.

Step 2 Now examine some other applets in the Control Panel:

a. In Windows 2000/XP, double-click the Display icon. This is the same window you see if you right-click the desktop and select Properties. Windows Vista uses the Personalization applet for many of the same functions.

b. Notice the tab headings in 2000/XP and list of links in Vista. Three are common to all flavors of Windows: Screen Saver, Appearance, and Settings. Windows 2000 also has Background, Web, and Effects tabs. Windows XP incorporates the contents of those three tabs into two tabs, named Themes and Desktop.

✖ Warning

Clicking an Advanced button in the Display applet can give you access to many special features of your particular monitor/video card, including the refresh rate. Be sure you know what you're doing before you change these settings!

✔ Hint

If you click the Apply button instead of the OK button after making a change, the Display applet will remain open after the change takes effect; this can be useful when you need to experiment a bit.

---

c. Return to the Control Panel and double-click the Sounds and Multimedia icon in Windows 2000, Sounds and Audio Devices icon in Windows XP, or the Sound icon in Windows Vista to open that dialog box.

d. Again, you'll see tabs at the top left of the dialog box. Most of your applets will be similar to this. Explore each tab, and become familiar with what each does. Make changes to see the results. Be sure you remember or record the original settings so that you can reset them.

e. Reset all of your experimental changes, and close the applet.

Step 3   Keyboard and mouse action settings are definitely a matter of personal preference. Be careful to tell the user if you make any changes to these settings. If you need to speed them up for your own use while troubleshooting a PC, remember to slow them down again so the user isn't frustrated by keys that repeat or a mouse cursor that races across the screen out of control.

To adjust the keyboard settings:

a.   Double-click the Keyboard icon in the Control Panel.

b.   Change the cursor's blink rate and test it.

c.   Change the key repeat rate and delay settings. A minor adjustment here can really help a heavy-fingered user.

d.   Close the Keyboard applet.

✔ Hint

The Mouse applet can have many different looks, depending on whether the system uses a default Windows driver or special drivers for the particular mouse. You may have to explore your applet to find these settings.

---

e.   Double-click the Mouse icon to open the Mouse applet.

f.   Change from a right-hand to a left-hand mouse. Try it out. Does that make your brain hurt? Well then, change it back. (Ahhh, that's better!)

g.   Change the double-click speed. Slow it down a bit. Is that easier? Slow it down more. Do you find that annoying? Now speed it up. Can you click fast enough?

h.   Change the mini-icons that represent your mouse pointer, such as the arrow, hourglass, and so on. Try a couple of different sets. Can you think of situations where some of these alternative icon sets might be useful?

_____

_____

i.   Change the pointer options. Change the speed at which the pointer travels across your screen. Everyone has his or her own sweet spot for this, so experiment to find yours. Turn on pointer trails. Do you find them cool, or annoying? If you have a Snap To option, turn that on. Now open a dialog box and watch the pointer jump to the active button. Is this convenient, or too much help? Turn off any features you don't want to retain.

j.   Now that you've tweaked your mouse performance, close the applet.

Step 4 The CompTIA A+ exams include questions about user accessibility. Know what settings you can change to accommodate the hearing and visually impaired, and where to find those settings:

a.   In Windows 2000 and XP, open the Accessibility Options applet (see Figure 4-19). In Vista, choose the Ease of Access Center applet and notice that you have all the previously mentioned items as well as many more! (See Figure 4-20.)

b.   Select the Display tab in Windows 2000/XP, or click *Make the computer easier to see* in Windows Vista.

c.   In Windows 2000/XP, check the Use High Contrast checkbox and click Settings (see Figure 4-21). In Windows Vista, check the box to enable the High Contrast key combination and then click Choose a High Contrast color scheme.

d.   Choose a scheme you like and click OK.

e.   Click Apply in the Accessibility Options dialog box to see how it looks. In Vista, you'll have to press LEFT ALT-LEFT SHIFT-PRINT SCREEN to activate High Contrast mode.

f.   Turn off the Use High Contrast option, then click Apply and OK.

g.   Close the Accessibility Options/Ease of Access dialog box.

FIGURE 4-19 The Accessibility Options dialog box

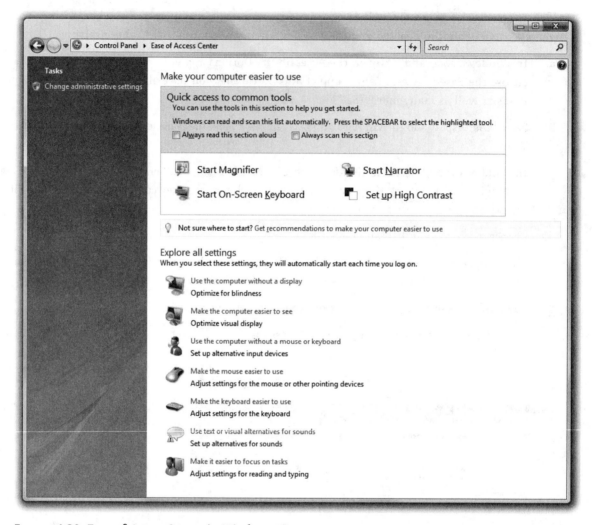

FIGURE 4-20 Ease of Access Center in Windows Vista

Step 5   One more commonly used applet is Date and Time.

Open the Date and Time applet in the Control Panel. This applet has been around since the dawn of time, more or less, when computers didn't automatically adjust themselves for Daylight Saving Time.

Adjust the date and time. Notice that you can do this either by scrolling with the arrows or by highlighting the fields. This feature can come in handy if you travel and want to change the time zone on a portable computer.

FIGURE 4-21 Setting the High Contrast option for the visually impaired

30 MINUTES

Lab Exercise 4.05: The Windows Microsoft Management Console (MMC) Toolbox

You're about to learn how to customize your Windows toolkit! Almost every profession requires a set of tools to get the job done. Some of these tools are necessary, and some are luxuries. If you were a carpenter, you might have a toolbox in which you keep your hammer, saw, screwdrivers, pliers, and so on. You could then buy new tools ("I really needed this pneumatic nail gun, and it was on sale!" is a common excuse) and add them to your toolbox—but you'd need to keep it all organized, or risk not being able to find the tool you need when you need it.

To help organize all of your PC technician's tools, Microsoft created a handy toolbox: the Microsoft Management Console, or MMC. The MMC not only organizes all of those useful tools, but also provides a consistent look and feel between different systems and even different operating systems, which makes it easier to use them.

✔ **Cross-Reference**

For details on working with the MMC, refer to the "Microsoft Management Console" section in Chapter 4 of *Mike Meyers' CompTIA A+ Guide to Managing and Troubleshooting PCs*.

Learning Objectives

In this exercise, you'll learn how to create an MMC. You'll also create a desktop icon that you can use to access this customized software toolkit whenever you need it.

At the end of this lab, you'll be able to

- Create an MMC

- Add tools (snap-ins) to the MMC

Lab Materials and Setup

The materials you need for this lab are

- A working computer running Windows 2000, Windows XP, or Windows Vista

Getting Down to Business

The MMC is a shell program that holds individual utilities called snap-ins. The first time you create an MMC, you get a default blank console. A blank MMC isn't much to look at—like any new toolbox, it starts out empty.

Step 1 To create your MMC, select Start | Run, type **mmc**, and then click OK. Voilà! You've created a blank console (see Figure 4-22).

You'll notice that the name in the upper-left corner is Console1. In Vista, you'll also notice a panel called Actions, which contains a list of actions that are available to users as you add snap-ins and select them.

Before you actually configure an MMC, you need to understand a few points. First, you can have more than one MMC; successive consoles will be given default names such as Console2, Console3, and so on. Second, you can rename the consoles that you create. Third, you can choose where to save the consoles, so that you can easily find them again. Finally, once you've created an MMC, you can modify it by adding or removing tools—just like your toolbox at home.

Follow these steps to practice working with MMCs:

a. Click File (Windows XP and Vista) or Console (Windows 2000) | Save As and fill in the boxes as follows:

- **Save in** Desktop

- **File name** My First MMC

- **Save as type** Microsoft Management Console Files (*.msc)

FIGURE 4-22 Blank MMCs in XP and Vista

b. Click Save to continue. (Don't exit the MMC!)

c. Notice in the upper-left corner of the open window that the name has changed.

d. Find the new icon that's been created on the desktop. This icon, which bears the same name as your new MMC, enables you to access the MMC in the future with just a double-click of the mouse.

Step 2 When you add snap-ins, they'll show up in the Add/Remove Snap-in dialog box (see Figure 4-23). You'll now add some snap-ins to your MMC:

a. Click File | Add/Remove Snap-in (Windows XP/Vista) or Console | Add/Remove Snap-in (Windows 2000).

b. Click Add, and let the fun begin (see Figure 4-24). I bet you haven't had this many selections since your last visit to Sears' hardware department!

c. Add the Device Manager as your first tool. Select Device Manager from the list and click Add.

Figure 4-23 Adding or removing snap-ins

Figure 4-24 Adding a standalone snap-in

✔ **Hint**

When you add a snap-in, you have a choice of adding it for either your local computer or another computer. With the proper access permissions, in other words, you can look at the Device Manager on a networked system. More than likely, you don't have the necessary permissions to do this, so stick with the local option for now.

    d.   Select Local Computer and click Finish.

✖ **Warning**

I can't emphasize strongly enough that the best way to get a systems administrator mad is to go snooping around on the network. As a technician, your main concern is to do no harm. If you accidentally find your way to an unauthorized area, it's your duty to report it to an administrator.

While you're here, you'll add one more snap-in: the Event Viewer. You'll use this tool in the labs for Chapter 17. Adding it here will provide an alternate way to access this tool:

    a.   Select Event Viewer from the list.

    b.   Select Local Computer and Finish to close out the wizard.

    c.   Click Add to close the list window, and click OK to close the Add/Remove window.

    d.   Your MMC should now show two snap-ins.

    e.   Be sure to save your MMC.

You now have a toolbox with quick access to Device Manager and Event Viewer. You can use these tools in the same way as if you navigated to them through the conventional methods.

Click Device Manager to expand the list of devices. Notice that it looks the same and works the same as it would if you opened it through the Control Panel.

Step 3 If everything has worked correctly up to now, continue with this step (if you had problems creating your MMC, review the instructions or ask your instructor for assistance):

    a.   Double-click the desktop icon for My First MMC.

    b.   Your Device Manager and Event Log are now available directly from your desktop (see Figure 4-25).

FIGURE 4-25 Accessing Device
Manager from a custom MMC

✔ **Hint**

I've only scratched the surface of creating an MMC here. Your customizing options are limited
only by the number of snap-ins available and your imagination. Try creating different groupings
of tools to organize similar tasks, maybe all the disk management tools together, or all the user,
group, and resource tools. Be creative!

 30 MINUTES

Lab Exercise 4.06: The Windows Registry

The Registry stores everything about your PC, including information on all the hardware in the PC,
network information, user preferences, file types, and virtually anything else you might run into with
Windows. The hardware, software, and program configuration settings in the Registry are particular
to each PC. Two identical PCs with the same operating system and hardware can still be remarkably
different because of user settings and preferences. Almost any form of configuration done to a Windows
system results in changes to the Registry.

✖ **Warning**

When changing the Registry, proceed with great care—making changes in the Registry can
cause unpredictable and possibly harmful results. To paraphrase the old carpenter's adage:
consider twice, change once!

Learning Objectives

Most of the common tools to modify the Registry are contained in the Control Panel. When you use the Display applet to change a background, for example, the resultant changes are added to the Registry. The Control Panel applets are what you should normally use to configure the Registry. However, there are times—a virus attack, perhaps, or complete removal of a stubborn application—when direct manipulation of the Registry is needed. In this lab, you'll familiarize yourself with the Windows Registry and the direct manipulation of the Registry using the REGEDIT command.

At the end of this lab, you'll be able to

- Access the Registry using REGEDIT

- Export, import, and modify Registry data subkeys and values

- Define the function of the five top-level Registry keys

Lab Materials and Setup

The materials you need for this lab are

- A working computer running Windows 2000, Windows XP, or Windows Vista

Getting Down to Business

A technician needs to know how to access the Registry and modify the configuration based on solid support from Microsoft or other trusted sources. As mentioned in the Learning Objectives, your main interface to the Registry is the Control Panel. Changes made through the applets in the Control Panel result in modifications to the Registry settings. To see what's going on behind the scenes, though, you'll explore the Registry directly in this exercise using the REGEDIT command.

✔ Cross-Reference

For more detail on the Windows Registry and working with REGEDIT and REGEDT32, refer to the "Registry" section in Chapter 4 of *Mike Meyers' CompTIA A+ Guide to Managing and Troubleshooting PCs.*

Step 1 You almost never need to access the Registry directly. It's meant to work in the background, quietly storing all the necessary data for the system, updated only through a few menus and installation programs. When you want to access the Registry directly, you must use the Registry Editor (REGEDIT or REGEDT32).

FIGURE 4-26 Starting the Registry Editor

✔ **Hint**

This lab exercise was written using a system running Windows XP Professional and works in Vista. Windows XP and all later versions have combined the two versions of the Registry Editor—REGEDIT and REGEDT32—into simply REGEDIT (although you can still use either command to open the editor. If you are working on a Windows 2000 Professional machine, you can explore the differences between REGEDIT and REGEDT32. Remember that no matter which version of Windows you are using, the Registry is a binary file, not a text file. You can't edit it using EDIT, Notepad, or any other text editor.

To edit the Registry directly, follow these steps:

a.   Select Start | Run, type **regedit**, and then click OK (see Figure 4-26) to start the Registry Editor.

b.   Note the five main subgroups or root keys in the Registry (see Figure 4-27). Some of these root key folders may be expanded. Click the minus sign by any expanded folders. Do a quick mental review—do you know the function of each Registry key? You should!

FIGURE 4-27 Viewing the five main subgroups of the Windows XP Registry

c. Now test your knowledge of the Registry. Referring to the textbook as necessary, match the listed keys with their definitions by writing the definition letter next to the corresponding key:

HKEY_CLASSES_ROOT   _____

HKEY_CURRENT_USER   _____

HKEY_LOCAL_MACHINE   _____

HKEY_USERS   _____

HKEY_CURRENT_CONFIG   _____

   A. Contains the data for non-user-specific configurations, and includes every device in your PC and those you've removed

   B. Contains the personalization information for all users on a PC

   C. Contains additional hardware information when there are values in HKEY_LOCAL_MACHINE such as two different monitors

   D. Defines the standard class objects used by Windows; information stored here is used to open the correct application when a file is opened

   E. Contains the current user settings, such as fonts, icons, and colors on systems that are set up to support multiple users

Step 2   One of the reasons you might want to edit the Registry directly would be to implement or expand a component of Windows that is not accessible through the Control Panel interface. A favorite of many techs is to enable the Rename function for the Recycle Bin. Expand the HKEY_CLASSES_ROOT key by clicking the plus sign. Notice that there are more subkeys underneath it, some of which have subkeys of their own, and so on. Search down to the CLSID subkey and expand the key by clicking the plus sign. You will see hundreds of long identification codes. Now use the Find utility (CTRL-F) and enter the following string into the text box: **645FF040-5081-101B-9F08-00AA002F954E**. Make sure you enter the numbers correctly. Expand the subkey and click the ShellFolder icon. You should see the information in Figure 4-28.

Before you start changing the Registry, it's a good idea to learn how to "back up" the keys by exporting and importing them. This will enable you to reset the subkey to its original state if you make a mistake in your entries.

   a. Highlight the ShellFolder subkey, and then select File | Export to open the Export Registry File dialog box. Save the key in a folder where you can find it again, and give it a useful name that you won't forget.

   b. Highlight the key again, and double-click the Attributes REG_BINARY file. Replace the hexadecimal number 40 01 00 20 with **50 01 00 20** and click OK.

   c. Double-click the "CallForAttributes" REG_DWORD file. Replace the 40 with **00** and click OK.

   d. Minimize the Registry Editor and find the Recycle Bin on your desktop.

FIGURE 4-28 Contents of the ShellFolder in REGEDIT

e. Right-click the Recycle Bin icon. In the drop-down menu there is now a Rename option (see Figure 4-29). Click Rename and change the name of the Recycle Bin. Fun, eh?

f. To return the Recycle Bin to its natural state, first rename it back to Recycle Bin. Now navigate to your exported Registry file and double-click the file. You will be asked if you are sure you want to add this information to the Registry. Click Yes. You should see a message that the information was successfully added to the Registry.

g. To confirm that your backup Registry information has taken effect, right-click the Recycle Bin. Can you still rename it? _____

FIGURE 4-29 The Recycle Bin's
newly added Rename option

Step 3 Imagine you're in the Control Panel adjusting your mouse settings, and you adjust the mouse double-click speed to the maximum (fastest) and close the window without testing it. When you try to use the system, you can't double-click the mouse fast enough even to get back into the Control Panel to fix it. (This is a bit of a stretch, as you could always use the keyboard to access the Mouse applet, but go with me here to see the Registry in action.) So, what do you do? Follow these steps to view your current Mouse applet double-click speed setting and then use REGEDIT to change it:

a. Access the Control Panel and open the Mouse applet.

b. Adjust the slider for the double-click speed to the middle position, and test to be sure it works.

c. Click Apply and then OK. Close the Mouse applet and Control Panel.

d. Open the Registry Editor, and make sure that My Computer is highlighted at the top of the left pane.

e. Select Edit | Find to search for the mouse double-click speed. In the Find What field, type **doubleclickspeed** (be sure to spell it as one word, no spaces). Check the Match Whole String Only box. Click Find Next. You want only the first occurrence it finds. There are other things with that name that you don't want to change.

f. When REGEDIT finds the file, right-click the word DoubleClickSpeed in the right pane and select Modify.

g. Change the value to something between 100 and 900 (milliseconds); 100 is very fast. Click OK and then close the Registry Editor.

h. Reopen the Mouse applet in the Control Panel. Did the slider move from where it was?

_____

i. For more practice, set your double-click speed to the fastest setting in the Control Panel and go to the Registry to slow it down.

✔ **Hint**

The Web site www.winguides.com/registry is full of working Registry fixes.

Lab Analysis Test

1. Your friend Brian calls you and asks if he can make his new Windows XP system look like the Windows 2000 system he uses at work. He says he doesn't like the bright, cartoonish style, and the Start menu is different. Explain to Brian what he can and can't do to change the look of Windows XP.

2. What's the purpose of the MMC? What is the added feature in Vista?

3. When you install Windows XP for the first time on Joe's PC, he notices that some desktop icons he's accustomed to seeing are missing. As a matter of fact, only the Recycle Bin icon is present. Where and how can you add the desktop icons he's used to seeing in Windows 2000?

4. One of your clients using Windows Vista called your help desk because he's experiencing difficulties using the mouse. He says his mouse moves too fast, and icons don't respond when he double-clicks them. What's wrong? Where would you direct him to go to fix this problem? Give the complete path.

5. Which is a safer place for trained technicians to make changes or modifications: the Control Panel or the Registry? Explain your choice.

Key Term Quiz

Use the following terms to complete the following sentences. Not all terms will be used.

Aero

Classic View

Control Panel

MMC

Recycle Bin

REGEDIT

snap-ins

Start button

taskbar

1. The Registry contains all the configuration data and can be accessed directly using _____.

2. When you delete files, Windows creates shortcuts to them in the _____.

3. The System, Display, and Mouse applets are found in the _____.

4. The various tools in the MMC are known as _____.

5. The Start button and the notification area/system tray are parts of the Windows _____.

6. With the proper video card installed in your computer running Windows Vista, you can take advantage of the _____ experience.

Chapter 5
Microprocessors

Lab Exercises

Many PC users are comfortable performing simple installation and upgrade tasks, such as adding RAM or installing a modem or sound card. When it comes to the more complicated tasks, however, such as installing or replacing a central processing unit (CPU), wise users turn to the experts—this means you!

Installing a CPU is one of the many tasks you'll find yourself performing as a PC tech. Whether you're building a new system from scratch or replacing the CPU on an existing computer, it's your job to know the important characteristics of the CPU, match the CPU to compatible motherboards, and confirm that the CPU in the PC is running properly.

In this set of lab exercises, you'll identify current CPU types, form factors, sockets, and practice installing a CPU/fan assembly on a motherboard. You'll then explore the specifications of the microprocessor with a freeware program known as CPU-Z.

It's time to find your anti-static wrist strap and get started with your exploration of CPUs!

🕐 30 MINUTES

Lab Exercise 5.01: Identifying CPU Characteristics

There you are, innocently strolling down the hall at work, following the smell of freshly brewed coffee, when you're ambushed by Joe the accountant, brandishing a CPU/fan unit. He wants to replace the CPU in his machine with this new one he bought on eBay, and he wants you to help him. When you're the resident computer tech geek, your coworkers will expect you to be able to deal competently with a situation like Joe's.

Staying on top of the many developments in CPU technology can be challenging, but it's also a necessary part of your job as a PC technician. By this point, you know that you can't just plug any CPU into any motherboard and expect it to work—you have to match the right CPU to the right motherboard. To accomplish this, you need to identify important CPU characteristics such as form factor, clock speed, and bus speed, as well as things like voltage settings, clock multiplier configurations, and cooling requirements.

Learning Objectives

In this lab, you'll practice identifying CPUs and CPU fan components.

At the end of this lab, you'll be able to

- Recognize the different kinds of CPUs

- Recognize different CPU fan attachments

- Identify the basic specifications of different classes of CPUs

Lab Materials and Setup

The materials you need for this lab are

- A notepad and pencil to document the specifications

- Optional: Access to a working computer with a word processing or spreadsheet application installed and access to the Internet, to facilitate research and documentation of the CPU specifications

- The disassembled, non-production PC computer system used in the lab exercises in Chapter 3

Getting Down to Business

In the following steps, you'll review your knowledge of CPU specifications, and then examine the CPU and fan attachment on a PC.

> ✔ **Cross-Reference**
>
> Use Chapter 5 of *Mike Meyers' CompTIA A+ Guide to Managing and Troubleshooting PCs* to help fill in the specifications for each CPU in the following charts.

Step 1 A good tech will not only learn the specifications of different CPU chips but will also master the use of reference tools such as the Internet, manufacturers' Web sites, product documentation, and reference books. A quick search of the Web or your motherboard book (a fancy name for your motherboard's manual) will generally yield a full list of specs for a given CPU.

See how many CPU chip features you can fill in given the maker and CPU type:

→ **Note**

CPUs have very short production lives. If some of these CPUs have become obsolete, use the extra rows provided to add more-modern processors to the assignment.

Maker	CPU Type	Package	Clock Speed(GHz)	FSB Speed (MHz or GT/s)	L2 Cache (MB)	Number of Cores
Intel	Core 2 Quad Q9650					
AMD	Phenom II X3 710					
AMD	Phenom II X4 965					
Intel	Celeron M 575					
AMD	Athlon X2 7550 Black Edition					
Intel	Pentium 4 650					
Intel	Atom 330					
Intel	Xeon X5570					
Intel	Core i7-960					

Step 2 Look at the CPUs pictured in Figure 5-1, making note of the differences you see. In particular, look for the following:

- Differing pin grid array (PGA) or land grid array (LGA) packages
- Orientation guide notches

Step 3 Many different types of fans can be attached to CPUs in many different ways. Describe the characteristics of the types of fans shown in Figure 5-2.

A. _____

B. _____

C. _____

FIGURE 5-1 Exploring different CPUs

Step 4   On your disassembled PC, locate the CPU and fan assembly. Make note of the type of CPU package and fan assembly. Also note the type of power connector used for the fan: Molex, three-prong motherboard plug, or none. Then replace the CPU into the anti-static bag and return the fan assembly to your work surface.

✔ **Hint**

Many users will argue that Intel is better than AMD, or vice versa. The best way to solve this dispute is to look it up for yourself. In fact, I challenge you to do as much research as possible before recommending one over the other. The most significant differentiation I've found is that AMD has better power management, whereas Intel is more power efficient. Again, look for yourself, interview many people, and don't forget to ask the client what they are primarily using the system for (that is, as a workstation, as a server, for gaming, and so forth).

A

B

C

FIGURE 5-2 Comparing different CPU fans

30 MINUTES

Lab Exercise 5.02: Recognizing CPU Sockets

Because you know your CPUs, you have identified Joe's purchase, but you explain to him that until you look at his motherboard, you can't say whether he'll be able to use it. CPU compatibility is determined largely by what the motherboard can support. Many motherboards enable you to upgrade the PC by replacing the existing CPU with a faster model of the same type. As a technician, your job is to make sure that the newer CPU has the same pin configuration as the motherboard. If you do not know where to begin, perform an online search for the maker of the motherboard. Still, in many cases, you must replace the entire motherboard if you want to move up to a faster microprocessor.

Learning Objectives

In this lab, you'll identify various CPU sockets.

At the end of this lab, you'll be able to

- Recognize different kinds of CPU sockets

- Know which CPUs require which sockets

Lab Materials and Setup

The materials you need for this lab are

- A notepad and pencil to document the specifications

- Optional: Access to a working computer with a word processing or spreadsheet application installed and access to the Internet, to facilitate research and documentation of the CPU socket specifications

This lab is more effective if you have access to different types of motherboards with different types of CPU sockets.

Getting Down to Business

In the following steps, you'll review your knowledge of CPU socket types.

Step 1   Identify and describe the different socket types in Figure 5-3. Include the socket number/letter and the make and model of CPU that would fit that socket.

A   B   C   D

Figure 5-3 Identifying sockets

Example: <u>Socket A (PGA-462), AMD Athlon 64 CPUs</u>

A. _____

B. _____

C. _____

D. _____

Step 2 Draw a line connecting each CPU to its corresponding socket type:

CPU	Socket Type
Intel Core 2 Duo	Socket 939
AMD Phenom II	Socket AM3
AMD Athlon X2	Socket LGA-1156
Intel Pentium 4 (1.8 GHz)	Socket 478
Intel Core i7-870	Socket AM2+
AMD Athlon 64 3000+	Socket LGA-775

 30 MINUTES

Lab Exercise 5.03: Removing and Installing a CPU

Luckily for Joe, his motherboard is compatible with his new CPU. Now he expects you to play your "computer expert" role and install the new CPU in his PC. As a PC tech, you must be comfortable with such basic tasks. In this exercise, you'll familiarize yourself with the procedure; using your disassembled PC, you'll practice removing and reinstalling the CPU and fan assembly.

Learning Objectives

In this lab, you'll practice removing and installing a CPU and CPU fan assembly.

At the end of this lab, you'll be able to

- Remove and install a CPU safely and correctly

- Remove and install a CPU fan assembly safely and correctly

Lab Materials and Setup

The materials you need for this lab are

- The disassembled, non-production PC you used in the lab exercises in Chapter 3

- An anti-static mat, or other static-safe material on which to place the CPU following removal

- An anti-static wrist strap

- Thermal paste

- A small slotted (flat-head) screwdriver

Getting Down to Business

Time to get your hands dirty! Removing and installing CPUs is one of the most nerve-wracking tasks that new PC techs undertake, but there's no need to panic. You'll be fine as long as you take the proper precautions to prevent ESD damage, and handle the CPU and fan assembly with care.

✖ Warning

Be careful not to touch any of the exposed metal contacts on either the CPU or the CPU socket.

Step 1   Using the disassembled PC, determine whether the process of reinstalling and removing the CPU and fan assembly will be easier with the motherboard on an anti-static mat or installed in its case; if you prefer, reinstall the motherboard into the case before proceeding. You may find that it is easier to work with the stubborn fan assembly clamp if the motherboard is secured in the case.

Step 2   In most cases you'll have to remove the fan assembly before you can remove the CPU. Screw-down fans are easier to remove than clip fans. Screw-down fans require only that you unscrew the securing hardware. Clip fans, found on many types of CPUs, require you to apply pressure on the clip to release it from the fan mount. Use a small slotted screwdriver to do this, as shown in Figure 5-4. Use caution when prying the clip open, and don't forget to unplug the CPU fan!

FIGURE 5-4 Using a screwdriver to remove a clip-type CPU fan from its mount

---

✔ **Hint**

You'll discover that releasing a fan clip takes way more force than you want to apply to anything so near a delicate CPU chip. Realizing this in advance, you can be sure to brace yourself and position the screwdriver carefully, to minimize the possibility of it slipping off and gouging something.

The CPU and fan assembly will have thermal paste residue on the surfaces that were previously touching. You cannot reuse thermal paste, so you'll need to apply a fresh layer when you reinstall the CPU fan. Using a clean, lint-free cloth, carefully wipe the thermal paste residue from the CPU and fan assembly, and then place the fan assembly on an anti-static surface.

Step 3 Before proceeding, notice the CPU's orientation notches. All CPUs have some form of orientation notch (or notches).

Now remove the CPU. Start by moving the end of the zero insertion force (ZIF) lever a little outward to clear the safety notch; then raise the lever to a vertical position. Next, grasp the chip carefully by its edges and lift it straight up and out of the socket. Be careful not to lift the CPU at an angle—if it's a PGA CPU, you'll bend its tiny pins. LGA CPUs don't have pins, but you can damage the pins on the motherboard, so still be careful! As you lift out the CPU, make sure that the ZIF lever stays in an upright position.

The recommendation to use an older, non-production PC for the disassembly and reassembly exercises may present you with the task of working with some older technology. PGA-style packages, even the early designs, are fairly similar from processor to processor. If your CPU is an Intel Pentium II or III, or an early AMD Athlon, you may have to work with a Single Edge Contact (SEC) cartridge inserted in a Slot 1 or Slot A socket.

Removing an SEC CPU that uses a slot interface normally does not require removing the fan, which is usually attached to the chip cartridge itself. To remove a slot CPU, first check for and release any retaining clips that may be securing it to the slot, and then grasp the cartridge firmly on both ends and pull straight up from the motherboard.

Step 4   Now that you have the CPU chip out, examine it closely. The manufacturer usually prints the chip's brand and type directly on the chip, providing you with some important facts about the chip's design and performance capabilities. If your chip is an AMD Athlon X2 dual core, for example, you know that its PGA packaging fits in a Socket AM2 (938 pins) and its bus speed is 200 MHz. Make a note of the relevant specs for your chip.

What is the CPU information printed on the chip package?

_____

✖ **Warning**

Always handle a CPU chip like a fragile old photograph: very gently, holding it only by the edges. Make sure you take *complete* ESD avoidance precautions, because even a tiny amount of static electricity can harm a CPU!

Step 5   Reinsert the CPU with the correct orientation, lock down the ZIF lever, and reattach the fan. Now remove the fan assembly and the CPU again. Practice this a few times to become comfortable with the process. When you're finished practicing, reinsert the CPU for the last time. Be sure to apply a thin film of fresh thermal paste onto the square in the center of the top of the CPU before you place the fan. Now reattach the fan assembly. Don't forget to plug the fan back in!

✔ **Hint**

If this were a production system with RAM and other components installed, this would be an ideal time to turn the system back on and make sure you have the CPU seated properly. In real life, you should always test your hardware before you put the case back on!

Step 6 You may leave your CPU/fan assembly installed on the motherboard and place the motherboard on your anti-static mat. Optionally, if you reinstalled the motherboard in the case, you may leave it assembled.

 30 MINUTES

Lab Exercise 5.04: Cooling Your CPU

Now that Joe has his processor, he needs to keep it cool, and since you've done everything else for him so far, you might as well make sure it's properly cooled, too! Someone new to the CPU cooling business might be tempted to think that CPUs come from the factory with a defined operating temperature. This isn't the case. The operating temperature depends tremendously on the way you cool the CPU. A far more reliable measurement is *power consumption*, the amount of power a CPU generates. CPU power consumption is measured in watts (W), with most desktop CPUs consuming in excess of 100 W. If you've ever tried to touch a 100-W light bulb, you can appreciate that this level of power consumption generates a tremendous amount of heat. If this heat isn't taken away from the CPU by some form of cooling, the CPU will begin to overheat. If a CPU gets too hot, it will automatically shut itself down to prevent permanent damage. You need to provide Joe's CPU with some form of cooling device.

Learning Objectives

In this lab, you'll identify the strengths and weaknesses of three CPU cooling options: OEM fans, third-party fans, and liquid cooling.

At the end of this lab, you'll be able to

- Determine the cooling needs of your CPU

- Decide on the form of cooling to use for your needs

Lab Materials and Setup

The materials you need for this lab are

- Access to a working computer with Internet access

- A notepad and pencil to document the specifications

Getting Down to Business

The three most common types of CPU cooling are original equipment manufacturer (OEM) fans, third-party fans, and liquid cooling. Each of the following steps gives you an opportunity to investigate each of these options for a particular CPU.

Step 1 For the purposes of this exercise, pick out any single modern CPU as a sample CPU—you'll use this to find the proper cooling devices. Any CPU will work, but you'll find more options if you choose one that's readily available on popular online stores. If you're not sure what online store to use, try www.newegg.com.

Individual CPUs are most commonly sold in what's known as a "retail box." This includes both the CPU and an OEM fan.

Step 2 Look online for third-party fan solutions for the CPU you've chosen. Look for the following popular brand names and see what third-party fans each of these manufacturers offer for your CPU:

Antec, Arctic Cooling, Cooler Master, Thermaltake, Zalman

Document the name, model number and price for each one and list some of the benefits it offers:

Manufacturer	Model Number	Price	Benefits
_____	_____	_____	_____
_____	_____	_____	_____
_____	_____	_____	_____
_____	_____	_____	_____
_____	_____	_____	_____

Step 3 Do some research on liquid cooling. Why would anyone want to use liquid cooling on a CPU?

_____

_____

Step 4 Using the same manufacturers listed in Step 3, try to find liquid cooling options for your CPU. Most liquid cooling options are either bolt-on (they can be added to an existing case) or case-integrated (they are built into a system case).

Manufacturer	Model Number	Price	Bolt-on or case?
_____	_____	_____	_____
_____	_____	_____	_____
_____	_____	_____	_____
_____	_____	_____	_____
_____	_____	_____	_____

30 MINUTES

Lab Exercise 5.05: Exploring CPU Specifications with CPU-Z

Joe is very impressed with your knowledge and expertise—and he's relieved that the CPU he purchased on eBay happened to work out. You explain that not only did it work out, but he has really improved the performance of his system with the upgraded CPU. In fact, to further display the characteristics of the CPU Joe has just purchased, you download and run a utility known as CPU-Z from www.cpuid.com. This utility reads the specifications of different PC components from information embedded in those components.

Learning Objectives

In this lab, you'll identify various CPU specifications.

At the end of this lab, you'll be able to

- Run the CPU-Z utility

- Recognize key characteristics of CPUs

Lab Materials and Setup

The materials you need for this lab are

- Access to a working computer with Internet access, to facilitate downloading and running the CPU-Z utility

- A notepad and pencil to document the specifications

- Optional: A word processor or spreadsheet application to facilitate the documentation

This lab is more informative if you have access to different types of systems with different classifications of CPUs.

Getting Down to Business

In the following steps, you'll download a reference utility known as CPU-Z and use it to further explore the characteristics of the CPU.

Step 1　Log on to a computer with Internet access and point your browser to the following Web site: www.cpuid.com. Follow the directions to download the current version of CPU-Z (the current version at this writing is 1.52). Unzip the file and launch CPU-Z.

Step 2　The CPU-Z utility displays a number of tabs across the top of the window (see Figure 5-5). At this time you are only concerned with the CPU and Cache tabs.

FIGURE 5-5 The CPU-Z utility

Using the data gathered by CPU-Z, record some of the pertinent information here:

Name _____

Code Name _____

Package _____

Core Speed _____

Multiplier _____

Bus Speed _____

L2 Cache _____

→ **Note**

The code name is used by the manufacturers to refer to different revisions of a chip. For instance, the Core 2 Duo line of CPUs has three main revisions: Conroe, Allendale, and Wolfdale.

✔ **Hint**

Because of variations in CPUs, chipsets, BIOS, and motherboards, CPU-Z may not be able to display all of the information about your CPU. In some cases, the information may actually be erroneous. The CPUID Web site has good documentation on some of the common incompatibilities.

Step 3   If possible, launch CPU-Z on various machines to compare the characteristics of different CPUs. Save the utility for use in future lab exercises.

Lab Analysis Test

1. James has an AMD Duron CPU motherboard and has bought a faster Intel Pentium D 820 from an eBay auction. He asks you to install the new CPU. What is your first reaction?

2. Joanna called you to say that ever since you installed her new CPU, the PC experiences intermittent problems when it runs. Sometimes it just quits and freezes up. What could possibly be wrong?

3. Theresa has an LGA 775 motherboard with an Intel Core 2 Quad 2.83-GHz processor and would like to put in a faster CPU. Can she install an Intel Core i7 2.93-GHz processor? Why or why not?

4. Lindscy runs CPU-Z on her system and notices that the processor's core speed is 2191.2 and the displayed multiplier is ×22. What is the speed of the system clock in Debbie's machine? How would the industry display this system clock speed?

5. David has been reading the trade magazines and keeps seeing all the hype over the "dual-core" processors. David decides, since he is a power gamer, that he will upgrade to a dual-core CPU to improve the performance of his system when playing his favorite game. Will a dual-core processor improve the performance in this scenario? Explain.

Key Term Quiz

Use the following terms to complete the following sentences. Not all terms will be used.

code name

CPU

fan assembly

land grid array (LGA)

Multi Core

package

pin grid array (PGA)

screw-down connector

water block

1. The Intel Core 2 Duo CPU uses a package known as a _____.

2. Both Intel and AMD have adopted the use of a _____ to distinguish among revisions of their CPUs.

3. You often need to remove the _____ to get to a system's CPU.

4. A _____ processor is designed to make multithreaded programs run faster.

5. A _____ is placed directly over the CPU in a liquid cooled system.

Chapter 6
RAM

Lab Exercises

One of the easiest and most cost-effective upgrades you can make to a PC is to add more memory. As such, RAM installation is probably the most common type of upgrade you'll perform as a PC tech.

RAM installation tasks include determining how much RAM the PC has installed, how much RAM the PC can support, and what type of RAM it uses, and then physically installing the RAM on the motherboard. The following labs are designed to give you practice working with RAM by using visual recognition of the different types and packages and by walking you through the steps of installing RAM.

 15 MINUTES

Lab Exercise 6.01: Determining the Amount of RAM in Your PC

There you are, a week after upgrading Joe's CPU, using your lunch hour to pummel your fellow PC techs in Team Fortress 2 (playing the good old Well map), when who should show up again but Joe, this time clutching a stick of RAM he got from a guy on the fourth floor. He wants you to install it in his system. You tell him you have to check on some things first, including how much RAM his system can handle and how much it already has, before you can help him.

✔ **Hint**

High-end PCs usually come straight from the factory equipped with hefty amounts of RAM. One of the ways in which makers of lower-cost PCs cut corners is by skimping on RAM.

Your first task in performing a RAM upgrade is determining how much RAM you need. Start by finding out how much RAM is currently installed in the system, and then consult the motherboard book to determine how much RAM the system supports.

Learning Objectives

In this lab exercise, you'll use various methods to determine how much memory is currently installed in your system, and how much it is capable of holding.

At the end of this lab, you'll be able to

- Find RAM measurements
- Identify how much RAM is installed in a system
- Determine how much RAM a particular motherboard supports

Lab Materials and Setup

The materials you need for this lab are

- A working Windows PC
- A notepad

✔ **Hint**

If you're in a computer lab or you have access to multiple PCs, you should practice on as many different PCs as possible.

Getting Down to Business

There are several ways to determine how much RAM is installed on a PC. First, you can check the RAM count during the boot process (some of the newer machines hide the RAM count, even if it's enabled in the BIOS). This tells you how much RAM the system BIOS recognizes during its check of the system. Second, you can check the amount of RAM that Windows recognizes from within the OS. And third, you can remove the PC case cover and physically examine the RAM sticks installed on the motherboard.

When you physically install RAM into slots on the motherboard, those slots are arranged into groups called *banks*. Depending on your computer's design, a bank might include one, two, or three slots. When you install new memory, you must fill every slot in a bank to take advantage of whatever RAM technology is using the banks. For example, if your computer uses triple-channel RAM with three-slot banks, you must install your RAM as a set of three or your RAM will not run at its ultimate speed. There are some big differences in RAM slots for each type of motherboard: be sure to read your motherboard book to determine how to install RAM in banks. Additionally, markings on the motherboard—either text labels or outlines—will identify the banks, if present.

Also keep in mind that motherboards support multiple types and speeds of RAM. In some situations, you might need to use the same type and speed of memory in every memory slot in your computer, even across different banks. Again, the motherboard book is your best friend here.

You'll find that computers leave any empty slots vacant. In older computers that used RDRAM, however, empty slots were filled with a continuity RIMM (CRIMM) module, a small circuit board designed to complete the electrical circuit but not add RAM to your system. (RDRAM is still covered on the CompTIA A+ exams, so even though it's not used in mainstream PCs anymore, you need to know about it.)

✔ **Cross-Reference**

To review the ways you can check the amount of RAM installed in a PC, refer to the "Determining Current RAM Capacity" section in Chapter 6 of *Mike Meyers' CompTIA A+ Guide to Managing and Troubleshooting PCs*.

Step 1   Turn on your PC, and watch the display as the system goes through its startup routine, otherwise known as a power-on self test (POST). Typically, the RAM count runs near the top-left side of the screen. Figure 6-1 shows an example of a typical RAM count.

Most BIOS programs display the RAM count in kilobytes (KB). To convert this figure to megabytes (MB), divide it by 1024.

Many systems run through the startup routine quickly, so the RAM count might appear on the screen for only a few seconds. Press the PAUSE/BREAK key to pause the boot process so you have time to write down the number accurately. When you want the boot process to resume, press the ENTER key.

What is the RAM count number displayed on your monitor? _____

✔ **Hint**

If you're starting the PC for the first time that day, the startup routine may run through the RAM count before the monitor has a chance to warm up. If this happens, just reboot the PC and try again.

```
  ● Award Modular BIOS v6.00PG, An Energy Star Ally
  ✎ Copyright (C) 1984-2005, Award Software, Inc

  GA-K8NP F13

  Processor : AMD Athlon(tm) 64 Processor 3200+
  <CPUID:00000F4A Patch ID:003A>
  Memory Testing : 3145728K OK
  CPU clock frequency : 200MHz

    Primary Master : WDC WD400BB-00JHA0 05.01C05
     Primary Slave : None
  Secondary Master : None
   Secondary Slave : LTN403 DQ19
```

```
  <DEL>:BIOS Setup/Dual BIOS, <F9>:Xpress Recovery
  09/08/2005-nForce-6A61CG0AC-00
```

FIGURE 6-1   Viewing a typical RAM count during boot-up

Depending on your system's BIOS, you may also see a RAM count in the system configuration summary. This is a screen that lists the PC's CPU type and clock speed, mass storage devices, port addresses, and so on. Typically, you'll also see an entry for the system's base memory (640 KB) and extended memory (the total amount of RAM installed).

Step 2   Use the following methods to determine the amount of RAM on your system from within any version of Windows.

a.   In Windows 2000/XP, right-click the My Computer icon and select Properties to see the amount of RAM in your system. In Windows Vista , open the Start menu, highlight Computer, right-click, and select Properties. The RAM count is under the System area (see Figure 6-2). You can also see other useful information here, like the processor type, Windows edition, the product ID, and more.

b.   You'll notice that Windows 2000 shows the amount of RAM in kilobytes, while Windows XP and Vista show it in gigabytes.

FIGURE 6-2   Viewing the RAM count in Windows Vista via Computer

Does the amount of RAM shown during the startup routine and that reported by Windows match?

Entry-level PCs and laptops often have onboard display adapters (the display adapter is built into the motherboard). Manufacturers include little to no video RAM on the motherboard, so the display adapter must "steal" some portion of the system RAM to be able to handle today's intense graphic applications.

If the amounts do not add up, and you see a number such as 448 MB or 992 MB, then your system has probably allocated some of the system memory to handle your display adapter's needs.

Another way to see the amount of memory installed is to follow this procedure:

a. Click Start | Programs (or All Programs) | Accessories | System Tools | System Information. In the System Summary, look for a value called Total Physical Memory (see Figure 6-3).

b. The amount of RAM will be listed in the displayed information.

How much memory is in your system? _____

Does this number agree with what you found in Step 1? _____

FIGURE 6-3 The System Information dialog box showing Total Physical Memory

We'll save the last method for determining how much RAM is installed for the next exercise in this lab. For the moment, let's talk about how to determine the maximum amount of RAM your system is capable of supporting.

Step 3   The amount of RAM you can install on a modern system depends on the limitations of the motherboard hardware. All new CPUs are capable of 64-bit processing, so new chipsets support very large amounts of RAM. The question is, how much RAM does your motherboard support?

Neither the CMOS setup utility nor the OS can help you determine how much RAM a PC is capable of handling. The best source for this information is the system's motherboard book, if you have it, or the PC maker's or motherboard manufacturer's Web site.

Examine the documentation that came with your PC, or visit the manufacturer's Web site, to determine how much RAM you can install on the system.

What is the maximum amount of RAM that your system can support? _____

 30 MINUTES

Lab Exercise 6.02: Identifying Types of RAM

Once you determine how much RAM is installed on Joe's PC, and how much his motherboard can handle, you conclude that there's room for more. But, you explain to Joe, this doesn't mean you can add his RAM stick, because not all RAM is the same. Having looked at the specs for his system, you know it takes 240-pin DDR2 SDRAM. Joe thinks the stick he got is the right size to fit, but you know it's 240-pin DDR3 RAM, so it won't. This is why they pay you the big bucks—and why you get to take the RAM stick Joe can't use and add it to your own machine! (Just kidding. Of course you'd give it back to Joe.)

RAM comes in several standardized form factors, each compatible with specific types of systems. Modern desktop systems use full-sized dual inline memory modules (DIMMs) of various pin configurations (168, 184, and 240). Laptop computers use scaled-down DIMM versions called small outline-DIMMs, or SO-DIMMs.

✔ **Cross-Reference**

For details on the various types of RAM found in modern systems, refer to the "DDR SDRAM," "Dual-Channel DDR," and "DDR2/3" sections in Chapter 6 of *Mike Meyers' CompTIA A+ Guide to Managing and Troubleshooting PCs*.

The steps for identifying the different types of RAM are presented in this lab exercise.

Learning Objectives

In this lab, you'll examine and compare different RAM packages.

At the end of this lab, you'll be able to

- Recognize and differentiate between different kinds of RAM packages

Lab Materials and Setup

The materials you need for this lab are

- The disassembled, non-production PC used in the lab exercises in Chapter 5

- Demonstration units of various RAM packages (optional)

✔ **Hint**

It is helpful to examine the RAM configurations in multiple PCs, if you have them available. Having a laptop with removable RAM is a plus.

Getting Down to Business

Let's do a quick review of the types of RAM packages you'll see on modern PCs. Then you'll check your PC or motherboard documentation to determine the type of RAM it uses.

All modern PCs use some form of DDR memory for their system RAM. As was discussed in the textbook, DDR stands for *double data rate*, which means that for every tick of the clock, two chunks of data are sent across the memory bus. This has the effect of giving you twice the performance without increasing the clock rate. A quick way to calculate that performance is to use this easy formula:

Transfer rate = (clock rate × transfer per cycle) × bus width / 8

Using this formula for a stick of 400-MHz DDR, for example, looks like this:

Transfer rate = (400 MHz × 2) × 64 bits / 8

When you run the numbers, you get a transfer rate of 6400 MB, or 6.25 GB.

Since the introduction of DDR, two major RAM upgrades have occurred, DDR2 and DDR3, each of which has double the throughput of its predecessor.

Another performance trick modern systems use to increase memory speed is dual- and triple-channel architectures. This enables the memory controller to access more than one stick of RAM at a time, thus increasing performance. In effect, the 64-bit bus acts like a 128-bit bus (for dual-channel) or a 192-bit bus (for triple-channel). To use these multichannel architectures, you must install memory in identical pairs or triplets. Check your motherboard book to see if your system supports dual- or triple-channel memory.

FIGURE 6-4   A 168-pin DIMM

Step 1   Typically, as older machines become obsolete and fall into disuse, they are easier to acquire for little or no cost. Many times, this is exactly the type of PC you have available to disassemble, so there is a good chance that it will use older memory (RAM) as well. If you are using an older, non-production machine for your exploration, there's a good chance the motherboard supports one of these older types of RAM packages (included here for your information):

- **168-pin DIMMs**   These are about five inches long and have 84 physical pins (edge connectors) on each side, and all 168 connectors are used. The board has two notches on the bottom: one near the center, and the other near an end (see Figure 6-4).

- **184-pin RIMMs**   Rambus Dynamic RAM (RDRAM) is the type of RAM you might find if you are working with an old Intel Pentium III or Pentium 4 motherboard. A stick of RDRAM is called a RIMM. RIMM is actually trademarked as a word; it's not an acronym like DIMM, despite what many people assume (see Figure 6-5).

If you are using a typical desktop system and it is relatively new (less than two years old), the motherboard will most likely support one of the following three types of RAM packages:

- **184-pin DDR DIMMs**   DDR RAM sticks are about five inches long and look a lot like 168-pin DIMMs, but with only one notch and more connectors. These are known as double data rate (DDR) memory. The notches are different from 168-pin DIMMs, so these RAM types are not interchangeable (see Figure 6-6).

- **240-pin DDR2 DIMMs**   DDR2 RAM sticks are physically the same size as the 184-pin DDR DIMMs, but the guide notch is in a different location and there are obviously more connectors. DDR2 uses a 240-pin DIMM (see Figure 6-7) that's not compatible with DDR RAM slots. DDR2 is expected to perform better than DDR due to lower voltage requirements, clock doubling on the chips' input/output circuits, and special prefetch buffers.

FIGURE 6-5   A 184-pin RIMM

FIGURE 6-6 A 184-pin DDR DIMM

- **240-pin DDR3 DIMMs** DDR3 RAM sticks are physically the same size as the 184-pin DDR DIMMs, but the guide notch is in a different location. DDR3 uses a 240-pin DIMM (see Figure 6-8) that's not compatible with DDR RAM slots or motherboards. DDR3 is triple-channel architecture and performs faster at higher frequencies but at lower voltages, thus generating less heat. The laptop version of DDR3 is called a 204-pin SO-DIMM.

→ **Note**

DDR3 DIMMs are not backward compatible—inserting a DDR3 module into a DDR2 socket can damage the DIMM and/or the motherboard.

Step 2 In your PC or motherboard documentation, or on the manufacturer's Web site, locate the section listing the type of RAM your system uses.

What speed of RAM does your system need? _____

Step 3 Using the disassembled PC at your workspace, locate the motherboard and the anti-static bag containing the RAM sticks, and make note of the following:

How many RAM slots does your motherboard have? _____

How many RAM slots are filled with RAM sticks? _____

Can you tell at a glance whether your system has DIMMs, RIMMs, DDR DIMMs, DDR2 DIMMs, or DDR3 DIMMs? _____

FIGURE 6-7 A 240-pin DDR2 DIMM

FIGURE 6-8 A 240-pin DDR3 DIMM

 30 MINUTES

Lab Exercise 6.03: Removing and Installing RAM

Taking pity on Joe, you've found a stick of RAM for him that works with his system, and now you have to install it.

Although RAM installation is one of the simpler PC hardware upgrades, it's still important that you follow the correct steps and take all appropriate safety precautions. You will once again practice using the disassembled, non-production system. This time, you will be removing and installing RAM sticks.

Learning Objectives

In this lab, you'll practice removing and installing RAM.

At the end of this lab, you'll be able to

- Remove RAM safely and correctly
- Install RAM safely and correctly

Lab Materials and Setup

The materials you need for this lab are

- The disassembled, non-production PC used in the lab exercises in Chapter 3
- An anti-static mat or other static-safe material on which to place the RAM
- An anti-static wrist strap
- A notepad

✔ **Hint**

If you're in a computer lab or you have access to multiple PCs, you should practice on a variety of systems.

Getting Down to Business

Removal and installation procedures vary depending on the type of RAM your system uses. DIMMs and RIMMs snap into the RAM slots vertically. The following steps describe the removal and installation procedures for DIMMs.

✖ **Warning**

Regardless of the type of RAM on your system, be certain to take measures to prevent ESD damage. Shut down and unplug your PC and place it on your anti-static mat. Strap on your anti-static bracelet and ground yourself. If necessary, remove any cables or components that block access to your system RAM before you begin.

✔ **Hint**

You should have already removed the RAM from your tear-down machine and safely stored it in an anti-static bag. You may either install the RAM in the sockets on the motherboard with the motherboard on the anti-static mat, or reinstall the motherboard into the case first. The following removal steps are listed for reference, especially if you have access to additional machines for exploration.

Follow these steps to remove DIMM or RIMM RAM from your PC:

Step 1 Locate the retention clips on either end of the RAM module.

Step 2 Press outward on the clips to disengage them from the retention slots on the sides of the RAM sticks (see Figure 6-9).

Step 3 Press down on the clips firmly and evenly. The retention clips act as levers to lift the DIMM sticks up and slightly out of the RAM slots.

Figure 6-9   Removing a 184-pin DIMM (DDR SDRAM)

Step 4   Remove the DIMM sticks and place them on your anti-static mat, or in an anti-static bag.

Step 5   Make note of the following:

How many pins does your RAM have? _____168_____

Where are the guide notches located? _____

What information is on the RAM's label? _____

Step 6   While you have your system RAM out, this is a good time to check the condition of the metal contacts on both the RAM sticks and the motherboard RAM sockets. Dirty contacts are fairly rare. If you see this problem, use contact cleaner, available at any electronics store.

Are the contacts free of dirt and corrosion? _____

After you've examined your system RAM and inspected the motherboard RAM sockets, reinstall the RAM as described next.

To install a DIMM or RIMM:

Step 1   Orient the DIMM or RIMM so that the guide notches on the RAM module match up to the guide ridges on the RAM socket.

Step 2   Press the RAM stick firmly and evenly straight down into the socket until the retention clips engage the retention notches on the ends of the RAM stick.

Step 3   Snap the retention clips firmly into place.

Step 4   Repeat these steps to install other RAM modules as appropriate. If you're using RIMM RAM, don't forget to install the continuity RIMM (CRIMM) sticks into any empty RAM slots.

KVR 133 X 64 C3/256

To finish a RAM installation professionally, specifically if you are on a production-level machine, follow these steps:

Step 1 Once your system RAM is in place, reattach any cables that you may have had to move, and plug in the system power cable. Do not reinstall the PC case cover until after you've confirmed that RAM installation was successful.

Step 2 Boot up the system and watch the RAM count to confirm that you correctly installed the RAM.

✔ **Hint**

If your system has any problems when you reboot, remember that you must turn off the power and unplug the computer again before reseating the RAM.

 30 MINUTES

Lab Exercise 6.04: Exploring RAM Specifications with CPU-Z

Now that you have Joe's system up and running with double the memory it had before, you can take a moment to analyze the re-inventoried memory on your machine. You've already downloaded the utility CPU-Z from the Internet in Lab Exercise 5.05; now you'll need to launch CPU-Z and examine the information on the Memory and SPD tabs.

Learning Objectives

In this lab, you'll identify various RAM specifications.

At the end of this lab, you'll be able to

- Recognize key characteristics of RAM

Lab Materials and Setup

The materials you need for this lab are

- Access to a working computer with the utility CPU-Z installed

- A notepad and pencil to document the specifications

- Optional: A word processor or spreadsheet application to facilitate the documentation

This lab is more informative if you have access to different types of systems with different types of RAM.

Getting Down to Business

In the following steps, you'll explore the different characteristics of RAM.

Step 1 Launch the CPU-Z application.

Step 2 Navigate to the Memory tab. The CPU-Z utility displays the current statistics of the RAM installed, as shown in Figure 6-10.

Using the data gathered by CPU-Z, record the following information:

Type _____SDRAm_____

Size _____256_____

CAS# Latency (CL) ___3.0 clocks_____

RAS# to CAS# Delay (tRCD) ___3 Clocks_____

RAS# Precharge (tRP) _____3 Clocks_____

Step 3 Click the SPD tab in CPU-Z.

FIGURE 6-10 CPU-Z showing RAM information

Step 4   The SPD tab, shown in Figure 6-11, lists a number of technical bits of information about a particular stick of RAM. This information is contained on every SDRAM stick on an additional chip called the serial presence detect (SPD) chip.

Using the data gathered by CPU-Z, record the following information for each of the system's RAM modules:

	Module 1	Module 2	Module 3	Module 4
Slot #	1			
Module size	256			
Maximum bandwidth	133 MHz			
Manufacturer	Kingston			

✔ **Cross-Reference**

To review how the SPD chip works with the system, refer to the "SPD" section in Chapter 6 of *Mike Meyers' CompTIA A+ Guide to Managing and Troubleshooting PCs.*

Figure 6-11 CPU-Z showing SPD information

Step 5 If possible, launch CPU-Z on various machines to compare the characteristics of different types of RAM. Save the utility for use in future lab exercises.

→ **Try This: PC Wizard**

On a computer with Internet access, point your browser to the following Web site: www.cpuid.com. Follow the onscreen directions and download a copy of PC Wizard.

Extract the files into a folder and launch the PC Wizard application. Once PC Wizard is running, find and click the Mainboard icon in the Hardware area. This brings up a list of components in the right pane of the application window. Click the Physical Memory item and then browse through the information displayed in the lower portion of the window.

Using this information, can you determine the maximum size for individual RAM modules allowed on this system, and the maximum amount of total memory that it supports? Does this correspond to the information you found earlier in the PC or motherboard documentation?

Note that because of variations in chipsets, BIOS, and motherboards, PC Wizard may or may not provide detailed information on the RAM. In some cases, the information may actually be erroneous. The CPUID Web site has good documentation on some of the common incompatibilities.

Lab Analysis Test

1. Jarel wants to upgrade his memory and calls you for help. He knows that he's using DDR RAM and that his system clock is 133 MHz, but he isn't sure what type of DDR SDRAM sticks he should purchase. What DDR RAM would you recommend that he use?

2. Theresa's Windows 2000 Professional system has 512 MB of RAM. She adds another stick with 512 MB of RAM, but the RAM count still only shows 512 MB. What could be causing this?

3. John's system has 512 MB of PC4200 DDR2 SDRAM. He recently installed an additional 512 MB of DDR2 SDRAM that a coworker gave him. He tells you that his system now boots up correctly and shows the correct amount of RAM, but then it freezes after several minutes. He notes that if he removes the new RAM, the system runs fine. What could be a possible reason for this?

4. Kyle has a system that supports dual-channel architecture (there are two blue DIMM slots on the motherboard). The motherboard has space for three sticks of RAM, so Kyle installs three 512-MB RAM sticks. What will be the result?

5. Joe has recently purchased a pair of 1-GB DDR3 RAM sticks. He's replacing an older pair of DDR2 RAM, but can't afford to replace the motherboard. Why won't this work?

Key Term Quiz

Use the following terms to complete the following sentences. Not all terms will be used.

168-pin DIMM

184-pin DIMM

240-pin DIMM

CRIMM

DIMM

DDR RAM

DDR2 RAM

DDR3 RAM

dual-channel

megabytes (MB)

RIMM

SDRAM

SO-DIMM

SPD

1. Today's PCs use DDR3 RAM, which comes in a(n) _____ package.

2. A RAM module used in a laptop is called a(n) _____.

3. A component known as a(n) _____ chip provides additional information about an SDRAM module.

4. A stick of _____ looks a lot like a 168-pin DIMM, but it has 184 pins.

5. The technology that uses two sticks of RAM together to increase throughput is known as _____ architecture.

6. When purchasing _____, you must realize that it is not backward compatible with _____ and new hardware must be considered.

Chapter 7
BIOS and CMOS

Lab Exercises

Basic input/output services (BIOS) provide the primary interface between the operating system's device drivers and most of its hardware. Although a modern BIOS is automated and tolerant of misconfiguration, a good PC technician must be comfortable with those occasional situations in which the BIOS may need some maintenance or repair.

Be aware that some viruses are written to erase the BIOS content from the PC, which makes the PC inoperative; that is, it will not be able to boot again. Some even attack the operating system and forbid it from reprogramming the BIOS so that it can operate again. The good news is that great utility programs are available to help you troubleshoot these issues if they arise. One program I've found to be trustworthy and great all around is PCDoctor Utilities, located at www.pcdoctor-tools.com. It's inexpensive and works well for dealing with systems corrupted by a virus. Lots of freeware programs are offered on the Web, but it's best to talk to a trusted IT professional to learn which ones work best before you download anything.

The PC needs the BIOS to tell it how each basic component is supposed to communicate with the system. At the beginning of the PC revolution, many different manufacturers developed BIOS for PCs, but over the years the BIOS business has consolidated to only two brands: AMI (American Megatrends, Inc.), and Phoenix Technologies (which absorbed the former third brand, Award Software). Both of these manufacturers provide a utility called the CMOS setup program (CMOS stands for *complementary metal-oxide semiconductor*, which is why everyone says "CMOS") that enables you to reconfigure BIOS settings for boot device order, amount of memory, hard disk drive configuration, and so on. Most of these configurations are automated, but as a PC tech, you'll find yourself reconfiguring BIOS settings more often than you might think!

As an example for the lab exercises in this chapter, suppose that the company you're working for is planning a mass upgrade from its current OS, Windows XP Professional, to Windows Vista. You've tested the upgrade process on a few lab machines and have found that systems with an out-of-date BIOS are having problems upgrading successfully. In preparation for the Windows Vista installation, besides upgrading any older BIOS versions you find, you'll disable any BIOS-level antivirus checking functions. You're also aware that the prior IT manager did not use consistent CMOS passwords, so you may need to reset the passwords on a few machines.

The lab exercises in this chapter will teach you to identify, access, and configure system BIOS.

 10 MINUTES

Lab Exercise 7.01: Identifying BIOS ROM

Having received your orders to do the big OS upgrade, your first task is to check the BIOS types and versions on every machines in your office, and then visit each BIOS maker's Web site to determine whether more recent versions are available.

The system BIOS is stored on nonvolatile memory called BIOS ROM. BIOS makers often (but not always) label their BIOS ROM chips prominently on the motherboard. In this exercise, you'll look at two different ways to identify your BIOS ROM chip.

✔ **Cross-Reference**

For details on the two big companies that manufacture BIOS on modern systems, refer to the "Updating CMOS: The Setup Program" section in Chapter 7 of *Mike Meyers' CompTIA A+ Guide to Managing and Troubleshooting PCs*.

Learning Objectives

In this lab, you'll learn two ways to identify your BIOS.

At the end of this lab, you'll be able to

- Locate the BIOS ROM chip on the motherboard

- Identify the BIOS manufacturer

- Determine the BIOS creation date and version

Lab Materials and Setup

The materials you need for this lab are

- A working PC

- An anti-static mat

- A notepad

Getting Down to Business

The first thing you'll do is remove your PC case cover and locate the BIOS ROM chip. Next, you'll make note of the BIOS information displayed during system startup.

✖ Warning

Any time you take the cover off your PC, remember to follow all proper safety and ESD avoidance precautions.

Step 1 Remove the case from the PC and locate the system BIOS ROM chip. Some motherboards label their chip with the name of the BIOS manufacturer. Compare your system BIOS ROM chip to the one in Figure 7-1.

Figure 7-1 A typical system BIOS ROM chip

Read the manufacturer's label *if you can*, and answer the following questions:

Who made the BIOS? _____

What year was the BIOS written? _____

Are there any other numbers on the label? Record them. _____

Does it look like you could easily remove the system BIOS chip, or does it look soldered to the motherboard? _____

Step 2   Replace the PC case cover and start the system. Be sure the monitor is turned on. When the first data appears on the screen, press the PAUSE/BREAK key on the keyboard. This suspends further operation until you press ENTER. Newer systems actually have instructions somewhere on the screen that indicate which key or keys to press to get into boot options, CMOS setup, and so forth.

Figure 7-2 shows an example of what you may see. At the top of the screen is the BIOS manufacturer's name and version number. At the bottom of the screen is the date of manufacture and the product identification number.

Make note of the following information:

Who made the BIOS? _____

What version is the BIOS? _____

What year was the BIOS written? _____

✔ **Hint**

Not all BIOS display the same type of information. Some BIOS makers modify the BIOS to show nothing more than their logos during the boot process.

```
        American      Released: 07/12/2000
        Megatrends    AMIBIOS (C)1999 American Megatrends Inc.,
6UX7-4X P15

Check System Health OK,
CPU ID:0683 Patch ID:0010
Pentium III - 667 MHz
Checking NVRAM..
393216KB OK

WAIT...
Auto-Detecting Pri Master..IDE Hard Disk
Auto-Detecting Pri Slave...IDE Hard Disk
Auto-Detecting Sec Master..ATAPI CDROM
Auto-Detecting Sec Slave...Not Detected
Pri Master: 3.02      ST310212A
           Ultra DMA Mode-4, S.M.A.R.T. Capable and Status OK
Pri Slave : 3.39      ST310211A
           Ultra DMA Mode-4, S.M.A.R.T. Capable and Status OK
Sec Master: YYS7      CDU5211
```

energy
EPA POLLUTION PREVENTER

FIGURE 7-2 A typical boot screen

Step 3   Press ENTER on the keyboard to continue booting. Once the system is up and running, go online and find out whether a more recent version of your BIOS is available. Your first stop should be your PC maker's Web site. If it does not have this information available, try your motherboard manufacturer or the BIOS maker.

> ✖ **Warning**
>
> Do *not* "flash" your system BIOS at this time!

 15 MINUTES

Lab Exercise 7.02: Accessing BIOS via the CMOS Setup Program

Once you've assessed the BIOS on each machine, but before you proceed with the Windows Vista installation, you should check to be sure the BIOS is properly configured using the special program for this purpose.

You don't access the hundreds of individual programs contained in the system BIOS directly, or from anywhere within the Windows OS. Instead, you use a utility that interfaces with the BIOS programs to enable you to reconfigure settings. This utility is the CMOS setup program.

Learning Objectives

In this lab, you'll go into CMOS and explore your BIOS configuration settings.

At the end of this lab, you'll be able to

- Enter the CMOS setup program
- Navigate the display screens of the setup utility

Lab Materials and Setup

The materials you need for this lab are

- A working PC whose BIOS settings you have permission to change

Getting Down to Business

In the following steps, you'll reboot your PC and access the boot options or CMOS setup program. Each BIOS maker has its own special way to do this, so how you go about it depends on which BIOS your system has installed. Common methods include the following:

- Press DELETE during the boot process.
- Press F2, F10, or F12 during the boot process.

- Press CTRL-ALT-INSERT during the boot process.

- Press CTRL-A during the boot process.

- Press CTRL-FI during the boot process.

There are four ways for you to determine which method works for your BIOS:

- Check your motherboard or PC documentation.

- Visit your motherboard or PC maker's Web site.

- Watch the screen display after booting your PC. Most BIOS direct you to press a specific key to enter CMOS.

- Use the trial-and-error method! Boot your system and go down the preceding list, trying each key or key combination until one works. You won't hurt anything if you get it wrong, but if you hold the wrong key down for too long you may get a keyboard error message. If this happens, just reboot and try again.

Step 1   Determine which method you need to use to enter the CMOS setup program. Then reboot your system and use that method to enter CMOS.

Step 2   Once you've entered the CMOS setup program, look at the screen and compare it to Figures 7-3 and 7-4. The Phoenix BIOS shown in Figure 7-3 opens immediately into the Main screen, whereas the Phoenix-Award BIOS in Figure 7-4 presents an initial menu. Although the screens for different CMOS setup programs may look different, they all contain basically the same functions.

FIGURE 7-3 Phoenix CMOS Main screen

```
           Phoenix - Award BIOS CMOS Setup Utility
                   Standard CMOS Features

   Date (mm:dd:yy)          Wed, Jun 7 2006    ▲        Item Help
   Time (hh:mm:ss)          13 : 19 : 35
                                                    Menu Level    ▶
 ▶ IDE Channel 1 Master    WDC WD1200JB-75CRA0
 ▶ IDE Channel 1 Slave     None                    Change the day, month,
 ▶ IDE Channel 2 Master    SONY    CD-CW  CRX17     year and century
 ▶ IDE Channel 2 Slave     TOSHIBA CD/DVDW SDR5
 ▶ IDE Channel 3 Master    None
 ▶ IDE Channel 4 Master    None
 ▶ IDE Channel 5 Master    WDC WD2000JS-00MHB0
 ▶ IDE Channel 6 Master    None

   Drive A                 1.44, 3.5 in.
   Drive B                 None
   Floppy 3 Mode Support   Disabled
   Halt On                 All , But Keyboard

   Base Memory                  640K
   Extended Memory          1047552K          ▼

▲▼▶◀:Move   Enter:Select    +/-/PU/PD:Value  F10:Save   ESC:Exit  F1:General Help
   F5:Previous Values        F6:Fail-Safe Defaults    F7:Optimized Defaults
```

FIGURE 7-4 Phoenix-Award BIOS opening screen

✖ Warning

Do not make any changes in BIOS settings during this lab exercise. You'll make changes in the next two lab exercises.

The CMOS setup program controls the "changeable" BIOS settings. Many settings depend on what hardware you add to the system. The following are some sample entries on your system that you can change or update (there are more, the specifics of which depend on your BIOS):

- Date

- Time

- Hard drive configuration

- Boot sequence

- RAM

- Serial and parallel port assignments

- Enable/disable onboard controllers

- Enable/disable supervisor and user passwords

Step 3 Explore each screen and make notes about what each setting does. Navigation, like the method to enter the CMOS setup program, varies from maker to maker. Most programs are navigable by keyboard only, but some (AMI, for instance) support a mouse. Look at the bottom of the CMOS setup program screen to see how to navigate in your particular CMOS utility.

✔ **Hint**

> Usually the arrow keys and the PAGE UP and PAGE DOWN keys will select and change settings. Sometimes the + and − keys or the SPACEBAR will toggle settings. The CMOS setup program screen usually provides a key to the navigation and selection keys; refer to it as well.

While navigating through the different setup screens, pay particular attention to any password or security menu that enables you to configure administrator/supervisor passwords and user passwords. Do not make any changes at this time; just make a note of where you configure these passwords. You will configure a password in the next lab exercise.

Step 4 Below is a list of common settings found in the CMOS. Know that each BIOS arranges its settings differently. View every screen of your CMOS setup utility to locate and record these settings and their location:

Drives Depending on your motherboard configuration, you will either set a primary master/slave drive or, if using SATA, get a list of the different drives attached and their name/type.

_____

Onboard Devices These settings allow you to configure onboard devices such as your USB ports.

_____

Performance Only common on better motherboards, this area allows you to tweak system timings for improved performance (also known as overclocking).

_____

Security This section allows you to set administrator or system passwords.

_____

Boot Sequence This setting lets you define the order your system looks for boot devices.

_____

Power Management This section defines when devices shut down and how they awaken.

_____

Once you're done exploring, press ESC a couple of times until you get the message "Quit Without Saving (Y/N)?" Press Y, and then press ENTER. The system will boot into your operating system.

🕐 30 MINUTES

Lab Exercise 7.03: Configuring and Clearing CMOS Setup Program Passwords

In many professional environments, the IT department doesn't want users to fool with any of the PC's settings, especially detailed items such as the BIOS settings. The IT manager may even devise a password to prevent entry to the CMOS setup utility by unauthorized users. Unfortunately, in your organization, the IT manager has resigned and was not very thorough about documenting these passwords.

When a CMOS setup utility has been password protected and its password has been subsequently lost, the typical way to clear the password is to shunt a jumper on the motherboard that clears either the password or the entire contents of CMOS.

Learning Objectives

In this lab, you'll learn how to configure CMOS setup utility passwords and how to clear the contents of the password and CMOS using the onboard CMOS-clear jumper.

At the end of this lab, you'll be able to

- Set a password using the CMOS setup utility

- Locate the CMOS-clear jumper on the motherboard

- Clear passwords and CMOS settings using the CMOS-clear jumper

Lab Materials and Setup

The materials you need for this lab are

- A working PC whose BIOS settings you can change, with access to the clear CMOS jumper on the motherboard

- An anti-static mat/wrist strap

- A notepad

Getting Down to Business

In the following steps, you'll reboot your PC and access the CMOS setup program using the key combination you verified in Lab Exercise 7.02. You will then navigate to the password or security menu and configure a CMOS setup utility password. Then you'll verify the password by rebooting the machine and entering CMOS setup. Finally, you'll open the case and reset the CMOS settings by physically shunting the CMOS-clear jumper.

✖ Warning

Any time you remove the cover from your PC, remember to follow all proper safety and ESD avoidance precautions.

Step 1   Reboot your system and use the appropriate key or key combination to enter the CMOS setup program.

Step 2   Once you've entered the CMOS setup program, navigate to the security or password menu (see Figure 7-5). Select the supervisor password and enter a four- to eight-character password. Save changes and exit CMOS setup.

Record your password here: _____

✔ **Hint**

Typically, two types of passwords can be set in CMOS, but a third is now appearing:

The *supervisor* password restricts access to the CMOS setup program so that only authorized personnel can change or modify BIOS settings. Organizations, especially schools, usually configure a supervisor password to keep curious users from causing system errors.

The *user* or *system* password restricts access to the PC itself, and is required every time the system boots (before an operating system is even loaded). This type of password is often used when an individual's PC is located in a public area.

The *hard drive* password is the third and newest password you'll find on some CMOS setups. Hard drive passwords prevent a user from accessing a hard drive unless they know the password.

Step 3   Reboot the PC and press the key or key combination required to enter the CMOS setup program. If you completed Step 2 correctly, you should be prompted to enter a password. Enter the password you configured in Step 2 and press ENTER. The main menu of the CMOS setup program will appear.

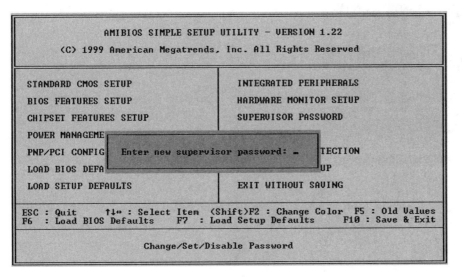

Figure 7-5 AMIBIOS supervisor password setup

Discard changes and exit the CMOS setup program.

✖ Warning

The next step will erase all CMOS settings! While you are in the CMOS setup program, take the time to write down important settings such as the CPU settings, boot order, which integrated peripherals are enabled/disabled, and the power management setup. Although the system should run fine using the default settings, taking notes now will help you get back to any custom settings that may have been configured.

Step 4   Shut down the PC and unplug the power cord from the PC and the wall outlet. Remove the case from the PC and, referring to the PC or motherboard documentation, locate the CMOS-clear jumper. Follow the instructions included with the documentation and move the jumper (see Figure 7-6) to clear the CMOS.

A less elegant alternative to using the CMOS-clear jumper is to remove the onboard battery for at least 30 seconds. Does your system have an onboard battery? Can it be removed easily?

Step 5   Replace the PC case cover, plug the system back in, and start the system. Press the appropriate key(s) to enter the CMOS setup program.

Were you prompted for a password? _____

Do you need to configure any of the other settings? _____

Figure 7-6 The clear CMOS jumper on a motherboard

🕐 30 MINUTES

Lab Exercise 7.04: Configuring BIOS Settings

If you find any issues when you examine the BIOS settings using the CMOS setup program, you'll need to reconfigure the settings. Remember also that you're preparing the PC for an upgrade to Windows Vista. BIOS-level virus checking is known to cause problems with the Windows 2000/XP/Vista installation process, so Microsoft advises that you disable it.

Many BIOS functions are unchangeable—such as keyboard and floppy drive recognition—and are therefore inaccessible via the CMOS setup program. Other functions are under your control. These include the boot sequence order and the date/time setting, as mentioned previously, but also some potentially hazardous settings such as BIOS shadowing and memory timing.

✔ Hint

> If you're not absolutely certain what a particular setting does, the best course of action is to leave it alone! If you have any doubts, you can always exit the CMOS setup program without saving.

Learning Objectives

In this exercise, you'll access the CMOS setup utility, navigate to find the various BIOS settings you would commonly need to modify, and practice disabling BIOS-level virus checking.

At the end of this lab, you'll be able to

- Modify the settings in BIOS

Lab Materials and Setup

The materials you need for this lab are

- A working PC whose BIOS settings you have permission to change

- If possible, a BIOS that includes virus checking

Getting Down to Business

In the following steps, you'll learn how to navigate to the CMOS setup program configuration screen that includes the virus-checking option. This example uses the Phoenix-Award BIOS CMOS setup program. Your CMOS setup program may vary, but all BIOS makers and versions should offer the same option.

✔ **Cross-Reference**

For more details about the features of CMOS setup programs, refer to the section "A Quick Tour Through a Typical CMOS Setup Program" in Chapter 7 of *Mike Meyers' CompTIA A+ Guide to Managing and Troubleshooting PCs.*

Step 1   Enter your CMOS setup program using the steps you learned in Lab Exercise 7.02.

Step 2   Check your notes and navigate to the configuration screen that has the BIOS-level virus-checking option. It's not always obvious where to find this option. For example, the Phoenix-Award BIOS CMOS setup program screen shown in Figure 7-4 doesn't give any hints about where to find the correct screen. As Figure 7-7 shows, virus checking can be disabled in this BIOS from the Advanced BIOS Features screen. Don't hesitate to explore.

Step 3   Follow the screen prompts to navigate to the correct configuration screen and find the virus-checking setting option. Highlight the option (using either the arrow keys or the mouse) and change it from Enabled to Disabled. Once again, your CMOS setup program's wording or appearance may be different, but the option to control BIOS-level virus checking should be common to all modern types of BIOS.

Step 4   Save and exit the CMOS setup program. After you exit, the system will reboot automatically. You have just made a change to BIOS.

The process you just followed is the same process you'll use for any changes you make to BIOS. Be sure to save the settings before exiting the setup utility.

```
          Phoenix - AwardBIOS CMOS Setup Utility
                    Advanced BIOS Features

   Virus Warning              [Disabled]    ▲        Item Help
   CPU Internal Cache         [Enabled]
   External Cache             [Enabled]          Menu Level  ▶
   CPU L2 Cache ECC Checking  [Enabled]
   Processor Number Feature   [Enabled]       Allows you to choose
   Quick Power On Self Test   [Enabled]       the VIRUS warning
   First Boot Device          [Floppy]        feature for IDE Hard
   Second Boot Device         [HDD-0]         Disk boot sector
   Third Boot Device          [CDROM]         protection. If this
   Boot Other Device          [Enabled]       function is enabled
   Swap Floppy Drive          [Disabled]      and someone attempt to
   Boot Up NumLock Status     [On]            write data into this
   Gate A20 Option            [Fast]          area , BIOS will show
   ATA 66/100 IDE Cable Msg.  [Enabled]       a warning message on
   Typematic Rate Setting     [Disabled]      screen and alarm beep
 x Typematic Rate (Chars/Sec) 6
 x Typematic Delay (Msec)     250
   Security Option            [Setup]
   APIC Mode                  [Enabled]   ▼

 ↑↓→←:Move  Enter:Select  +/-/PU/PD:Value  F10:Save  ESC:Exit  F1:General Help
      F5: Previous Values   F6: Fail-Safe Defaults   F7: Optimized Defaults
```

FIGURE 7-7 Disabling BIOS-level virus checking

Lab Analysis Test

1. What can you do in a pinch to clear the CMOS settings if you are unable to find the clear CMOS jumper?

2. After running Windows XP for a few years, Chris has decided to perform a clean install of Windows Vista. After backing up his important files, he places the Windows Vista DVD in the DVD/CD-ROM drive and reboots his machine—but it just boots into Windows XP like normal. What setting will he most likely need to configure in the BIOS to correct this situation?

3. Arnold has just installed a new sound card. He boots his system to install the drivers, but his system does not recognize the new card. What BIOS settings might he change using CMOS setup?

4. Alex has just finished making changes to the BIOS-level virus checking and would now like to save these changes. Name two ways to save BIOS settings after making changes in the CMOS setup program.

5. Ryan is working on an older Pentium II system. What key or keys should he press to enter the CMOS setup program?

Key Term Quiz

Use the following terms to complete the following sentences. Not all terms will be used.

AMI

Award Software

BIOS (basic input/output services)

BIOS ROM

CMOS (complementary metal-oxide semiconductor)

CMOS setup program

DELETE key

PAUSE/BREAK key

Phoenix Technologies

1. The system BIOS is stored on nonvolatile memory called _____.

2. Technicians configure the BIOS using the _____.

3. Press the _____ to suspend operation of the POST.

4. _____ provides the primary interface between the operating system's device drivers and most of the system's hardware.

5. A common way to enter CMOS setup is to press the _____ during startup.

Chapter 8
Expansion Bus

Lab Exercises

One of the many things that make PCs so useful is their amazing versatility. Modern PCs support a wide array of peripheral devices and attachments that expand their capabilities and boost performance. Peripherals attach to the PC via the expansion bus.

The expansion bus is the pathway that enables you to plug new devices and device controllers into the motherboard. This pathway can be split up into two groups: the internal expansion bus and the external expansion bus.

The most common internal expansion buses include the Peripheral Component Interconnect (PCI) bus, the PCI Express (PCIe) bus, and the Accelerated Graphics Port (AGP) bus, which was used exclusively for video cards on older systems. The most common external expansion buses include the Universal Serial Bus (USB) and the IEEE 1394 (FireWire) bus. You'll explore the external expansion bus in great detail when you work through the lab exercises for Chapter 18.

→ **Note**

Serial ATA (SATA) provides connections for drives and includes an external connection called eSATA for plugging in external hard disk drives. Chapter 11 goes into more detail on eSATA.

In these lab exercises, you'll learn how to determine which expansion slots are available in a system, and how to install and remove expansion cards properly. This will help you gain confidence in handling expansion card issues in the real world.

For the purposes of this chapter, suppose that you've befriended the owner of a small Internet café. Currently, the café has 12 PCs of various makes and models, all running Windows Vista Business. Paul, the owner, wanted the systems to perform well, so he ensured that each system had at least a 2.8-GHz processor and 4 GB of memory. In an attempt to keep the initial cost under budget, however, he purchased the systems without upgraded graphics or sound, so they are using the onboard graphics and sound.

Paul has noticed that many of the patrons seem to be using the systems to play games against each other in addition to the normal Internet surfing. Some of them have asked if there's any way to improve the performance of the systems so that they can play more advanced games. Paul has been thinking of branching off into hosting LAN parties anyway, so he asks you to look into what it will take to upgrade the machines.

→ **Note**

A "LAN party" is where a group of people play games on computers connected to a small network. LAN parties are nerdy, but fun! Chapter 23 goes into more detail on networking.

You would enjoy recommending that Paul buy new PCs with the latest high-performance components—what tech wouldn't want to play with the latest and greatest tech toys?—but since the machines are fairly new and well appointed, you decide to experiment with some upgrades. Because PC games are graphics- and sound-intensive, you believe that installing individual cards, such as a PCIe (or possibly AGP) graphics card and a PCI sound card, will improve the overall performance. You begin by assessing what expansion slots (PCI, AGP, and/or PCIe) are available on the current machines. You ask Paul for some cash up front, and choose two of the machines to test your theory.

 30 MINUTES

Lab Exercise 8.01: Identifying Internal Expansion Slots

Unless you've got X-ray vision, the best way to examine the expansion slots is to remove the PC case cover. In this exercise, you'll identify the type of expansion slots on your disassembled system, your working system, and as many systems (or motherboards) as you're authorized to examine. Does your system use a PCIe, AGP, or PCI graphics card, or does it use onboard video as in our lab scenario? Check to see how many other expansion slots are available for adding a sound card and (if required) upgrading the graphics adapter.

✖ **Warning**

Remember to use proper safety and electrostatic discharge (ESD) avoidance procedures when working inside the PC case.

Learning Objectives

In this exercise, you'll properly identify expansion slots and the basic features of each type of expansion technology.

At the end of this lab, you'll be able to

- Identify PCI expansion bus slots and component cards
- Identify the AGP expansion bus slot and video card
- Identify PCIe ×1 and PCIe ×16 expansion bus slots and component cards

Lab Materials and Setup

The non-production, disassembled PC and the working PC are adequate for this exercise, but it's more beneficial to be able to see motherboards inside different systems.

The materials you need for this lab are

- Your non-production, disassembled PC

- A working PC (or more than one if possible)

- An anti-static mat

- A notepad

- Optional: Some sample motherboards

Getting Down to Business

Start with the disassembled PC. Since the only components you have reinserted are the CPU and RAM, you should have a very clear view of the expansion bus slots and connections. You should also locate any expansion cards you removed during disassembly to identify what functions they serve. If the motherboard is still removed from the case, place it on the anti-static mat for exploration. If you have installed the motherboard into the case, lay the case down on the anti-static mat and follow all ESD precautions.

After completing the steps using the tear-down machine, switch over to your working PC. Shut down your PC and unplug it from the wall. Place it on your anti-static mat, remove the PC case cover, and take a good look inside. Your aim is to determine what type of expansion slots your motherboard has, and what peripheral card components are currently installed.

Step 1   Here are the physical characteristics of PCI expansion slots:

- About three inches long

- Usually white in color (modern motherboards may use bright colors like yellow or green to enhance the visual appeal of the motherboard)

- Offset from the edge of the motherboard by about one inch

Figure 8-1 shows PCI slots on a modern motherboard.

Record the following information:

How many PCI slots are on your motherboard? _____

What PCI devices are installed on your system? _____

How many PCI slots are empty? _____

FIGURE 8-1 A group of PCI slots

Step 2   See if you can locate a 32-bit AGP slot. As the name suggests, the AGP slot is used for one component only—the graphics adapter. Here are the physical characteristics of the AGP slot:

- One slot per motherboard

- A little less than three inches long

- Usually brown in color

- Offset from the edge of the motherboard by about two inches

Figure 8-2 shows an AGP slot in its natural habitat. While popular on slightly older motherboards, AGP slots have been all but ousted by PCIe, and your motherboard may not have one.

Record the following information:

Is there an AGP video card slot on your motherboard? _____

What can you tell about the type and brand of video card without removing it?

_____

Step 3   Take a look at your motherboard and see if there are any PCIe ×1 or PCIe ×16 slot connectors. These are fairly new (circa 2004), so you may not see them on all the motherboards you are exploring. PCIe is very interesting, offering a theoretical throughput of 2.5 Gbps per lane and supporting from 1 to 32 lanes. The first devices to take advantage of PCIe are graphics cards using the 16-lane configuration. The physical characteristics of the PCIe expansion slots depend on the number of lanes. Figure 8-3 shows PCIe slots on a modern motherboard.

PCIe ×1 slots have the following characteristics:

- About one inch long

- Often brightly colored (blue and white being fairly common)

- Offset from the edge of the motherboard by about 1.25 inches

FIGURE 8-2 An AGP slot

PCIe ×16 slots have the following characteristics:

- About 3.5 inches long

- Often brightly colored (blue and white being fairly common)

- Offset from the edge of the motherboard by about 1.25 inches

Record the following information:

Are there any PCIe slots on your motherboard? _____

If yes, how many PCIe ×1 slots are there? _____

How many PCIe ×16 slots are there? _____

Are there any PCIe cards installed in the system? _____

PCIe ×16

PCIe ×1

FIGURE 8-3 A motherboard with both PCIe ×1 and PCIe ×16 expansion slots

---

 Cross-Reference

For more detail about the PCI, AGP, and PCIe buses, refer to the "PCI" section in Chapter 8 of *Mike Meyers' CompTIA A+ Guide to Managing and Troubleshooting PCs.*

After you've completed your inventory of installed expansion bus devices, put the case cover back on your PC, plug it back in, and restart the system.

⏱ 30 MINUTES

Lab Exercise 8.02: Installing Expansion Cards

There are five steps to installing any expansion card device properly:

1. Arm yourself with knowledge of the device before you install it. Is the device certified to run on the Windows OS that you're running? Is it compatible with your motherboard and other hardware? Depending on your Windows version, be sure to check the Windows Catalog, Windows Vista Compatibility Center, or Windows Logo'd Product List (which can be found at http://winqual .microsoft.com/HCL/Default.aspx?m=x) before you do anything.

2. Remove the cover from your PC case and install the device. As always, follow all ESD and safety precautions, and handle the card with care.

3. Assign system resources to the device. In approximately 99.99 percent of cases (a rough estimate), you won't have to do this because plug and play (PnP) takes care of it for you, but if you're working with an old, mid-1990s era system, then you may have to assign resources manually to accommodate the old, non-PnP device.

4. Install device drivers for the component. Windows comes with a large device drivers catalog, so it may try to help you by installing the driver that it thinks the device needs. In most cases, you should visit the card manufacturer's Web site, download the latest drivers for the card and your operating system, and then install the updated drivers. You can also install the card and then use Microsoft/Windows Update, which may find and download a copy of the latest driver from the manufacture.

5. Verify that the device is functional and that it's not creating any conflicts with other devices on your system.

The following exercise is a somewhat abridged version of this procedure; instead of installing a new device, you'll remove and reinstall devices that are already on your system.

✔ **Cross-Reference**

To review the details of device installation, refer to the "Installing Expansion Cards" section in Chapter 8 of *Mike Meyers' CompTIA A+ Guide to Managing and Troubleshooting PCs*.

Learning Objectives

In this lab, you'll practice removing and installing internal expansion cards.

At the end of this lab, you'll be able to

- Remove and install expansion cards in a system correctly and safely

Lab Materials and Setup

The materials you need for this lab are

- At least one working Windows computer with expansion cards installed

- A Phillips-head screwdriver

- An anti-static mat and wrist strap

- Anti-static storage bags

- A notepad

→ **Note**

As usual, if you have access to more than one system, take advantage of it—with one exception. You may be asking yourself, "Hey, how come I'm not reinstalling the cards into this disassembled PC I have sitting here?" That's a very good question!

In the next chapter, you'll be practicing removing the motherboard from the case and reinstalling it. This process would be complicated by having a card or two sticking out of the motherboard. After you complete your practice on the motherboard, you can check back with this chapter and reinstall the expansion cards in the disassembled PC.

Getting Down to Business

In this exercise, you'll physically remove expansion card devices from your PC. You'll then make note of any important information you can find on the device's label: device maker, version, and so on. Finally, you'll reassemble and restart the system. In Lab Exercise 8.03, you'll use the Device Manager to make sure everything is working properly.

Shut down the system and unplug the power cable, and then place it on your anti-static mat. Once you remove the PC case cover and strap on your anti-static wrist strap, you're ready to start.

Step 1   Check your notes from Lab Exercise 8.01 and draw a sketch showing which device is installed in which slot on the motherboard (assuming that you are using the same working machine from Lab Exercise 8.01).

Step 2   Remove the cards one at a time from your system. For each card, follow these procedures:

   a.   Remove the retaining screw and store it safely. Check for any latches on the expansion slot (see Figure 8-4) and release them when removing the video card.

✔ **Hint**

You'll see two main types of screws used in PCs. At first glance, they may look the same, but while these screws are the same overall size, they have different sizes of threads. Screws with the larger threads, commonly called *coarse-threaded* screws, are generally used to secure expansion cards, hard drives, power supplies, and case covers. Screws with the smaller threads, commonly called *fine-threaded* screws, are typically used to secure storage devices such as floppy disk drives and optical drives into their respective bays.

   b.   Taking hold of the card by its edges, carefully and firmly pull it straight up and out of its slot.

✔ **Hint**

These cards can be difficult to remove. If a card seems stuck, try rocking it back and forth (from front to back in the direction of the slot, not side to side).

FIGURE 8-4 Releasing a latch holding in the video card

    c.   Holding the card only by the edges and the metal flange, place it in an anti-static bag for safekeeping.

Step 3   Examine each of the cards you removed from your system and record the pertinent information. Do any of the cards have writing or labels on them? If so, what information do these labels provide?

_____

_____

_____

Can you identify the manufacturers of the cards? If so, list each card and its manufacturer.

_____

_____

_____

Are there any version numbers or codes on the cards? If so, list this information for each card.

_____

_____

_____

What kind of interface does each card use? List whether it is a PCI, AGP, PCIe (or something else).

_____

_____

_____

Step 4   Reinstall into your system the expansion cards you removed. For each card, follow these procedures:

    a.   Check your notes to confirm where to reinstall the card.

    b.   Align the card over its motherboard slot, making sure that the metal flange is aligned properly with the case slot. Holding the flange with one hand, place the heel of your hand on the top edge of the card and push the card firmly into the expansion slot.

    c.   Once the card is in the slot and the flange is flush with the case, replace the screw that holds the card in place. Don't be tempted to skip the screw! It keeps the card from working loose over time.

✖ Warning

After you have reinstalled all the expansion cards, take a look at the back of your system (where you can see input/output connections for the cards). Are there any holes where no cards are installed and a slot cover has not been used? It's very important to install slot covers wherever an expansion card is not installed. This ensures that air will flow properly through the computer case, keeping your critical components cool.

30 MINUTES

Lab Exercise 8.03: Managing Hardware with Device Manager

Windows is capable of utilizing a universe of peripherals and expansion cards—everything from modems to TV tuners. Management of this massive collection of hardware in Windows is handled by the Device Manager.

The Device Manager provides a centralized location for dealing with all aspects of the computer's hardware. This includes a simple inventory of all installed devices, notification of malfunctioning devices, and the capability to install and update drivers.

This exercise will cover some of the more useful features of the Device Manager.

✔ **Cross-Reference**

If you need a refresher on system resources, refer to the "System Resources" section in Chapter 8 of *Mike Meyers' CompTIA A+ Guide to Managing and Troubleshooting PCs*.

Learning Objectives

In this lab, you'll use the Device Manager to examine and update a system.

At the end of this lab, you'll be able to

- Use the Device Manager to examine devices on your system, check for problems, and update drivers

Lab Materials and Setup

The materials you need for this lab are

- A working computer running Windows

- Access to the Internet

✔ **Hint**

As usual, if you have access to more than one system, take advantage of it.

Getting Down to Business

In this exercise, you'll use the Device Manager to view the system resource settings on your PC.

Step 1 Open the Windows Control Panel. In Windows 2000/XP, click the icon for the System applet. Select the Hardware tab and then click the Device Manager button; this brings up the Device Manager in a separate window (see Figure 8-5). In Windows Vista, select System and Maintenance, and then choose Device Manager. If Control Panel is set to Classic View, select the Device Manager applet directly. Note that you can also access this applet by pressing the Windows key and the PAUSE/BREAK key at the same time.

Step 2 Check for any missing devices, or devices marked with error icons:

- A device marked with a black "!" on a yellow circle means that the device is missing, Windows does not recognize it, or there is a driver issue.

- A device marked with a red "X" means the device is disabled. It has either been turned off or damaged.

Step 3 Download and install the latest device drivers for each of your expansion cards. There are many methods you can use to accomplish this task, but the two that follow are the most common.

- If your working PC is connected to the Internet, you can use the Update Driver Wizard from the device's Driver tab in the Device Manager to connect to Windows Update. Open the Device Manager and select *View device by type*. Locate the device that matches the expansion card you have installed, and open its properties. Select the Driver tab, and then click Update Driver as shown in Figure 8-6. This brings up the Hardware Update Wizard, as shown in Figure 8-7; from here you can follow the directions to download the signed driver from the Windows Update site.

FIGURE 8-5 Device Manager in Windows XP

FIGURE 8-6 The Driver tab from the device
properties in Windows

- If your working PC is not connected to the Internet, or the device does not have a signed
  driver available through Windows Update, you will have to follow these instructions before
  clicking Update Driver. Using a computer with Internet access, find and connect to the
  manufacturer's Web site. Using the model number of the device, locate and download the
  correct driver for the operating system on the PC where the device is installed. Save the driver
  to a floppy disk or USB thumb drive, remove the floppy or thumb drive from that system, and
  insert it into your working PC. Open Device Manager and select *View device by type*. Locate the
  device that matches the expansion card you have installed, and open its properties. Select the
  Driver tab, and then click Update Driver. When prompted to connect to the Internet, choose *No,
  not this time*, and follow the directions to locate and load the new device driver (see Figure 8-8).

FIGURE 8-7 Accessing the Windows Update site

FIGURE 8-8 The Hardware Update Wizard searching for device drivers on removable media

---

✔ **Hint**

Many manufacturers include installation wizards for their devices, so that is yet another method that you can use to update device drivers. Many times, the manufacturer will include related applications along with the drivers to enhance the performance of the device. A good example of this is an inkjet printer that includes the driver and utilities for adjusting print quality, performing printer maintenance, and so on.

Lab Analysis Test

1. When you examined the two machines from the Internet café, you were very pleased to find that one of them had a PCIe ×16 expansion slot. What is the advantage of the PCIe expansion bus, and how will it contribute to providing a solution at the Internet café?

2. John has a system that runs at 3.2 GHz and uses a 128-MB AGP video card. He uses Windows XP Professional and wants to try its multiple-monitor support feature. Can he add another AGP video card?

3. You've installed a NIC and a PCI FireWire controller card on Susan's Windows XP Professional system. The system starts up fine, but when you check the Device Manager, you see a yellow circle with a black exclamation mark beside the NIC icon. What is the problem?

4. Given the scenario in the preceding question, what steps should you take to rectify the problem?

5. Tim has installed a new PCIe sound card. He boots the machine and navigates to the Device Manager, only to find a red X icon next to this device. What should Tim do next?

Key Term Quiz

Use the following terms to complete the following sentences. Not all terms will be used.

AGP

device drivers

DMA

expansion card

I/O address

IRQ

PCI

PCIe

system resources

memory address

1. Most current motherboards continue to provide several _____ slots.

2. Older systems use the dedicated _____ slot for video cards.

3. The settings for I/O addresses and IRQs have pretty much become automated with the introduction of PnP. These, along with DMA and memory addresses, are collectively known as _____.

4. The _____ bus provides for ×1, ×2, ×4, ×8, ×16, and ×32 lanes of bidirectional communication.

5. The Hardware Update Wizard makes it easy to update the _____ for a device.

Chapter 9
Motherboards

Lab Exercises

With all due respect to the CPU, system RAM, power supply, hard drive, and all the other sundry pieces of a typical PC, the motherboard is the real workhorse of the system. Every component on the PC plugs into the motherboard either directly or indirectly. Every bit and byte of data that moves between devices passes through the motherboard's sockets and traces. The motherboard is what brings all of the individual parts of the PC into a working whole. As such, replacing a motherboard is one of the most challenging tasks a PC tech will face.

Luckily, only a couple of circumstances require you to undertake this chore. The first is when the motherboard malfunctions or is damaged; modern motherboards aren't made to be repaired, so when they go bad, they must be replaced as a whole unit. The other is when you want to upgrade the PC with a more powerful CPU than its current motherboard supports. In either of these cases, you've got a bit of work ahead of you! Installing a motherboard requires more effort than any other type of installation—more preparation, more time performing the installation, and more cleanup afterward. Still, you shouldn't be intimidated by the prospect of replacing a motherboard—it's a common and necessary part of PC repair. In this chapter, you'll go through the process from start to finish.

In the following lab exercises, you'll make preparations for a motherboard installation, including labeling cables and connectors, removing the motherboard from a working PC, and exploring its features. You'll then research new motherboards, reinstall your motherboard, and explore your motherboard more thoroughly using CPU-Z.

🕐 15 MINUTES

Lab Exercise 9.01: Removing and Labeling Components and Cables

You are consulting for a small graphics firm that's upgrading its PCs to accommodate a major software upgrade and network restructuring. While assessing the company's PC stock, you discover that a number of its systems lack sufficient CPU power to run an important new CAD program. To remedy this, you must replace the motherboards of these systems with models that support newer and faster CPUs.

→ **Note**

CAD, or computer-aided design, refers to any software that helps users draw or draft designs, usually of a technical nature. This type of software is commonly used by engineers and architects.

The first step, however, is to remove the motherboard, which can be daunting. To get to the motherboard, you have to remove the installed expansion cards and cables first. Many of us have had the experience of taking something apart only to wind up with leftover parts after we put it back together. To avoid this result when you disassemble a PC, you should get into the habit of properly storing and labeling any parts that you remove from the system. This includes everything from the major components to the screws that hold them in place and the cables that connect them to the motherboard.

✔ **Hint**

If you are using the disassembled non-production machine for this lab, you have already removed and organized the components and cables from the machine. Use this step to review the labeling and storage of components and cables in preparation for removal and installation of the motherboard. If you are using a second machine for this exercise, make use of this lab to build the "good habit" of organization. Of course, you don't need to attach a label to each individual screw, but do keep them organized in labeled containers to avoid confusion!

Learning Objectives

In this lab, you'll remove and label expansion card components, cables, and connectors in preparation for removing the motherboard.

At the end of this lab, you'll be able to

- Remove and label expansion cards

- Remove and label data cables and connectors

- Remove and label power cables

Lab Materials and Setup

The materials you need for this lab are

- A working computer

- The motherboard book or online documentation for the motherboard

- Sticky notes and a pen

- A Phillips-head screwdriver

- An anti-static mat and anti-static wrist strap

- Anti-static bags

Getting Down to Business

Starting with your system shut down (and, as always, the power cable unplugged from the wall and the case), set your system on the anti-static mat, remove the PC case cover, and strap on your anti-static wrist strap. Have your labeling materials handy and perform the following steps.

Step 1 Following the procedure laid out in Lab Exercise 8.03 in the previous chapter, remove any expansion cards from the PC. Label each one with a sticky note that identifies the card, and store it in an anti-static bag.

Step 2 Disconnect and label the following data cables:

- Hard drive cables

- Optical drive cables

- Floppy drive cable

- Sound cable (runs from the optical drive to the sound card)

- USB front panel connector dongle (if applicable)

Step 3 Disconnect and label the following power cables:

- Hard drive cables

- Optical drive cables

- Floppy drive cable

- Power plugs for CPU fan, power supply fan (if present), and case fan (if present)

- Motherboard power (P1 and P4)

Step 4 Disconnect and label the front panel control wires (also called the *harness wires*) from the motherboard. Be certain to use the motherboard book to properly label these wires! Front panel control wires typically include the power button, reset button, front panel LEDs (power, hard disk activity, and so on), and system speaker.

✔ **Hint**

To label wires, use the small sticky notes, or cut the square ones into strips. Write on it, fold the sticky part of the sticky note over the wire, and stick it to the back to make a tag.

Step 5   Depending on your system, you may have to remove other devices to ensure that you have sufficient clearance to lift the motherboard out of the PC case in the next exercise. Visually confirm that there aren't any components blocking a path for easy removal. Are any hard drives or optical drives in the way? Is the power supply in the way? Remove anything that could block the motherboard's exit or bump into important attached components (namely the RAM or CPU fan) during removal.

 15 MINUTES

Lab Exercise 9.02: Removing a Motherboard

With all of your PC components and cables safely tucked away, the next step in your upgrade job is to remove the old motherboard so that you can replace it. Techs will tell you that motherboard removal is the exercise that separates the geek from the meek and the true PC tech from the wannabe, but don't let that intimidate you! Motherboard removal is completely straightforward and simple.

✔ **Hint**

Once again, if you're using the disassembled non-production machine, you have already removed the motherboard from the case, but you should use this exercise to review. If you're using a different machine for this exercise, follow the instructions.

Learning Objectives

In this lab, you'll remove your PC's motherboard.

At the end of this lab, you'll be able to

- Remove a motherboard safely and correctly

Lab Materials and Setup

The materials you need for this lab are

- The computer on which you performed Lab Exercise 9.01
- A Phillips-head screwdriver

- An anti-static mat and anti-static wrist strap

- A large anti-static bag

Getting Down to Business

Following the same ESD avoidance procedures listed in the previous exercise, you'll now remove the mounting screws for the motherboard and lift it out of the PC case.

Step 1   Locate and remove the screws holding the motherboard to the frame of the case. There are most likely six to nine screws, which may also have small washers. Be sure not to lose these washers because they help prevent over-tightening the screws during installation. Some systems may use small plastic or metal supports called *standoffs* between the motherboard and the frame. Remove these and store them in a labeled container.

✖ Warning

Remember to handle the motherboard as you would any printed circuit board: gently, by the edges, as if you were holding a delicate old photograph.

Step 2   Carefully remove the motherboard from the PC case and place it on your anti-static mat. You should place the motherboard in a large anti-static bag for the best protection.

 15 MINUTES

Lab Exercise 9.03: Identifying Motherboard Features

At a glance, one motherboard pretty much looks like any other. Of course, as a PC tech, you know that many differences may exist: Two identical-looking motherboards can have completely different feature sets. Chipsets, bus speed, CPU socket type, and clock speed are just some of the important features that separate one motherboard from another. These differences aren't always obvious, but you can turn to your motherboard book to identify your motherboard's features, as described in the following steps.

Learning Objectives

In this lab, you'll become familiar with different motherboard features.

At the end of this lab, you'll be able to

- Recognize different motherboard features

- Identify the location of motherboard features

Lab Materials and Setup

The materials you need for this lab are

- A motherboard, such as the one you removed in Lab Exercise 9.02

- The motherboard book or online documentation for that motherboard

Getting Down to Business

In the following steps, you'll identify the location of key features on your motherboard.

✔ Hint

If you're using the motherboard you removed in the previous lab, take this opportunity to clean any dust off of it, using canned air, before you begin.

Step 1   Note the location of the make and model information on the motherboards in Figure 9-1. Compare this to your motherboard and locate the manufacturer name and model number.

✔ Cross-Reference

For details on chipsets, refer to the "Chipset" section of Chapter 9 of *Mike Meyers' CompTIA A+ Guide to Managing and Troubleshooting PCs*.

What is the name of your motherboard manufacturer? _____

What is the model number of your motherboard? _____

What CPU socket do you have on your motherboard? _____

What type of chipset do you have on your motherboard? _____

Keep this information handy! Having the make and model of your motherboard readily available makes it easy to search the Web for drivers and updated BIOS.

FIGURE 9-1 Two examples of model number information printed on motherboards

Step 2   Look for any charts or numbers printed on the surface of the motherboard.

Are there any jumper blocks? _____

What are some of the settings that can be configured using jumpers?

_____

_____

_____

Step 3   Locate the following on your motherboard:

- System clock battery

- BIOS

- RAM slots (What type? Dual-channel or triple-channel support?) _____

- SATA or RAID (if present) _____

- Graphics adapter support (onboard, PCI, AGP, PCIe?) _____

 30 MINUTES

Lab Exercise 9.04: Researching New Motherboards

While the motherboard may be the backbone of a PC, all good upgrade efforts should begin with the CPU. Trying to pick out a motherboard and *then* a processor that goes with it is a little like choosing a new car stereo before you choose a new car—you can do it, but you might end up having to modify the dashboard to make it fit. In other words, it's much less painful to work from CPU to motherboard, especially when your goal is to increase performance. Don't tie yourself down by doing it backwards.

There are a lot of variables to cover when searching for a new CPU and motherboard. Ensuring compatibility is key. Once you've picked the latest and greatest processor from Intel or AMD, you need to find a motherboard that will play nicely with it. This involves matching the socket type of the processor to the socket type of the motherboard. You must also make sure that the motherboard's form factor is compatible with your case. And even after you've narrowed it down to that, there is still the matter of picking a manufacturer and determining which features you want the motherboard to have.

Learning Objectives

In this lab, you'll become familiar with different motherboards and their compatibility with various processors and cases.

At the end of this lab, you'll be able to

- Recognize different motherboard form factors

- Understand considerations for upgrading a system with a newer motherboard

Lab Materials and Setup

The materials you need for this lab are

- The disassembled, non-production PC computer system used in the lab exercises in Chapter 3

- A PC with Internet access

- An anti-static mat and anti-static wrist strap

✔ **Hint**

As usual, if you have access to multiple systems, take advantage of it. It's most useful to have a variety of motherboards to study.

Getting Down to Business

The following steps will lead you through the process of determining which motherboard you need to obtain to update your client's systems. You'll also see that a motherboard is not an island unto itself, but one piece of the archipelago that is a PC.

Step 1 Go to www.newegg.com (or another online PC component store) and search for a newer, faster processor. When selecting a new processor, be sure to keep track of important specifications so that you can refer to them when you need to pick out a motherboard. Record the following information:

Manufacturer _____

Series _____

CPU socket type _____

Step 2 Search the online PC component store for a new motherboard. Keep in mind that the CPU's socket type must match the motherboard's, otherwise they will be incompatible. You'll find more than one that is compatible, but for now, pick one and record the following information:

Manufacturer _____

CPU socket type _____

Form factor _____

Expansion slots _____

_____

Step 3 The next step to finding a new and compatible motherboard is to make sure that it will work with the form factor of your client's system cases.

Current PC motherboards come in a few different styles, or *form factors*: ATX (Advanced Technology eXtended), microATX and FlexATX, BTX (Balanced Technology eXtended), and proprietary form factors from companies such as Dell and Sony. Each motherboard form factor has a corresponding case it is compatible with, but some motherboards will fit in a case with a different form factor. ATX motherboards are what you find in most PCs on the market.

ATX, microATX, and FlexATX are all in the same family. The FlexATX is physically the smallest in size, the microATX is in the middle, and the ATX is the largest. Typically, all three will work in the large ATX case because all three variations retain the same form factor for the external connections.

From 2005 to around 2007, BTX looked as though it would be the next big thing in motherboard form factors. Sadly, the BTX standards were so strict that manufacturers simply could not fit newer chipsets onto a BTX motherboard. But some BTX boards are still out there, so you may still encounter them. These are essentially the same components rearranged for better cooling, but this form factor requires a BTX case, so it is not interchangeable with ATX.

Your client's cases are all ATX. Is the motherboard you picked compatible? _____

What if the client wants to switch over to microATX cases in the future—would the same motherboard still work? Why? _____

_____

Step 4 Look at a few different (but still compatible) motherboards. Compare their features. What makes them different? Does one have more expansion slots than the other? Does one have fewer RAM slots? Are there other features, such as support for NVIDIA's SLI or ATI's CrossFire dual-graphics card technology, that would influence your choice? Using the motherboard you already selected, record the following information:

Number of memory slots _____

Maximum memory supported _____

SATA ports _____

Onboard video chipset _____

Other features _____

_____

 30 MINUTES

Lab Exercise 9.05: Installing a Motherboard

Now you get the real test of your tech skills: installing the new motherboards and reconnecting everything so that the computers work again! Don't be intimidated, though. Everything you need to install a motherboard (in your case, probably the motherboard you just removed in Lab Exercise 9.02) is right in front of you.

Over the past few labs, you have concentrated on hardware removal and installation, using either the disassembled non-production system or a working non-production system—or in some cases both. It is very easy to become casual or even careless about technique and organization since these machines are noncritical.

One of the really important concepts to remember is that all of these efforts—the studying, the labs, and the CompTIA A+ certification itself—are designed to help you become the highest-quality tech that you can be! It's very important that you develop and practice patience, attention to detail, and finesse while working through the lab exercises.

To this end, when you remove and replace a motherboard in a system, you interact with almost every component of the computer system. In the field, you must not only successfully disassemble/assemble the hardware, but also verify that the system powers up and operates properly afterward. Many competent techs, when installing a new motherboard, will check for proper operation along the way. Here's a good checkpoint: After you've installed the CPU and RAM, configured any jumpers or switches, and installed the motherboard in the case, insert the power connections and test the system. A POST card is a real timesaver here, but you can also connect the PC speaker, a graphics card, monitor, and a keyboard to verify that the system is booting properly.

Learning Objectives

In this lab, you'll install a motherboard. You can use the motherboard and system you disassembled in Lab Exercise 9.03.

At the end of this lab, you'll be able to

- Install a PC motherboard and connect all its associated components

Lab Materials and Setup

The materials you need for this lab are

- The disassembled, non-production PC computer system used in the lab exercises in Chapter 3
- A working system from which the motherboard has been removed
- Components and cables previously connected to the removed motherboard
- The motherboard book or online documentation for the motherboard
- An anti-static mat and anti-static wrist strap
- A notepad and pen

Getting Down to Business

Physically installing the motherboard itself is mostly a matter of being careful and methodical. The more complex part of the task is reattaching all the cables and cards in their proper places.

✖ **Warning**

Motherboards are full of delicate electronics! Remember to follow the proper ESD avoidance and safety procedures.

✔ **Hint**

When installing a motherboard, it's handy to use your notepad to check off assembly steps as you go along.

Step 1 Carefully line up the motherboard inside the PC case and secure it in place with the mounting screws. Be sure to use the washers and plastic/metal standoffs, if supplied.

Step 2 Insert the front panel control wires in their appropriate places. These should include your power button, reset button, front panel LEDs (power, hard disk activity, and so on), system speaker, and so on. Refer to the labels and your motherboard documentation for the proper connections.

✔ **Hint**

At this point, if you're working on the disassembled, non-production system, skip to Step 5, install the expansion cards, and then set the system aside. You will continue to build the disassembled system in future lab exercises where you will explore the power supply, hard drives, removable storage, and audio/video components.

Step 3 Connect all power cables to the hard drive, optical drive, floppy drive, CPU fan, main motherboard, and so on.

Step 4 Connect data cables to the hard drive, optical drive, and floppy drive, as well as the sound cable and USB connector dongles, if applicable.

Step 5 Following the procedure laid out in Lab Exercise 8.02 in the previous chapter, install the expansion card components.

Step 6   Now comes perhaps the most important step: Double-check all of your connections and cards to make sure that they're properly seated and connected where they're supposed to be! If something is wrong, it's definitely better to discover it now than to smell smoke after you've hit the power switch.

Step 7   If you're using the working PC you previously disassembled, you can now replace the case cover on your PC. Then plug the keyboard, mouse, and monitor back in, plug the power cable back in, and finally turn on the PC. Assuming you've done everything correctly, your system will boot up normally.

 15 MINUTES

Lab Exercise 9.06: Exploring Motherboard Features with CPU-Z

Now that you've completed the analysis and upgrade of your client's systems with new motherboards and CPUs where needed, you can verify some of the characteristics and features the motherboard manufacturer has promoted. You already downloaded the CPU-Z utility from the Internet, so you can launch that to examine the information on the Mainboard tab.

✔ **Hint**

Over the years, motherboards have been called many names—and not just the bad names you might use when one doesn't work properly! Early motherboards were sometimes called the *planar board*. A motherboard can be referred to as the *system board*, *mainboard*, and sometimes just *board* or *mobo*. Regardless of the name, these terms refer to the large printed circuit board (PCB) used to connect all the components in a computer system.

Learning Objectives

In this lab, you'll identify various motherboard features.

At the end of this lab, you'll be able to

- Verify motherboard features

Lab Materials and Setup

The materials you need for this lab are

- Access to a working computer with the CPU-Z utility installed

- A notepad and pencil to document the specifications

- Optional: A word processor or spreadsheet application to facilitate the documentation

This lab is more informative if you have access to different systems using various motherboards.

Getting Down to Business

In the following steps, you'll verify the features of your motherboard.

Step 1 Launch CPU-Z and navigate to the Mainboard tab.

Step 2 The CPU-Z utility displays some of the key features of your motherboard, as shown in Figure 9-2.

Using the data gathered by CPU-Z, record as much pertinent information as possible:

Manufacturer _____

Model _____

Chipset _____

Southbridge _____

Sensor _____

BIOS brand _____

Graphic interface version _____

Step 3 If possible, launch CPU-Z on various machines to compare the features of different motherboards.

FIGURE 9-2 CPU-Z displaying motherboard information

→ **Try This: PC Wizard**

Using the system from Chapter 6, launch the PC Wizard application. Once PC Wizard is running, click the Mainboard icon. This brings up a number of items (components) in the top-right pane of the window. Click the Mainboard item to display detailed information in the lower-right pane of the window, as shown here:

Using this information, can you determine the integrated devices supported by your motherboard? Does this correspond to the information in the PC or motherboard documentation?

Lab Analysis Test

1. Jonathan is building a system using an Intel Core 2 Duo processor, and he's purchased a new motherboard from ASUS. He would like to use an old (but working!) ATX power supply he has lying around to power the system. Why might this *not be a good idea?*

2. Keith bought a fancy new case for his system. He removed the motherboard from his old case, but discovered it wouldn't fit in the new one. What did Keith forget to check?

3. Dianne is trying to install an ATX motherboard in a new, empty ATX case. She tries to set it down in the bottom of the case, but it won't fit—the ports on the side are too low to poke out the back of the case, and she can't make the screws work at all. What has she forgotten?

4. After Erik reassembled his PC and turned it on, he noticed that the green LED and the disk active LED never light up, but everything seems to work okay. What is the problem?

5. Jeremy wants to upgrade his system by replacing the CPU. His friend works at a local computer shop and has offered him a Pentium D processor for a great price! Jeremy's current system uses a Pentium 4 2.54-GHz CPU. Will this work? Why or why not?

Key Term Quiz

Use the following terms to complete the following sentences. Not all terms will be used.

AT

ATX

BTX

CPU-Z

FlexATX

microATX

motherboard book

P1 power connector

P4 power connector

P8/P9 power connector

sockets

1. The power supplies for modern ATX motherboards connect using the _____.

2. To check the technical specifications of a motherboard, consult its _____.

3. _____ is a handy tool for finding out information about your system.

4. _____ are the areas where CPUs are installed on motherboards.

5. One motherboard design has reconfigured the components and layout to maximize the cooling properties of the system; this is known as the _____ motherboard.

Chapter 10
Power Supplies

Lab Exercises

The term "power supply" is somewhat misleading. After all, the power supply in a PC does not actually *supply* power; it just takes the alternating current (AC) supplied by the power company and converts it to the direct current (DC) used by the computer system. Local power companies supply AC to the outlet in your home or office, and some conversion must take place to supply the lower operating voltages and DC power required for the PC to function.

As a PC technician, you need to understand the difference between AC and DC power. You should be able to measure the AC power at the wall outlet and determine whether the hot, neutral, and ground wires are properly connected. You must also measure the DC output of the power supply inside the PC case to determine whether the power supply is providing the correct DC voltage.

The power supply in a PC is an electronic device that converts the higher voltage—120 volts of alternating current (VAC) in the United States or 240 VAC outside the United States—into the three power levels of 12, 5, and 3.3 volts of direct current (VDC) used in today's PC systems. The 12-volt level is traditionally used for devices that have motors to spin, such as hard drives, floppy drives, CD/DVD-ROM drives, and cooling fans. The 5-volt and 3.3-volt power usually supports all of the onboard electronics. Modern CPUs often use less than 3.3 volts, so there are further step-down regulators and filters to provide core voltages as low as 1.4 volts.

The various versions of the ATX power supplies are, by far, the most common power supplies you will see on desktop computer systems. These include ATX (with a 20-pin P1 power connector), ATX 12V 1.3 (which added the AUX 4-pin connector commonly referred to as P4), and the ATX 12V 2.0 (which added the 24-pin P1 connector and dropped the P4 connector).

Higher-end computers such as servers and gaming systems with multiple high-powered graphics processing units (GPUs) often require much more current, so you may start to see the Server System Infrastructure (SSI)–developed, non-ATX-standard motherboard with a power supply named EPS 12V; it uses a 24-pin P1 connector, a 4-pin P4 connector, and a unique 8-pin connector.

Suppose a client calls you saying that her PC keeps locking up. After walking her through a few simple troubleshooting steps, you rule out a virus or a misbehaving application. This leaves hardware as the likely culprit, and in all likelihood, it's the power supply. In these lab exercises, you'll practice the procedures for measuring power going to the PC, testing the PC's power supply, and replacing a PC power supply.

✔ **Hint**

The CompTIA A+ exams show their American roots in the area of electrical power. Watch for power questions that discuss American power standards—especially ones related to household voltage and outlet plug design.

The exams will also typically refer to the power supply using the abbreviation PSU (power supply unit) or the acronym FRU (field replaceable unit). FRU can describe any component that would be replaced in the field by a technician.

---

 30 MINUTES

Lab Exercise 10.01: Electricity

Troubleshooting power-related problems is one of the trickier tasks you'll undertake as a PC tech. Your first step is to go right to the source, so to speak, and make certain that the power being supplied to the PC from the electrical outlet is good.

✔ **Cross-Reference**

For details on AC power from the power company, refer to the "Supplying AC" section in Chapter 10 of *Mike Meyers' CompTIA A+ Guide to Managing and Troubleshooting PCs*.

Learning Objectives

At the end of this lab, you'll be able to

- Determine if the AC wiring is correct at a wall outlet

- Determine if the AC voltages are correct at a wall outlet

Lab Materials and Setup

The materials you need for this lab are

- An AC electrical outlet tester

- A multimeter

Getting Down to Business

Measuring the voltage coming from an AC outlet is a nerve-wracking task even for experienced techs! Sticking objects into a live power outlet goes against everything you've been taught since infancy, but when done properly, it really is completely safe.

Be sure to use common sense and appropriate safety procedures. If you're not familiar with using a multimeter, please review the "Supplying AC" section in Chapter 10 of *Mike Meyers' CompTIA A+ Guide to Managing and Troubleshooting PCs*, or ask your instructor for a demonstration.

✔ **Hint**

If a PC is having unexplained errors and you suspect the power supply, don't be too hasty in replacing it. First check the wall outlet. In some buildings, especially older ones, the wiring can be improperly connected or otherwise provide poor power.

Step 1   Look at Figure 10-1, and compare it to your electrical outlet.

FIGURE 10-1 A typical AC electrical outlet

A typical electrical socket has three openings: hot, neutral, and ground. The hot wire delivers the juice. The neutral wire acts as a drain and returns electricity to the local source (the breaker panel). The semi-rounded ground socket returns excess electricity to the ground. If your outlet doesn't have a ground socket—and outlets in many older buildings don't—then don't use it! Ungrounded outlets aren't appropriate for PCs.

✖ Warning

Take all appropriate safety precautions before measuring live electrical outlets. In a classroom, you have the benefit of an instructor to show you how to do these exercises the first time. If you're doing these on your own with no experience, seek the advice of a trained technician or instructor.

Step 2 Determine whether or not your electrical socket is "live." Do this with your electrical outlet tester. Plug your outlet tester (see Figure 10-2) into the electrical outlet or power strip where you plug in the PC. Look at the LED indicators. Are they showing good power?

Step 3 Now measure the voltage between the hot and neutral openings of the outlet. Start by setting your multimeter to AC voltage; do not proceed until you're sure you have done this correctly! If you aren't sure, ask your instructor for guidance. Referring to Figure 10-3, take the black probe and place it in the neutral opening of the wall socket. Make sure you have good contact inside the outlet. The metal probe tip must contact the metal connector inside the outlet.

Figure 10-2 A circuit tester for AC electrical outlets

FIGURE 10-3 Multimeter probe locations when testing an AC outlet's hot-to-neutral circuit

Next, place the red probe inside the hot opening. Again, you must make good metal-to-metal contact. You may have to reposition the probes to get a good connection and proper reading for the AC circuit. Your reading should be somewhere between 110 and 120 V.

What is your reading? _____

Step 4   Measure the voltage in the hot-to-ground circuit. Place the black probe into the ground opening of the outlet, as shown in Figure 10-4. Make sure you have good contact. Then place the red probe into the hot opening. Move the probes around until you get a good reading for the AC voltage. Again, your reading should be in the 110- to 120-V range.

What is your reading? _____

Step 5   The last measurement you need to take is the voltage in the neutral-to-ground safety circuit. When the neutral wire is broken or missing, the ground wire is the only way for wayward electrons to depart safely. Any electricity on both the neutral and ground wires should have a direct path back to earth, so there should be no voltage between these wires.

Place the black probe into the ground opening of the outlet. Make sure you have good contact. Place the red probe into the neutral opening (refer to Figure 10-5). Move the probes around until you get a good reading for the AC voltage. You should get a reading of 0 V.

What is your reading? _____

FIGURE 10-4 Multimeter probe locations when testing an AC outlet's hot-to-ground circuit

FIGURE 10-5 Multimeter probe locations when testing an AC outlet's neutral-to-ground circuit

Step 6 Measure another outlet in the same building, and repeat the previous steps. Are the readings similar? If the readings from your electrical outlets are outside of the ranges described, it's time to call an electrician. Assuming your reading is showing good power, go to the next exercise.

 30 MINUTES

Lab Exercise 10.02: Power Supply Output

Once you've determined that the AC power going to your client's PC is good, the next troubleshooting step is to test whether the DC power traveling from the power supply to the rest of her system is good.

✔ **Hint**

Since this lab exercise takes you through the steps you would perform on an actual trouble ticket, the scenario has you working on a machine that is completely assembled. If, however, you are working on the disassembled, non-production machine, you should proceed to Lab Exercise 10.03 ("Replacing a Power Supply") and reinstall the power supply in the tear-down machine. You may then return here and perform the power supply output exercises.

Learning Objectives

At the end of this lab, you'll be able to

- Identify the connectors of a PC power supply

- Measure the output of a PC power supply

Lab Materials and Setup

The materials you need for this lab are

- The disassembled, non-production PC computer system used in the lab exercises in Chapter 3 (with the power supply reinstalled)

- A multimeter

- A PC power supply tester

- Optional: A working PC with an ATX power supply

Getting Down to Business

There are two ways to determine whether a power supply is providing the proper voltages to the components of the computer. One is the traditional method, using a multimeter to measure the actual voltages. Another method growing in popularity is the use of a PC power supply tester.

✔ Cross-Reference

For details on DC power from the power supply, refer to the "Supplying DC" section in Chapter 10 of *Mike Meyers' CompTIA A+ Guide to Managing and Troubleshooting PCs*.

In the following steps, you'll measure DC voltage coming from the PC power supply. The two places to measure power supply output are at the Molex power connectors and at the motherboard power connector. Molex power connectors plug into devices that need 5 or 12 volts of power. These include hard drives and CD- or DVD-media drives. Mini power connectors also carry 5 or 12 volts, but on modern systems these are used only for floppy drives. On most recent systems, the power supply will provide two motherboard power connectors: the 20- or 24-pin P1 and the smaller P4 (see Figure 10-6). Both of these power connectors are used on motherboards requiring an additional 12 V power supply.

You'll then plug the P1 power connector into a PC power supply tester and verify that the readings you measured with the multimeter are within tolerance. The power supply tester has LEDs that will glow green for each of the voltages that it passes.

✖ Warning

Although the power coming out of the PC power supply is considerably less lethal than that coming directly out of the electrical outlet, you should still take all appropriate safety precautions before taking measurements.

FIGURE 10-6 Motherboard power connectors: P1 (left) and P4 (right)

Step 1 Set the multimeter to read DC voltage. Find a Molex connector that's not being used for a device. If no Molex connectors are unused, turn the system off and disconnect the one from the CD- or DVD-media drive, and then turn the PC back on.

Step 2 Referring to Figure 10-7, place the black probe into either one of the holes on the Molex connector that is aligned with a black wire. Now place the red probe into each of the other three holes of the Molex connector in turn, first the other black wire, then the red, then yellow, and record your findings.

Black wire to black wire: _____ V

Black wire to red wire: _____ V

Black wire to yellow wire: _____ V

Step 3 Measuring the voltage from the motherboard connector is a little trickier. Leave the power connector plugged into the motherboard and push the probes into the end of the connector that the wires run into. You must push the probe deep enough to touch the metal contact pins, but be careful not to push too deeply or you might push the pin out of the connector.

Push the black probe into the motherboard connector alongside any black wire, and leave it there. Insert the red probe into each of the other wires, and record your findings. Depending on your motherboard connector, you may not have all of these wires.

Black wire to red wire: _____ V

Black wire to yellow wire: _____ V

Figure 10-7 Measuring the voltage in a Molex connector

Black wire to purple wire: _____ V

Black wire to white wire: _____ V

Black wire to black wire: _____ V

Black wire to blue wire: _____ V

Black wire to green wire: _____ V

The voltages generated by the power supply must be within a tolerance (range) level; readings outside these ranges mean the power supply should be replaced. The 5 V connections have a tolerance of ±2 percent (4.9 to 5.1 V is okay), and 12 V connections have a tolerance of ±6 percent (11.25 to 12.75 V is okay).

✔ **Hint**

A single reading from your power supply may not be enough to pinpoint a power-related problem. Sometimes a power problem becomes evident only when the power supply is placed under a heavier-than-normal load, such as burning a CD or DVD. Also, some RAM-related errors mimic a failing power supply.

The other method to verify that the power supply is operating properly and supplying all the voltages within tolerance is to use a power supply tester. There are many styles of PSU testers on the market, so make sure you follow the specific directions included with your tester as you complete the steps.

Step 1   Starting with the P1 connector, follow the directions for connecting it to your specific PSU tester. Verify that all of the voltages provided through the P1 connector are acceptable (usually an LED will light to verify voltage present and within tolerance).

✔ **Hint**

When connecting and disconnecting the power supply connectors, always take care to insert the connector with the proper orientation. Most power connectors are keyed to make it difficult to install the connector backwards, but if you use excessive force, you may be able to insert the connector improperly. This applies to powering the motherboard, plugging in devices, and even using the PSU tester.

Step 2   Now, depending on your tester and power supply, plug either the 4-pin, 6-pin, or 8-pin auxiliary connector into the appropriate socket on the PSU tester and verify the voltages provided through this connector. Once they are verified, remove the connector from the socket.

Step 3 Plug the Molex connector into the PSU tester and verify the voltages provided through this connector. Once they are verified, remove the connector from the socket.

Step 4 Plug the SATA HDD power connector into the appropriate socket and verify the voltages provided through this connector. Once they are verified, remove the connector from the socket.

Step 5 Finally, plug the mini floppy drive power connector into the PSU tester and verify the voltages provided through this connector. Once they are verified, remove the connector from the socket and remove the P1 from the socket.

 30 MINUTES

Lab Exercise 10.03: Replacing a Power Supply

Let's assume that you've found a variance in the 12 V range that explains your client's system lockups. You know that power supplies aren't user-serviceable components—you don't fix them, you replace them as a unit—so it's time to replace her power supply. Next to the motherboard, the power supply is the most time-consuming component to replace, simply because of all those wires! Nonetheless, replacing the power supply is a simple operation, as described in this exercise.

Learning Objectives

At the end of this lab, you'll be able to

- Determine the total wattage requirements of the system and select the proper power supply

- Replace a power supply

Lab Materials and Setup

The materials you need for this lab are

- The disassembled, non-production PC computer system used in the lab exercises in Chapter 3

- A Phillips-head screwdriver

- A labeled container for holding screws

- Optional: A working PC with an ATX power supply

Getting Down to Business

One of the areas where PC manufacturers cut corners on lower-end systems is power supplies. High-end systems typically come with higher-wattage power supplies, whereas entry-level PCs typically have lower-wattage power supplies. This might not be evident until you add power-hungry components to the system, placing a heavier load on the power supply and causing an early failure.

In the following steps you'll determine the wattage of the power supply on your system, calculate the power usage of your PC, and then remove and reinstall the power supply.

Step 1   To find out what the wattage rating of your power supply is, look at the label on the power supply (see Figure 10-8).

Locate the watts rating. If you don't see a clear wattage rating as shown in Figure 10-8, or if you see something less evident, like the smaller "430 W" marking on the label, the power supply rating may be hidden in the model number, which in this example is "Neo HE430."

✔ **Hint**

All power supplies have a wattage rating. If it is not apparent on the power supply itself, search the Internet using the model number for reference.

What is the wattage of your power supply? _____

Step 2   When it comes time to replace a power supply, don't skimp on the wattage! Modern power supplies typically range from 300 watts to 1000 watts or more; 300-watt power supplies are the bare minimum you would use on a system that has only a few installed components (such as a single hard drive and CD- or DVD-media drive), while the 1000-watt models are usually found on server systems that have multiple hard drives (such as a RAID array), multiple processors, or other power-hungry components. Many gaming systems with high-performance graphics cards and processors, and SATA RAID configurations will use PSUs that provide 550–650 watts to meet these systems' power requirements. As a general rule, get the highest-wattage replacement you can afford while maintaining compatibility with your system. Remember, the system will draw only the current it requires, so you will never damage a system by installing a higher-wattage power supply.

Figure 10-8 Typical ATX power supply ratings label

> ✖ **Warning**
>
> Never replace a PC's power supply with one of lower wattage!

Use the following table to calculate the overall wattage needed for your system. Add the numbers for each component and determine the lowest and highest wattage requirements.

Component	Requirement	Voltage(s) Used
PCIe video card	45–75 W	3.3 V
AGP video card	30–50 W	3.3 V
PCI card	5–10 W	5 V
10/100/1000 NIC	4 W	3.3 V
SCSI controller PCI	20 W	3.3 V and 5 V
Floppy drive	5 W	5 V
7200 rpm IDE hard drive	5–20 W	5 V and 12 V
7200 rpm SATA hard drive	5–20 W	5 V and 12 V
10,000 rpm SCSI drive	10–40 W	5 V and 12 V
CD/DVD/Blu-ray media drive	10–25 W	5 V and 12 V
Case/CPU fans	3 W (each)	12 V
Motherboard (without CPU or RAM)	25–40 W	3.3 V and 5 V
RAM	10 W per 128 MB	3.3 V
Intel Core i7-860	95 W	12 V
Intel Core 2 Duo 3.0GHz	65 W	12 V
AMD Phenom II X4 965	140 W	12 V

If the highest total exceeds the power supply wattage rating, you may run into problems. When selecting a new power supply, you should multiply the load by a factor of 1.5. The multiplier provides a safety factor and allows the power supply to run more efficiently. A power supply is more efficient at 30 to 70 percent of its full capacity rating. Thus, a 450–watt PSU works best when only 135 to 315 watts are being used.

What wattage is appropriate for your system? _____

✔ **Hint**

Depending on the design of your PC case, you may have to remove data cables or components before you can get to the power supply. Make certain that you have plenty of room to work inside the case!

Step 3 Shut down the system and remove the power cable from the back of the power supply. Then remove the power supply.

   a.   Disconnect the Molex, SATA, and mini connectors from your drive devices, then unplug the main power connector from the motherboard.

   b.   If your power supply uses a P4 connector, disconnect it from the motherboard.

   c.   Unscrew the four screws holding the power supply onto the PC case (remembering to support it while you remove the last one!), and remove the power supply from the case. Store the screws in a labeled container.

Step 4 Take this opportunity to inspect and clean the power supply. Check for any rust or corrosion on the power supply casing or on any of the contacts. Inspect the wires for damage or frayed insulation. Use canned air to blow dust and dirt out of the intake and exhaust vents.

Step 5 Reinstall the power supply by performing the preceding steps in reverse order. If you had to remove data cables or other components to get at the power supply, be sure to reattach them.

🕐 30 MINUTES

Lab Exercise 10.04: Power Protection

You've successfully fixed your client's power-problem-plagued PC (say that five times fast!), but now you've noted that she has nothing in the way of power protection for her system, nor do any of her coworkers. None!

When you mention this to her, she tells you that her boss never really saw the point of spending money on surge protectors, uninterruptible power supplies, or any of "that stuff." With a straight face, she asks, "Do those things really do any good?"

Now it's your task to sell the boss on the idea of power protection. To do this, you must explain the types of power problems that lurk in the bushes just waiting to pounce on unwary users without power protection, and suggest precautions that they can take to prevent power-related damage.

Learning Objectives

At the end of this lab, you'll be able to

- Explain the need for power protection
- Explain the types of power protection available for a PC

✔ **Cross-Reference**

For details on power protection, refer to the "Surge Suppressors" and "UPS" sections in Chapter 10 of *Mike Meyers' CompTIA A+ Guide to Managing and Troubleshooting PCs.*

Lab Materials and Setup

The materials you need for this lab are

- A working PC

Getting Down to Business

Too often, PC users take for granted the electricity that powers their system. After all, there's not much you can do about the electricity, is there? Not so! Armed with the knowledge of the types of power conditions that can affect your PC, you can best determine what precautions to take.

Step 1 Describe the following types of power conditions and the types of damage they can cause.

Power spike: _____

_____

Brownout: _____

_____

Blackout: _____

_____

Step 2 Describe the following types of power protection equipment.

Surge suppressor: _____

Online uninterruptible power supply (UPS): _____

_____

Standby UPS: _____

_____

Lab Analysis Test

1. Your client calls you and says that her PC is unusually quiet and keeps rebooting for no apparent reason. What should you ask her to check?

2. Athena lives in an area where the power is often interrupted. She bought a good surge protector strip, but that does not seem to help. What does she need to prevent her system from shutting down unexpectedly?

3. Your assistant technician calls you and says he suspects a bad power supply in one of your client's systems. He said the multimeter readings are 12.65 volts and 4.15 volts. What should he do?

4. One of your clients has an older Pentium 4 system with a single IDE hard drive and 512 MB of RAM. He had been using this PC as his main workstation, but he's recently purchased a newer system and now wants to redeploy the older system as a file server on his network. He has ordered a PCI SCSI controller board and three SCSI hard drives, so that he can configure a RAID array, and an additional 2 GB of RAM. He also ordered two Y adapters for the power supply connectors. He asks for your advice about any additional hardware he should order. What do you tell him?

5. What are the power requirements of the following system?

   - AMD Athlon 64 X2 CPU and 512 MB RAM
   - Two SATA hard drives and one floppy drive
   - One CD-RW drive and one DVD-ROM drive
   - PCIe video
   - PCI sound card
   - NIC

Key Term Quiz

Use the following terms to complete the following sentences. Not all terms will be used.

3.3 V

5 V

12 V

20-pin P1

24-pin P1

Molex connector

P4

P8/P9

power sags

power spikes

power supply

UPS

1. The ATX 12V 2.0 power supply plugs into the motherboard using the _____ connector(s).

2. PC devices with motors, such as hard drives and CD/DVD-ROM drives, usually require _____ of DC electricity from the power supply.

3. Hard drives and CD/DVD-ROM drives connect to the power supply with a _____.

4. A surge protector prevents damage from _____ in the voltage.

5. Pentium 4 motherboards have both _____ and _____ power connectors.

Chapter 11
Hard Drive Technologies

Lab Exercises

As the primary storage area for the operating system, applications, and vital data, the hard drive takes on a level of importance to PC users that borders on reverence. Considering the fact that the death of a drive can mean many hours or days of tediously rebuilding your OS install, reloading applications, and re-creating data, such strong feelings make sense. And that reverence can turn quickly to agony if the user hasn't backed up his or her data in a while when the hard drive dies!

Every tech must know how to connect, configure, maintain, and troubleshoot hard drives of all types. A fully operational drive requires proper hardware setup and installation, CMOS configuration, and software setup (usually performed by tools that come with the operating system). The first few labs in this chapter cover physical installation and CMOS configuration of the mainstream hard drive technology, namely Integrated Drive Electronics (IDE), in both parallel and serial flavors, and solid-state drives (SSDs). You will then conduct research on the developments of the rapidly changing Small Computer Systems Interface (SCSI), primarily used for large, fault-tolerant data storage. The next exercise will have you troubleshoot installations, and finally you'll install additional hard drives in preparation for an exercise in the next chapter. You'll work with the software aspects of all hard drives—partitioning, formatting, and running drive utilities—in Chapter 12.

 60 MINUTES

Lab Exercise 11.01: Installing Parallel ATA Hard Drives

The local nonprofit organization where you volunteer has received a donation of ten used PCs. Most of them have tiny hard drives, so they need an upgrade before you can distribute them to the various workers at the agency. All of the motherboards have built-in parallel ATA (PATA) controllers; some even have the better ATA/100 controllers. Your boss breaks out a stack of donated hard drives and tells you to get to work!

Installing a PATA hard drive successfully requires little more than connecting data and power cables to the drive and plugging the other end of the data cable into the motherboard. Sounds simple enough on the surface, but because all PATA drives give you options to install two on each motherboard controller, unwary techs get tripped up here. This lab walks you through the physical installation of the hard drive.

✔ **Hint**

As you know from Chapter 11 of your textbook, IDE drives have several names that techs use pretty much interchangeably: IDE, EIDE, and ATA. You'll see all three terms in this lab manual and on the CompTIA A+ Certification exams. Except for discussions of very old technology, the terms describe the same type of hard drive today.

Learning Objectives

In this lab exercise, you'll identify the different components of PATA hard drives and cables and learn installation procedures.

At the end of this lab, you'll be able to

- Remove a hard drive safely and correctly

- Describe PATA cables and connectors

- Describe the geometry of a hard drive

- Calculate the capacity of a hard drive

- Describe jumper settings

- Identify the major parts of a hard drive

- Install a hard drive safely and correctly

Lab Materials and Setup

The materials you need for this lab are

- The disassembled, non-production computer system from the lab exercises in Chapter 3, with at least one PATA hard drive

- A working PC with a PATA hard drive installed

- The Windows operating system installed on the PC

- Optional: Access to one or more broken hard drives that have the covers removed for observation of the internal parts

Getting Down to Business

Grab your handy screwdriver and anti-static wrist strap; it's time to remove a hard drive! As in previous labs, if you are using the disassembled, non-production PC for this lab, you have already removed the hard drives, optical drive, and floppy drive (if present). You should gather together the drives you removed from the system, along with all associated cables and mounting hardware, to facilitate their reinstallation at the end of this exercise. The following removal instructions are included for clarification; however, you will use the drives and cables to work through the identification steps that follow.

Step 1   Shut down your system and remove the system cover, following proper electrostatic discharge (ESD) avoidance procedures.

Step 2   Disconnect all the ribbon cables from the hard drives and optical drives, but first note which device is connected to which cable and where the orientation stripe is located on each device. Be careful but firm. Grasp the cable as closely as possible to the connector on the drive and pull, rocking the connector gently from side to side.

Examine the connector on the end of the ribbon cable. Use Figure 11-1 to help you.

How many holes does your connector have for pins? _____

Are any of the holes in your connector filled in? Does your connector have a raised portion on one side so that it only fits one way? In other words, is it keyed? _____

Take a close look at the top connector in Figure 11-1.

How many connectors are on your ribbon cable? _____

Do you have a 40-wire or 80-wire ribbon cable? _____

Disconnect the power supply from all of the PATA devices by unplugging the Molex connector from each one.

FIGURE 11-1 ATA cables: Comparing 80-wire and 40-wire ribbon cable connectors

✖ **Warning**

Molex plugs can be difficult to remove and brutal on the fingers. Little "bumps" on each side of the plug enable you to rock the plug back and forth to remove it.

✔ **Hint**

You will explore removable storage devices (CD-ROM, DVD-ROM, USB thumb drives, floppy drives) and associated media in Chapter 13.

Step 3 Now look at the motherboard connections, and note the orientation of the cable connectors. Disconnect the ribbon cables from the motherboard. Be careful but firm. Grasp the cable as closely as possible to the connector on the motherboard and pull, rocking the connector gently from side to side. Lay the cables aside for later reinstallation.

Step 4 Look at the PATA connections on your motherboard; they may be labeled "IDE" (see Figure 11-2).

How many PATA controllers do you see on your motherboard? _____

Look closely at your motherboard and see if you can find writing on the board next to the IDE connections. Are the interfaces grouped into pairs? Are any of them dedicated to special configurations such as RAID? _____

What color are the IDE connections on the motherboard? _____

FIGURE 11-2 Viewing the PATA connectors on a motherboard

Step 5 Remove a hard drive from the system. Be careful to note the type of screws you removed and store them for safekeeping. Also be sure to use proper ESD avoidance procedures when removing the drive from your system.

Because of the variety of cases, caddies, bays, slots, and so on, it's not possible to give detailed instructions on how to remove the drive from your particular system. Look closely for caddy releases or retaining screws. Close inspection and a little logic will usually make it clear how to remove the drive. Make notes of how the drive comes out, as you'll have to reinstall it later.

Step 6 With the hard drive out of the system and on a static-free surface, ground yourself, pick up the drive, and examine it carefully.

Note its dimensions. It should measure about 6" × 3.5" × 1". Some drives may be larger than this, measuring 6" × 5.25" × 1"—these are known as *bigfoot drives*. Some drives are smaller, but those are used mostly in laptops.

Look at the largest surfaces of the drive (the top and bottom). The bottom is where the printed circuit board with a ROM chip is located. This circuitry is the hard drive controller. The top side of the drive normally has a label or another means of listing the specifications for the drive, but this is not always the case.

Write down all the information on the label. Be sure to include the manufacturer and the model number for future reference.

Usually the label lists the total capacity of the hard drive and the power requirements of the drive (voltage and current). On older drives, the label lists the three main measurements of hard drive geometry: the number of cylinders, the number of heads, and the number of sectors per track. Together these measurements may be listed simply as CHS.

✔ **Cross-Reference**

For more information about CHS, refer to the "Geometry" section in Chapter 11 of *Mike Meyers' CompTIA A+ Guide to Managing and Troubleshooting PCs*.

Using these three measurements, you can calculate the capacity of the hard drive. The formula is cylinders × heads × sectors per track × 512 = bytes of data. (The number of bytes in one sector is 512.)

For example, an older drive has the following information on the label. What is the total capacity of this drive?

- C = 859
- H = 16
- S = 63

$$859 \times 16 \times 63 \times 512 = 443{,}326{,}464 \text{ bytes}$$

To convert this to megabytes, divide the answer by 1,048,576, as shown here:

$$443{,}326{,}464 / 1{,}048{,}576 = 422.8 \text{ MB}$$

A Seagate ST310211A PATA hard drive has CHS values of 16383, 16, and 63. What is its total capacity in

Bytes: _____

Megabytes: _____

Gigabytes: _____

(To convert from megabytes to gigabytes, divide the number of megabytes by 1024.)

Step 7 Look at the end of the drive where the ribbon cable connects. Find the markings for where pin 1 of the ribbon cable should go.

Is it closer to the center (near the power connector), or to the side, of the drive? _____

Does your hard drive have jumpers like the ones in Figure 11-3? _____

Notice that the drive in Figure 11-3 has the jumper set to CS (which stands for *cable select*).

Each PC system that boots from a PATA hard drive should have the hard drive located on the first PATA interface (IDE1). Normally the jumper must be set to Master so that the system can recognize it as the boot drive. A second drive (hard drive or optical drive) can be on the same cable, but must be set to Slave.

How are the jumpers set on your hard drive? _____

How are the jumpers set on your optical drive? _____

Can you have two master drives in the system? _____

FIGURE 11-3 Locating the PATA hard drive jumper setting

For the purposes of this exercise, make sure you leave your hard drive jumpered as it was when you removed it.

Step 8 Locate a broken hard drive (if you're in a class, ask your instructor for one) and remove its cover.

✖ Warning

Never remove the cover from a functioning hard drive! Hard drives are extremely sensitive, so merely exposing the inside to the air will cause irreparable damage.

Notice the round polished platters that spin in the middle of the drive. This is where the data is stored magnetically.

The actuator arms that move across the platters have tiny coils of wire attached to their ends. These coils hold the read/write heads.

How many surfaces does your sample drive have (one platter = two surfaces)? _____

How many physical heads does your sample drive have? _____

Both answers are most likely the same because usually there is a read/write head for each surface.

Look at Figure 11-4 and identify the following parts by number.

Read/write heads _____

Platters _____

Voice coil motor _____

FIGURE 11-4 The internal parts of a hard drive

Figure 11-5 The external parts of a hard drive

Now look at Figure 11-5 and match the numbered components.

Enhanced Integrated Drive Electronics (EIDE) controller _____

Molex connector _____

PATA connector _____

Master/slave jumper _____

Step 9 Insert the drive back into your system, and secure it with the proper screws. Connect all the ribbon cables to all the drives, and pay attention to the proper alignment of the connectors. Connect the Molex power connectors.

Leave the system case off until you verify that everything works properly.

If you used a working machine for the prior steps, you can verify that you've reinstalled the drives correctly by going to the next major step in the process of hard drive installation: CMOS configuration. Lab Exercise 11.03 in this chapter covers the CMOS details, but if you just can't wait, try Step 10. This bonus step should work on newer motherboard models.

Step 10 Turn on the system and wait for it to boot to the desktop. Double-click the My Computer/Computer icon, and confirm that the icons for the reinstalled drives are displayed. The fact that you were able to get to the desktop confirms that you've reinstalled the boot drive correctly, but do the other drives (if you have them) and your optical drive work?

✔ **Hint**

If you cannot boot the system or the optical drive does not work, the first and obvious place to start is to verify all the cable connections. Any kind of disk errors at this time were most likely caused by the technician; after all, it worked before you touched it!

45 MINUTES

Lab Exercise 11.02: Installing Serial ATA Hard Drives

A wealthy donor has just given your nonprofit organization a dozen brand-new desktop machines. Since these are new machines, their motherboards have built-in serial ATA (SATA) controllers, but the SATA hard drives have yet to be installed or configured. You're tasked to do the job!

Installing SATA hard drives is a simple matter of plugging in the data and power cables to the drive and attaching the other end of the data cable to the SATA controller card or motherboard connection. You don't have to pull the power from the PC. You don't even have to shut down Windows. No, really—it's that simple! Let's go through the steps.

Learning Objectives

This lab is designed to introduce you to the two current flavors of SATA and walk you through the straightforward installation.

At the end of this lab, you'll be able to

- Explain key features of SATA I and SATA II

- Install a SATA hard drive

Lab Materials and Setup

The materials you need for this lab are

- A newer PC system with an onboard SATA I or SATA II controller and Windows installed

- At least one additional SATA hard drive

- Optional: A PCI SATA controller may be installed into an older PC system

Getting Down to Business

To start, you'll review the features and specifications of SATA, and then you'll compare and contrast the technology with PATA. Keep that screwdriver handy, because you'll finish with the installation and hot-swap of a SATA drive.

✔ **Cross-Reference**

To help in answering the following questions, reference the "ATA-7" section in Chapter 11 of *Mike Meyers' CompTIA A+ Guide to Managing and Troubleshooting PCs*.

Step 1 Using your reference materials, review the features and specifications of SATA hard drive technology. Then answer these questions:

What is the speed of data transfer with ATA/133 drives? _____

What is the speed of data transfer with SATA I (SATA 1.5Gb) drives? _____

What is the speed of data transfer with SATA II (SATA 3Gb) drives? _____

What is the maximum length of a SATA cable? _____

How many wires are in a SATA cable? _____

What is the maximum length of an 80-wire PATA cable? _____

How many drives can a single SATA cable support? _____

SATA RAID has waltzed into the mainstream today. Motherboards are now being sold with a SATA RAID controller built-in, from Promise or another company, but you can also readily buy a PCIe or PCI SATA RAID controller at your local computer parts store. You'll install additional hard drives in Lab Exercise 11.06, and you'll explore the implementation of a software RAID solution in Chapter 12.

Step 2 It's time to get working with some SATA drives. Shut down your system and remove the system cover, following proper ESD avoidance procedures.

Step 3 Disconnect the data cable(s) from the SATA hard drive(s), as shown in Figure 11-6. Grasp the cable as closely as possible to the connector on the drive and pull, rocking the connector gently from side to side.

Disconnect the power supply from the SATA drive(s) by unplugging the SATA connector from each one. Is the power supply a newer model with SATA connectors directly attached, or is there a Molex-to-SATA power adapter like the one shown in Figure 11-7?

Figure 11-6 Removing the SATA data cable

FIGURE 11-7 Molex-to-SATA power adapter

Step 4 Now look at the motherboard connections and note the orientation of the connectors. Disconnect the data cables from the motherboard, being careful but firm. Grasp the cable as closely as possible to the connector on the motherboard and pull, rocking the connector gently from side to side.

Lay the cables aside for later reinstallation.

Step 5 Look at the SATA connections on your motherboard (see Figure 11-8).

How many SATA connectors do you see on your motherboard? _____

Look closely at your motherboard, and see if you can find writing on the board next to the SATA connectors.

Are the interfaces grouped into pairs? Are any of them dedicated to special configurations such as RAID?

_____

Step 6 As in the previous exercise, remove the hard drive from the system, note the type of screws you removed, and store the screws for safekeeping. Be sure to use proper ESD procedures when removing the drive from your system.

FIGURE 11-8 The SATA connectors on a motherboard

Because of the variety of cases, caddies, bays, slots, and so on, it's not possible to give detailed instructions on how to remove the drive from your particular system. Look closely for caddy releases or retaining screws. Close inspection and a little logic will usually make it clear how to remove the drive. Make notes of how the drive comes out; you'll have to reinstall it later.

Step 7   With the hard drive out of the system and on a static-free surface, ground yourself, pick up the drive, and examine it carefully.

Note its dimensions; it should measure about 6" × 3.5" × 1", the same as a PATA drive. Here, too, the bottom of the drive boasts the hard drive controller, and the top of the drive is normally labeled with the drive's specifications.

Write down all the information on the label. Be sure to include the manufacturer and the model number for future reference.

Step 8   To demonstrate one of the benefits of SATA—hot-swapping—you will now reinstall all the drives you removed and, if necessary, install an additional SATA drive to be hot-swapped. With the PC still powered down, insert all of the original drives back into your system, and at least one additional SATA drive with no critical data. Secure the drives with the proper screws, connect all the data cables, and connect the SATA power connectors using Molex-to-SATA adapters if required.

Leave the system case off, to verify that everything is working properly and to facilitate the last steps.

✔ **Hint**

If you are performing this lab using a PCIe or PCI SATA controller card, you'll have to install the expansion card and load the drivers for the card. If you haven't loaded drivers for the SATA controller, you should do so now. Otherwise, this is going to be a very frustrating lab for you!

Power up the PC and boot into Windows. Windows should pick up the drive(s) with no problems at all. Check My Computer/Computer to verify that the drive is installed and functional. If the drive has no partition, then of course it won't show up in My Computer/Computer; if this is the case, you can use the Computer Management console to verify that the drive works.

Step 9   With Windows still running, disconnect the SATA data cable from the additional drive. What happened? _____

Step 10   Plug the data cable back in. Does Windows see the drive? _____

Step 11   Try the same hot-swap test with the SATA power cable—unplug it, then plug it back in. Does this produce the same effect as the hot-swap with the data cable?

 30 MINUTES

Lab Exercise 11.03: Configuring CMOS Settings

After installing either PATA or SATA devices, the second step you'll want to perform is the configuration of the BIOS to support these devices. On most motherboards, the BIOS automatically detects devices, so you will primarily be confirming the detection of all the devices and configuring advanced features such as RAID, S.M.A.R.T., and boot options. Autodetection does not render CMOS irrelevant, though; you can do or undo all kinds of problems relating to hard drives using CMOS setup. This lab walks you through the important configuration options.

Learning Objectives

At the end of this lab, you'll be able to

- Configure the CMOS settings for the hard drive

- Confirm that the hard drive is indeed installed properly

Lab Materials and Setup

The materials you need for this lab are

- A fully functioning PC with PATA and/or SATA devices installed

- Optional: A second drive with no important data

Getting Down to Business

There are many possible CMOS settings for the hard drive, depending on the BIOS installed on the motherboard. For example, every motherboard gives you the option to disable the built-in hard drive controllers. Why is this relevant? You can install a drive into a perfectly good system, but it won't work if the controllers are disabled!

Step 1   Turn on your system, and enter the CMOS setup utility by pressing the appropriate key(s) while your system is booting.

Select the Integrated Peripherals option from the main menu, or the Drive Configuration option from the Advanced menu (you may have to hunt around for where you enable the PATA/SATA devices in your CMOS setup program), and look for the various controllers. You can enable or disable the controllers here.

✔ Hint

This option may look somewhat different depending on the version of CMOS you are using. Look for a menu option such as one of these:

- Onboard Primary PCI IDE

- Onboard Secondary PCI IDE

- PCI Primary and Secondary IDE

- Onboard IDE

- Use Automatic Mode

- SATA Port 0

When the controllers are disabled in CMOS, no device attached to them can be used—not even optical drives. This is why some systems will not let you disable the controllers at all.

If you are performing the labs in sequence, and have arrived at this lab directly from Lab Exercise 11.01 or Lab Exercise 11.02, here's where you find out whether or not you installed and jumpered the drive correctly.

Make sure all controllers are enabled, and then look for the Autodetection option in the CMOS settings. Older systems have a separate category in CMOS, appropriately named Autodetect or something similar; newer systems have it integrated into the main settings screen. Run this utility now. If your hard drive shows up in Autodetect as the drive you thought it would be—primary master, secondary master, SATA Port 0, or what have you—then you installed and (if necessary) jumpered it properly (see Figure 11-9).

Step 2   Save your settings, exit CMOS, and reboot your PC. You should boot into Windows normally. Check My Computer/Computer to verify that you can see and access all drives.

Step 3   Reboot your PC and go into CMOS. Access the settings to enable or disable the various controllers, and disable them all. (This won't affect your data; it will just prevent drive access for the next couple of steps in this lab.)

```
              Phoenix - Award BIOS CMOS Setup Utility
                      Standard CMOS Features

    Date (mm:dd:yy)       Wed, Jun 7 2006     ▲      Item Help
    Time (hh:mm:ss)       13 : 19 : 35
                                                  Menu Level    ▶
  ▶ IDE Channel 1 Master  WDC WD1200JB-75CRA0
  ▶ IDE Channel 1 Slave   None                    Change the day, month,
  ▶ IDE Channel 2 Master  SONY     CD-CW  CRX17    year and century
  ▶ IDE Channel 2 Slave   TOSHIBA CD/DVDW SDR5
  ▶ IDE Channel 3 Master  None
  ▶ IDE Channel 4 Master  None
  ▶ IDE Channel 5 Master  WDC WD2000JS-00MHB0
  ▶ IDE Channel 6 Master  None

    Drive A               1.44, 3.5 in.
    Drive B               None
    Floppy 3 Mode Support Disabled
    Halt On               All , But Keyboard

    Base Memory                 640K
    Extended Memory         1047552K          ▼

▲▼▶◀:Move   Enter:Select   +/-/PU/PD:Value  F10:Save   ESC:Exit   F1:General He
    F5:Previous Values     F6:Fail-Safe Defaults   F7:Optimized Defaults
```

FIGURE 11-9   Various drives and their roles as listed in CMOS setup

Step 4   Save your settings, then exit CMOS to reboot the system. Making sure there is no floppy disk in the floppy drive, reboot normally and watch the monitor display for messages.

What message is displayed last? _____

With most systems, the PC searches its various storage devices for a way to boot. It looks for a bootable drive (connected to an EIDE, SATA, or SCSI controller), a bootable optical or floppy disk, or a network connection—not necessarily in that order—and then stops if it cannot find the operating system. It then displays a message indicating "no bootable device" and waits for your instructions to continue.

✖ Warning

If your system is connected to a network and uses the network boot option, disconnect the network cable for this exercise to get the desired results. Be sure to plug the network cable back in when finished.

When the system is not able to find a disk (because you disabled the controller), it will probably hang for a long period of time and then return a Primary Hard Drive Failure code or error message. Some systems try to recognize that you have a hard drive regardless of the disabling of features, but this is rare.

Okay, so the system can't find your hard drive. You obviously know why—you turned off the controller!

Step 5   Reboot your system, entering the CMOS setup utility by pressing the appropriate keystroke combination while your system is booting. Navigate to the menu where you disabled all of the controllers and reenable them.

Step 6   Now that the controllers are enabled, go back to the Autodetection utility and look for any drives connected.

If Autodetection still does not see a hard drive, save your settings, reboot your system, and reenter the CMOS setup utility. Then try it again.

Do you now see all of the storage devices that are installed in the system?

Step 7   While you're still in CMOS, navigate to the menu where all of the storage devices can be configured. Use this screen (sometimes there are multiple screens) to examine the device settings and answer the following questions:

Are there any devices listed as ATA/IDE devices (Primary Master, Primary Slave, Secondary Master, or Secondary Slave)? _____

Are there any SATA controllers present? If yes, are there any SATA devices installed on the system (SATA Port 0, SATA Port 1, and so on)? _____

Is the motherboard capable of implementing RAID? If yes, how is it currently configured?

_____

Exit CMOS without saving changes and let the PC reboot.

Step 8   At this point, if you did everything as described and if you started with a known good hard drive containing a working operating system, the system will boot back into the operating system. Otherwise, you'll have to wait until you partition and format the drive to see if everything's working as it should (for example, if your instructor gave you, to use, a demo hard drive with nothing on it).

✔ **Cross-Reference**

For details about partitioning and formatting drives, refer to Chapter 12 in *Mike Meyers' CompTIA A+ Guide to Managing and Troubleshooting PCs*.

 30 MINUTES

Lab Exercise 11.04: Comparing Solid-State Drives and Magnetic Hard Drives

PATA and SATA hard disk drives store data magnetically and have moving parts, but solid-state drives (SSDs) store data on dynamic RAM (DRAM) or flash memory boards and have no moving parts. In other words, SSDs use nonvolatile memory—memory that retains data even when it's not powered on—to store data and emulate a hard drive. Most common uses have been in what are called flash drives or thumb drives, but now PC users are installing SSDs as their primary storage in desktops and laptops. SSDs have no moving parts, which makes them tougher, quieter, and oftentimes faster than hard disks.

Learning Objectives

This lab explores the differences between solid-state drives and magnetic hard drives and is designed to help you recommend drives to clients as the need arises.

At the end of this lab, you'll be able to

- Explain solid-state drives

- Explain magnetic hard drives

- Discern which one will be best for your clients

Lab Materials and Setup

The materials you need for this lab are

- Access to a PC system and the Internet

- A solid-state drive and a magnetic hard drive

Getting Down to Business

It's so cool to see how technology has changed over the years and migrated to smaller, less noisy equipment. Heck, I remember when we used to have to park the heads to move a hard drive, and now we just pull them out and put them in our pocket—what will they think of next?

In this scenario, your boss is not convinced that SSDs are all that great, so your job is to explain why you think SSDs are better than magnetic hard drives.

Step 1   Search the Internet for "solid-state drives." Use manufacturer and retailer Web sites to find the information listed in the following table. Record your findings.

Maker	Cost	Capacity	Pros	Cons	Unique Features

Step 2   Now do the same thing for "hard drives" and note whether it's a PATA or SATA drive.

Maker	Cost	Capacity	Pros	Cons	Unique Features

Step 3   Now that you've compiled some hard facts about SSDs and magnetic hard drives, prepare (electronically) a proposal to your boss explaining why you think SSDs are superior to magnetic hard drives. Be prepared to share your proposal with the class.

 60 MINUTES

Lab Exercise 11.05: Exploring SCSI and RAID

As you inventory the machines that were just donated to your nonprofit organization, you discover two additional machines with small computer system interface (SCSI) controllers. You want to use them in a RAID array, but don't know much about either technology.

Learning Objectives

This lab touches on important tech skills, helping you research hardware so you can provide good information to clients. With the introduction of the SATA interface, the need for SCSI implementation on desktop machines is quickly fading. However, SCSI—which is well over 20 years old—still rules the hot-swappable, large-capacity, data server environment.

At the end of this lab, you'll be able to

- Explain key features of SCSI
- Define the levels of RAID

Lab Materials and Setup

The materials you need for this lab are

- Access to a PC system and the Internet

- A trip to the local computer store for research

- A notepad and pen to take notes at the store

Getting Down to Business

Limber up your surfing fingers, as you'll start your search on the Internet. Then you might want to make a visit to the local computer store to explore further how the technologies of SCSI and RAID are being used in today's computing environments.

Step 1 Access the Internet and search for information on parallel SCSI devices, primarily hard drives. Use keywords such as *Ultra320*, *Ultra640*, *white paper*, *controllers*, and *storage solutions*. Then answer the following questions:

What speed of data transfer can be achieved with parallel SCSI? _____

How many drives can be attached to a single controller? _____

What is the price range of parallel SCSI drives? _____

What is a SCSI chain? _____

✔ **Cross-Reference**

For more information on SCSI, refer to the "SCSI: Still Around" section in Chapter 11 of *Mike Meyers' CompTIA A+ Guide to Managing and Troubleshooting PCs*.

Step 2 As you surfed around to the different sites on SCSI, you probably noticed that many of these drives are implemented in different RAID configurations. With the overall cost of hard drives dropping, many desktop motherboard manufacturers (ASUS, Gigabyte, Intel, and so on) are incorporating RAID controllers into their motherboards. Visit a few of the motherboard manufacturers' Web sites and research their implementation of RAID. Use the following questions to refine your focus.

✔ **Cross-Reference**

For more information on RAID, refer to the "Protecting Data with RAID," "RAID," and "Implementing RAID" sections in Chapter 11 of *Mike Meyers' CompTIA A+ Guide to Managing and Troubleshooting PCs*.

What are the most popular implementations of RAID used on desktop machines?

_____

How many drives are required to support the various RAID levels? _____

Can you configure desktop RAID using both PATA and SATA drives? _____

What are the two goals when implementing a RAID solution?

_____

_____

Step 3 Gather the information you've found in your Internet research and head to your local computer store. Explore the current trends, based on the systems and components your local supplier is promoting. Write (on a separate sheet of paper) a brief summary of your findings and share it with your instructor and classmates.

 45 MINUTES

Lab Exercise 11.06: Troubleshooting Hard Drive Installations

The newest tech in your office has had trouble installing hard drives properly. In fact, he's tried it on four different machines with eight different drives and succeeded only once! You've been tasked to troubleshoot his failed installations and patiently explain the proper installation process to him. What fun!

Learning Objectives

This lab walks you through the errors new techs typically make on hard drive installation, particularly with PATA drives. The lab also addresses the main problems with SATA drives—usually faulty hardware—and how to address this in the field.

At the end of this lab, you'll be able to

- Troubleshoot hard drive installation problems effectively
- Explain the proper installation techniques for PATA and SATA drives

Lab Materials and Setup

The materials you need for this lab are

- Access to a PC system with PATA and SATA interfaces
- At least one PATA or SATA hard drive (preferably two or more)

Getting Down to Business

It might seem odd to mess up a hard drive installation deliberately, but you can't hurt anything, so give it a whirl. Seeing how the PC responds to mistakes when you know specifically what's wrong can help you when you run into similar situations later in the field.

Step 1   You must have a properly functioning PC for this lab to be effective, so verify first that you have a system up and running with one or more hard drives installed.

Step 2   Power down the system. Disconnect the data cable for the hard drive used to boot the system, then power up the system. What happens? Will the PC autodetect the drive?

It is difficult to imagine not connecting the data cables to hard drives, but many times to add RAM or new devices, we have to disconnect the cables to gain access to the component. It is easy to miss reconnecting one of the cables after installing the new device.

Disconnecting the cable also simulates a broken IDE or SATA cable. These cables are somewhat delicate, and can fail after a sharp crease or a crimp from the system case. If you're having unexplained problems with your drive, check the cables prior to replacing the drive.

Step 3   Power down the PC and put the cable back on properly.

Step 4   On a PATA drive, change the jumper for the primary master hard drive to slave, and then power on the PC. What happens? Will the PC autodetect the drive? How should the jumper be installed?

Step 5   Power down the PC and put the jumper back on properly.

Step 6   Install a second PATA drive onto the primary controller, and set the jumpers on both drives incorrectly. Try variations: both as master; both as standalone; both as slave; both as cable select. Power on the PC and test each variation. What happens? Will the PC autodetect the drives? How should the jumpers be set for two PATA drives to work properly on the same controller?

30 MINUTES

Lab Exercise 11.07: Installing Multiple Hard Drives in Preparation for RAID

Remember those two extra machines you discovered—the ones with the dual CPUs and the SCSI controllers? Well, each of them has eight 150-GB SCSI hard drives ready to be installed. You haven't had the opportunity to configure a RAID system before, so you ask a colleague for advice. She recommends that you install some additional drives in one of the workstations and then practice configuring RAID 0 using the software solution that comes with Microsoft Windows. This should help build your confidence before tackling the hardware RAID controllers on the servers.

Learning Objectives

In this lab, you will install additional hard drives—PATA, SATA, or both—in an existing system. You will access CMOS to verify that all of the drives have been recognized by the system. You will then set the system aside to be used in Lab Exercise 12.05, "Implementing Software RAID 0 with Disk Management," in Chapter 12.

At the end of this lab, you'll be able to

- Install multiple hard drives in computer systems

- Verify multiple drives in CMOS

Lab Materials and Setup

The materials you need for this lab are

- A working PC with PATA or SATA interfaces and Microsoft Windows 2000 Professional, Windows XP Professional, or Windows Vista installed

- At least two additional, system-compatible hard drives—PATA or SATA as appropriate

Getting Down to Business

Even though you haven't been reminded during the last few exercises, you know that you should always take the proper anti-static precautions when opening the system case and working with the delicate components inside. Take those precautions now, and get ready to install a few extra hard drives into your system. In this exercise, you'll make sure these drives are recognized by the system; in the next chapter's labs, you'll configure them.

✔ Hint

For many of the exercises in the next chapter, it is very important that you have a working system with either Windows 2000 Professional, Windows XP Professional, or Windows Vista installed. Obviously, you will need to keep the system partition and boot partition intact (usually these are the same partition, and are the first partition on the first hard drive of the system) with the operating system running.

Even if you have available space on the first hard drive, it is much cleaner if you can install at least two additional hard drives. That way, you can partition, format, and convert to dynamic disks to your heart's content, without the worry of losing data (or the operating system).

Follow these steps to install an additional PATA drive.

Step 1 Determine on which controller, and in which order, you will be installing the drives.

Step 2 Set the jumpers properly for both the master and slave drives. (Usually, the boot device is the master drive on the primary controller, whereas the optical drive is the master drive on the secondary controller, so the new drive is likely to be a slave to one of those drives.)

Step 3 Physically install the second drive, connecting the power and data cables properly.

Follow these steps to install additional SATA drives.

Step 1 Determine which controller you will use for the first additional drive and connect the SATA data cable to the controller on the motherboard.

Step 2 Physically install the first additional drive and connect the SATA power and data cables to the new drive.

Step 3 Determine which controller you will use for the second additional drive and connect the SATA data cable to the controller on the motherboard.

Step 4 Physically install the second additional drive and connect the SATA power and data cables to the new drive.

Follow these steps to verify the drives in CMOS.

Step 1 After installing all of the hard drives, plug the power back in and boot the machine.

Step 2 Press the appropriate key(s) to enter CMOS setup, and navigate to the configuration screen for installed devices.

Step 3 Perform autodetection if required, and confirm that all of the installed devices are present. If any of the devices are missing (and you remembered to reboot the machine if your system requires it), power the machine down, disconnect the power, and double-check all of the cables and drive settings.

Lab Analysis Test

1. Matthew has decided to use the RAID integrated into the SATA controller on his new system. He uses the system for high-end video editing, and would like to improve the performance of the system for this task. What implementation of RAID would you recommend to improve performance?

2. In what situation(s) might it be appropriate to disable the motherboard's hard drive controllers?

3. Brock, a new tech in your firm, informs you that the PC he's working on can't autodetect a hard drive he installed. He thinks the motherboard is broken. What's the more likely problem here?

4. The second SATA hard drive on your company's server has just died. You have a replacement drive, but it's critical that the server remain up and functioning. What, if anything, can you do to resolve this problem and get the second drive replaced?

5. Sean would like to install four additional hard drives in his system. His motherboard has two IDE controllers and two SATA controllers. There is one SATA drive installed, and the CD/DVD-RW drive is an IDE device. How would you configure Sean's system?

Key Term Quiz

Use the following terms to complete the following sentences. Not all terms will be used.

autodetect

cable select

CHS

master

PATA

platters

RAID

SATA

Slave

SSD

1. A(n) _____ uses memory chips to store data and has none of the moving parts of traditional hard drives.

2. The data in a traditional hard disk drive is actually stored magnetically on disks called _____.

3. One type of IDE drive transfers data in a parallel fashion. The other type of IDE drive transfers data in a serial fashion. These two types are known as _____ and _____, respectively.

4. To secure data in servers and high-end PCs, use a(n) _____ controller.

5. A great way to determine whether a new drive is installed and configured correctly is to run _____.

Chapter 12
Implementing Hard Drives

Lab Exercises

Once you've installed a new drive on a PC and it has been recognized by the system, you have two more steps to complete before you can start storing data: partitioning and formatting.

✔ **Hint**

The tasks of partitioning and formatting have really become automated into the installation of the operating system (and the tools included in the operating system). Many of the steps are now completed in sequence, blurring the line between partitioning and formatting. Make sure you're clear on the distinction between partitioning and formatting, because you must do them in the proper order. Partitioning the disk simply means defining physical sections that are used to store data. Formatting the disk means *configuring the partition* with a file system.

In the early days of DOS, Windows 3.*x*, and Windows 9*x*, your hard drive had to be partitioned and formatted before you could run the installation setup routine. Windows now incorporates these disk-preparation steps into the installation routine itself. However, it's still important for you to be able to perform these tasks from scratch as part of your basic PC tech repertoire.

You have a number of tools at your disposal for performing partitioning and formatting tasks. If you are working with a fresh hard drive, you need to get to these tools without necessarily having an operating system installed (this may be the first disk in the system, and you are preparing it for the OS installation). The first of these tools is the Windows installation media. Also, a number of third-party utilities are available for partitioning and formatting, such as Avanquest's Partition Commander, Easeus Partition Master, and the open source Linux tool Gnome Partition Editor, affectionately known as GParted. These specific tools are beyond the scope of the CompTIA A+ exams; however, a good tech should develop skills in the use of these tools. The second tool you'll explore in this chapter is a live CD of GParted.

Once you have an operating system up and running, you should have some type of partitioning and formatting tool that you can run from the GUI. Windows uses a tool known as the Disk Management utility. Disk Management enables you to create, modify, and format partitions. You can also format partitions from within My Computer/Computer on the Windows desktop.

After looking at how to create and format partitions using the Windows installation media and the live CD of GParted, you'll start up Windows to look at how to accomplish these tasks using the built-in tools. Next, you'll use the Disk Management utility to convert basic disks to dynamic disks and implement a RAID 0 stripe set. Then you'll look at the procedures for performing regular hard drive maintenance and troubleshooting tasks.

✔ **Hint**

The following exercises walk you through the basic management of hard drive storage available on your system. If you have only one drive installed, you will need to install the operating system after the first few exercises to perform the later exercises. In Lab Exercise 11.07, you installed two additional hard drives into a machine with Windows installed. I recommend that you use this machine for all of the implementation labs (being careful not to partition or format the first drive, which should contain the operating system). Not only will this enable you to practice creating and deleting partitions and formatting and reformatting those partitions, it will also enable you to verify the partitions and file systems with the Disk Management tool in Windows.

 30 MINUTES

Lab Exercise 12.01: Creating and Formatting Partitions with the Windows 2000/XP and Vista/7 Installation Media

As you'll recall from the labs in Chapter 11, you have just worked with a number of donated machines, physically installing and configuring multiple hard drive technologies, primarily PATA and SATA hard drives. Once these drives have been recognized in CMOS, you are only halfway to your goal of using the drives for data storage. You must now partition each drive into usable space (even if only one partition uses all of the available drive space) and then format each partition with a file system.

In this lab, you will use the Windows installation media to partition and format hard drives in your system. You will be left with blank partitions, one of which needs an operating system. In the labs for Chapter 14, you will complete the process of installing the operating system.

✔ **Cross-Reference**

For details about partitioning and formatting drives with the Windows installation disc, refer to the "Partitioning and Formatting with the Windows XP Installation CD" and "Partitioning and Formatting with the Windows Vista Installation DVD" sections in Chapter 12 of *Mike Meyers' CompTIA A+ Guide to Managing and Troubleshooting PCs.*

Learning Objectives

In this exercise, you'll use the Windows installation media to partition a hard drive and format the partition for use.

At the end of this lab, you'll be able to

- Set up a primary partition on a hard drive

- Format the partition with the NTFS file system

Lab Materials and Setup

The materials you need for this lab are

- The PC from Lab Exercise 11.07 with a primary hard drive that holds your Windows OS, and the two blank hard drives that you can partition and format to your heart's content

- Optional: A system with one hard drive that you can safely erase

- The Windows 2000/XP or Vista/7 installation media

✖ Warning

Partitioning and formatting a hard drive destroys any data on it! Practice this lab using only drives that don't store any data you need.

Getting Down to Business

In this exercise, you'll start the system by booting from the Windows installation media (you will have to configure your system CMOS to boot from the optical drive or, if available, a USB device). You'll partition a portion of one of the hard drives and format it with the NTFS file system, as if you're preparing to install the operating system.

The instructions for Windows 2000/XP are first, followed immediately by the instructions for Windows Vista/7.

Step 1 Enter the CMOS setup program and configure the boot order, selecting the CD-ROM drive as the first boot device. Also make sure that the setting called "Boot Other Device" (or something similar) is enabled; otherwise, your system may not recognize the CD-ROM drive as a bootable drive.

Step 2 Place the Windows installation CD in the optical drive tray and boot the machine. Windows Setup copies a number of files and then presents you with the screen shown in Figure 12-1. Press ENTER to set up Windows now.

Step 3 Press F8 to accept the license agreement and enter the main partitioning screen.

```
Windows XP Professional Setup

   Welcome to Setup.

   This portion of the Setup program prepares Microsoft(R)
   Windows(R) XP to run on your computer.

      •  To set up Windows XP now, press ENTER.

      •  To repair a Windows XP installation using
         Recovery Console, press R.

      •  To quit Setup without installing Windows XP, press F3.
```

```
   ENTER=Continue   R=Repair   F3=Quit
```

FIGURE 12-1 The first Windows XP Setup screen

✔ **Hint**

If you are using the machine configured in Lab Exercise 11.07, Windows XP has been installed on one of the drives in the system. Setup asks if you would like to repair this installation, and advises you to press ESC if you want to install a fresh copy. Press ESC to progress to the next step—partitioning the drive.

The screen displays the installed drives and any partitions and/or file systems that have been configured on the drives prior to this session (see Figure 12-2).

Step 4 If any partitions exist on the drives you have installed to practice this lab (and the data on these drives is expendable), delete them at this time.

To delete a partition, simply select the partition, press D to delete, and then press L to commit the delete process. The partition will be returned to unpartitioned space.

Step 5 To create a partition, follow these steps:

a. Press C.

b. Select the size of the partition you want to create (10 GB is a good size for a system partition or a boot partition, but you should try multiple sizes).

c. Press ENTER.

d. The new partition should appear in the partitioning screen.

Congratulations! You have created a partition.

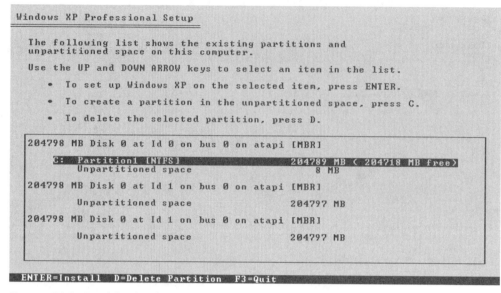

FIGURE 12-2 Partitioning screen

Step 6 Press ENTER to see a list of file system options, as shown in Figure 12-3. Choose a file system (NTFS is the default) and indicate whether you will perform an exhaustive formatting process or the "Quick" formatting process.

Press ENTER. Windows formats the partition and proceeds with the operating system installation. You can shut down the PC once this step is completed.

```
Windows XP Professional Setup

    The partition you selected is not formatted. Setup will now
    format the partition.

    Use the UP and DOWN ARROW keys to select the file system
    you want, and then press ENTER.

    If you want to select a different partition for Windows XP,
    press ESC.

        Format the partition using the NTFS file system (Quick)
        Format the partition using the NTFS file system




















    ENTER=Continue   ESC=Cancel
```

FIGURE 12-3 Format screen

Step 7 Reboot the machine and allow your Windows OS to boot. Then use the Disk Management tool to verify the partition(s) you have created with the installation CD. Alternatively, you can verify the partitions you created and the file systems you configured when you use the GParted tool in the next lab.

Step 8 Practice deleting, creating, and formatting different combinations of partitions and file systems to become comfortable with the tools used in this exercise. Have fun!

Here are the same instructions, but for Windows Vista/7.

Step 1 Enter the CMOS setup program and configure the boot order, selecting the optical drive (or, if necessary, a USB device) as the first boot device. Also make sure that the setting called "Boot Other Device" (or something similar) is enabled; otherwise, your system may not recognize the optical drive as a bootable drive.

Step 2 Place the Windows installation media in the optical drive tray and boot the machine. Set your language and regional preferences on the first screen, and then click Next.

Step 3 Click the large Install Now button on the next page. Setup will then ask for a product key, but you do not need to enter one right now. Click Next to move on.

Step 4 Pick the edition of Vista/7 you wish to install. Your product key will only activate the edition that you purchased. Click Next to continue, and then agree to the license agreement on the next page.

Step 5 Click the Custom install button on the following screen. The screen displays the installed drives and any partitions and/or file systems that have been configured on the drives prior to this session (see Figure 12-4).

Step 6 If any partitions exist on the drives you have installed to practice this lab (and the data on these drives is expendable), delete them at this time.

To delete a partition, simply select the partition, click Drive options (advanced), and then click Delete. The partition will be returned to unpartitioned space.

Step 7 To create a partition, follow these steps:

    a. Click the Drive options (advanced) button.

    b. Click New.

    c. In the Size field, type **50000** and click Apply to end up with a 50-GB partition.

Step 8 Click the Format button. The installer will automatically set up an NTFS file system for the partition and proceed with the operating system installation.

Step 9 Reboot the machine and allow your Windows OS to boot. Then use the Disk Management tool to verify the partition(s) you have created with the installation disc. Alternatively, you can verify the partitions you created and the file systems you configured when you try using the GParted tool in the next lab.

Step 10 Practice deleting, creating, and formatting different combinations of partitions and file systems to become comfortable with the tools used in this exercise. Enjoy!

FIGURE 12-4 Where do you want to install Windows?

⏱ 30 MINUTES

Lab Exercise 12.02: Creating and Formatting Partitions with Gnome Partition Editor (GParted)

As a competent tech, you want to keep up with the newest methods for accomplishing old tasks. Using the donated computers as an example, you might want to partition and format all of the machines before installing an operating system and deploying the machines to users. To accomplish this task, it might be easier to use a standalone partitioning/formatting tool such as the open source Gnome Partition Editor (GParted). Gnome is one of the many versions of the Linux operating system. GParted uses a basic, bootable version of Gnome with disk management tools built in. This method is somewhat beyond the scope of the CompTIA A+ exams, but the skills and techniques you will practice in this lab are valuable to a real-world tech, and can help you gain a deeper understanding of partitioning and formatting hard drives.

✔ Tech Tip

Many techs, and specifically techs employed by the IT departments of small to large businesses, often use one of the popular drive-imaging tools such as Symantec's Norton Ghost. Drive imaging is used to roll out the operating system and applications on multiple machines expediently. This method creates the partition, and copies the OS, applications, and user profiles onto the file system that was used to make the image, all in one step. This method is also beyond the scope of the CompTIA A+ exams, but you should explore drive imaging for completeness.

In this exercise, you will use the live CD of GParted to partition and format the two additional hard drives installed in your lab system. If you are working in a classroom setting, the instructor should be able to provide copies of the GParted live CD to you for this exercise. Alternatively, you could jump ahead to Lab Exercise 13.05, where you will create a live CD by burning a CD with an ISO image.

✔ Cross-Reference

For additional details about the GParted live CD, refer to the "Third-Party Partition Tools" section in Chapter 12 of *Mike Meyers' CompTIA A+ Guide to Managing and Troubleshooting PCs*.

Learning Objectives

In this exercise, you'll use the GParted live CD to partition a hard drive and format the partition for use.

At the end of this lab, you'll be able to

- Set up primary and extended partitions on hard drives
- Format the partitions with various file systems

Lab Materials and Setup

The materials you need for this lab are

- The PC from Lab Exercise 11.07 with a primary hard drive that holds your Windows OS, and the two blank hard drives that you can partition and format to your heart's content
- Optional: A system with one hard drive that you can safely erase
- A GParted live CD

✖ Warning

Partitioning and formatting a hard drive destroys any data on the drive! Practice this lab only on drives that don't store any data you need.

Getting Down to Business

In this exercise, you'll start the system by booting from the GParted live CD. (You will have to configure your system CMOS to boot from the CD.) You'll then partition a portion of one of the hard drives and format it with the file system of your choice.

Step 1 Enter the CMOS setup program and configure the boot order, selecting the CD-ROM drive as the first boot device. Also make sure that the setting called "Boot Other Device" (or something similar) is enabled; otherwise, your system may not recognize the CD-ROM drive as a bootable drive.

Step 2 Place the GParted live CD in the optical drive tray and boot the machine. GParted displays an introduction screen, as shown in Figure 12-5. Press ENTER to boot; Gnome Linux should begin to load. As the system loads, you will be queried a number of times for settings related to boot options, language, keyboard, and screen depth and resolution. Unless told to do otherwise by your instructor, select the defaults for these settings by highlighting OK and pressing ENTER.

GParted should finish booting and arrive at a screen displaying various menu items, icons, and the current drive focus with strange Linux names such as /dev/hda1, /dev/hda3, and so forth. Notice the item at the far right of the menu bar; here, you can click the drop-down arrow to select which physical drive the GParted screen is focused on (see Figure 12-6).

Step 3 Now change the focus to the second or third drive installed on your system. This will probably be labeled /dev/hdb or /dev/hdc in the drop-down list of hard drives.

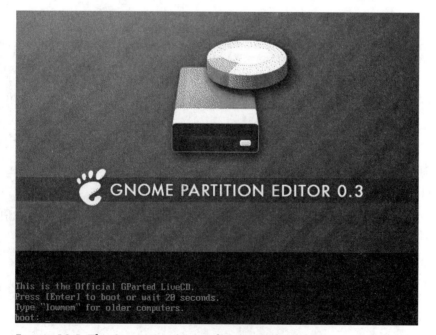

FIGURE 12-5 The Gnome Partition Editor initial screen

FIGURE 12-6 Selecting a drive on the main GParted partitioning/formatting screen

✔ **Hint**

If you are using the machine that you configured in Lab Exercise 11.07, Windows has been installed on one of the drives in the system (most likely the first drive). When GParted first launches, the screen focus will be on this drive and the label will probably read /dev/hda1. Make sure that you use the menu drop-down list to select one of the drives that has been set up to be partitioned and formatted, or you'll find yourself reinstalling Windows.

The screen now focuses on the drive you've selected and shows any partitions and/or file systems that have been configured on that drive prior to this session. If any partitions are displayed, highlight the partition, right-click, and select Delete.

Step 4 GParted requires that you commit any changes that you make to the partitions on the disk, so after deleting the partition, you must click the Apply button to apply the settings and actually delete the partition.

When you click Apply, GParted applies the pending operations. You should now have a drive visible with all of the available space denoted as unallocated space.

Step 5 Select the unallocated space, right-click, and select New. Then follow these steps:

  a. Enter the size of the partition in megabytes; either type a number or use the up and down arrows to select a size. For the purposes of practice, 4000 MB (4 GB) to 10,000 MB (10 GB) is a good size for the partition.

  b. Select Primary Partition or Extended Partition; primary is a good choice for the initial partition on the drive.

  c. Select the NTFS file system.

d.   Click the Add button. The new partition with the formatted file system should appear on the screen.

e.   Click Apply to create the formatted partition. A message box will pop up, asking you to confirm that you want to apply the pending operations. Click Apply again, and then watch as the Applying pending operations dialog box appears, shows you the status of the operation, and then disappears.

f.   Click Close.

Congratulations! You should now have a drive with a formatted partition visible in the main screen (see Figure 12-7).

Step 6   There is one last step, which depends on whether you plan to use this partition to boot the machine with an OS (active partition) and which file system you have selected.

With the partition highlighted, right-click the partition and select Manage Flags. A small window appears in which you'll see a number of flags that you can set (see Figure 12-8). Many of these apply to operating systems other than Windows, but one of them must be set if you are to use the partition in Windows: boot. This flag must be set if the partition is to be the active partition in the system (this is usually the first partition on the first hard drive in the system).

Set the appropriate flags for your partition and file system and close the Manage flags window. Notice that you will not have to apply changes, as the settings take effect immediately.

Step 7   Reboot the machine and allow your Windows OS to boot. You can then use Disk Management to verify the partition(s) you have created with GParted.

Step 8   Practice deleting, creating, and formatting different combinations of partitions and file systems to become comfortable with the GParted program.

FIGURE 12-7 The GParted screen with a newly partitioned and formatted drive

FIGURE 12-8 The Manage flags window in GParted

30 MINUTES

Lab Exercise 12.03: Using Windows Tools to Create and Format Partitions

Once you have all of the donated machines' drives configured, partitioned, and formatted, and you've installed Windows, working with hard drive storage becomes much more intuitive. Windows includes tools that let you create, modify, and format partitions "on the fly" from within Windows. One of these utilities is called Disk Management.

✔ **Cross-Reference**

For details about creating and formatting partitions using Disk Management, refer to the "Disk Management" section in Chapter 12 of *Mike Meyers' CompTIA A+ Guide to Managing and Troubleshooting PCs.*

This lab exercise assumes that you want to create a partition on the second or third hard drive installed on the Windows lab system and then format that partition with a file system. Disk Management will enable you to format the partition right away; however, you can also use another Windows utility that you should be intimately familiar with by now: My Computer/Computer. Follow the steps in this lab exercise to create and format a new partition.

✔ Hint

Each version of Windows can read from and write to the FAT16, FAT32, and NTFS file systems. However, only Windows 2000/XP can be installed to a FAT16 or FAT32 partition—Windows Vista/7 must be installed on an NTFS partition.

Learning Objectives

In this exercise, you'll use the Disk Management program to partition a hard drive and format the partition with a file system.

At the end of this lab, you'll be able to

- Set up a primary, active partition on a hard drive
- Set up an extended partition and logical drives in that partition
- Format partitions with various file systems

Lab Materials and Setup

The materials you need for this lab are

- The PC from Lab Exercise 11.07, with a primary hard drive that holds your Windows installation and the two blank hard drives that you can partition and format

---

✖ Warning

Partitioning a hard drive destroys any data on it! Practice this lab only on drives that don't contain any data you need.

Getting Down to Business

The steps for partitioning drives and formatting partitions in each version of Windows are very similar.

Step 1 Right-click the My Computer/Computer icon and select Manage to open a Computer Management window. Under the Storage node, click Disk Management.

Step 2   As in prior lab exercises, if there are any existing partitions on the second or third drive, highlight the partitions and either right-click and delete the partitions or simply press DELETE.

Step 3   Start the process of creating a partition by right-clicking an unpartitioned section of drive space and, in 2000/XP, selecting New Partition (see Figure 12-9). In Vista/7, select New Simple Volume. This will start the New Partition Wizard or the New Simple Volume Wizard, depending on the OS.

Step 4   Click Next, and, in Windows 2000/XP, select Primary Partition (in Windows Vista/7, you will not have to select Primary Partition). At the next screen, enter the size of your new partition in megabytes.

Step 5   You can now assign a drive letter or mount the partition to an empty folder. For now, go with the default drive letter assignment and click Next again.

Step 6   The next screen offers you the option to format the new partition with a file system. Select a file system: FAT, FAT32, or NTFS. (Note that Windows will not allow Disk Management to create a FAT16 partition larger than 4 GB or a FAT32 partition larger than 32 GB.) Then enter a volume label if you want and click OK. Figure 12-10 shows this selection screen in the Disk Management utility.

Step 7   The utility warns you that formatting will erase all data on the drive. Click OK to begin formatting.

FIGURE 12-9 Creating a new partition in Disk Management

Figure 12-10 Formatting a partition in Disk Management

Step 8   You can also format partitions in My Computer/Computer, but generally speaking you'll use this method only to format removable media such as floppy disks, Zip disks, USB thumb drives, and so on.

Right-click a drive icon in My Computer/Computer and select Format to open the Formatting dialog box (see Figure 12-11). Now proceed as in Step 6.

Step 9   Practice deleting, creating, and formatting different combinations of partitions and file systems to become comfortable with the Disk Management utility.

Figure 12-11 Formatting a partition in My Computer

As you've no doubt noticed, I keep warning you to protect your data because you'll lose it when you create or format a partition. While the partitioning and formatting utilities you've practiced with thus far are destructive to data, it is possible to resize a partition without losing data; programs such as GParted (http://gparted.sourceforge.net) can do this.

There's also a way to convert earlier file systems to NTFS without the loss of data. Windows has a built-in command called CONVERT that you can use to change a partition from FAT32 to NTFS. You will perform this conversion in the lab exercises for Chapter 15.

 30 MINUTES

Lab Exercise 12.04: Converting Basic Disks to Dynamic Disks with Disk Management

In Lab Exercise 11.07, you configured two additional hard drives in a system to facilitate a software implementation of RAID. Windows 2000, Windows XP Professional, Windows Vista Business/Ultimate, and Windows 7 Professional/Ultimate require that a disk be converted to a dynamic disk to allow the implementation of RAID. In this lab, you will prepare the two additional drives to be used in the next lab exercise by using Disk Management to perform the simple, nondestructive conversion from basic disks to dynamic disks.

✔ Cross-Reference

To learn more about dynamic disks, refer to the "Dynamic Disks" section in Chapter 12 of *Mike Meyers' CompTIA A+ Guide to Managing and Troubleshooting PCs*.

Learning Objectives

In this exercise, you'll use the Disk Management utility to convert basic disks to dynamic disks.

At the end of this lab, you'll be able to

- Convert basic disks to dynamic disks

Lab Materials and Setup

The materials you need for this lab are

- The PC from Lab Exercise 11.07 with a primary hard drive that holds your Windows installation (converting to dynamic disks requires Windows 2000, Windows XP Professional, Windows Vista Business/Ultimate, or Windows 7 Professional/Ultimate) and the two blank hard drives that you will convert to dynamic disks

Getting Down to Business

The steps to convert a basic disk to a dynamic disk are really quite simple.

Step 1 Open the Disk Management utility as in the previous exercise.

Step 2 Select the first drive to be converted. Position the mouse pointer over the left-hand drive icon, right-click, and select Convert to Dynamic Disk (see Figure 12-12).

Step 3 Follow the wizard's instructions to complete the dynamic disk conversion. Reboot the PC (if necessary) and then open Disk Management again. The disk should now be labeled as a dynamic disk instead of a basic disk (see Figure 12-13).

Step 4 Repeat Steps 2 and 3 on the third drive in the system (you will need two dynamic disks to implement a RAID 0 stripe set), and then proceed to Lab Exercise 12.05.

FIGURE 12-12 Selecting Convert to Dynamic Disk in the Disk Management utility

FIGURE 12-13 Disk Management showing basic and dynamic storage

30 MINUTES

Lab Exercise 12.05: Implementing Software RAID 0 with Disk Management

It's finally time to flex your RAID muscles in preparation to deploy the two server machines—remember, these are the systems with dual CPUs and SCSI controllers. Windows 2000, Windows XP Professional, Windows Vista Business/Ultimate, and Windows 7 Professional/Ultimate allow you to configure software RAID implementations using Disk Management and multiple hard drives. Windows XP Professional offers only RAID 0, a stripe set, which offers improved disk access time but no fault tolerance. At the end of this lab, you will have configured a stripe set using two disks.

✔ **Cross-Reference**

Additional information on RAID 0, 1, and 5 may be found in the "Dynamic Disks" section in Chapter 12 of *Mike Meyers' CompTIA A+ Guide to Managing and Troubleshooting PCs*.

This lab exercise guides you through the creation of a RAID 0 stripe set using free, unpartitioned space on the second and third hard drives installed on the Windows lab system. These are the same disks that you converted from basic disks to dynamic disks in the prior exercise. Disk Management allows you to configure simple volumes, spanned volumes, and striped volumes on dynamic disks.

✔ **Hint**

Microsoft's dynamic storage provides five types of volumes: simple volumes, spanned volumes, striped volumes, mirrored volumes, and RAID 5 volumes. The first three—simple, spanned, striped—are the only volumes currently available in Disk Management on Windows 2000, Windows XP Professional, and Windows Vista Business/Ultimate.

- Simple volumes on dynamic disks are equivalent to primary partitions on basic disks. Simple volumes use a contiguous area of a single drive and are represented by one drive letter or mount point.

- Spanned volumes enable you to extend the size of a simple volume to include any unallocated space (contiguous or noncontiguous) on one or more dynamic disks. Spanned volumes are represented by one drive letter or mount point and fill the volume sequentially.

- Striped volumes use two or more dynamic disks, and spread data across all of them. Striped volumes are represented by one drive letter or mount point and will speed up disk access times due to concurrent disk write and read operations. The more disks in the stripe set, the faster the throughput.

Learning Objectives

In this exercise, you'll use the Disk Management program to configure a RAID 0 striped volume.

At the end of this lab, you'll be able to

- Create and configure a RAID 0 striped volume

Lab Materials and Setup

The materials you need for this lab are

- The PC from Lab Exercise 11.07 with a primary hard drive that holds your Windows installation (Windows 2000, Windows XP Professional, Windows Vista Business/Ultimate, or Windows 7 Professional/Ultimate) and the two blank hard drives that have been converted to dynamic disks

---

✖ **Warning**

Partitioning a hard drive destroys any data on the drive! Practice this lab only on drives that don't contain any data you need.

Getting Down to Business

You're in the home stretch now! Once you've worked with the Disk Management tool and converted basic disks to dynamic disks, it's just a matter of using the Disk Management New Volume Wizard, choosing the size allocated to the striped volume, and formatting the striped volume.

Step 1 Launch the Disk Management utility and right-click the unallocated space on the first disk of the planned striped volume. Select New Volume and then select Striped (see Figure 12-14).

Step 2 The wizard asks you to select at least one additional dynamic disk for the striped volume. You will then select the size of the volume you want to create and decide what file system to use to format the striped volume.

Are there any restrictions on the size of the volume? _____

Step 3 Disk Management now allocates the space on the drives and formats them with the file system you've selected. You should now have a healthy, formatted, striped volume.

Step 4 Practice deleting and creating various sizes of striped volumes using various file systems. Can you format a striped volume with FAT? Why or why not?

_____

_____

FIGURE 12-14 The Select Volume Type screen from the New Volume Wizard

60 MINUTES

Lab Exercise 12.06: Maintaining and Troubleshooting Hard Drives

Of all the devices installed in a PC, hard drives tend to need the most attention. Maintaining and troubleshooting hard drives is one of the most common tasks you'll undertake as a PC tech, but also one of the most important.

After all, the loss of other components such as video cards or NICs is inconvenient, but hardly disastrous. The loss of a hard drive, on the other hand, means the loss of data. This data might be as trivial as your favorite bookmarked Web pages or a saved Half-Life 2 game. But it could be as important as your business records, family photos, or the 1200-page novel that you've spent the last two years writing! Unless you want to spend valuable time and money trying to retrieve data from a damaged or corrupted hard drive, you should familiarize yourself with the built-in Windows drive maintenance tools. These tools include

- **Error-checking** This GUI tool enables you to examine the physical structure of the drive and retrieve data from bad clusters. Command-line utilities that perform the same duties are called CHKDSK and ScanDisk.

- **Disk Defragmenter** This tool reorganizes disorganized file structures into contiguous clusters.

- **Disk Cleanup** This tool reclaims wasted space on the hard drive by deleting unneeded files and compressing files that are rarely accessed.

Learning Objectives

At the end of this lab, you'll be able to

- Use error-checking to scan for and fix physical errors on the hard drive

- Use the Disk Defragmenter utility to reorganize the hard drive's file structure

- Use the Disk Cleanup utility to reclaim wasted disk space

Lab Materials and Setup

The materials you need for this lab are

- A fully functioning Windows PC

Getting Down to Business

Performing regular maintenance on your hard drives can keep them running more smoothly and efficiently. If you're getting obvious disk-related errors (such as error messages indicating that your disk has bad clusters or cannot be read), or if files are missing or corrupt, a tune-up is in order. Another sign that your drive needs maintenance is excessive disk activity, or disk "thrashing." It's also a good idea to do some maintenance after a serious system crash or virus infection by scanning your drive for damage or fragmentation.

✔ **Tech Tip**

In a computer system, the hard drive wins the prize as the most critical storage device and for having the most moving parts of any of the components. For this reason, it is extremely important that you not only perform routine preventive maintenance (error checking, defragmentation, and disk cleanup), but also regularly back up critical data.

You will work with some backup techniques and tools in the lab exercises for Chapters 17 and 26.

Step 1 To scan a hard drive for physical problems, open My Computer/Computer and right-click the drive's icon. Select Properties, and then select the Tools tab, shown in Figure 12-15. Click Check Now to start the error-checking utility.

In the Check Disk dialog box, you can opt to fix file system errors automatically, scan for and attempt to recover bad sectors, or both. When you've made your selections, click Start.

FIGURE 12-15 Disk Properties Tools tab

✔ **Hint**

The error-checking utility must have *exclusive* access to the drive to finish scanning it. If you have services or applications running in the background, the utility will halt. In some cases, the utility will schedule itself to run the next time you restart your PC.

The error-checking utility has two command-line equivalents: CHKDSK (used on Windows 2000/XP and Vista/7) and ScanDisk (used on older Windows 9x systems). There's no inherent advantage to running these utilities as opposed to the GUI version, except that you can launch the utilities as part of a scripted batch file.

Step 2   To launch the Disk Defragmenter, click Defragment Now. The Windows 2000/XP version of the Disk Defragmenter is shown in Figure 12-16.

Disk Defragmenter offers you a choice: You can click Analyze to examine the disk to see if a defragmenting operation is needed, or simply click Defragment to start the process without first analyzing the drive.

Step 3   Click the General tab, and then click Disk Cleanup. Disk Cleanup calculates the space you'll be able to free up, and then displays the Disk Cleanup dialog box, shown in Figure 12-17.

FIGURE 12-16 Disk Defragmenter

FIGURE 12-17 Disk Cleanup

Near the top of the dialog box you can see how much disk space (maximum) you could free up using Disk Cleanup. But look carefully! Depending on which categories in the *Files to delete* list are checked, the actual amount of disk space you'll gain could be much smaller than the estimate at the top. As you select and deselect choices, watch this value change. Disk Cleanup can remove hibernation files, Recycle Bin files, and temporary Internet files, and can also compress old files.

Lab Analysis Test

1. Name at least two indicators that you should perform maintenance on your hard drive.

2. What are the two command-line versions of the Windows error-checking utility?

3. Amanda argues that a hard drive must be formatted before you can set up the partitions. Samantha says the drive must be partitioned first. Who is correct, and why?

4. Kyle is running out of disk space on his hard drive on a Windows XP Professional system. He has installed and configured a third hard drive in the system to increase the total storage. He is planning on converting his current drive to dynamic storage and extending the storage space to the newly installed drive (also dynamic storage). Pablo argues that the conversion is destructive and that Kyle would not be able to extend the volume anyway. Is Kyle going to be able to make this work?

5. Sean has created a RAID 0 stripe set using three drives on a Windows 2000 Professional system. After running the system for a few years, he arrived at work one day to find one of the three drives had failed. He thought that if only one drive failed, he would still be able to access his data. What facts about RAID did Sean misunderstand?

Key Term Quiz

Use the following terms to complete the following sentences. Not all terms will be used.

basic disk

CHKDSK

defragmentation

Disk Cleanup

Disk Management

dynamic disk

error-checking

FDISK

format

GParted

partition

ScanDisk

volumes

Windows installation media

1. To partition and format a hard drive when no operating system has been installed, you may use either _____ or _____ to boot the system and run disk setup utilities.

2. Use a(n) _____ tool to fix noncontiguous file clusters on a hard drive.

3. The _____ tool enables you to partition and format drives in Windows.

4. Microsoft supports two types of storage configurations now; the _____ uses partitions, whereas the _____ uses _____.

5. If your hard drive is running out of free space, you should use the _____ utility.

Chapter 13
Removable Media

Lab Exercises

Removable media storage is one of the fastest-changing components of the PC, and these days it's also very much in the public eye. With the advent of USB thumb drives, iPods, and digital cameras using CompactFlash and Secure Digital memory cards, all kinds of people—from children to great-grandmothers, from artists to zookeepers—are using removable storage. With the high resolution of today's audio and video files, photographs, and games, the need for portable large-capacity storage is greater than ever.

The lowly floppy drive has the distinction of being the only component of a modern PC to employ basically the same technology as the original IBM PC. It's hard to believe, but when the first PCs came out, the entire data storage system consisted of a single floppy drive and multiple floppy disks holding a little more than 300,000 bytes of data each! Floppy drives (and disks) have been around ever since, but with the recent advances in storage technology, the floppy is finally entering its twilight, due mostly to its tiny capacity.

Technicians were the last holdout in keeping floppy drives around. Although hard drives can contain trillions of bytes of data, they can also fail; until recently, techs could still depend on the floppy drive, and a disk that can hold less than 2 MB of data, to boot a failed system and provide troubleshooting utilities that might breathe life back into the PC. While techs still need these tools, they now come in the form of bootable CDs, DVDs, and even U3 bootable USB thumb drives.

As a budding tech, you'll work with all types of removable media. The labs in this chapter will introduce you to the installation, configuration, and use of optical drives, burners, and media. You'll work with thumb drives and even learn to install the venerable floppy drive—this is important, as many corporations still order floppy drives with new machines. The final lab in the chapter looks at some troubleshooting techniques for removable media.

✔ **Hint**

Do you still have that non-production, disassembled PC from the lab exercises back in Chapter 3? Well, if you haven't done so already, you should have it completely assembled and running again after the floppy and optical drive installation lab exercises in this chapter. You can still use it to explore the hardware of video and sound cards in future chapters, and if you can install an OS on it, so much the better!

 30 MINUTES

Lab Exercise 13.01: Installing Floppy Drives

Your boss recently approved the purchase of a number of new workstations, all without floppy drives. "Times are changing," he explained, "and floppies just hold too little data. Plus they're slow and cumbersome!" But the employees assigned to the new machines complained so much that the boss has decided to retrofit all the new workstations with 3.5-inch floppy drives. Many manufacturers offer external USB 3.5-inch floppy drives, but you found a supply house close-out on old, original floppy drives. You've been assigned the task of installing them into each system.

✔ **Cross-Reference**

To review the details of floppy drive installation, refer to the "Installing Floppy Drives" section in Chapter 13 of *Mike Meyers' CompTIA A+ Guide to Managing and Troubleshooting PCs.*

Learning Objectives

In this lab, you'll practice removing and installing a floppy drive.

At the end of this lab, you'll be able to

- Remove a floppy drive safely and correctly

- Install a floppy drive safely and correctly

Lab Materials and Setup

The materials you need for this lab are

- A working computer system with a floppy drive installed

- A known good floppy disk with data

Getting Down to Business

Although this lab starts with a working floppy drive installed in a PC—a likely scenario in a classroom setting—you would obviously need to install one yourself when building a system. On a new system (or if you are reassembling the disassembled, non-production machine from Chapter 3), you'd start this lab at Step 5.

Step 1 Begin with the PC turned on and the standard Windows desktop displayed. To verify that the floppy drive works, insert a known good floppy disk containing files into the drive, and then view the files on it by following these steps:

a. Double-click the My Computer/Computer icon on the desktop.

b. Double-click the 3½ Floppy Disk Drive (A:) icon in the window (see Figure 13-1).

c. Observe the files and folders displayed.

Do you see files displayed? _____

FIGURE 13-1 Accessing the contents of a floppy disk in Windows Vista

✔ **Hint**

If no files are displayed, try another floppy disk. Also, be sure to insert the disk properly. You should hear a ratcheting sound when you double-click the floppy drive icon. This is the sound of the read mechanism opening the metal cover so that it can read the data on the disk.

Step 2 Properly shut down the system, unplug the main power cable, and open the case following good ESD procedures.

Step 3 Carefully disconnect the two cables from the back of the floppy drive. One is the four-wire cable from the power supply (with its mini power connector), and the other is the flat ribbon cable that carries the data to and from the drive.

✖ **Warning**

Be sure to notice the seven-wire twist in the ribbon cable before you disconnect it. Is the twist closer to the drive or to the motherboard? If you put this cable back on incorrectly, the floppy drive will not work. The end with the twist (see Figure 13-2) always goes closest to the floppy drive.

✔ **Hint**

If your lab has gone high-tech and uses rounded data cables rather than the traditional flat ribbon cables, you can safely assume that one of the connectors will have a marking for the A: drive.

Floppy B

Floppy A

Floppy Controller Plug

Figure 13-2 The twist in one end of the floppy drive ribbon cable

Now disconnect the other end of the ribbon cable from the motherboard. These cables can be quite firmly attached to the motherboard, so use caution! Grab the connector, or grab as close to the connector as you can, and pull straight up firmly but gently. Sometimes a connector will seem to stick on one side—make sure that you don't pull unevenly, or you may bend the pins on the motherboard.

How many wires make up the ribbon cable? (Go ahead, count 'em!) _____

Is one of the wires a different color from the rest, and if so, what does that mean?

_____

Look at the motherboard where the cable was attached, and examine the pins. How many pins do you count? _____

Look at the shape of the connection. Is it symmetrical, meaning you can plug the connector in either direction, or is one side of the connector keyed to prevent you from inserting it backward?

_____

Locate pin 1 (where the colored wire attaches) and pin 34. The thirty-fourth pin is the drive change signal/disk change signal. It indicates when a disk has been physically changed. If this wire is broken or not connected, the system will read the initial disk placed in the floppy drive after power is applied and remember the contents for that disk, no matter how many times you change disks during a session, until you reboot the system.

Compare your motherboard connection for the floppy drive with the one shown in Figure 13-3.

Step 4   Remove the floppy drive from the case. There are so many different ways that floppy drives are held into system cases that it would be impossible to list all of the various carriers, caddies, bays, and so on that might be used to hold your floppy drive.

Almost all floppy drives are secured to these carriers, caddies, and bays with fine-threaded screws. The threads on these screws are narrower than those on the screws commonly used to secure expansion cards and the case cover. There should be two screws in each side of the floppy drive for support.

Figure 13-3 The orientation of the floppy drive connector on the motherboard

✔ **Hint**

Get in the habit of storing screws safely while you're changing out or inspecting hardware. You can use a small plastic bowl, a coffee cup, or an empty baby food jar or breath mint tin—but if you let those screws roll around loose, you may not have enough of them the next time you need to install a device!

Step 5   Now that you've removed the floppy drive, give it a thorough inspection. Look at the area where the cables connect (see Figure 13-4).

Is this ribbon cable area keyed or notched? _____

Find the indicator for the location of pin 1 on the floppy drive. What and where is it?

_____

On which side of the connector does the red (or other colored) orientation stripe of the cable go—toward the center or toward the outside?

_____

How many physical pins are on your floppy drive? _____

Look at the area where the power is attached. How many pins are there? _____

Take a moment to experiment to see if you can insert the power connector into the floppy drive incorrectly. Be gentle!

Can you connect it upside down? _____

Can you connect it without covering every pin? _____

On which side of the mini connector does the orientation stripe go—toward the center or toward the outside?

_____

FIGURE 13-4 Examining the connections for the ribbon cable (top) and power cable (bottom) on the back of a floppy drive

> ### ✖ Warning
>
> It is possible to force the power connector on incorrectly, which will cause damage to the drive. Practice how it feels to make this connection properly and improperly, so that when you do it from an odd angle (for example, lying on your back under a desk), you know how it should feel.

Step 6 Reinstall the floppy drive by placing it back where you found it in the case. Be sure to use the proper fine-threaded screws to secure the drive.

Now attach a mini connector to the floppy drive to provide power, and attach the 34-pin ribbon cable securely to the drive.

Attach the ribbon cable to the motherboard. Make sure it is secure and all the pins are covered.

Did you make sure that pin 1 was connected properly at both ends of the ribbon cable? _____

Are the connectors properly aligned so that pin 34 is connected on both ends of the cable? _____

Step 7 Once everything is back in place, leave the system cover off so that you can make adjustments if needed. Start the system, and watch the green LED on the front of the floppy drive.

If the green LED does not turn on at all during the boot process, then check your power connection.

If the green LED comes on and stays on all the time, then the ribbon cable is not connected properly (it is probably reversed either on the motherboard or on the floppy drive).

Is everything working properly? _____

After you confirm that everything is working, place the cover back onto your system. Start Windows and test your floppy drive as you did in Step 1 of this lab.

 30 MINUTES

Lab Exercise 13.02: Installing Optical Drives

Your supervisor calls you in one day and announces that he wants to simplify the daily database backup procedures for your company. You will still use tape backups for archival backups, but he wants all the CD-R/RW drives on your company's servers replaced with DVD-R/RW drives. The increased storage capacity of this type of drive will enable you to back up onto a single disc most of the critical files that change during the day. To accomplish this task, you must physically uninstall all the existing CD-R/RW drives and replace them with DVD-R/RW equivalents.

You should be comfortable removing and installing optical drives. Many optical drives still use the popular PATA interface to connect to your system, making the installation process fairly simple. If you are lucky enough to be working with a newer system, you will probably uninstall and install SATA optical drives. The CompTIA A+ exams assume you know how to install both PATA and SATA optical drives!

Learning Objectives

In this lab, you'll remove and inspect an optical drive, and then reinstall the drive.

At the end of this lab, you'll be able to

- Remove and install an optical drive safely and properly
- Identify the physical features of an optical drive

Lab Materials and Setup

The materials you need for this lab are

- A working computer with Windows and an optical drive of some type installed (what type you use doesn't matter, but it's helpful if you have both a PATA and a SATA drive)

Getting Down to Business

Removing an optical drive is almost too easy. The only real secret here is to remember which cable you removed and how the cable ends were oriented, to make sure you can put it back! Also, PATA optical drives use the standard master/slave jumpers—these also need to be inspected to make sure that the drive runs properly on the PATA connection! For a quick look at jumper settings for PATA or SATA drives, check out the PDF at www.wdc.com/en/library/eide/2579-001037.pdf.

Step 1 Properly shut down your system. As I've mentioned before, there are so many different ways that drives are held into system cases that it would be impossible to list all of the various carriers, caddies, bays, and so on that might be used to hold your drive. Using whichever method is appropriate, remove the cover from the PC case so that you can access the screws on both sides of the drive. Using proper ESD procedures, perform the following steps to remove the drive from your system:

   a. Unplug the connections. First unplug the Molex or SATA power connection from the back of the drive, and then disconnect the PATA ribbon cable or SATA cable from the drive. Unplug the audio cable coming from the sound card (if present) that plugs into the back of the drive.

   b. Using a Phillips-head screwdriver, remove the screws holding the drive in place. Notice that the screws are small-threaded screws—the same type you encountered when you removed and installed your floppy drive.

✔ **Hint**

Some optical drives are held in their bays by rails. Simply squeeze the rail toggles (sticking out of the front) and remove the drive by pulling it forward.

Step 2 Inspect the optical drive. Look at the front of the drive. Do you see a tiny hole near the edge of the tray door? Most drives have such a hole. You can take a straightened-out paper clip and push it into this hole to release the tray. This is handy in case you accidentally leave a disc in the drive when you remove it from the system. Go ahead and push a straightened-out paper clip into the hole to eject the tray.

Look at the back of the drive. You should see several areas for connections:

- The Molex or SATA power connection

- The connection for the flat ribbon or SATA cable

- An audio connection for a cable to the sound card (there may be more than one connector because of different styles of cables, but only one cable should be connected)

- Jumper settings: master, slave, and cable select (PATA only)

✔ **Hint**

Look for the orientation of pin 1. It is usually closest to the power connection.

Step 3 Reinstall the optical drive into your system. It can be a master drive or a slave drive, depending on what other PATA devices are installed. Figure 13-5 shows a properly installed drive.

Now answer these questions:

Did you fasten the drive using the correct screws? _____

Is the master/slave jumper set correctly? _____

Is the PATA/SATA cable connected properly? _____

Is the power plug fully inserted? _____

Is the audio cable connected to the drive? _____

Step 4 Leave the cover off the system and boot the PC to the Windows desktop.

Step 5 Select My Computer/Computer. Notice if the drive's icon is present. If so, all is well. If not, repeat Steps 2 and 3. The most common problem when installing hardware is a loose connection, so recheck your cable ends and try again. Replace the PC cover once the drive is recognized in Windows.

FIGURE 13-5 Viewing a properly installed optical drive

 30 MINUTES

Lab Exercise 13.03: Working with USB Thumb Drives

Your company is finally being forced to provide larger-capacity removable storage for all of the sales organization staff. In the not-so-distant past, PowerPoint presentations were moved from machine to machine via floppy disks, and then CD-Rs. With the ease of use and convenient size of USB thumb drives, all sales personnel will now be issued 2-GB thumb drives. Your mission (should you choose to accept it) is to teach the field sales personnel how to properly use their new thumb drives.

✔ **Cross-Reference**

For a primer on USB flash memory drives (often called thumb drives), see the "USB Thumb Drives" section in Chapter 13 of *Mike Meyers' CompTIA A+ Guide to Managing and Troubleshooting PCs.*

Learning Objectives

In this lab, you'll learn to insert, use, and safely remove USB thumb drives.

At the end of this lab, you'll be able to

- Insert and remove USB thumb drives
- Save and transfer data using USB thumb drives

Lab Materials and Setup

The materials you need for this lab are

- A Windows PC

- A USB thumb drive

Getting Down to Business

In Lab Exercise 13.01, you physically removed and reinstalled a floppy drive, but as you are aware, this technology is quickly being retired. This lab exercise uses the newest technology to replace the function and ease of the floppy disk, the USB flash drive (thumb drive). You will use a USB thumb drive to transfer a large file by inserting the drive into a Windows system, copying some data onto it, removing it, and reinserting it into a new system (or the same lab machine) and transferring the data to the new machine.

Step 1   USB thumb drives come in many shapes and colors, as well as many data capacities. An older thumb drive might be as small as 256 MB, and a newer thumb drive might be as large as 256 GB. They are typically a few inches long, and most provide protection for the USB connector using either a cover of some type or a retractable mechanism as shown in Figure 13-6.

Boot your lab system and allow it to finish displaying the Windows desktop. Insert the USB thumb drive and note any activity on the screen.

Did a window appear asking what you want Windows to do? _____

If yes, what were some of the options you could choose? _____

_____

Close the options window.

Figure 13-6 A USB thumb drive with a retractable connector

✔ **Hint**

Current USB thumb drives support the USB 2.0 specification, allowing a faster transfer of data (480 Mbps). Some systems (motherboards, specifically) offer both USB 1.0 and USB 2.0 ports, so when you insert the USB thumb drive into a USB 1.0 port, you may see a pop-up message in the system tray (notification area) pointing out that this device can perform faster if inserted into a USB 2.0 port.

Step 2 Open an application on your PC, such as Word or PowerPoint, and select and open a file. If you can find a file larger than 1.44 MB, you can experience firsthand the benefit of USB thumb drives over floppy drives.

Step 3 In the application window, select File | Save As. In 2000/XP, click the drop-down arrow for the Save in field. You will see a number of folders and drives where you could choose to save the file. One of these should be the thumb drive, as shown in Figure 13-7. Select the thumb drive and save the file. In Vista, click Browse Folders. In the list that appears, click Folders. Then scroll until you see the thumb drive. Select it and save the file. Close all open windows.

Step 4 In the system tray, find and click the Safely Remove Hardware icon, which in Windows 2000/XP is a green arrow and a gray rectangle, and in Vista is a white checkmark on a green circle in front of a tiny USB symbol. A tiny pop-up message appears adjacent to the icon, listing all removable devices; click the name of the thumb drive. In 2000/XP, an information balloon with a *Safe to Remove Hardware* message should notify you that you can now remove the USB mass storage device. In Vista, an announcement will appear with the same message.

Remove the thumb drive from the USB port.

FIGURE 13-7 The Windows XP Save As dialog box showing a Lexar Media thumb drive

✔ **Hint**

If you forget to close one or more windows with a focus on the thumb drive, you will receive an error message: *The device 'Generic Volume' cannot be stopped right now. Try stopping it later.* If you receive this message, just click OK, close all open files and folders on the thumb drive, and try again.

If you have some open files or folders on the thumb drive and you just pull it out of the machine, you may receive an error message such as *Fail Write Delay.* Most of the time the files and folders will remain intact, but this is not the recommended removal method.

Step 5   At this point, if you have a second machine where you can plug in the thumb drive, it will make the lab exercise more realistic. If you don't, you can just use the same system again for this step. Insert the thumb drive into a USB port and again note any activity on the screen. This time, double-click *Open folder to view files using Windows Explorer.*

Step 6   Double-click the file you saved previously; if the file has an associated application, this should launch that application and open the file.

You have now successfully used a USB thumb drive—also referred to as a *jump drive*—to "jump" files from one machine to another.

 30 MINUTES

Lab Exercise 13.04: Configuring Removable Media Drives

A new client has very specific needs for the boot order and access to removable media in his computer center's seven computers. For the two servers, the floppy drive and USB ports will be installed, but the floppy drive will be disabled in CMOS. Three of the five workstations need the optical drive set as the first drive in the boot sequence, but the other two need the USB drive to be first in the boot sequence, with the optical drive second. It's your job to set up these PCs properly, so get to work!

Learning Objectives

In this lab, you'll use the CMOS setup program to configure the settings for the floppy drive, USB devices, optical drive, and boot order.

At the end of this lab, you'll be able to

- Locate the CMOS setup screens for configuring the floppy drives, USB devices, optical drives, and boot order

- Configure various scenarios for the floppy drive, USB devices, optical drive, and boot order

Lab Materials and Setup

The materials you need for this lab are

- A working computer system with a floppy drive, an optical drive, and USB device support

Getting Down to Business

This lab exercise involves the floppy drive controller, optical drive, and USB controller, and shows you how to configure these devices and the boot order of these devices in CMOS.

Depending on your BIOS manufacturer and version, you may or may not be able to perform all of the following steps. Explore the different screens to discover whether you can enable/disable the floppy drive controller (FDC) and the USB controller, and which devices you can put in the boot order (floppy drive, optical drive, hard drive, and possibly USB devices).

Step 1 You will start by disabling the floppy drive. Enter the CMOS setup program by pressing the appropriate key or key combination (which you should remember from Lab Exercise 7.02) while your system is booting.

Having previously browsed through your version of CMOS, you should be able to locate the screen that contains settings for the FDC. If you can't remember which screen deals with the FDC, browse through the CMOS screens until you find it.

Do you have an option in CMOS to disable the FDC? _____

Under what title heading did you find this option? _____

_____

How do you disable this setting?

_____

Now disable it.

✔ Hint

Disabling the FDC is a good way for a network administrator to prevent users from using floppy disks to either take information off the network or introduce viruses into the network.

Step 2 Restart your system and see if you can access the floppy drive. Did the LED on the front of the floppy drive turn on as the system booted up?

Step 3 Re-enter the CMOS setup utility and turn the FDC back on. Reboot the system, and test the floppy drive. Does it function properly?

Step 4 One of the most important aspects of removable media is that you can boot a nonfunctioning system from a device other than the hard drive with the diagnostic and troubleshooting tools included. The next CMOS setting to play with is the boot sequence.

When you boot up a PC, the system needs to know where to get the operating system software to load into memory. The three standard places to store this software are the floppy drive, the hard drive, and the optical drive. USB thumb drives have emerged as the next big bootable media. In some cases, the needed software is stored in another location, such as a network server.

Using the CMOS setup utility, you can designate the order in which your system will check the devices for the operating system software. Specifying the proper boot sequence—that is, the search order—saves time by telling the system where to look first. After all, why should your system waste time looking on the optical or USB thumb drive every time you boot, if your operating system is on the hard drive?

Enter the CMOS setup utility, and look for a screen that includes a boot sequence setting.

How many different boot sequences can you configure in CMOS? _____

How many different devices can be in the search sequence? _____

Set your system to boot from the optical drive first (see Figure 13-8).

Step 5   Restart your system. Typically, the boot screen will prompt you with the message *Press any key to boot from the CD*. If there is a bootable CD in the drive, the system will boot from that disc. Leave this boot order in place for the next lab exercise, in which you'll learn to create bootable CDs.

Step 6   Re-enter the CMOS setup utility, and note whether your system will allow you to boot from a USB device, such as a USB thumb drive.

If your machine is capable, you can substitute a USB thumb drive for the optical drive in the next lab exercise and create a live USB of the GParted partition editor. For now, leave the optical drive as the first device in the boot order and shut down the machine.

```
            Phoenix - Award BIOS CMOS Setup Utility
                    Advanced BIOS Features

   Quick Power On Self Test      Enabled             Item Help
 ▶ Hard Disk Boot Priority       Press Enter   ┌─────────────────────┐
   First Boot Device             CDROM         │ Menu Level    ▶     │
   Second Boot Device            Hard Disk     │                     │
   Third Boot Device             Floppy        │ Allows the system to│
   Boot Other Device             Enabled       │ skip certain tests  │
   Boot Up Floppy Seek           Disabled      │ while booting. This │
   Boot up NumLock Status        On            │ will decrease the time│
   Security Option               Setup         │ needed to boot the  │
   MPS Version Control For OS     1.4          │ system              │
   Delay For HDD (Secs)          0             │                     │
   Full Screen LOGO Show         Disabled      │                     │


▲▼►◄:Move   Enter:Select    +/-/PU/PD:Value  F10:Save  ESC:Exit  F1:General Help
     F5:Previous Values     F6:Fail-Safe Defaults    F7:Optimized Defaults
```

FIGURE 13-8 Boot sequence screen from CMOS with optical drive as first boot device

60 MINUTES

Lab Exercise 13.05: Burning Optical Discs

PCs today are used more than ever for storage of digital photographs, music, and video, in addition to more traditional types of data. Even a modest collection of MP3 files, family photos, and home video clips requires many gigabytes of space! Hard drives do have space limits, and at some point they tend to fail, so wise PC users turn to recordable CDs, DVDs, and Blu-ray drives. These discs provide an affordable large-capacity portable storage option; you can put your important data onto a disc, or make multiple copies of that disc to store in two or more secure locations.

This lab will introduce you to the process by which we record, or *burn*, optical discs. Rather than burning a disc full of your favorite tunes or photos, you'll be making the type of disc that a technician would have in his toolkit when troubleshooting a machine that won't boot.

→ Note

If your systems have Blu-ray drives, you will be burning your disc the same way. However, be aware that Blu-ray Discs are better armed than current DVDs. They come equipped with a secure encryption system—a unique ID that protects against video piracy and copyright infringement.

✔ Cross-Reference

For additional information on burning optical discs, refer to the "Applications" section in Chapter 13 of *Mike Meyers' CompTIA A+ Guide to Managing and Troubleshooting PCs.*

Learning Objectives

In this lab, you'll use a third-party burning program to create bootable ISO images on recordable optical discs.

At the end of this lab, you'll be able to

- Work with optical discs and burning tools
- Create a bootable optical disc

Lab Materials and Setup

The materials you need for this lab are

- A working computer system with a CD-RW or DVD-RW drive installed

- Internet access (preferably a high-speed connection) for downloading

- An optical disc burning application such as ISO Recorder, Nero Burning ROM, or freeware CDBurnerXP

- Blank optical discs (more than one if possible)

Getting Down to Business

In Chapter 12, you were asked to prep a number of newly donated PCs by preparing their hard drives for the installation of an operating system; you already partitioned and formatted the drives. To do that, you used the open source utility called GParted. GParted is a Gnome Linux live CD with the Gnome Partition Editor application installed. Your instructor may have provided you with the bootable CD, or you may have jumped ahead to this lab to make it yourself. In this lab you will burn the ISO image of the open source, bootable live CD of Gnome Linux and the utility GParted.

Step 1   Ensure that you have optical disc burning software that will allow you to burn ISO images. An ISO image is a complete copy of a disc, including all of the boot information in the boot record. Popular third-party products include the freeware ISO Recorder for Windows XP or Vista (http://isorecorder .alexfeinman.com/isorecorder.htm) and the commercial Nero Burning ROM (www.nero.com).

You can also try CDBurnerXP, an excellent freeware burning tool that supports the burning of ISO images; it's available at www.cdburnerxp.se. Just go to the CDBurnerXP Web site, follow the instructions, and run the installation. After you've successfully installed the program, you should have all the tools necessary to burn ISO images (see Figure 13-9).

✔ **Hint**

Microsoft is constantly updating operating systems and applications such as Internet Explorer and Windows Media Player, so don't forget to check occasionally to see if they have updated the built-in burning application with the ability to handle ISO images.

Step 2   Now visit the GParted Web site at gparted.sourceforge.net. Click Downloads and follow the instructions. You can download the full ISO, or download the .zip file to improve transfer times (remember you will have to expand the .zip file after it's on your system).

Step 3   Once you have the ISO image, open the tray on your optical drive and insert a blank optical disc. Close the tray and launch your optical disc burning software. Navigate to the GParted ISO file and follow the instructions to burn the ISO image onto the optical media. Most programs will eject the tray with the disc once the writing process is complete.

FIGURE 13-9 CDBurnerXP

Step 4 Place the newly created disc into the optical drive tray, close the tray, and reboot the computer. If all has gone well, GParted will boot, detect your hard drives, and give you the option to partition and format these drives.

✖ Warning

Remember, any time you format a hard disk, you delete the data currently on that disk. Do not run GParted on the disk containing your operating system unless you have been instructed to delete this system's OS.

→ Try This: Ultimate Boot CD

Now that you have an understanding of why you might want to boot a machine from removable media—to perform low-level diagnostics, troubleshoot, or just prep the disk before installing an operating system—take a cruise over to www.ultimatebootcd.com.

You can download the ISO image of Ultimate Boot CD (UBCD), which has over 100 different freeware tools, all placed on a live CD. Use the method you learned in this exercise to burn the ISO image to a CD, boot a machine with the UBCD, and explore some of the tools. You might find that using some of the drive manufacturer's low-level formatting tools will bring a dead drive back to life.

Lab Analysis Test

1. Jovan installed an optical drive on the same cable as his primary hard drive, and now the system will not boot. What could be causing this?

2. While looking around in the BIOS settings, Kaitlin set the PIO and DMA settings to Auto. Will this affect the system in any way? Explain.

3. Cecelia is a freelance Web designer who is delivering some files to a client. She sits down at a Windows XP system in the client's office and plugs in her trusty USB thumb drive, but nothing happens—Windows doesn't acknowledge the device at all. The thumb drive has been working perfectly well as recently as this morning. What is most likely the reason that the USB thumb drive won't connect with the client PC?

4. When Philip puts his CD-RW disc in the drive and copies files to and from it, he notices that the drive speeds up and slows down. Is this normal? If not, what should he do to fix it?

5. After removing an optical drive for replacement, you remember that you left a disc in the drive. You look for a hole to insert the paper clip into, but there is none. How do you remove the disc?

Key Term Quiz

Use the following terms to complete the following sentences. Not all terms will be used.

Blu-ray

CMOS

disc

DMA

label

optical drive

scratches

spiral

surface

USB 1.0

USB 2.0

1. An optical drive must be identified in the _____ settings.

2. _____ discs can hold and play back large quantities of high-definition video and audio, as well as photos, data, and other digital content.

3. Any drive that uses a laser of some sort to read data from a disc is called a(n) _____.

4. The _____ version of thumb drives supports a throughput of 480 Mbps.

5. The reflective aluminum layer of an optical disc can be damaged by _____.

Chapter 14
Installing and Upgrading Windows

Lab Exercises

As a PC technician, you'll spend a lot of time installing and upgrading operating systems. For this reason, it's important that you become familiar with the tasks involved; otherwise, you might find yourself in a tight spot when Windows won't install on the laptop that your boss needs to have working for a presentation this afternoon.

A number of different operating systems are in use today, including Apple Macintosh OS X, several different flavors of Linux, and of course the Microsoft Windows family. Because the CompTIA A+ certification focuses primarily on Microsoft products—and because Microsoft products represent the majority of the market—these lab exercises are dedicated to the installation of Windows.

Just about anyone can install software if everything goes right and no problems come up during the process; plenty of people with minimal software knowledge have upgraded Windows without the slightest incident. Even an experienced technician may have problems, though, if the system has incompatible expansion cards, broken devices, or bad drivers. As a PC technician, you have to be prepared to handle both the simple installations—the ones with only new, compatible components—and the more complex installations on older and more problematic systems.

Installing and upgrading Windows is more than popping in the installation disc and running the install program. You need to plan the installation thoughtfully, check for component compatibility, and thoroughly understand the installation options and how to configure them. Good planning up front will give you the best chances for a successful installation or upgrade.

Be sure to have everything you need before you start, from the installation disc to the discs containing your device drivers. Remember the old adage, "Measure twice, cut once." Believe me, it's no fun to start over on an installation or upgrade if you mess it up! Do it right the first time—you'll be glad you did.

 30 MINUTES

Lab Exercise 14.01: Installing/Upgrading Considerations

Your client has asked you to upgrade his system to Windows Vista Business. He's currently running Windows XP Professional, and everything works fine. He has the documentation that came with his system, which states that it has an ASUS P4G8X Deluxe motherboard. He isn't sure how fast the processor is, but he does know that he's already using 512 MB of memory. Where do you start the planning process?

✔ **Cross-Reference**

To review the details of pre-installation planning, refer to the "Preparing for Installation or Upgrade" section of Chapter 14 of *Mike Meyers' CompTIA A+ Guide to Managing and Troubleshooting PCs*.

Learning Objectives

In this lab exercise, you'll become more familiar with using the Internet to help answer pre-installation questions.

At the end of this lab, you'll be able to

- Access the Microsoft support Web site
- Determine the minimal requirements for a system installation
- Determine whether to perform an upgrade installation or a clean installation

Lab Materials and Setup

The materials you need for this lab are

- A working PC
- Internet access
- A notepad and pencil

Getting Down to Business

The first step in a successful Windows installation or upgrade is to determine whether the hardware meets the requirements of the new operating system. Your first stop in this process is the Microsoft support Web site.

Microsoft has invested massive amounts of energy and time in building its support Web site. Sometimes digging through all of the articles on the huge number of Web pages can be overwhelming, but I'm a firm believer in this site's usefulness. When I have a question that directly concerns a Windows operating system (or any Microsoft product, for that matter), I check this site first, and I'm rarely disappointed. In fact, while searching for the answer to a problem or question, I usually learn two or three new, sometimes unrelated, things just by reading through the search results. Also, my search techniques improve with each visit. I consider the Microsoft support Web site an invaluable tool and resource.

Step 1   You'll first need to make sure that your client's computer is capable of running Windows Vista Business. To do this, go to www.microsoft.com/windows/windows-vista/get/upgrade-advisor.aspx and click the Download Windows Vista Upgrade Advisor button, which will take you to the actual download page. Click Download and save the file to your computer.

When the file is downloaded, double-click it to start the installation process, and then follow the onscreen prompts to install the Upgrade Advisor. When it's finished installing, it should start up automatically, so just click the Start Scan button and wait for it to complete.

Once the scan completes, click the See Details button to view the results of the scan. The top of the screen (see Figure 14-1) will tell you whether or not your system is Vista-capable, and further down the page you can click buttons to view details about the system requirements, device compatibility, and program compatibility. The left side of the screen enables you to view details about the various editions of Vista, so click Business and then check out the details pages.

✔ Hint

Web sites are infamous for losing information that was once relevant to a particular subject—or sometimes disappearing altogether. If the Microsoft Web site should change significantly from the time this book was printed to the time you're reading this, and you find that a link listed here is no longer valid, a quick search of the site should get you where you need to be.

Once you've seen the scan's results, answer the following questions about Windows Vista Business:

What's the recommended CPU speed? _____

What's the recommended amount of RAM? _____

How much available hard drive space is required? _____

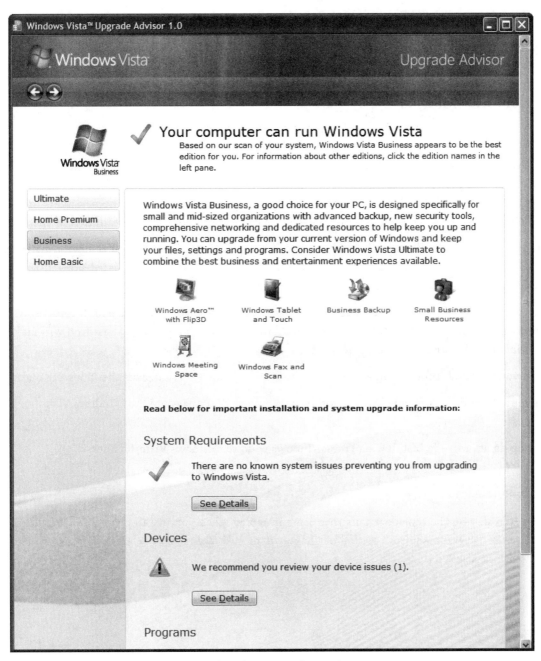

Figure 14-1 A Windows Vista Upgrade Advisor scan's results

How much video memory is required? _____

At a minimum, what other devices are recommended?

_____

→ **Note**

If you search around for the requirements for Windows 7, you'll actually find that it's a slightly less demanding operating system than its predecessor, particularly in hard drive space. Microsoft offers a Windows 7 Upgrade Advisor, too, but in general, if your computer can run Vista, it can run Windows 7.

Step 2 Now that you know whether or not your client's computer can run Vista Business, and, if not, what you need to upgrade in order to get it to run Vista Business, you need to find out whether you can do an upgrade installation (called an in-place installation by Microsoft), where the new OS is installed on top of the old one, or a clean installation, where the drive is erased before installation of the new OS.

Doing an upgrade installation is based both on the version of Windows XP you're upgrading from and the edition of Windows Vista that you're upgrading to, so it's a fairly complicated subject. In order to find out the possible upgrade paths, you'll need to do a bit of searching.

Go to www.microsoft.com/ and do a search for Vista Upgrade Paths. The first search result should give you the information you need, but if not, search around a little. This sort of research will make up a substantial part of your life as a tech, so get used to it!

When you've found information about Windows Vista upgrade paths, answer the following questions:

Can your client do an upgrade installation from Windows XP Professional to Windows Vista Business? _____

Can you do an upgrade installation from Windows 2000 to Windows Vista Business? _____

✔ **Cross-Reference**

For a refresher on the considerations that come into play when you install or upgrade Windows, refer to the "Upgrade Advisor" section of Chapter 14 of *Mike Meyers' CompTIA A+ Guide to Managing and Troubleshooting PCs*.

---

 30 MINUTES

Lab Exercise 14.02: Using Windows Easy Transfer

You're about to upgrade a client's computer from Windows XP to Windows Vista, but the client doesn't want to lose any of her important data. She doesn't have a lot of data to transfer, just a gigabyte or so, but that data is absolutely essential to the operation of her business. Fortunately, you're a savvy tech and you know that Windows Easy Transfer will enable you to back up her documents onto a flash drive and then transfer them to her new OS after it's installed.

Learning Objectives

You'll learn how to use Windows Easy Transfer effectively to back up files and transfer them to a new operating system.

At the end of this lab, you'll be able to

- Use Windows Easy Transfer to back up files onto a USB thumb drive
- Use Windows Easy Transfer to transfer files onto a new OS installation

Lab Materials and Setup

The materials you need for this lab are

- A PC running Windows XP Professional
- A PC running Windows Vista
- Access to the Internet
- A USB thumb drive (1 GB or more)

Getting Down to Business

Microsoft's Windows Easy Transfer has made moving data to a new computer as easy as it could be, but it's still a somewhat complicated program. In this lab, you'll learn all the necessary steps you need to take to move a customer's data from one computer to another. If you ever work as a tech in a retail store, this sort of information will be vital when trying to convince customers to upgrade their PCs.

Step 1 The first thing you need to do to use Windows Easy Transfer, of course, is to get a copy of Windows Easy Transfer. Microsoft offers Windows Easy Transfer as a free download, so go to www .microsoft.com/downloads and do a search for "Easy Transfer Wizard" to locate the specific version for Windows XP. Click the search result and then download the program to your hard drive. I'd give you the direct link to the download page here, but you wouldn't thank me after typing in a nonsensical URL for ten minutes.

After you've downloaded a copy of Windows Easy Transfer to your XP machine, run it and follow the onscreen prompts to install the program. Once it's installed, run it from the All Programs menu. The first screen (see Figure 14-2) gives you information about the transfer process, so once you've read all of that, click the Next button.

Step 2 The next screen (see Figure 14-3) offers you several different options from which to choose how you want to transfer the files and settings to your new computer, whether by Easy Transfer Cable (a special USB cable sold by Microsoft), a network connection (useful if you're transferring between two computers on a local area network), or by CD, DVD, or other removable media. Since you're using a USB flash drive, a type of removable media, select the third option.

FIGURE 14-2 Running Windows Easy Transfer

FIGURE 14-3 How do you want to transfer your files?

Once you've selected the removable media option, the wizard asks for you to be a bit more specific. At this point, you can choose to use either a CD or DVD (even though the wizard doesn't specifically list DVDs, you are still able to use them), a USB flash drive, or a network location (see Figure 14-4). If you haven't yet, plug in your USB flash drive now, and once the USB flash drive option is clickable, click it.

On the next wizard page (see Figure 14-5), choose your thumb drive from the drop-down list. If several drives appear in the list, make sure you select the right one! You can also set a password on your data if you're transferring sensitive information that you don't want falling into the wrong hands. Set a simple password and then click Next.

The next page enables you to select which type of files and settings you want to transfer, whether files and settings for all of the computer's user accounts, just the files and settings for the current user account, or, by selecting an advanced option, any files and settings you want. Since all your client needs is her My Documents folder, click My user account, files, and settings only. You'll then be asked to review your selected files and settings, so just click Transfer on the next page and your selected files and settings will start transferring (see Figure 14-6).

Step 3   Once you've transferred all your files onto your USB thumb drive, you can remove the drive and move it to your PC running Vista. If you don't have a PC with Vista already installed, skip to Lab Exercise 14.04 and then come back when you're finished with it. Once you're on your Vista PC, open Windows Easy Transfer by going to Start | All Programs | Accessories | System Tools | Windows Easy Transfer.

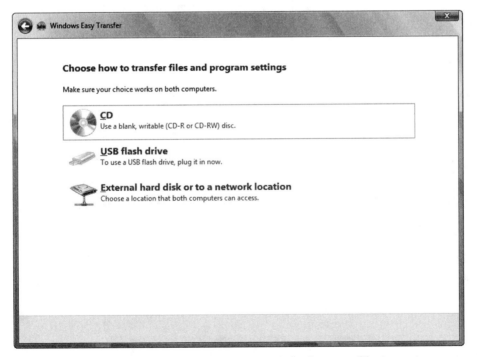

Figure 14-4 For real now, how do you want to transfer your files?

FIGURE 14-5 Select your USB drive and type a password.

FIGURE 14-6 Review your selection.

When the wizard starts, you can once more click Next past the welcome screen. The next screen will be a bit different from what you saw when you ran the wizard in XP, as it asks you whether you would like to start a new transfer or to continue a transfer that's already in progress. Since you've already backed up the files from the old computer, select Continue a transfer in progress (see Figure 14-7).

The next screen asks you how you are going to transfer your files, so select the second option, *No, I've copied files and settings to a CD, DVD, or other removable media*. When the next screen comes up, plug in your USB thumb drive if you haven't already and then select the USB flash drive option.

Next, you will once again be asked which drive the files are on. Select the appropriate drive, type in your password, and click Next, at which point the wizard will scan your disk for any files.

When it finishes scanning, the wizard will ask you to type in a user account name for the new computer. Since this is a step you've likely already completed when setting up Vista, you probably already have an account name. If so, select it from the drop-down list and click Next. If you want to create a new account, type an account name in the box and then click Next (see Figure 14-8).

After the account name page, you will be asked to review the selected files and settings for transfer, so check them over and then click Transfer. When the transfer is finished, the wizard will notify you, and will ask you to log off your account if you changed the account name.

FIGURE 14-7 Running Windows Easy Transfer in Vista

FIGURE 14-8 Select an account name.

1.5 HOURS

Lab Exercise 14.03: Upgrading a Windows Operating System

A client of yours, who has a high-end system but still uses Windows XP Professional, decides to modernize by moving to a more recent OS. He asks you to upgrade his system to Windows Vista Business. You agree to upgrade the system for him.

Learning Objectives

You need to finish at least one complete upgrade, both for practice and to prepare for questions asked on the CompTIA A+ exams.

At the end of this lab, you'll be able to

- Upgrade an operating system

✔ Cross-Reference

To refresh your memory about the ins and outs of performing a Windows upgrade, read the "Installing or Upgrading to Windows 2000 Professional," "Installing or Upgrading to Windows XP Professional," and "Installing or Upgrading to Windows Vista" sections in Chapter 14 of *Mike Meyers' CompTIA A+ Guide to Managing and Troubleshooting PCs*.

Lab Materials and Setup

The materials you need for this lab are

- A working Windows XP Professional PC with a hard drive that you can write to without negative consequences (make sure it can also run Windows Vista)

- A Windows Vista installation disc

✔ **Hint**

A Windows Vista installation disc has every edition of Windows Vista on it, and you can install any edition you want on your computer for a 30-day trial without a product key. So if you don't have a product key for Vista Business, don't worry—you can just install a trial!

Getting Down to Business

You'll need quite a bit of time to complete this lab; most of that time will be spent waiting for Windows to install files. The exercise will walk you through upgrading a Windows XP Professional system to Windows Vista Business. Depending on the systems and software licenses you have available, you may not be able to do this lab exactly as it's laid out here. The important thing is that you actually perform a Windows upgrade, to see the questions that are asked during the installation and to become familiar with the process so that you're prepared for the CompTIA A+ certification exams.

Step 1 You've completed the compatibility exercise in the earlier labs, and you know whether or not your system can handle Windows Vista. Since you won't actually be *using* Vista, just installing it, the main consideration for performing this installation is hard drive space. Make sure you have at least 40 GB of hard drive space available on the computer you're upgrading. Whereas it will be important in later labs to have a PC that can capably run Vista, you can complete this lab if you don't have a Vista-capable PC.

The first step to doing an upgrade installation of Windows Vista is to make sure your computer is booted into XP. Because an upgrade installation is meant to be installed on a computer with a preexisting OS, Vista will not allow you to do an upgrade installation unless you start the installation while booted into another Windows OS. So, with your computer booted up, insert the Vista installation disc, wait until the Setup program starts, and click Install now.

Step 2 When asked whether or not you want to download the latest updates for installation, choose the second option, *Do not get the latest updates for installation*. Ordinarily, you would agree to do this, but it can take a long time to complete this download, and you'll be updating this computer in Lab Exercise 14.05, so you don't need to bother right now.

Step 3 If you have a legitimate Vista product key, enter it on the next screen (see Figure 14-9). If not, just click Next and then answer No to the dialog box that pops up asking you if you want to enter your product key.

Step 4 Select Windows Vista BUSINESS from the next screen asking which edition of Vista you purchased, click the checkbox at the bottom of the page, and then click Next.

Step 5 The next screen is the End User License Agreement (EULA), shown in Figure 14-10. This document enumerates the deal made between you and Microsoft that you agree to by installing their software. EULAs typically contain a great deal of legalese, and are generally quite lengthy, and the Vista EULA is no exception. You are certainly free to read through it if you like, but you don't have to. When you're done, check the box that says *I accept the license terms* and click Next.

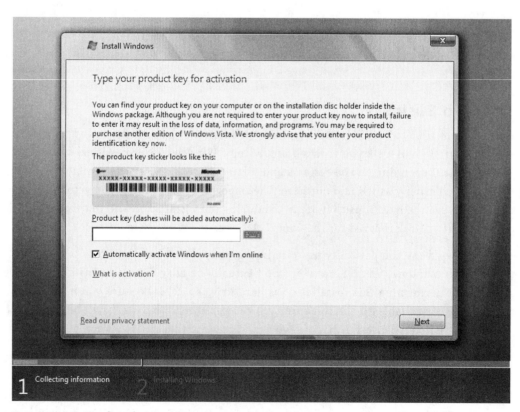

FIGURE 14-9 Product key screen

Figure 14-10 Vista EULA agreement screen

Step 6 The next screen enables you to choose either an upgrade installation or a custom installation. For this lab, you're doing an upgrade installation, so select that box. This option may or may not be available to you based on the version of Windows XP that you're starting with and the edition of Vista you're installing to, as you saw in the first lab in this chapter. The Vista installer may give you an error at this point, and if it does, follow any instructions it gives you and start the installation process again. If there are no errors, click Next.

Step 7 Wait around for a while as Windows installs itself.

Step 8 Wait some more.

Step 9 Twiddle your thumbs.

Step 10 Why does it have to copy files and then "gather" them? What does that even mean?

Step 11 Oh, hey! It finished! Once the installer's done copying files, it will ask you how you want to set up Windows Update. Generally, there's no reason not to select the first option, Use recommended settings, so click that now.

Step 12 Now you're asked to set your time zone, the time, and the date. Make sure all the settings are correct and click Next.

Step 13 If your computer has network access, the installer will ask you whether you are on a home, work, or public network. Answer appropriately.

Step 14 You're done! Click Start and enjoy the Vista experience. After installing Vista, you will have 30 days to run the Windows Activation Client to activate Windows, or else the OS will stop functioning, so keep that in mind, especially if you didn't enter a product key.

 60 MINUTES

Lab Exercise 14.04: Performing a Clean Installation

Your boss has traditionally ordered new workstations already assembled and loaded with the desired Windows OS. She recently decided that with her great in-house techs, she should be buying PC parts from a wholesaler instead, and having you and your team build the systems. You've enjoyed choosing the various hardware components and building these custom machines, but now it's time to bring your creations to life! You need to load Windows Vista Business onto these new machines that have never seen the light of day.

Learning Objectives

You should complete at least one clean Windows installation, both for the experience and to prepare for questions asked on the CompTIA A+ exams.

At the end of this lab, you'll be able to

- Install a Windows operating system on a blank hard drive

Lab Materials and Setup

The materials you need for this lab are

- A working PC with a blank hard drive, or with a hard drive that you can write to without negative consequences

- A Windows Vista installation disc

Getting Down to Business

In this exercise, you'll be putting an operating system onto a hard drive that doesn't currently have one. Even if the hard drive has an operating system on it, doing a clean installation will format that drive and erase all its data, so be sure you've backed up any important files!

Step 1 Insert the Windows Vista installation DVD into the optical drive, close the tray, and wait for the Install Windows screen to appear. Vista will first ask you to select your preferred language (see Figure 14-11). After you do so, click Next. Then, click Install now.

FIGURE 14-11 Language selection screen

Step 2   This process is almost identical to the upgrade installation, with a few key differences, so if you start to feel a sense of déjà-vu, just stick with it. Here are the steps for performing a clean installation of Windows Vista:

a.   If you have a legitimate Vista product key, enter in the appropriate box. If not, just click Next and then answer No to the dialog box that pops up asking you if you want to enter your product key.

b.   If you didn't enter a product key, select Windows Vista BUSINESS from the next screen asking which edition of Vista you purchased, click the checkbox at the bottom of the page, and then click Next.

c.   The next screen is your old friend, the End User License Agreement (EULA). When you're done reading it, check the box that says *I accept the license terms and click Next.*

d.   The next screen, shown in Figure 14-12, is the fork in the Windows Vista installer's road. You've already tried the Upgrade button (which should be grayed out, since you booted from the installation disc), so go ahead and click Custom (advanced) to do a clean installation.

e.   The next screen is the disk partitioning page, where you can select which drive to install Vista to, as well as how to partition that drive. You should already be familiar with partitioning drives using this screen, but that's not important for now. Simply select the drive you wish to install to and click Next.

f.   Wait once again for Windows Vista to install itself (it shouldn't take quite as long this time).

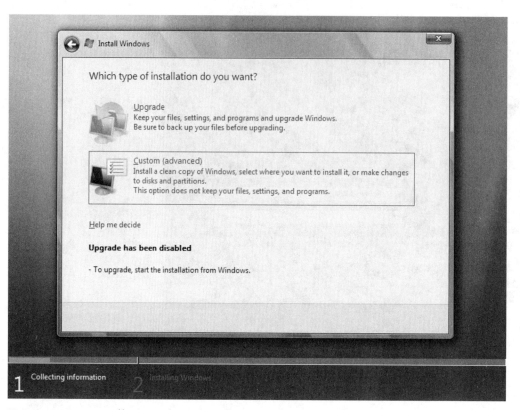

FIGURE 14-12 Installation selection with grayed out upgrade option

g.   Hey, that was pretty fast! Once the installer's done copying files, it will ask you for a user name and password. Type in your name and a password that you can remember, and click Next.

h.   The next screen asks you for a computer name, which you can generally leave as the default, unless you have a good reason to change it. You can also select one of Vista's other desktop wallpapers here, so do that if you want, and then click Next.

i.   Now you're back in familiar territory, at the screen asking how you want to set up Windows Update. Generally, there's no reason not to select the first option, *Use recommended settings*, so click that now.

j.   Now you're asked to set your time zone, the time, and the date. Make sure all the settings are correct and click Next.

k.   If your computer has network access, the installer will ask you whether you are on a home, work, or public network. Answer appropriately.

l.   You're done! Click Start and enjoy the Vista experience.

1-3 HOURS

Lab Exercise 14.05: Post-Installation Tasks: Drivers and Updates

As a tech, you will run into countless well-meaning, industrious, but ultimately hopeless customers who have taken their OS installation into their own hands, only to find that some critical piece of hardware doesn't work properly post-installation. Because of this, you absolutely must become well versed in the art of finding and installing hardware drivers and Windows updates.

Imagine, then, that you have a friend who has been happily using Windows XP Professional on his custom-built PC for a few years, but recently got a little cocky and decided that he'd do his own upgrade to Windows Vista, which seemed to go pretty well. Only now, his wireless networking card doesn't work. And his graphics card seems to be acting kind of funny. And he can't hear any sound. And ... you get the picture. Because you're an excellent tech, you instantly recognize the problem, and you graciously let him know that the problem is a result of his not properly following up his Windows installation with the appropriate driver installations. Then, of course, you offer to help him out.

✔ Cross-Reference

To review the process of installing drivers and updates, refer to the "Post-Installation Tasks" section in Chapter 14 of *Mike Meyers' CompTIA A+ Guide to Managing and Troubleshooting PCs*.

Learning Objectives

In this exercise, you'll learn how to finish up an installation by installing hardware drivers and operating system updates.

At the end of this lab, you'll be able to

- Find and install the correct hardware drivers for your operating system
- Install updates to the operating system

Lab Materials and Setup

The materials you need for this lab are

- A working Windows Vista PC
- Internet access
- A notepad and pencil
- Possibly a second PC and a thumb drive or other removable media

Getting Down to Business

The first thing you should do post-installation is to upgrade your operating system, so you'll learn how to do that before you move on to finding and installing drivers.

Step 1 When you install Windows Vista, it installs basic drivers for a wide range of products, so it's highly likely that Vista will immediately have Internet access. If that isn't the case, you will have to use another computer to find network drivers for your Vista PC, and then use a thumb drive or other removable media to transfer them over. For more information on how to do that, see the next step of this lab.

Once you have Internet access, click Start | All Programs | Windows Update. Over the years, Microsoft has made this a fairly painless process, so all you have to do is click the Check for updates button and wait.

When Windows Update has finished finding updates for your OS, click the Install updates button to begin the installation process. If you're curious about the updates being installed, you can click the View available updates button for more information.

After clicking the Install updates button, you may be asked to agree to further license agreements, which you should agree to. Then, Vista will download and install any updates it found. Note that for a just-installed OS, this can take a long time, so you may have to be patient for this step.

Once the updates have all been downloaded and installed, you will be asked to restart your computer. Do so, and you're done. Sometimes, it's a good idea to run Windows Update again after updating, just to make sure it got everything, but that's really up to you.

Step 2 Once you've got your operating system updated (or if you need drivers to access the Internet), it's time to install hardware drivers. On a custom-built PC, this step can be pretty intimidating, since you can't just go to, say, Dell's Web site and download all the drivers in bulk. Instead, you have to track down drivers for each and every component in your system. This can be a time-consuming process, but there are a few tools that all good geeks should know about that can drastically reduce the frustration of this process.

The first thing to do when looking for drivers is to check Device Manager to get an idea about what drivers you should be looking for. To get to Device Manager, right-click My Computer, go to Properties, select the Hardware tab, and click Device Manager (in Vista, just open the Start menu, type Device Manager into the Smart Search bar, and then click the Device Manager icon).

If you see "Video controller (VGA compatible)" listed in Device Manager with a yellow question mark next to it, you know you need to look for graphics drivers. If you see "Ethernet controller" listed, you know you need to look for drivers for your network interface card, and so on. Most of the missing-driver descriptions should give you a hint as to what they are for.

To find the drivers, shut down your computer, open the case, and look at the motherboard, graphics card, and any other expansion cards the PC may have, like sound cards, TV tuners, and so forth. Often, these parts will have a manufacturer and model number on them somewhere, such as Gigabyte

GA-MA790GPT-UD3H written on your motherboard, or NVIDIA GeForce GTX 260 on your graphics card. Write those things down and then do a Google search for them. If you can find the manufacturer, just go to its Web site, look up your product, and follow the link to download drivers.

Sometimes, you're not lucky enough to get a manufacturer or model number, but just about every device out there should have a sticker with some sort of part number or serial number on it. Usually, doing a quick Google search for that number and the word "driver" will get you the results you need. Finding drivers can be pretty frustrating, but keep searching and you're almost guaranteed to find what you're after.

In today's computing world, if you can find your motherboard's chipset drivers, most of the unknown driver icons in Device Manager will go away, so concentrate on finding your motherboard drivers first, and the expansion cards second.

Lab Analysis Test

1. Phyllis wants to do an upgrade installation from Windows XP Professional to Windows Vista, and the Windows Vista Upgrade Advisor says her computer is eligible for an upgrade installation. However, when she boots her computer from the Vista installation disc, the Upgrade option is grayed out. Why is that?

2. What's the recommended CPU speed and amount of RAM needed to install Windows Vista Business?

3. Dwight wants to upgrade his old Windows XP system to Windows Vista, but he isn't sure whether his hardware is sufficient to support Vista. What Microsoft tools would you recommend that he use to check his system?

4. Michael is about to replace his aging Windows XP Home machine with a hotrod PC running Windows Vista Ultimate, but he wants to transfer all his documents to the new computer. What tool can you recommend that he use to do that?

5. What happens if you don't run the Windows Activation Client for Windows Vista within 30 days of installation?

Key Term Quiz

Use the following terms to complete the following sentences. Not all terms will be used.

1 GHz

installation

network drive

optical drive upgrade

Upgrade Advisor

Windows 2000 Professional

Windows XP Home Edition

Windows XP Professional

Windows Vista Business

Windows Vista Home Premium

Windows Vista Ultimate

1. If you plan to install Windows Vista onto a system, it must have a(n) _____.

2. You can start with a blank hard drive to perform a clean _____ of Windows Vista.

3. You can use the _____ to see if your computer is capable of running Windows Vista.

4. Installing Windows Vista on a system currently running Windows XP is known as a(n) _____.

5. _____ can be upgraded to any edition of Windows Vista.

Chapter 15
Working with the Command-Line Interface

Lab Exercises

Although the CompTIA A+ certification exams have dropped the requirements of working with the MS-DOS operating system, they do stipulate that PC technicians should know some of the basic commands and functions available at the command-line interface in all versions of Windows. Why? Because they still work, and good techs use the command line often. You'll need a solid understanding of several basic command-line commands, and a few advanced tasks. Commands such as CD, COPY, and ATTRIB, as well as the tasks of starting and stopping services, editing files, and converting file systems, should be part of your PC tech arsenal.

If you have a system crash and are able to gain access to the machine using Windows XP's Recovery Console or Windows Vista's System Recovery Options, you'll really need to know the proper commands for navigating around your drives, folders, and files, and launching utilities that will get your OS up and running again. Also, when you start working with networks, the command-line interface on all Windows systems is invaluable.

✔ **Cross-Reference**

You will further explore the use of the Recovery Console and System Recovery Options in the lab exercises for Chapter 17. You will also have the opportunity to work with additional networking command-line utilities in the lab exercises for Chapter 23.

The command line can often provide a quicker way to accomplish a task than the graphical alternative. In cases where a virus, hard drive failure, or OS problem prevents you from booting to Windows, you need to know how to get around with the command line. The following labs are designed to give you the chance to practice your basic command-line skills so that when the need arises, the command line will be your friend.

✔ **Hint**

As you have worked through the labs in this manual, I have recommended often that you explore features, options, and components not specifically covered in the lab exercises. You have embarked on the journey to become a CompTIA A+ certified technician! Natural curiosity, enthusiasm, and determination will go a long way toward developing the understanding and experience you need to become a competent technician and pass the exams. These qualities are especially important when it comes to working with the command-line interface. As you navigate through the following labs, it is easy to take a left when you should have taken a right and get lost in subdirectories, mistype a command, or delete a file you didn't want to. Don't let it discourage you.

Making mistakes while learning is good, and learning from those mistakes is great! If you get lost, explore ways to get back to where you need to be—you're unlikely to hurt anything. If you really get lost, work with your instructor or a more experienced classmate to determine where you went astray, then work through it again.

 30 MINUTES

Lab Exercise 15.01: Configuring the Command-Line Window

Before you can use the command line, you need to know the basics: ways to access it, manipulate and customize the look of it within the GUI, and close it down properly. This lab covers those basics.

Learning Objectives

In this lab, you'll practice opening, resizing, customizing, and closing a command-line window.

At the end of this lab, you'll be able to

- Open a command-line window from within the Windows operating system

- Resize the command-line window

- Customize the look of the command-line window

- Exit the command-line window

Lab Materials and Setup

The materials you need for this lab are

- A PC with Windows installed

Getting Down to Business

The first thing you'll need to do, obviously, is get to a command line. Spend the next several minutes becoming familiar with accessing the command-line window.

✔ Cross-Reference

For details on how to access the command-line interface, refer to the "Accessing the Command Line" section in Chapter 15 of *Mike Meyers' CompTIA A+ Guide to Managing and Troubleshooting PCs*.

Step 1　Turn on your system, and wait for the Windows desktop to appear. Then follow these steps:

    a.　In Windows 2000/XP, select Start | Run, then type **CMD** (see Figure 15-1). In Windows Vista, select Start, then type **CMD** into the Search box.

    b.　In 2000/XP, click OK to open a command-line window. In Vista, press ENTER.

Step 2　There are three ways to change the size of the command-line window for better viewing:

- Use the resize arrows along the edges of the windows (this will not work when the window is maximized).

- Use the minimize/maximize button in the upper-right corner of the window.

- Press ALT-ENTER to toggle between the full screen mode and a window.

Step 3　In Windows 2000, you should be looking at a black screen with your operating system information in the upper-left corner and a C prompt (C:\>) below. Windows XP will have a different prompt (C:\Documents and Settings\username>), and the Windows Vista prompt will display C:\Users\ username>. This just means that in Windows 2000, the command line opens as a default at the root of the C: drive, whereas Windows XP and Windows Vista open with the focus pointing to the user's personal area in the Documents and Settings or Users folder, respectively.

FIGURE 15-1　Opening the Windows XP command-line window

To the right of the prompt, you'll see a flashing cursor indicating that it's waiting for your input. There's also a scroll bar along the right side of the window. Sometimes your command causes more information to be displayed than the window can hold, and it's really useful to be able to scroll back up and see what messages were displayed.

You'll now execute a few commands, for the purpose of exploring the scrolling issue. The Change Directory command (CD) lets you change the focus of the working directory displayed in the command-line window. The Directory command (DIR) lists the filename, extension, file size (in bytes), and creation date/time of the files in the current folder.

You are going to change from the current working directory to a subdirectory with hundreds of files. Type **CD C:\WINDOWS\SYSTEM32** (C:\ is the root directory, WINDOWS is the system folder, and SYSTEM32 is where many of the system configuration and driver files are stored). You may have to use a different drive letter or system folder name to arrive at the SYSTEM32 directory.

Now type **DIR** and press ENTER. The SYSTEM32 folder contains over 1000 files, so the command-line window will not be able to display all of the information at once. If there's more than one screen's worth of information, it will keep scrolling out of sight until everything has been displayed. You can use the scroll bar to go back a few screens' worth—give it a try.

If you were actually trying to work with a few of the files in the folder, you'd probably be out of luck, because you can't scroll back more than a few screens. To address this problem, there's a command you can use that forces the information to be displayed one screenful at a time. Type **DIR /P** and then press ENTER. Adding the /P switch to the command tells it to pause after each screenful of text. Press the SPACEBAR to display the next screenful. You can't go back if you're too quick with the SPACEBAR, so take a good look at each screen! If you tire of paging through the screens, you can end the command by pressing CTRL-C.

Step 4 Just as with most applets in the Windows environment, if you right-click the title bar and select Properties, you can configure some of the features of the command-line window:

- **Options** Configure the cursor size, command history, display options, and edit options.

- **Font** Select from a limited set of command-line fonts and sizes.

- **Layout** Set the screen buffer size and window size, and position the window on the monitor screen.

- **Colors** Configure the color of screen text, screen background, pop-up text, and pop-up background.

→ **Note**

Some features differ depending on which operating system you are using. For example, Windows Vista does not offer the Display Options panel in the Command Prompt Properties dialog box.

Explore some of the settings you can change, and feel free to set up the command-line window to your personal taste. I grew up on early IBM machines, in the days when owning a color monitor meant that you had an electric green or bright orange character on a black monochrome screen. See if you can re-create this wonderful look!

Step 5 There are two common ways to close a command-line window:

- Click the × in the upper-right corner of the window. This method isn't recommended if the window is actively running a program. You should wait until you see the prompt before clicking the ×.

- Type **EXIT** at the command line, and press ENTER. I prefer this method, because I can be sure the window is inactive when I quit.

 30 MINUTES

Lab Exercise 15.02: Navigating Basic Commands

Before you can really use the command line, you must know the basic commands needed to navigate around a drive to locate and modify files. In this lab exercise, you'll learn more basic command-line commands that you would need to know when troubleshooting your or your client's PC.

✔ Hint

For the most part, mistakes such as spelling a command or filename incorrectly won't be disastrous for you. But it is possible to misspell just incorrectly enough to delete the wrong file, or something similar, especially if you're using wildcards (I'll get to those in a bit). Typically, though, if you misspell a command or filename, the command line won't know what you're asking it to do and therefore won't do anything, or won't know what file you're asking to work with, and will return an error message.

Learning Objectives

In this lab, you'll learn or review commands for directory and file management while using the command line.

At the end of this lab, you'll be able to

- Use commands to view, navigate, create, and delete directories using the command line

- Use commands to copy, move, rename, and delete files using the command line

Lab Materials and Setup

The materials you need for this lab are

- At least one working computer running Windows

✔ Hint

Any version of Windows will work just fine for this exercise, as long as you understand that the results may appear differently on your screen.

Getting Down to Business

Hundreds of commands and switches are available to you from the command-line interface. Although it is beyond the scope of these exercises to explore every possible command and its associated switches, you should spend the time in this lab exercise working with the specific ones that form the cornerstone of command-line navigation. These are the basic commands you'll use most often when working with the command line.

Step 1 Follow these steps:

a. Launch the command-line interface in Windows 2000/XP by typing **CMD** in the Run dialog box and either clicking OK or pressing enter. In Windows Vista, access the command-line interface through the Start menu Search box with the same command.

b. When you first open the command-line window, your prompt might not be focused on the root directory. Because you want to focus on the root directory at this time, you must change directories before continuing.

The CD (Change Directory) command changes the directory the system is focused on. When you use the CD command, you must type the command followed by a space and then the name of the directory you want to view. This is true of all command-line commands. First, type the command followed by a space and then any options. Because you want to focus on the root of C: and the name of the root is the backslash (\), you'd type in the following and press ENTER (assuming that you're in the C: drive to begin with):

```
C:\Documents and Settings\username>CD \
```

Notice that the prompt has changed its focus to C:\> (see Figure 15-2).

Step 2 Probably the most frequently typed command is the request to display the contents of a directory (DIR). Because the command-line interface doesn't continually display everything the way a GUI does, you have to ask it to display specific information. The way you display the contents of a directory is to focus on the particular directory or subdirectory, and enter the command **DIR**.

Let's take a look at the contents of your root (C:\) directory. You should already be focused there from the previous step in this exercise. Type **DIR** at the command prompt and press ENTER.

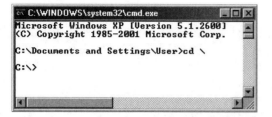

FIGURE 15-2 Changing the command-line focus

 Hint

From now on, when you see an instruction to type a command, you should assume that you should press ENTER afterward to complete the request (command). Otherwise, the command line will sit there, waiting patiently until the sun grows cold.

Now here's where it gets a little gray. Because I don't know what's in your root directory, there's no way to predict exactly what your C:\ contents will look like—but it's a good bet that *something* will be different from what I show you here! In theory at least, your display should be similar to Figure 15-3. Windows 2000, XP, and Vista will have the same basic look.

Notice that using the DIR command in any Windows operating system gives you the following information:

- Filename
- File extension

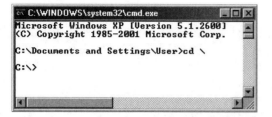

FIGURE 15-3 Viewing a sample Windows XP root directory

- Date and time of creation

- Size in bytes

- Designation as either a directory (<DIR>) or a file

- The number of files in the directory

- The amount of free space on the drive

Look at your particular results and note the mixture of files, which display a size in bytes, and directories, which have the annotation <DIR> after their name. In the preceding examples, AVG7QT.DAT is a file of 12,288,463 bytes, and WINDOWS, Program Files, and Documents and Settings are all names of directories.

Note whether you see the following files or folders in your root (C:\>) directory (you won't see them all):

	Yes	No
AUTOEXEC.BAT		
CONFIG.SYS		
WINNT		
WINDOWS		
Documents and Settings		
Program Files		

List the names of all the directories you see displayed in your root directory:

_____   _____
_____   _____
_____   _____
_____   _____
_____   _____
_____   _____

Step 3   The biggest challenge when working with the command prompt is remembering what exactly to type to achieve your goal. Learning the commands is one thing, but each command can have switches and options that modify it somewhat. Also, you may have noticed that the screen fills up and scrolls from top to bottom, making it difficult to view all the information you might need. Let's look at a command to clear the screen and another to provide assistance with how to use the commands.

Type the command **CLS**. What happened? _____

Type the command **DIR /?**. What happened? _____

The question mark (/?) is a standard help switch for most commands. Even though I've used these commands for decades, I still use the /? switch occasionally to remember what options are available for a specific command.

✔ Hint

Be careful not to confuse the backslash (\) and the forward slash (/). In a command-line world, the path uses the backslash and command switches use the forward slash.

At this point, a huge amount of help information is displayed (see Figure 15-4), so you may feel like you're in command overload! Take comfort in the fact that DIR is the most complex command. Other commands are more straightforward with their help. You don't need to know what all the switches are—just know how to use the help switch (/?) to find them! The main thing to learn is the syntax of the commands.

Everything in brackets ([ ]) is optional for the command. Notice that DIR is the only mandatory part in that command even though there are several optional switches and parameters. This is the same for all the commands. The system will use defaults if you don't specify a switch or optional parameter. It's the defaults that can cause problems if you're not careful when using these commands. Now follow these steps:

a.   Put a known good disc with files in your optical drive and let it spin up and come to rest. Cancel any windows that automatically open and proceed to the next substep.

b.   Type **DIR**, and examine the resulting list of files and folders. Did they change from the previous step? _____

FIGURE 15-4 Viewing the syntax of the DIR command

Do you think it read the disc? Probably not, because your prompt is still focused on the root directory of the hard drive.

c. **Type DIR D:** (replace D: with the appropriate drive letter for your optical drive, if necessary) and examine the resulting list of files and folders. Did they change this time? Aha! The option of [drive:] was needed to change the focus of the DIR command to the optical drive.

The [drive:] option will work for any of the drive letters. Floppy diskettes, CDs, DVDs, USB thumb drives, and Zip drives are all fair game as well. When you use this option, you can look at those other drives without switching from the directory you're in.

Step 4 Type **DIR /?** to look at two more optional switches: /P and /W. The /P switch is used when all the information will not fit on one screen, and /W is used to see a condensed listing of the directory.

Let's focus on a different directory. Remember, the CD command will let you change the directory you want to focus on:

a. Type **CD \WINDOWS**.

b. Type **CLS**.

c. Type **DIR** at the command prompt. This shows way too much data for the screen to display all at once.

d. Type **DIR /P** at the command prompt. This very useful switch causes the display to stop scrolling (pause) after each screen, waiting until you press the SPACEBAR to show you more. In directories with lots of files, this is a lifesaver!

✔ **Hint**

If you want to stop a process that seems to be running forever, you can press CTRL-C. The process will end, and you'll get the prompt back.

e. Type **DIR /W** at the command prompt. This switch is convenient when you're simply looking to see if a particular file resides in a particular directory, because it shows a "wide" list with filenames but no details.

f. Now practice moving around in the command window. Right now you're focused on the WINDOWS directory. Go back to the root directory by typing **CD **. To change the focus to another directory, use the CD command as you've learned. Use the DIR command to see what directories you have available in your current folder.

g. Try going to a subdirectory in another subdirectory and listing the contents. Look back at the list of directories you made previously and select one. Issue the CD command followed by a backslash (\) and the name of the target directory. For example, to switch to the Documents and Settings directory in the previous listing, type this:

```
C:\WINDOWS>CD \DOCUMENTS AND SETTINGS
```

Do this using several of the directory names you wrote down previously, and then type **DIR** to see what's there. Are there any subdirectories in this directory? Make a note of them.

_____　_____

_____　_____

_____　_____

✔ Hint

After you've changed the prompt focus many times, you may become confused about exactly where you are. You can always get to the root directory from any focus by typing **CD **.

Step 5　A Windows installation creates a Drivers directory, within a directory called System32, under the WINDOWS directory in the root of the C: drive. To go to the Drivers directory, you don't have to do the CD command three times unless you really want to. If you know the path, you can go directly to the subdirectory with one CD command.

Go to the Drivers subdirectory by typing this at the command prompt:

```
C:\>CD \WINDOWS\SYSTEM32\DRIVERS
```

Your prompt should now look like Figure 15-5.

Type **DIR** to see what's there.

One final navigation hint—you can change directories going back up toward the top level without returning directly to the root. If you want to go up a single directory level, you can type **CD** followed immediately by two periods (sometimes referred to as *CD dot dot*). For example, typing this takes you up one level to the System32 directory:

```
C:\>\WINDOWS\SYSTEM32\DRIVERS>CD..
C:\>\WINDOWS\SYSTEM32>
```

Do it again to go to the Windows directory:

```
C:\>\WINDOWS\SYSTEM32>CD..
C:\>\WINDOWS>
```

```
C:\Windows\System32\drivers>
```

FIGURE 15-5 Focusing on the Drivers subdirectory

Type the command once more to arrive at the root directory:

```
C:\>\WINDOWS>CD..
C:\>
```

Take a minute and practice using the CD command. Go down a few levels on the directory tree, and then jump up a few, jump back to the root directory, and then jump down another path. Practice is the only way to get comfortable moving around in a command-prompt environment, and a good PC technician needs to be comfortable doing this.

Step 6   Sometimes a technician needs to make a directory to store files on the system. This could be a temporary directory for testing purposes, or maybe a place to store something more permanently (diagnostic reports, for example). In any case, it's important that you know how to create and remove a directory. The CompTIA A+ exams will test you on this. Follow these steps:

a.   Be sure you're in the root directory. If you aren't there, type **CD ** to return to the root directory, where you'll add a new top-level directory. Actually, you can make a directory anywhere in the file structure, but you don't want to lose track of where it is, so make your new directory in the root. Do this using the MD (Make Directory) command.

b.   Type **MD /?** to see how the command is structured and view the available options (see Figure 15-6).

c.   At the command prompt, type the following:

```
C:\>MD CORVETTE
```

d.   When the command line just presents a fresh prompt, it means that everything worked correctly. But to verify that the directory was actually made, type **DIR** to see your new directory in the list. It's as simple as that!

✖ **Warning**

Be careful—the new directory will always be created wherever the prompt is focused when you issue the command, whether that's where you meant to put it or not.

e.   Be sure you're in the root directory (type **CD**), and prepare to remove your new CORVETTE directory.

```
C:\>md /?
Creates a directory.

MKDIR [drive:]path
MD [drive:]path
```

Figure 15-6 Using the MD command

Removing a directory requires the RD (Remove Directory) command and two conditions: First, the directory must be empty, and second, your system must not currently be focused on the directory about to be deleted.

f. Type this command:

`C:\>RD CORVETTE`

The directory has been deleted.

g. Type **DIR** to confirm that CORVETTE has been removed.

✔ Hint

Be *very* careful when you remove directories or delete files in the command line. It isn't as forgiving as Windows, which allows you to change your mind and "undelete" things. When you delete a file or directory using the command line, it's gone. If you make a mistake, there's nothing left to do but pout. So think carefully before you delete, and be sure you know what you're deleting before you do it—you'll save yourself a great deal of agony. Also pay attention to the directory you're currently focused on, to ensure that you're in the correct one.

Step 7 Sometimes you know the name of the file you want to use, but you don't know in which directory it's located. In this case, working with files and directories can become quite tedious. To help you locate files more easily, here are some switches and wildcards you can use with the DIR command:

a. Look again at the results of the DIR /? command, and find the /S switch. The /S switch will look for a file(s) in the specified (focus) directory and all subdirectories under that directory.

b. Windows has a file named XCOPY.EXE somewhere on the drive. Locate the path to the XCOPY. EXE file using the /S switch.

c. Start with your command prompt at the root directory (CD \).

d. Type this command:

`C:\>DIR XCOPY.EXE`

If the file isn't in the root directory, nothing will be displayed.

e. Now try the new switch you just learned about to search all subdirectories. Type this command:

`C:\>DIR /S XCOPY.EXE`

f. On my system, the file shows up in two places: in the C:\WINDOWS\system32 directory and in the C:\WINDOWS\system 32\dllcache directory (see Figure 15-7).

Another way to look for a file is to use a *wildcard*. The most common wildcard is the asterisk character (*), which you can use in place of all or part of a filename to make a command act on more than one file at a time. Wildcards work with all commands that use filenames.

FIGURE 15-7 Locating the XCOPY.EXE file

The * wildcard replaces any number of letters before or after the dot in the filename. A good way to think of the * wildcard is "I don't care." Replace the part of the filename that you don't care about with *.

For example, if you want to locate all the README files on a hard drive and you don't care what the extension is, type the following:

C:\>**DIR /S/P readme.***

The result is a list of all the README files on the hard drive. Notice that I used the /S switch to look in all the directories and used the /P switch so that I can view one screenful of results at a time (see Figure 15-8).

FIGURE 15-8 Using a wildcard to locate files

```
C:\ D:\WINDOWS\System32\cmd.exe - DIR /S/P *read*.*                          _ □ X
 Volume in drive C is LOCAL DISK
 Volume Serial Number is FC74-59D7

 Directory of C:\Program Files\E-Color\3Deep

05/07/2001  04:43 PM              4,966 Readme.txt
05/07/2001  04:43 PM              4,966 ReadmeNT.txt
               2 File(s)          9,932 bytes

 Directory of C:\Program Files\E-Color\E-Color Indicator

05/02/2001  04:39 PM              4,802 ReadMe.txt
               1 File(s)          4,802 bytes

 Directory of C:\Work Files

10/20/2001  12:30 PM              6,895 Style Guide Proofreader's and Editor's Sy
mbols.htm
02/21/2003  01:02 PM    <DIR>           Style Guide Proofreader's and Editor's Sy
mbols_files
               1 File(s)          6,895 bytes

Press any key to continue . . . _
```

FIGURE 15-9 Using a wildcard to locate *READ*.* files

You can use the * wildcard for any number of characters. For example, not all companies use README.TXT as the help filename. Some use READ.ME, and others may use READ.

Because READ is common to all those variations, let's find all the files with READ in the filename. You should be prepared to see a long list of every file with READ in the name, not just the README files.

Type the following:

```
C:\>DIR /S/P *read*.*
```

Figure 15-9 shows the first screenful of results from my system. I found 104 files with READ somewhere in the filename. How many files and directories did you find with READ as part of the name?

 30 MINUTES

Lab Exercise 15.03: Using Command-Line Tools

Commands such as TYPE, COPY, MOVE, RENAME, and DELETE are used for manipulating files, such as you would be doing while troubleshooting a client's PC. These are more of the commands that every working tech should know by heart.

Learning Objectives

In this lab, you'll use commands for file management.

At the end of this lab, you'll be able to

- View text (.TXT) documents from the command-line interface
- Rename files using the command-line interface
- Copy files using the command-line interface
- Move files using the command-line interface
- Delete files using the command-line interface

Lab Materials and Setup

The materials you need for this lab are

- At least one working computer running Windows

Getting Down to Business

You might refer to these as the "second-tier" commands. Once you've used commands such as DIR, MD, and CD to navigate and create folders, you can use the following commands to manipulate individual files.

Step 1   In Lab Exercise 4.02, you created a text document using Notepad that you can safely use to explore file commands in this chapter. You will now navigate to your My Documents folder and verify that the file is there and contains readable text:

   a.   If you don't already have the command-line window open, get to a command prompt.

   b.   Enter the following commands:

```
C:\>CD \Documents and Settings\%USERNAME%\My Documents

C:\Documents and Settings\%USERNAME%\My Documents\>DIR /P
```

✔ Hint

To locate the file you created in Lab Exercise 4.02 and saved to My Documents, you should be logged on as the same user. The variable %USERNAME% (including the preceding and trailing percent signs) in the command-line syntax represents the user name you're currently using. Microsoft has assembled many variables that can be used in this manner, such as %SYSTEMROOT% to represent the system folder (usually named WINNT or WINDOWS). You may actually use the variable in the command-line syntax to have the system insert your user name (the folder where all of your personal settings and saved documents are) in the path. I have included a generic example of the use of this variable in Figure 15-10.

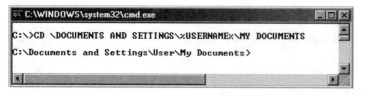

FIGURE 15-10 Using an environment variable to insert the user name

Do you see the file you created in Lab Exercise 4.02? (It should be called Command Line Test.TXT.)

_____

Now you will use another command to verify that the file is a text file containing readable text. There are many ways to do this; you'll use one of the simplest methods. The TYPE command displays the contents of a text file, but doesn't allow you to edit or manipulate the text in any way.

c.   Enter the following (carefully enter the line in the exact syntax as shown, including the quotation marks):

```
C:\Documents and Settings\%USERNAME%\My Documents\>TYPE "COMMAND LINE TEST.TXT"
```

You should see the text that you entered in Notepad during Lab Exercise 4.02. All of the text should be displayed, although you may have to resize your command-line window to see all of it, and even then it won't be pretty.

The other thing you may have noticed is that to access the text file, you had to add quotation marks to the beginning and the end of the filename. This is because the command line only understands spaces as breaks between commands and operators or switches. Leave the quote marks out of the command line and run the **TYPE** command again. What happened? _____

You should see something similar to the output in Figure 15-11.

You're going to use this file in the next few steps, and it will be easier to work with if its format conforms to the 8.3 rule. In the early days of MS-DOS, filenames could only be eight characters long, with a three-character extension after the period. The three-character extension has remained throughout all versions of Microsoft operating systems, but you can now use up to 255 characters

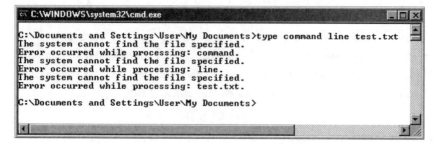

FIGURE 15-11 Results of running TYPE without using quotation marks

(with spaces) as the filename. To make this file easier to work with in the command line, you'll use the REN (Rename) command to change the filename.

d.   Type the following command:

C:\Documents and Settings\%USERNAME%\My Documents\>**REN "COMMAND LINE TEST.TXT" CMDLNTST.TXT**

e.   Now confirm that this has worked by typing the following command:

C:\Documents and Settings\%USERNAME%\My Documents\>**TYPE CMDLNTST.TXT**

Great! Now you will be able to type the filename more quickly as you complete the rest of the exercise.

Step 2   At the command prompt, type **CD ** to change your focus to the root directory.

You'll now create a new directory called STUDY in the root so that you can do some copying and moving. The only difference between copying and moving is that COPY leaves the original file in the same place (as a backup) with a duplicate made elsewhere, whereas the MOVE command relocates the original file to a new location with no backup available. They're otherwise similar, so once you've learned the COPY command, you've pretty much learned the MOVE command too! Follow these steps:

a.   Make a directory named STUDY by typing the following:

C:\>**MD STUDY**

b.   Verify that the directory is there by using the DIR command.

Now follow these steps for copying your file named CMDLNTST.TXT to the new STUDY directory:

c.   Change the focus of the command prompt to the STUDY directory:

C:\>**CD STUDY**

d.   Copy the CMDLNTST.TXT file to the STUDY directory:

C:\STUDY>**COPY "C:\DOCUMENTS AND SETTINGS\%USERNAME%\MY DOCUMENTS\CMDLNTST.TXT" C:\STUDY\CMDLNTST.TXT**

Here, COPY is the command, C:\DOCUMENTS AND SETTINGS\%USERNAME%\MY DOCUMENTS\ CMDLNTST.TXT is the current location and name of the file (notice the use of the quotation marks and the %USERNAME% variable once again), and C:\STUDY\CMDLNTST.TXT is the target location and name of the file.

The entire command and response will look similar to Figure 15-12.

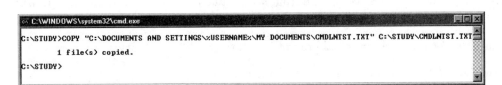

FIGURE 15-12 COPY command and response

e.   Run the DIR command to see if you copied the file. If the file isn't there, carefully repeat the previous steps or ask your instructor for help.

f.   Change your directory focus back to the My Documents folder (**CD \DOCUMENTS AND SETTINGS\%USERNAME%\MY DOCUMENTS**) and run the DIR command to see if the original CMDLNTST.TXT file is still there.

✔ **Hint**

If you're already in the target directory, you don't need to include the target path in the command. My idea of copying or moving files is to start in the directory to which you want to copy the files. Then you can bring the files to where you are. Each time you copy or move a file, you can run the DIR command to see if it's actually there. The other way of sending a file to a directory can be troublesome if you're moving files, because you may accidentally send them to a wrong directory and waste time looking for them.

Another good use of the COPY command is to make a backup copy of a file and rename it at the same time, so that the two files can reside in the same directory.

g.   To make a backup of the CMDLNTST.TXT text file, type the following command:

```
C:\STUDY\>copy CMDLNTST.TXT CMDLNTST.BAK
```

You now have three copies of the same file; you will clean these up in the last step.

Step 3   The last two commands you will work with in this step are the MOVE and DEL (Delete) commands. First, you will delete the copy of CMDLNTST.TXT that you copied into the STUDY folder in the last step. You will then move the file permanently from the My Documents folder to the STUDY folder. Follow these steps:

a.   Change the focus of the command prompt to the STUDY directory:

```
C:\>CD STUDY
```

b.   Delete the CMDLNTST.TXT file from the STUDY directory:

```
C:\STUDY\>DEL CMDLNTST.TXT
```

c.   Run the DIR command to see if you deleted the file. If the file isn't there, you deleted it.

Now you will follow the steps to move the file from My Documents to the STUDY folder. You will then verify that the file is in the STUDY folder and no longer in the My Documents folder.

d.   Make sure the focus of the command prompt is still the STUDY directory.

e.   Move the CMDLNTST.TXT file to the STUDY directory:

```
C:\STUDY>MOVE "C:\DOCUMENTS AND SETTINGS\%USERNAME%\MY DOCUMENTS\CMDLNTST.TXT"
C:\STUDY\CMDLNTST.TXT
```

In this case, MOVE is the command, C:\DOCUMENTS AND SETTINGS\%USERNAME%\MY DOCUMENTS\CMDLNTST.TXT is the current location and name of the file (notice the use of the quotation marks and the %USERNAME% variable once again), and C:\STUDY\CMDLNTST.TXT is the target location and name of the file.

f. Run the DIR command to see if you moved the file. If the file isn't there, repeat the previous steps or ask your instructor for help.

g. Change your directory focus back to the My Documents folder (**CD \DOCUMENTS AND SETTINGS\%USERNAME%\MY DOCUMENTS**) and run the DIR command to see if the original CMDLNTST.TXT file is still there. Do you see it? _____ Why or why not?

_____

You should now have two copies of the file in the STUDY directory, CMDLNTST.TXT and CMDLNTST.BAK. The file should have been moved from the My Documents directory.

🕐 60 MINUTES

Lab Exercise 15.04: Advanced Command-Line Utilities

In Windows, you can perform many tasks either from the GUI or from the command-line window. The CompTIA A+ exams want you to be comfortable with both methods to accomplish these tasks. To practice your skills with the command-line versions of these tasks, work through the following scenarios and steps to explore the attributes, the Print Spooler service, and the NTFS file system, all with the view from the command prompt.

Learning Objectives

In this lab, you'll work through three scenarios.

At the end of this lab, you'll be able to

- Work with the ATTRIB and EDIT utilities
- Start and stop services with the NET command
- Convert file systems

Lab Materials and Setup

The materials you need for this lab are

- At least one working computer running Windows
- A hard drive with at least 1 GB of unallocated space, or a 1-GB or greater partition formatted with the FAT32 file system

> ✔ **Hint**
>
> If the machines configured with multiple hard drives are still available from Lab Exercise 12.05, "Implementing Software RAID 0 with Disk Management," you can convert these back to basic disks and format them with FAT32 to use in Step 3 of this exercise.

Getting Down to Business

Working through commands as you have in the prior exercises is an excellent method to explore the commands and their usage, but it can seem a little sterile since the commands are isolated and out of context. The next few steps are built around scenarios common in the workplace, requiring you to perform tasks that incorporate both commands you have learned in prior exercises and new commands that will be introduced as needed.

Step 1   In the steps that follow, you will use the ATTRIB command to alter the attributes of a text file.

   a.   Create a new folder in the root directory. Name it **Folder**. Inside that folder, create a new text document and name it **TEXT.TXT**.

   b.   Using your favorite method, launch the command prompt and change your focus to the new folder you created.

   c.   To list the files and all of their attributes, use the ATTRIB command:

   `C:\FOLDER>`**`ATTRIB`**

   Because the folder contains one file, the only file that should be listed is your new text document. Notice the *A* to the left of where TEXT.TXT is listed. This means that the Archive attribute has been applied. To make this blank text file more secure, we'll add two more attributes: R (Read Only) and H (Hidden). For more options, type **ATTRIB /?**.

   d.   To change the attributes for TEXT.TXT, type the following command:

   `C:\FOLDER>`**`ATTRIB +R +H TEXT.TXT`**

   This will add the Read Only and Hidden attributes to the text file. Verify this by using My Computer/Computer to navigate to the folder and checking its contents. Do any files show up in the folder? _____

   e.   Now change the attributes for TEXT.TXT again so that it's not Read-only or Hidden anymore. Type the following command:

   `C:\FOLDER>`**`ATTRIB -R -H text.txt`**

   Return again to the folder in My Computer/Computer and verify that the text file has reappeared.

Step 2   One recurring problem you will run into in the field is that one of the services in Windows will stall—in particular the Print Spooler. The Print Spooler is a holding area for print jobs, and it's especially important for network printers. If the print device runs out of paper while printing a document, you may have to stop and start the Print Spooler to allow the print device to receive jobs again. Typically, you just open the Computer Management console, select Services, and restart the service. However, there may be times when it is more convenient or just plain necessary to accomplish this task from the command-line interface.

The following steps walk you through stopping and starting the Print Spooler from the command-line interface:

a.   Launch the Services console by opening the Control Panel, launching the Administrative Tools applet, and double-clicking Services.

b.   Scroll down and highlight the Print Spooler, then select Action | Properties. You should see that the Print Spooler is started and running (see Figure 15-13).

c.   Launch the command-line interface and change the focus to the root directory.

d.   Type the following command at the prompt:

C:**NET STOP SPOOLER**

The command line should inform you that the Print Spooler service is stopping, and then that the Print Spooler service was stopped successfully (see Figure 15-14).

FIGURE 15-13 The Print Spooler Properties window

FIGURE 15-14 Stopping the Print Spooler service from the command-line interface

✔ **Cross-Reference**

You will explore the NET command-line utility in the lab exercises for Chapter 23. If you would like to explore the NET command while working on this lab, type NET /?.

e. Using ALT-TAB, change your focus to the Print Spooler Properties window you opened earlier. You should be able to confirm that the Print Spooler service has been stopped (see Figure 15-15).

FIGURE 15-15 The Print Spooler Properties window after stopping the service

f.   Change the focus back to the command-line window, and type the following command at the prompt:

```
C:\NET START SPOOLER
```

The command line should inform you that the Print Spooler service is starting, and then that the Print Spooler service was started successfully (see Figure 15-16).

In the real-world scenario, your Print Spooler service would be restarted, and you should have a healthy, functioning print server once again. Now you just have to figure out where you stored the extra toner!

Step 3   Many of the legacy systems in the field started out as Windows 98 or Windows 2000 machines. Often, these systems' hard drives were partitioned and formatted with the FAT32 file system. As you upgrade these systems, you may want to leave the FAT32 file system intact until you verify that the upgrade has been successful. After successful completion of the upgrade, it is recommended that you convert the file system to NTFS. This is a nondestructive, one-way conversion! Once you switch to NTFS, you will have to delete the data and reformat the partition if you want to revert to FAT32.

In this step, you will create a FAT32 partition (unless you already have one from earlier labs) and then use the command-line utility called CONVERT to convert the partition to NTFS.

a.   Boot a computer system with at least 1 GB of unallocated hard drive space. If you have access to the system you used to explore RAID 0 (striping), you can use the extra hard drives installed in the system.

b.   Launch the Disk Management console. Right-click My Computer/Computer and select Manage.

c.   Click Disk Management.

d.   Right-click an area of unallocated space and select New Volume from the drop-down menu.

e.   Follow the wizard instructions to create a FAT32 partition of at least 1 GB.

✔ **Cross-Reference**

To refresh your Disk Management skills, refer to Chapter 12, Lab Exercise 12.03, "Using Windows Tools to Create and Format Partitions."

Figure 15-16 Starting the Print Spooler service from the command-line interface

f. Close the Disk Management console and double-click My Computer/Computer. Create and save a text file to the new drive to verify that the drive is accessible. Right-click the drive and select Properties; notice the tabs and file system (see Figure 15-17).

Now that you have a FAT32 partition, you can launch the command-line window and convert the file system from FAT32 to NTFS. You will then verify that the conversion was indeed nondestructive by opening the text file you created in Step f.

g. Launch the command-line window and change the focus to the root directory using the **CD ** command.

h. Type the following command at the prompt (substitute the drive letter for your FAT32 partition):

C:**CONVERT E: /FS:NTFS**

Your result should look similar to Figure 15-18.

i. Exit the command-line window and double-click My Computer/Computer.

j. Right-click the drive that you just converted and select Properties. Your drive should now be formatted with the NTFS file system. Notice the additional tabs for Security and Quota (see Figure 15-19).

k. Close the Properties window and double-click the drive. The text document you created in Step f during the setup should still be there and accessible.

FIGURE 15-17 FAT32 partition properties

FIGURE 15-18 Converting a partition from FAT32 to NTFS

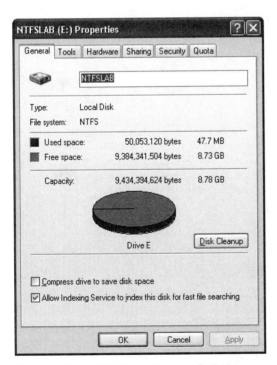

FIGURE 15-19 NTFS partition properties

Lab Analysis Test

1. Nate would like to make backup copies of all of his Word documents in the root directory. He types the following at the command prompt:

    `C:\>COPY A:\*.DOC`

    Will this command work? Why or why not? What will it do? Are there any limitations?

2. Which command(s) would you use to make a full copy of a file in the same directory under a different name?

3. The XCOPY.EXE file is in the SYSTEM32 directory, which is in the WINDOWS directory that's in the root directory of the primary hard drive. What's the complete command-line path to the file?

4. Explain the 8.3 rule. What does the 8 mean? How about the 3?

5. Thomas was messing around one day and deleted a file named CRITICAL.DLL from the SYSTEM32 directory. His friend gave him a copy on a floppy disk. What's the exact command he'd use to copy it back to the correct place?

Key Term Quiz

Use the following terms to complete the following sentences. Not all terms will be used.

/?

/P

/W

CD

COPY

DEL

DIR

MD

RD

REN

1. The command to create a new directory is _____.

2. The command used to create a duplicate file is _____.

3. The _____ switch is used to get help about command syntax.

4. When there are too many files to show on the screen while using the DIR command, add the _____ switch.

5. For a listing of a directory's contents that displays only the filenames, use the _____ command with the _____ switch.

Chapter 16
Securing Windows Resources

Lab Exercises

Not every computer is a part of some vast corporate network. Not everyone logs on to a domain and manipulates multiple file servers to carry out their business. Sometimes, a system stands alone. And lest you take pity on this lonely PC—or worse, ignore it entirely—its security must still be considered. Even without a network, a single computer contains plenty of vital data, and it is these very systems that will be accessed by multiple users (because, well, it's the only one). Without taking the necessary security precautions, your data could easily be stolen or destroyed by anyone else who uses that computer. This is why user accounts, permissions, and encryption in Windows are so important.

As a PC tech, you may be called upon to set up a new user account. But simply adding a new user is just the beginning. You will need to keep in mind what sort of powers or permissions you want each user to have—do they need to be able to install new software, or is just being able to open and edit files enough?

But sometimes, the general set of abilities granted by each type of user account isn't specific enough—maybe there are certain files or folders that should be accessed only by certain users, or groups of users. Then there are the files that should only be seen or touched by you, with access granted by your password alone. Or the opposite—maybe some folders need to be shared so that everyone on that PC can get to them. This chapter will show you how to implement these security features in Windows so that a single system can have multiple users working with and sharing files securely.

🕐 15 MINUTES

Lab Exercise 16.01: Managing Users in Windows

Any time you access a PC, you do so through a local user account, whether Windows makes it obvious or not. A lot of home PCs have only one user without a password, so this process becomes transparent. But that would not be the ideal setup for the workplace, unless you want everyone to be able to go through everyone else's bank records, e-mail messages, personal photos, and so on. Having local user accounts provides a means of authentication—making sure that Steve *is* Steve—and authorization—allowing Steve to delete this, but not install that.

Learning Objectives

In this lab, you'll practice creating and managing new users.

At the end of this lab, you'll be able to

- Create and manage a new local user account
- Work with user groups

Lab Materials and Setup

The materials you need for this lab are

- A PC with Windows

Getting Down to Business

Your client is a small business with four employees and one computer. They each need their own user account so that they can keep their personal data private and so that they stop accidentally deleting everything while logged in as an administrator. Adam is the only one with enough knowledge of computers to have a more powerful account. Betsy, Carol, and Dale each need more limited accounts, because they aren't tech savvy and could easily break something.

This exercise works with any version of Windows, but for the sake of instruction, the steps will be repeated for Windows 2000, Windows XP, and Windows Vista.

✔ **Cross-Reference**

For more information on users and groups, refer to the "Managing Users in Windows 2000," "Managing Users in Windows XP," "Managing Users in Windows Vista," and "Managing Users in General" sections in Chapter 16 of *Mike Meyers' CompTIA A+ Guide to Managing and Troubleshooting PCs.*

Step 1 Follow these steps to create a new user account for Adam in Windows 2000:

    a.   First, make sure to sign in as an administrator; otherwise, you won't be able to create the user account. Then click Start | Settings | Control Panel.

    b.   Double-click Users and Passwords to open the Users and Passwords applet, shown in Figure 16-1.

    c.   Check the box (if it is not already) at the top of the Users tab, *Users must enter a user name and password to use this computer.*

    d.   Click Add. In the Add New User wizard that opens (see Figure 16-2), enter a user name, full name (usually the user's real name), and a description, such as a job title. Then click Next.

    e.   You would normally have the user (Adam in this case) enter his password at this point, but for the sake of the lab, create a memorable password, retype it in the next box to confirm it, and then click Next.

    f.   Because Adam seems to be the only one who knows his way around computers, his user account should be designated as a Standard User. This will place his user account in the Power Users Group, allowing him to install and delete software and access other important Windows features. After you've selected Standard User, click finish.

    g.   The list of user names should now include Adam, and his group should be listed as Power Users.

    h.   Click the Advanced tab. Under Secure Boot Settings, make sure the *Requires users to press Ctrl-Alt-Delete before logging on* box is checked (see Figure 16-3). This forces the user to clear any malicious programs from memory before logging on.

FIGURE 16-1 Windows 2000 Users and Passwords applet

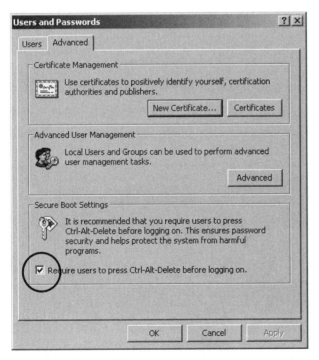

FIGURE 16-2 Add New User wizard

FIGURE 16-3 Requiring users to press CTRL-ALT-DELETE before logging on

Step 2   Follow these steps to create a new user account for Betsy in Windows XP:

     a.   Again, make sure to sign in as an administrator, so that you can create the user account. Then click Start | Control Panel.

     b.   If Classic View is not enabled in Control Panel, enable it now by clicking Switch to Classic View.

     c.   Double-click User Accounts. Then click *Change the way users log on or off*. Deselect the *Use the Welcome screen* option (see Figure 16-4). This also disables Fast User Switching. Now each user will have to type in their user name and password at the login screen. Click Apply Options.

     d.   Click *Create a new account*. Enter a user name, and then click Next.

     e.   For the account type, choose Limited. Then click Create Account (see Figure 16-5).

     f.   Windows XP creates user accounts without passwords by default, so you need to add this manually. Select the user you just created by clicking her icon. Then click *Create a password*. Type in a memorable password and confirm it. Then create a hint phrase to remind you of the password if you forget it. *Do not* use the password as the hint phrase, since this makes having a password pointless. Click Create Password.

Step 3   Follow these steps to create a new user account for Carol in Windows Vista:

     a.   As usual, make sure to sign in as an administrator, so that you can create the user account. Then click Start | Control Panel. Click Switch to Classic View, and then double-click User Accounts.

     b.   Select *Manage another account* (see Figure 16-6). Then click *Create a new account*.

     c.   Type in a new account name. Standard user should already be selected. Click Create Account.

     d.   Select Carol's user account from the Manage Accounts screen. Click *Create a password*. Type in a memorable password, confirm it, and then create a password hint to remind yourself in case you forget. Click *Create password*.

FIGURE 16-4 Disabling the Windows XP Welcome screen

FIGURE 16-5 Choosing Limited for account type

FIGURE 16-6 Selecting the Manage another account link

Step 4   Now that Carol has been set up as a standard user, your client decides that he really needs another administrator besides Adam. Carol turns out to know more about computing than previously indicated, so her account will be upgraded to Administrator.

   a.   As usual, make sure your account is set to Administrator. Then, in 2000, right-click My Computer and select Manage. In XP and Vista, click Start, right-click My Computer/Computer, and select Manage.

   b.   On the left side of the screen, select Local Users and Groups. On the right side, double-click Groups, and then double-click Administrators.

   c.   In the Administrators Properties window, click Add. Windows 2000 will give you a list to select from. Find Carol's user account on the list, double-click it, and then click OK. In Windows XP and Windows Vista, type the user name (Carol) in the *Enter the object names to select* box, and then click *Check Names*. Click OK.

   d.   Click OK in the Administrators Properties window. Find the name of the group that Carol had been in previously, most likely Users. Double-click it to open the Properties window.

   e.   Find the user name in the list, click it, and then click Remove. Click OK. Now Carol is an Administrator!

 15 MINUTES

Lab Exercise 16.02: Defining NTFS Permissions

Now that you've learned how to set up authentication, it's time to talk about authorization—what a user can do with files, folders, or any other resource. Granting NTFS permissions is a powerful and complex tool that allows you to define precisely who can do what on a system. Depending on your needs, this can quickly become a complicated and sticky web of overlapping settings that you don't want to deal with. But it's important to know how to define these permissions so that each user has the specific powers and limitations he requires. It's best to start thinking about it one folder at a time: who can open it, and who can edit it?

Learning Objectives

In this lab, you'll use NTFS permissions to define which users can access specific files and folders.

   At the end of this lab, you'll be able to

   •   Set up NTFS permissions for files and folders

Lab Materials and Setup

The materials you need for this lab are

   •   A PC with Windows 2000, Windows XP Professional, or Windows Vista Business/Ultimate on an NTFS partition

Getting Down to Business

Now that your client has a set of user accounts for his employees, he wants to set up a folder on the C: drive for everyone to use. But there's one text file he doesn't want Dale to touch—he doesn't even want Dale to be able to open it, let alone make any changes. He's asked you to set up the file with the right permissions so that Dale can't access the file.

Setting up permissions for files and setting up permissions for folders are very similar procedures. In this exercise, you'll work with setting up permissions for a text file, but the same procedure will also work with folders.

Step 1 The rest of the steps in this lab will be more straightforward if you first deactivate simple file sharing (in Windows XP only). To do so, open any folder in Windows Explorer, such as My Documents. Select Tools | Folder Options. Switch to the View tab. At the bottom of the list of Advanced settings is the *Use simple file sharing (Recommended)* option. Deselect the box. Click OK.

Step 2 If you haven't done so already, create an account for Dale on your computer using Lab Exercise 16.01. Make sure Dale *isn't* an administrator and *you* are. Then navigate to My Computer/ Computer and double-click the C: drive. Right-click an empty area in the right pane of the window and select New | Folder. Rename it **Work**.

Step 3 Open the Work folder you just created. Right-click an empty area again and select New | Text Document.

Step 4 Right-click the text document and select Properties. Then open the Security tab. Click Edit. This opens a more detailed version of the tab you were just looking at. Listed should be several users and groups, but Dale might not be listed. To add him, click Add. Type **Dale** in the *Enter the object names to select* box (see Figure 16-7) and click Check Names. Click OK.

Step 5 Now that Dale is on the list, you can set his permissions. Select Dale from the list of Group or user names. The bottom half of the window shows a list of permissions for Dale. Everything should be set to Allow. Scroll until you see Read. Check the Deny box next to Read. Click Apply. A dialog box will pop up explaining how this will change the permission of this file and how it could affect other files. Choose Yes.

Figure 16-7 The Select Users, Computer, or Groups applet

Step 6 Log off of the administrator account and log in as Dale. Go back into My Computer/Computer, double-click the C: drive, and open the Work folder you created. Double-click the new text file.

What happens? _____

If all goes well, Notepad should open, but Windows should deny you (Dale) access to the text file. Congratulations! You just set a permission!

🕐 10 MINUTES

Lab Exercise 16.03: Sharing Files and Folders

There are plenty of times when delving into specific NTFS permissions is overkill. Sometimes, you just want to share a folder, one that everyone can freely add to, edit, and so on. Windows makes it incredibly easy to share a folder with multiple local user accounts. Most versions even come with a folder set up for this purpose, like Public Documents in Windows Vista. But one shared folder isn't always enough.

Learning Objectives

In this lab, you'll use sharing in Windows to set up a folder that can be accessed by all users.

At the end of this lab, you'll be able to

- Set up a shared folder

Lab Materials and Setup

The materials you need for this lab are

- A PC with Windows XP Professional or Vista Business or greater

Getting Down to Business

In the previous lab, you created the Work folder on the C: drive of your computer. But the only account that has complete control of that folder is the one used to create it. Your client wants to make sure that every user on that system has full access to the contents of that folder. The easiest way to accomplish that is to use the share feature of Windows.

This is pretty easy, but to make it clear, the exercise will be divided between Windows 2000/XP and Windows Vista.

✔ **Hint**

Just because you know how to set up sharing in one operating system doesn't mean you shouldn't practice in another. Remember that the CompTIA A+ certification exams aren't just testing you on the OS you already know. Take time to check out all the differences.

Step 1   Windows makes the basic process of sharing files and folders over a network pretty easy, but don't think that because it's easy, it's simple. File sharing in Windows is an incredibly deep and complex topic, and you're only going to scratch the surface in this lab. Entire books have been written about share permissions and proper sharing security. With that said, here are the basic steps for sharing a file over a Windows network:

 a. In Windows 2000/XP, navigate to the C: drive in My Computer. If you haven't already done so, create a Work folder in the root folder of the C: drive. Then right-click the folder and click Properties.

 b. Open the Sharing tab. Select Share This Folder. Then click Permissions. From the choices given, select Everyone. On the bottom half of the window, under Permissions for Everyone, check the Allow box next to Full Control. Click OK. Now you are sharing the Work folder with everyone!

→ **Note**

If you have XP Professional, but aren't seeing these options in the Sharing tab, it's because you're using simple file sharing. To fix this, go to the Control Panel and open the Folder Options applet. At the bottom of the View tab, you will see a checkbox that says *Use simple file sharing (Recommended)*. Uncheck this and click OK.

Step 2   The process for sharing folders in Windows Vista has changed significantly. Here are the steps for accomplishing in Vista what you did in XP in Step 1:

 a. In Windows Vista, navigate to the C: drive in Computer. If you haven't already done so, create a Work folder in the root folder of the C: drive. Then right-click the folder and select Share.

 b. Select *Change sharing permissions*. From the drop-down menu, select Everyone. Click Add. Then, in the list of Names and Permission Levels below, click Everyone. Open the drop-down menu for the Permission Level and select Co-Owner. Then click Share. Done!

 10 MINUTES

Lab Exercise 16.04: Encrypting Important Data

So far, you've gone through several methods of securing data on a machine accessed by multiple users. But these features don't secure the data itself as much as put a wall around it to keep people out. The data inside is (as of yet) defenseless. If a system has two administrator accounts, and one administrator sets up file permissions to keep the other out, the second administrator has the power to undo those permissions and access the data—unless you activate encryption.

When you encrypt a file, it becomes absolutely secure from everyone else but you or, more specifically, your password. If you were to lose your password, or an administrator were to change it for you, that data would be lost forever, because that password is *the only way* to get it back. So be careful!

Learning Objectives

In this lab, you'll use encryption to protect sensitive data.

At the end of this lab, you'll be able to

- Use the Encrypting File System in Windows

Lab Materials and Setup

The materials you need for this lab are

- A PC with Windows 2000, Windows XP Professional, or Windows Vista Business/Ultimate

Getting Down to Business

Your client has several personal documents that she keeps copies of on her computer at work. But she isn't the only administrator on that system, so to fully secure the data, she wants it to be encrypted.

Thanks to the Encrypting File System introduced with NTFS, encrypting files in Windows is simple. Be warned, however, that if you lose access to the user account that you used to encrypt the files, you will lose those files forever!

✔ Hint

The Home versions of Windows, such as Windows XP Home and Windows Vista Home Premium, do not include a utility to encrypt data. If you are using one of these operating systems and still want to or need to use encryption, check out TrueCrypt. Open source (and free), TrueCrypt provides advanced encryption features across multiple platforms. Check it out at www.truecrypt.org.

Step 1 Navigate to the files or folder in question (for the purposes of the lab, use the Work folder you already created). Right-click the Work folder and select Properties. Next to the Attributes checkboxes, click the Advanced button. At the bottom of the Advanced Attributes applet, check the box for *Encrypt contents to secure data* (see Figure 16-8). Click OK.

Step 2 Now switch to another user, even another administrator. Navigate back to the folder that you just encrypted. Try opening it.

What happens? _____

Figure 16-8 The Advanced Attributes applet

Lab Analysis Test

1. Jonas has an administrator account and sets up the permissions of a folder on the C: drive to deny anyone else from accessing it but himself. If another administrator account was created, would the folder still be secure? Why or why not?

2. Reginald needs to set up a folder that can be seen by the administrator and two standard users, but can only be edited by the administrator. How would he make this work?

3. Why should you force users to press CTRL-ALT-DELETE before logging in to Windows?

4. Nina created several user accounts in Windows XP for her family, but forgot to give each of them passwords. List the steps to take to add a password to a user account in Windows Vista.

5. What makes encryption the strongest security feature in Windows?

Key Term Quiz

Use the following terms to complete the following sentences. Not all terms will be used.

administrator

authentication

authorization

group

limited user

NTFS permissions

simple file sharing

standard user

Users group

Welcome screen

1. A(n) _____ cannot install software or delete system files.

2. Typing your user name and password is a means of _____.

3. The account with the most power is the _____.

4. _____ are used to define specific rules for which users and groups can and cannot access files and folders.

5. What a user can and cannot do on a system is called _____.

Chapter 17

Maintaining and Troubleshooting Windows

Lab Exercises

Imagine that your company has just acquired a small architectural firm. One of the principals of the firm informs you that they haven't really had any IT support to speak of in a few years. You visit the new office and determine that the computers are about three years old. They were good machines when they were purchased, and as long as the hardware is not failing, they should be more than adequate for a year or two more. The architects do complain that their machines are running slowly and that it's affecting productivity. You would like to avoid a complete rollout of new PCs, since you're looking at a replacement expense of thousands of dollars. Consequently, you decide it would be worthwhile to spend a day trying to figure out if anything can be done to make the machines run faster.

After checking out a few of the systems, you determine that they could definitely benefit from additional memory, but that's not the only issue—none of the systems have been updated in over three years! Even though most versions of Windows are optimized when they're installed, time and use can alter that fact significantly. It's important, therefore, to be able to take what you know about navigating and manipulating the Windows environment and put it to work figuring out what needs to be fixed, updated, or improved. Sometimes a simple tweak is all it takes to make a sluggish system run like it's fresh out of the box.

One of the first tasks is to make sure that all of the systems have the latest service packs and Windows updates. Before you do that, however, it's recommended that you back up all of the data on the systems, as this can be a pretty major upgrade. Another item that needs to be checked is whether the device drivers are all up to date. Neglected PCs will definitely require updated device drivers.

First, you will learn how to back up and restore your system as preparation for updating and optimizing Windows. You'll then explore the various troubleshooting tools included with Windows. It's time to drop a few sticks of memory into the pilot machines, back them up, run them through the service packs and updates, and get this office back on its feet!

 60 MINUTES

Lab Exercise 17.01: Performing a Backup and Restoration

Windows offers both simple backup/restoration utilities that you can use to back up system data and program data and files, and an advanced recovery feature, in case the system becomes so unstable that it won't even boot.

Windows 2000 uses the Emergency Repair Disk (ERD), Windows XP introduced the Automated System Recovery (ASR) routine, and Windows Vista uses the Backup and Restore Center. The ERD and ASR only create nonbootable disks with tools to restore a system in case of a major failure, whereas Vista's Backup and Restore Center will make a full (or partial) backup of your entire system that is restored using the System Recovery Options. It is important to understand—and the CompTIA A+ certification exams expect you to know this—that none of these options are bootable.

This lab introduces you to the ASR process in Windows XP Professional and the Backup and Restore Center in Windows Vista.

> **✖ Warning**
>
> The ERD and ASR processes do not back up or restore program data or files! After the system restoration process is complete, the program data and files must be restored separately from previously created backup media.

Learning Objectives

Performing backups of any kind is a critical responsibility of a PC technician. The Windows XP Professional Automated System Recovery and the Vista Backup and Restore Center are excellent representations of the steps required to back up and restore an OS.

At the end of this lab, you'll be able to

- Prepare a backup
- Perform a restoration

Lab Materials and Setup

The materials you need for this lab are

- A working PC with Windows XP Professional or Windows Vista installed
- Some form of backup media/device (CD/DVD drive, tape drive, network drive, separate partition)
- A blank, formatted floppy disk (XP only)
- The Windows XP Professional or Windows Vista installation media

Getting Down to Business

The time to prepare a backup is while the system and data are in a state of complete integrity. It's when they crash or get corrupted that you'll need the backup! The following steps create an ASR set and then use that ASR set to restore a Windows XP system to working condition. The steps for the Windows Vista Backup and Recovery Center will follow.

AUTOMATED SYSTEM RECOVERY PREPARATION

Step 1 Launch the Windows Backup or Restore Wizard by clicking Start | Run and typing **ntbackup.exe** in the dialog box. Alternatively, you can click Start | All Programs | Accessories | System Tools | Backup. Click the Advanced Mode text link to bring up the screen shown in Figure 17-1.

FIGURE 17-1 Windows XP Backup Utility's Advanced Mode screen

Step 2 Launch the Automated System Recovery Wizard and perform the following steps:

    a. Click Next, and in the *Backup media or file name* dialog box, type or browse for the location in which you want the backup to be placed. Then name the backup file, being careful to preserve the .BKF file extension. If you are using a separate partition, for example, you might enter D:\MyASRBK.BKF to create the file on the D: drive.

    b. Click Next and then click Finish to start the backup of your system files.

    c. When the backup completes, the ASR Preparation Wizard instructs you to insert a formatted 1.44-MB floppy disk. Click OK. ASR copies the required files onto the floppy disk.

    d. When instructed, remove and label the floppy disk and then click OK. You have completed the preparation for an Automated System Recovery.

AUTOMATED SYSTEM RECOVERY RESTORE

Step 1 Boot the system using the Windows XP Professional installation CD-ROM.

Step 2 When prompted with *Press F2 to run Automated System Recovery (ASR)*, press the F2 key.

Step 3 Insert the ASR floppy disk and press any key when ready.

Step 4 The Windows XP Installer will copy files to a temporary folder, format the partition where XP will be installed, and prompt you to remove the installation CD-ROM and reboot.

Step 5 After rebooting, the Windows XP installation continues.

    a. During the installation, you'll be prompted for the location of the ASR backup file.

    b. Enter the file location or use the Browse button to enter the location and name of the ASR backup file.

    c. Click OK.

    d. The installation now completes. All of the Windows XP configuration settings and preferences should be as they were on the original system.

BACKUP AND RESTORE CENTER

Step 1 Open Control Panel. Switch to Classic View (if you haven't already) and double-click Backup and Restore Center.

Step 2 To set up the backup, decide first whether to back up certain files or the whole computer. The Back Up Files wizard will open. Select where to save the backup and click Next. If you chose only a partial backup, select the file types you wish to back up from the list provided. Click Next. For partial backups, Windows also asks how often you want the backup to be updated. Click Save settings and start backup.

Step 3 To restore files, choose whether to restore only certain files or to restore a Windows Complete Backup and Restore image. (To do a complete restoration, you must reboot your system and open the System Recovery Options from the installation media.) If you are performing a partial restoration, click Restore files. Select whether to restore the latest backup or an older one. Click Next. Then select where to restore the backup files to and click Start Restore. If you are overwriting any files, a window will pop up asking how to resolve the conflict.

30 MINUTES

Lab Exercise 17.02: Upgrading to Windows Vista SP2 and Configuring Automatic Updates

These systems have been around for some time, so there are probably a number of outdated patches and drivers. Windows Vista went through a major upgrade with Service Pack 2, so this is where you'll start. If you are working with a new installation of Windows Vista, Service Pack 2 should already be incorporated into the cabinet files, but these are old machines, so they will need some attention. Upgrading to Service Pack 2 is imperative to keeping the system up and running, secure, and compatible with new technology. To bring the OS up to date, you will first manually download and install Service Pack 2, and then configure Automatic Updates so Windows will take care of future updates on its own.

Learning Objectives

A competent technician should understand the importance of upgrading an OS with the latest service pack.

At the end of this lab, you'll be able to

- Upgrade Windows Vista to Service Pack 2

- Configure Windows Automatic Updates to update drivers, security patches, and utilities

Lab Materials and Setup

The materials you need for this lab are

- A working PC with Windows installed

- An Internet connection

→ **Note**

The procedures for updating Windows and setting up Automatic Updates are very similar between Windows XP and Windows Vista. Although this lab describes a Windows Vista upgrade, the concept remains the same for Windows XP.

Getting Down to Business

You will begin by downloading and installing Service Pack 2 for Windows Vista. Then you will learn how to configure Automatic Updates.

Step 1 You will need to procure Windows Vista Service Pack 2. Go to Microsoft's Web site and search for **vista service pack 2**, or go straight to http://technet.microsoft.com/en-us/windows/dd262148.aspx. The search should return a page with the title Service Pack 2 for Windows Server 2008 and Windows Vista; follow the directions on this page to download Service Pack 2. You may also order this update on optical disc—this can come in handy if you have a slower Internet connection. (You'll look at getting updates through Automatic Updates next.)

Step 2 Once the download finishes, or your optical disc has arrived, log on to the system that you want to update. Open the folder where you have placed the files and complete the following steps:

    a.   Double-click the setup file you downloaded.

    b.   The Windows Vista Service Pack 2 setup wizard welcome screen appears (see Figure 17-2). Click Next to continue.

    c.   The End User License Agreement screen displays next. Accept the agreement and click Next to continue.

    d.   The setup wizard now inspects your machine, installs files, and upgrades your system. When the upgrade is complete, the wizard informs you that *Windows Vista Service Pack 2 is now installed on your computer* (see Figure 17-3).

    e.   Click Finish and let the system reboot.

Figure 17-2 Welcome to the Windows Vista Service Pack 2 setup wizard

FIGURE 17-3 Completing the Windows Vista Service Pack 2 setup wizard

f.   After the machine reboots for the first time with Service Pack 2 installed, Windows gives you the opportunity to turn on Automatic Updates before it presents the logon screen. Decline this option for now; you will manually configure this in the next step.

Step 3   You will now configure the system to perform automatic updates. Log on to Windows and complete the following steps:

a.   In Windows XP, click Start | All Programs | Accessories | System Tools | Security Center. In Windows Vista, type **Security Center** in the Start Search box. This opens the Windows Security Center window, where you'll find the configuration utility for Windows' Automatic Updates feature. Click Automatic Updates.

✔ **Cross-Reference**

You will have the opportunity to work with antivirus software in Chapter 26.

---

b.   This brings up the Automatic Updates configuration screen (see Figure 17-4) in Windows XP. Click *Automatic (recommended)* and then click Apply. In Windows Vista, select Change Settings, and then choose Install Updates Automatically.

FIGURE 17-4 Automatic Updates configuration screen

c.   The Windows Security Center screen now indicates that Automatic Updates is set to On, and the yellow security shield should disappear from the notification area (system tray).

d.   If your system is connected to the Internet, you can visit the Microsoft Windows Update Web site. There, you can choose to install all critical Windows updates, or select specific updates to install.

30 MINUTES

Lab Exercise 17.03: Installing Device Drivers in Windows

Installing new devices under Windows is easier than it has ever been. Assuming, of course, that you start with compatible hardware, Windows will detect the new device and install the correct driver with little prompting. If that doesn't work, it is often just a matter of updating the driver, using driver rollback, or adjusting the settings for driver signing. It's best to check the Internet for new drivers whenever you install a new device.

Even after a device has been installed, you should check for newer drivers periodically, even for devices that have been working fine. Manufacturers occasionally release new drivers aimed at optimizing the device or enabling it to work with some new technology. Keep in mind, however, that a new driver may cause unexpected problems with your operating system. Because of this, Windows XP introduced a feature that enables you to roll back to the previous (working) driver if something should go wrong with a driver update. Microsoft attempts to protect the system by qualifying devices and drivers through the Windows Hardware Quality Labs (WHQL) and Windows Logo Program and digitally signing the drivers as approved for the OS. Driver signing allows you to configure how the system will handle the installation of untested drivers.

One of two wizards will assist you when you need to load a driver: the Found New Hardware Wizard or the Add New Hardware Wizard. Windows starts the Found New Hardware Wizard when it discovers some new hardware device while booting. If Windows has a driver in its database, it proceeds on its own. If not, the Found New Hardware Wizard will prompt you for one. The Add New Hardware Wizard enables you to add or update hardware manually at any time. There's a lot of overlap in how the two wizards work, so you'll look at just the Add New Hardware Wizard, which you can activate at any time.

Learning Objectives

Loading and removing device drivers is one of the basic skills that any good PC tech should have. The following lab exercise walks you through the process.

At the end of this lab, you'll be able to

- Load a device driver in Windows

- Roll back to a previously working driver in Windows XP and Windows Vista

- Explore driver signing

Lab Materials and Setup

The materials you need for this lab are

- A working PC with Windows XP or Windows Vista installed

- An Internet connection

Getting Down to Business

The following labs cover the steps for installing and updating device drivers. You'll also look at the steps to roll back (uninstall) device drivers that turn out to be incompatible, and explore the settings for how Windows handles unsigned drivers.

Step 1   The first step before you begin installing any new device is to make sure it's compatible with your current Windows OS. It is best to check the http://www.microsoft.com/windows/compatibility/windows-vista/ Web site before purchasing a device for your Windows PC.

Step 2   Now you'll walk through the process of adding a device using the Add Hardware Wizard:

a.   From the Control Panel, double-click Add Hardware.

b.   On the Add Hardware Wizard's welcome screen, click Next.

✔ **Hint**

If the wizard doesn't find any new hardware, it asks, "Have you already connected this hardware to your computer?" Select Yes or No, and follow the directions.

---

c.   Select the device you want to install or update by either selecting from the given list or choosing the Add a New Hardware Device item in the list box. For this lab, select the last item in the list—*Add a new hardware device*—and then click Next.

d.   Click the *Install the hardware that I manually select from a list (Advanced)* option button, and then click Next.

e.   Select the type of hardware you're trying to install or update from the list. If your device doesn't fit the descriptions, select the Show All Devices item. When you've made your selection, click Next.

f.   If you chose the Show All Devices item, the wizard displays the *Select the device driver you want to install for this hardware screen*. If you chose a specific type of hardware, you'll be led off into a series of options for that type of hardware.

g.   Choose the Windows driver for your device, or click Have Disk and point to the location of the new driver you want to install. This driver generally is located either on the installation CD-ROM that came with the device, if you have it, or on your hard drive if you downloaded it from the manufacturer's Web site.

h.   Click Next. Windows is ready to install the driver.

i.   Click Next again, and click Finish when the installation is complete.

You should now have a driver that runs your newly loaded device. If the device isn't working properly and you're sure the driver loaded correctly, you can check online and see if there's a newer driver that you can download from the manufacturer's Web site.

Step 3   What if you have a device already installed and you want to update the driver to address a problem, improve performance, or just add a new feature? This step will take you through updating new drivers.

a.   Begin by locating the updated driver. In most cases, the best way to obtain the updated driver is to search the Internet for the manufacturer's Web site. Search its site for your specific model, and download the most recent driver.

b.   Go to Device Manager and expand the appropriate device category. Locate the device you want to update.

c.   Double-click the device.

d.   Select the Driver tab and click the Update Driver button (see Figure 17-5). This launches a wizard similar to the Add New Hardware Wizard.

✔ **Hint**

In Windows XP and Vista, you can right-click the device in question in Device Manager and update the driver without accessing its properties.

For Windows XP, select *Install from a list or specific location (Advanced)* and click Next. Select *Include this location in the search*, and browse to where you have saved the new driver.

For Windows Vista, click *Browse my computer for driver software*. Then choose *Let me pick from a list of device drivers on my computer*. Click the Have Disk button and then click Browse. You can locate the file from there.

You may be wondering, "What if I load a new driver, and my system doesn't work correctly anymore?" Well, if you're using Windows XP or Windows Vista, you're in luck! Read the next step, and your question will be answered.

FIGURE 17-5 The Windows Vista Update Driver button

Step 4   If a driver is corrupt or if the wrong driver is installed, Windows has a bad habit of stopping dead in its tracks, rendering your PC useless. Windows XP and Vista have a feature that keeps track of the drivers you install on a system and allows you to roll back to a previous one when a new one isn't working as it should.

    a.   Go to the Device Manager and locate the device you want to roll back.

    b.   Double-click the device.

    c.   Select the Driver tab. You can revert to the previous driver by clicking Roll Back Driver (see Figure 17-6).

Step 5   Windows 2000 introduced a feature for Windows known as driver signing. Driver signing verifies that a device driver has been tested by the Windows Hardware Quality Labs (WHQL) or Windows Logo Program and will work with the OS as tested. More important, Windows allows you to configure how the OS will handle unsigned drivers! You can direct Windows to ignore, warn, or block new unsigned drivers. The following steps explore this feature:

    a.   In Windows 2000 or XP, open the Control Panel and launch the System applet.

    b.   Click the Hardware tab (see Figure 17-7).

    c.   Click the Driver Signing button to open a dialog box with the various options (see Figure 17-8).

    d.   Select Warn and click OK.

FIGURE 17-6 Windows XP's Roll Back Driver button

FIGURE 17-7 Hardware tab under System Properties

FIGURE 17-8 The Driver Signing Options dialog box

Note that these options don't exist in Windows Vista—you will always be warned about installing unsigned drivers. Also, 64-bit versions of Windows do not allow the installation of unsigned drivers at all.

At this point, you should be pretty familiar with drivers and how to load and update them. More and more devices are being sold as hot-pluggable, but I doubt that user-installed drivers will be going away in the near future.

 30 MINUTES

Lab Exercise 17.04: Examining and Configuring Log Files in Event Viewer

Windows Event Viewer is a valuable tool to anyone who maintains or troubleshoots systems. It's mostly run as a standalone program, but it can also be added as a snap-in to the MMC.

Event Viewer monitors various log files and reveals things about the health of the operating system. This utility reports real-time statistics, but normally this data is only used with servers. Desktop computer users are less proactive and usually depend on the after-the-fact log files to help determine the cause of a problem.

Event Viewer displays important events from three log files: Application, Security, and System. (More log files are available in the server versions of Windows.) Figure 17-9 shows the contents of the System event log in Event Viewer.

FIGURE 17-9 Viewing the System log in Event Viewer

Notice in Figure 17-9 that there are three kinds of log entries for the System and Application logs: Information, Warning, and Error. The Security event log shows two types of entries: Success Audit and Failure Audit. These types of events are only logged when auditing is turned on; again, this is normally done only on servers.

Learning Objectives

You'll become familiar with using Event Viewer to analyze the different logs kept by the system.

At the end of this lab, you'll be able to

- Run the Event Viewer program
- Examine an event log entry
- Save the event log

Lab Materials and Setup

The materials you need for this lab are

- A working PC with Windows installed

Getting Down to Business

In Windows 2000 and XP, you can start Event Viewer from the Control Panel by double-clicking the Administrative Tools applet and then double-clicking Event Viewer. In Windows Vista, go to the Search box in the Start menu and type **Event Viewer**. Click the program that appears in the search results.

Step 1 Follow these steps to change the size of a log file:

a.   In Event Viewer's left panel, right-click System and select Properties.

b.   Change the number in the *Maximum log size* box to **1024** KB (512 is the default) and select *Overwrite events as needed* (see Figure 17-10).

c.   Do this for all three event logs: Application, Security, and System.

d.   Sometimes the log can be completely full before you get a chance to look at the entries. Scrolling through all the events can be a little boring and time consuming, but you can fix that with filter settings. Click the Filter tab, and look at the filter settings (see Figure 17-11).

You can filter events based on type, source, category, ID, user, computer, and date. This only controls what Event Viewer displays; all the events information will still be logged to the file, so you can change your mind about filter settings. Click OK to close the Properties dialog box.

Step 2 To clear, archive, and open a log file, follow these steps:

a.   Clear the System log by right-clicking System and selecting *Clear all Events* (see Figure 17-12).

b.   When you're prompted to save the System log, click Yes.

FIGURE 17-10 Changing the size of a log file

c.   You can archive log files using different filenames each time (recommended) and select a
location other than the default. Give your file a name you can remember and save it.

d.   To open a saved file, click the Action menu and select Open Log File. Select the file and log type
(System, Application, or Security) and click Open.

FIGURE 17-11 Viewing Event Viewer's settings

FIGURE 17-12 Clearing the System log

⏱ 45 MINUTES

Lab Exercise 17.05: Using the Advanced Options Menu and the Recovery Console

An errant upgrade or a poorly written driver can cause the system to lock up. Some software problems, such as corrupt Registry files, will even prevent the system from booting. This means that you must be ready to use alternative methods to boot the system to make repairs or replace files.

Windows has several ways to boot, and these ways are as different as the operating systems themselves. A Safe Mode boot is available in every version of Windows. There's also a nice recovery tool that comes with Windows 2000 and Windows XP known as the Recovery Console. Windows Vista uses the System Recovery Options on the bootable installation media. One of the options available is access to the Command Prompt, which works just like the Recovery Console, but with more power.

Learning Objectives

You'll become familiar with alternative methods of booting a faulty system.

At the end of this lab, you'll be able to

- Boot to Windows' Advanced Options Menu and enable Safe Mode

- Install the Recovery Console

- Repair the Registry using the Recovery Console/Command Prompt

Lab Materials and Setup

The materials you need for this lab are

- A working PC with Windows 2000 or XP installed (preferably a non-production system, as you will be corrupting and repairing the Registry)

- The Windows 2000/XP installation media

Getting Down to Business

If your system won't boot normally because of some system problem, you need a way to gain access to the hard drive and your files to troubleshoot the problem. There are, happily enough, troubleshooting tools that give you access to these files if the normal boot process won't work. You'll begin this exercise with the first line of defense, the Advanced Options Menu, and boot to Safe Mode. You will then install and explore the Recovery Console, eventually repairing the Registry manually.

Step 1   Power up a machine with Windows installed. After the POST messages, but before the Windows logo screen appears, press F8. Depending on your system, you will see a number of different boot options. Record the various modes and provide a short description for each:

_____

_____

_____

_____

_____

_____

✔ **Cross-Reference**

> For definitions of each of the boot modes, refer to the "Advanced Startup Options" section in Chapter 17 of *Mike Meyers' CompTIA A+ Guide to Managing and Troubleshooting PCs.*

Step 2   Select Safe Mode and press ENTER.

The system will proceed to boot into the operating system, but it will inform you many times that it is running in Safe Mode (see Figure 17-13).

Safe Mode is often used when video settings have been changed and render the display unusable. In Safe Mode, a standard VGA driver is installed, and the minimal settings (16 colors, 640×480 resolution)

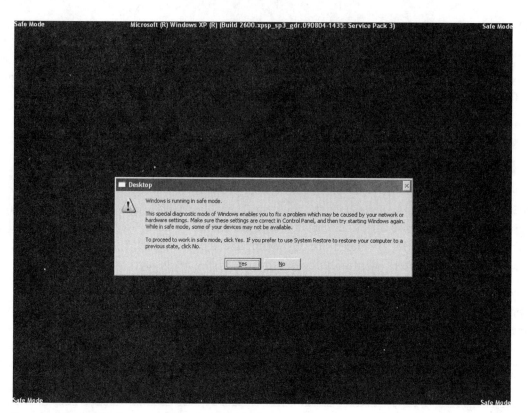

FIGURE 17-13 Windows running in Safe Mode

are set. This enables you to revert to previous drivers, and/or correct the settings for the current display or monitor you are using. Complete the following steps to explore the display properties:

a. Right-click somewhere in the empty space of the desktop and select Properties from the drop-down menu. This brings up the Display Properties dialog box.

b. Click the Settings tab and note the display, color, and screen resolution settings. Record your settings here: _____

c. Click Cancel to close the Display Properties dialog box.

d. Click Start | Shut down.

Step 3 Next, you will explore using the Repair menu item from the Windows installation media to launch the Recovery Console.

a. Insert the Windows installation disc and then reboot the system, making sure your CMOS is set to boot from your optical drive. The installation program loads a number of files and then displays a screen with the following information. These steps were completed using a Windows

2000 Professional installation, but a Windows XP installation will be very similar. The steps for accessing Windows Vista's System Recovery Options follow.

```
Welcome to Setup
This portion of the Setup program prepares Microsoft
Windows 2000™ to run on your computer
        To set up Windows 2000 now, Press ENTER.
        To repair a Windows 2000 installation, press R.
        To quit Setup without installing Windows 2000, press F3.
```

b. Because the operating system is already installed, press R to select the Repair function. The next screen offers two choices:

```
To repair a Windows 2000 installation by using
        the recovery console, press C.
To repair a Windows 2000 installation by using
        the emergency repair process, press R.
```

c. Press C to open the Recovery Console.

You'll now see a command-line interface asking which installation you want to access. If you have a dual-boot system, you'll have to choose an operating system; type its number from the list and press ENTER. Then type the administrator's password. This is the password for the first account created when you initially installed the operating system. You now have a command-line prompt from which to work.

✖ **Warning**

Be sure you know what you're doing here. You have access to files that you can add, change, rename, or delete. The old DOS command set is only partially available.

---

d. To see a list of commands, type **help** and note the results.

e. Type a command followed by **/?** to get an explanation of that command. You'll explore some of these commands later when you install the Windows XP Recovery Console.

➜ **Note**

The Recovery Console operates very similarly to the Windows Command Line that you learned about in Chapter 15.

---

f. Type **exit** to quit the Recovery Console; the system will reboot.

To access the Command Prompt through Windows Vista's System Recovery Options, follow these steps:

a. Boot from the installation media. After you choose your language settings, click Next.

```
Please select the operating system to start:

    Microsoft Windows XP Professional
    Microsoft Windows Recovery Console

Use the up and down arrow keys to move the highlight to your choice.
Press ENTER to choose.
```

FIGURE 17-14 Recovery Console option in Windows 2000 startup

b.   Select *Repair your computer* and then click Next. The System Recovery Options menu should appear.

c.   From the list of options, choose the Command Prompt.

Step 4   Although you can run the Recovery Console by booting directly to it from the Windows 2000/XP installation disc, it's much more convenient to set it up as a startup option on your boot menu (see Figure 17-14). In this step, you'll install the Windows XP Recovery Console as a boot option. You can do the same thing using the same steps for Windows 2000. (Windows Vista's System Recovery Options are either preinstalled or located on the installation media.)

✔ **Hint**

To install the Recovery Console, you must have administrative rights on the computer.

---

a.   Put your Windows XP (or Windows 2000) installation CD-ROM into the CD-ROM drive; if it autostarts, select Exit. You can also press and hold SHIFT until the CD-ROM stops loading.

b.   Select Start | Run.

c.   In the Open box, type **D:\I386\WINNT32.EXE /CMDCONS** (where D is the drive letter for your CD-ROM drive).

d.   A Windows Setup dialog box appears, which describes the Recovery Console option. The system prompts you to confirm installation. Click Yes to start the installation procedure.

e.   When the installation is complete (see Figure 17-15), restart the computer. You will see a Microsoft Windows Recovery Console entry on the boot menu.

Microsoft Windows XP Professional Setup

The Windows Recovery Console has been successfully installed.

To use the Windows Recovery Console, restart your computer and then select Windows Recovery Console from the Startup Menu.

For a list of commands you can use with the Recovery Console, type HELP at the Recovery Console command prompt.

[OK]

FIGURE 17-15 Completing the Recovery Console installation in Windows XP

→ **Note**

When you're installing the Recovery Console, you must use a Windows installation CD-ROM with the same version of Windows that was used for the system's main OS installation. For example, if you used a Windows XP Service Pack 2 CD-ROM to install Windows on this system, you cannot use a pre–Service Pack 2 CD-ROM for this procedure.

It's wise to install the Recovery Console on important servers and on critical workstations.

Step 5 For Windows 2000/XP machines, reboot your system, and at the boot menu screen, select the Recovery Console. For Windows Vista users, either boot from the installation media and open the System Recovery Options, or open the Advanced Boot Options menu and access it there. Then open the Command Prompt.

To see a list of the commands, type **help** at the command prompt. Type a command followed by **/?** to get an explanation of the command's use.

Several commands are worth reviewing; for the CompTIA A+ exams, you should know what the following commands do:

- **CHKDSK** Checks the clusters and sectors of a disk (fixed or removable) and, if possible, repairs bad clusters or sectors

- **DISKPART** The Windows 2000 equivalent to FDISK

- **EXIT** Closes the Recovery Console and restarts your computer

- **EXPAND** Extracts copies of single files from the CAB files

- **FIXBOOT** Writes a new partition table

- **FIXMBR** Equivalent to FDISK /MBR

- **HELP** Displays a Help screen

✔ **Hint**

Many techs resort to the Recovery Console when a system fails to boot in the normal fashion (from the hard drive). Three of the commands, FIXBOOT, FIXMBR, and CHKDSK, are particularly important when it seems that the hard disk, the master boot record, or the system partition are missing, corrupt, or damaged. If you come across a system exhibiting these symptoms (and you will), follow good troubleshooting procedures, but remember that you have these tools available to you.

→ **Note**

Windows Vista replaced FIXMBR and FIXBOOT with the BOOTREC command. They are still functionally identical, but to access them, you must use BOOTREC /FIXMBR and BOOTREC /FIXBOOT. Other available options include /SCANOS, which scans for Windows installations not in the boot configuration store, and /REBUILDBCD, which does the same but allows you to add the installation to the boot configuration store.

The files that make up the Recovery Console reside on the system partition, making the Recovery Console useless for a system partition crash. In such a situation, you would use the optical drive to access the Recovery Console/Command Prompt. The Recovery Console/Command Prompt shines in the business of manually restoring Registry files, stopping problem services, rebuilding partitions (other than the system partition), or using the EXPAND program to extract copies of corrupted files from removable media.

Step 6 As mentioned in the previous step, the Recovery Console/Command Prompt is excellent when you need to restore Registry files. In the following steps, you will crash a system by deleting the SYSTEM folder, and then repair the folder and recover the system.

✖ **Warning**

As mentioned in the "Lab Materials and Setup" section for this lab exercise, you are going to purposefully delete/corrupt the SYSTEM folder of a working Windows system. For this reason, the system you use must be a noncritical, non-production system. Don't risk your family's financial records or your 40-GB photo archive—find another system to use for this exercise!

✔ **Cross-Reference**

The following steps use many components of Windows and the Recovery Console/Command Prompt. To understand better the files, folders, and Registry components involved, be sure to read the "Registry" section in Chapter 17 of *Mike Meyers' CompTIA A+ Guide to Managing and Troubleshooting PCs*.

Microsoft has also gathered invaluable information in their Knowledge Base articles (a component of TechNet). The following lab steps incorporate valuable information from Knowledge Base articles 307545 and 309531. As previously mentioned, Web sites change over time, so if you don't find these exact articles, use your favorite search engine and locate similar articles related to the Recovery Console/Command Prompt and repairing the Registry.

a. Some preparation may be required to complete the steps to corrupt and restore your Registry folders. In Windows 2000/XP, open My Computer, then select Tools | Folder Options. In Windows Vista, select Start, then type **Folder Options** in the Start Search box and press ENTER. Click the View tab. Turn on *Show hidden files and folders*, turn off *Hide extensions for known file types*, and turn off *Hide protected operating system files (Recommended)*. Click OK.

b. Boot to the Recovery Console/Command Prompt, and after logging on as Administrator (if needed), type the following commands at the prompt:

```
MD C:\%SYSTEMROOT%\TMP
COPY C:\%SYSTEMROOT%\SYSTEM32\CONFIG\SYSTEM C:\%SYSTEMROOT%\TMP\SYSTEM.BAK
DELETE C:\%SYSTEMROOT%\SYSTEM32\CONFIG\SYSTEM
EXIT
```

c. At this point the Recovery Console/Command Prompt closes. Restart Windows. Allow Windows to boot normally. Did anything inhibit the normal loading and startup of Windows?

_____

d. Boot to the Recovery Console/Command Prompt once again, log on as Administrator (if needed), and type the following commands at the prompt:

```
COPY C:\%SYSTEMROOT%\REPAIR\SYSTEM C:\%SYSTEMROOT%\SYSTE32\CONFIG\SYSTEM
EXIT
```

e. The Recovery Console/Command Prompt again closes. Reboot Windows. Allow Windows to boot normally. Did Windows boot properly this time? _____

→ **Note**

Windows Vista's System Recovery Options also includes a handy tool called Startup Repair. It is able to scan your computer for any problems and automatically repair them. The next time you think you need to delve into Vista's Command Prompt to fix any startup-related troubles, try Startup Repair first—it might just save you from having to type all of those backslashes!

→ **Try This: Create a Batch File to Restore a Corrupted Registry**

Though floppy drives are becoming scarce, the use of the Recovery Console and some form of accessible, removable media will enable you to semi-automate the restoration of the critical Registry folders. Create the following batch file and save it to a floppy disk.

1. Open a text editor, type the following lines of code exactly, and save your work as a text file (located on a floppy disk) called MyRegBak.txt:

```
MD TMP

COPY C:\%SYSTEMROOT%\SYSTEM32\CONFIG\SYSTEM C:\%SYSTEMROOT%\TMP\SYSTEM.BAK

COPY C:\%SYSTEMROOT%\SYSTEM32\CONFIG\SOFTWARE C:\%SYSTEMROOT%\TMP\SOFTWARE.BAK
```

```
COPY C:\%SYSTEMROOT%\SYSTEM32\CONFIG\SAM C:\%SYSTEMROOT%\TMP\SAM.BAK

COPY C:\%SYSTEMROOT%\SYSTEM32\CONFIG\SECURITY C:\%SYSTEMROOT%\TMP\SECURITY.BAK

COPY C:\%SYSTEMROOT%\SYSTEM32\CONFIG\DEFAULT C:\%SYSTEMROOT%\TMP\DEFAULT.BAK


DELETE C:\%SYSTEMROOT%\SYSTEM32\CONFIG\SYSTEM

DELETE C:\%SYSTEMROOT%\SYSTEM32\CONFIG\SOFTWARE

DELETE C:\%SYSTEMROOT%\SYSTEM32\CONFIG\SAM

DELETE C:\%SYSTEMROOT%\SYSTEM32\CONFIG\SECURITY

DELETE C:\%SYSTEMROOT%\SYSTEM32\CONFIG\DEFAULT


COPY C:\%SYSTEMROOT%\REPAIR\SYSTEM C:\%SYSTEMROOT%\SYSTEM32\CONFIG\SYSTEM

COPY C:\%SYSTEMROOT%\REPAIR\SOFTWARE C:\%SYSTEMROOT%\SYSTEM32\CONFIG\SOFTWARE

COPY C:\%SYSTEMROOT%\REPAIR\SAM C:\%SYSTEMROOT%\SYSTEM32\CONFIG\SAM

COPY C:\%SYSTEMROOT%\REPAIR\SECURITY C:\%SYSTEMROOT%\SYSTEM32\CONFIG\SECURITY

COPY C:\%SYSTEMROOT%\REPAIR\DEFAULT C:\%SYSTEMROOT%\SYSTEM32\CONFIG\DEFAULT
```

2. Place the floppy with your text file in the machine that needs restoration. Launch the Recovery Console, locate the text file, and execute the following batch command to restore the Registry to a working state:

```
C:\%SYSTEMROOT%\BATCH A:\MyRegBak.TXT
```

 30 MINUTES

Lab Exercise 17.06: Troubleshooting Startup Problems

When it comes to troubleshooting tools, the latest versions of Windows inherited the best of both the Windows NT and 9x OS families. They have vintage tools such as the Last Known Good Configuration startup option for startup failures and the Task Manager for forcing errant programs to close. There is also the Recovery Console/Command Prompt, and Windows Help.

I'll leave the finer details of these tools for you to explore through Windows Help, the main textbook, and other labs. In this lab, you'll explore a simple tool known as the System Configuration utility. The System Configuration utility has been around for some time, having been introduced in Windows 98. It was never incorporated into Windows NT or 2000, but it is included in Windows XP and Windows Vista/7.

Learning Objectives

You'll be reintroduced to some troubleshooting tips using a vintage tool with Windows XP.

At the end of this lab, you'll be able to

- Use the System Configuration utility to perform diagnostic startups

Lab Materials and Setup

The materials you need for this lab are

- A working Windows XP or Windows Vista system

Getting Down to Business

Many systems have way too many startup options enabled. This isn't only a source of boot problems; it can also slow down the boot process and hog RAM from programs that need it. When Windows experiences failures during startup, consider using the System Configuration utility to discover and fix the problem.

Step 1   In Windows XP, select Start | Run, type **msconfig**, and then press ENTER. In Windows Vista, select Start, type **msconfig** into the Start Search box, and then press ENTER.

The System Configuration utility opens (see Figure 17-16).

FIGURE 17-16 Using the System Configuration utility

Notice that on the General tab, you can select Diagnostic Startup. This is useful if you have just added new hardware that's causing intermittent problems, because it enables you to boot with only basic devices.

The Selective Startup feature is also nice; it lets you bypass some configuration files to see which one contains the errors that are causing problems.

Notice the SYSTEM.INI and WIN.INI tabs, which provide settings that enable you to change the load sequence of your drivers and edit the entries when you find an error.

> → **Note**
>
> The SYSTEM.INI and WIN.INI tabs are not present in Windows Vista.

Step 2 The BOOT.INI tab (labeled Boot in Windows Vista) is powerful (see Figure 17-17) and goes well beyond the CompTIA A+ exam requirements, but there are a couple of options you should know about.

One important option for troubleshooting is to create a log of what transpired during the boot process. On the BOOT.INI tab, you can enable a BOOTLOG to be created each time the system boots.

FIGURE 17-17 The BOOT.INI tab

FIGURE 17-18 Using the Services tab with Microsoft Services hidden

If you're troubleshooting a problem and you need to start in Safe Mode every time, instead of pressing F8, you can enable the /SAFEBOOT option.

Step 3 One item that I find useful is under the Services tab. Microsoft has many services that you can disable during bootup if you believe they're causing problems. The Hide All Microsoft Services option, when enabled, only displays those services you've installed—like my VMware Tools Service driver in Figure 17-18.

Step 4 The Startup tab is perhaps the most useful. You can enable or disable any of the Terminate and Stay Resident (TSR) programs that are installed. This is a good place to look if some unexplained program is trying to load every time you boot, even though you thought you'd uninstalled it.

Notice in Figure 17-19 that one program on the list doesn't have a name. I'm kind of suspicious about what this program might be doing! If you find questionable entries in your Startup tab listing, you should fire up a browser and do some research to see whether or not they're harmful.

✔ **Hint**

You can also run the System Configuration utility in Safe Mode. If you're having problems, you can boot to Safe Mode and then use this utility to identify the source of the problem.

FIGURE 17-19 Checking your startup programs

 30 MINUTES

Lab Exercise 17.07: Working with Windows System Restore

The prior labs dealt with upgrading Windows and optimizing device drivers. In some cases, installing a service pack or updating a device driver can cause problems, in which case the best thing you can do is to put the system back to the state it was in before you started. You've already worked with Safe Mode and the Recovery Console/Command Prompt when the system will not boot; this lab focuses on restoring the system to a previously working state when you can still access the system.

Learning Objectives

The successful technician knows how to restore a working Windows system that has encountered problems beyond those associated with installation and configuration problems.

At the end of this lab, you'll be able to

- Manually create a restore point in Windows

- Restore a Windows system to a restore point

Lab Materials and Setup

The materials you need for this lab are

- A working PC with Windows XP or Windows Vista installed

Getting Down to Business

Windows has a great utility to help you restore your system after a botched program or driver installation. It watches for any system changes and basically records them in a diary. To restore a system to a previous state, you can just open the diary and point to a date and time to which you want to return.

Step 1   In this step, you'll manually create a restore point in Windows. The OS automatically creates restore points each day, as well as any time you install an application, update a driver, or add a piece of hardware. In Windows XP, you also have the option to create your own restore points whenever you want and give them unique names that are meaningful to you. You might decide to create a restore point before tweaking a bunch of settings in the Display applet, for example, and name the restore point "VideoBack" in case your changes should have a dire effect on your video display.

a.   To create a restore point (Windows XP only), select Start | All Programs | Accessories | System Tools | System Restore to open the System Restore utility (see Figure 17-20).

b.   At the welcome screen, choose *Create a restore point* on the right side of the screen and click Next.

c.   Type **My Test Restore Point** and then click Create.

d.   The system takes some time building the restore file information and then displays a confirmation screen (see Figure 17-21). Click Close to exit the System Restore utility.

FIGURE 17-20 Using System Restore

FIGURE 17-21 Confirming the new restore point

You're done! That was easy, wasn't it?

Step 2 To restore the system to an earlier time, return to the System Restore utility, but this time, select *Restore my computer to an earlier time* in Windows XP. In Windows Vista, access System Restore by typing **System Restore** into the Start Search box and pressing ENTER. Then click Next.

When you click the Next button, the Select a Restore Point screen displays, with a calendar view of restore points in Windows XP (see Figure 17-22) and a list view in Windows Vista. Based on your knowledge of when your system started having problems, select a restore point and follow the prompts to complete the restore operation.

System Restore is pretty powerful. Even if you crash hard and can only boot to Safe Mode, you can still run the System Restore utility to recover your system. It sure beats the alternative!

FIGURE 17-22 Choosing a restore point

Lab Analysis Test

1. John complains that his Windows Vista system gives him a lot of grief. He tries to tweak the settings and then forgets what he changed, and it takes him days before he can straighten it back out. What tool would you recommend that he use in the future to enable him to retrace his steps and revert his system back to its former settings?

2. You've installed a new network card and sound card. Every time you boot, the system locks up, and you must boot into Safe Mode to get to a GUI. What tool can you use to assist you in locating the source of the problem?

3. Tim is a Windows XP user who feels he's really a programmer at heart—he always seems to be opening the Registry with REGEDIT and changing settings directly in the Registry. Today, it doesn't go so well, and he ends up with the Blue Screen of Death (BSOD). What can Tim use to get back to a working system?

4. Laurie has been given six computers in various stages of disrepair. Not one of the systems will boot, even though they are Windows 2000 and XP systems. A friend gives her some floppy disks labeled "ERD" and "ASR," and recommends that she boot the machines using these floppies. When she tries it, the machines display the message *Non-System disk or disk error, replace and press any key when ready*. Why?

5. William has been running his Windows XP system for a few days and notices a small yellow shield icon in the system tray/notification area. He calls you to ask what it might be.

Key Term Quiz

Use the following terms to complete the following sentences. Not all terms will be used.

ASR

automatic updates

driver signing

ERD

Event Viewer

MSCONFIG

Recovery Console

service packs

System Restore

WHQL

1. To assist in the recovery of a system crash, Windows 2000 uses the _____ process, while Windows XP uses the _____ process. Both processes require a floppy disk to store critical system files.

2. The _____ can be added as a boot menu option.

3. As operating systems age, many of the system files, drivers, and utilities are updated. It is recommended that Windows always has the latest _____ installed.

4. Microsoft qualifies devices and drivers through its _____, which approves and digitally signs drivers that are proven to work properly with Windows.

5. The _____ provides three log files—System, Security, and Application—to assist with the troubleshooting of a Windows operating system.

Chapter 18

Input/Output

Lab Exercises

One of the most important functions in any type of computing is getting information (data) in and out of the computer system. If it weren't for data moving in and out, your computer would be a boring (and pretty useless) device! You need two items to make input/output work on your PC: a peripheral device and a way to connect that peripheral device to your system unit. The typical desktop PC comes with a number of peripherals: keyboard, mouse, monitor, printer, speakers, and often a cable that runs to a network. These peripherals all come with some form of cabling/connection system.

Many of these connections are unique pairings. For example, a monitor uses either a 15-pin VESA (also called VGA) connector or a DVI connector, whereas a sound card uses S/PDIF or mini-RCA connectors—you won't see any other device commonly using these types of connectors. CompTIA wants you to have a solid understanding of these types of peripherals and their unique connections: printers using parallel connections, networks using twisted-pair cabling, monitors using VGA or DVI, and speakers using mini-RCA or S/PDIF. Entire chapters of this lab manual address these specific peripherals in more detail, but there's much more to the world of input/output than just those devices.

The most common PC input devices are keyboards and mice. Other, more exotic input devices include scanners, touch screens, and biometric readers. More general-purpose connections used by many types of peripherals include serial, USB, and FireWire. This chapter takes a look at those "other" peripherals and connections that don't really fit well into any of the other chapters.

⏱ 30 MINUTES

Lab Exercise 18.01: Exploring USB Drivers

USB's incredible ease of use makes it the most popular type of general-purpose connection used on PCs. USB is so popular that every type of peripheral (other than monitors) has someone making a USB version. The downside to this ease of use is that it can be a challenge to deal with USB when it doesn't work as specified.

Learning Objectives

At the end of this lab, you'll be able to

- Diagnose and repair common USB driver failures

- Recognize the limitations of built-in Windows USB device drivers

Lab Materials and Setup

The materials you need for this lab are

- A Windows system using USB

- At least one "human interface" USB device, such as a mouse or keyboard

- At least one mass storage USB device, such as a USB thumb drive

- At least one USB device that is neither a human interface device nor a mass storage device (for example, a wired NIC, Bluetooth hub, wireless NIC, or PDA synching cradle)

- A notepad and pencil

Getting Down to Business

The biggest problems you'll see with USB are the result of improper drivers. If you know how to recognize these problems from error messages or by using third-party tools, you shouldn't have too much trouble fixing them.

Windows comes with very good built-in support for what it calls human interface devices (HIDs), such as keyboards and mice. It also does a good job supporting most USB mass storage devices such as USB thumb drives. However, once you move outside these two classes of devices, Windows really needs the drivers supplied by the manufacturer to work properly, if at all.

✔ **Cross-Reference**

For more information on setting up USB devices, refer to the "USB Configuration" section in Chapter 18 of *Mike Meyers' CompTIA A+ Guide to Managing and Troubleshooting PCs*.

Step 1   Connect any HID or mass storage USB device to the Windows system, *without* first installing the supplied driver. Does the device work as expected? Is it missing any features? Does the device even come with drivers? Write down your conclusions and unplug the device.

_____

_____

_____

Step 2   Check the Web site of the manufacturer of the USB device you just installed to see if a driver exists. If there is a driver, download it and install it into your system. Now connect the device again. Does the device work the same as it did before?

_____

_____

Step 3   Select another USB device—specifically, one that is neither a HID nor a mass storage device—and connect it to the same system *without* first installing the supplied driver. Does the device work as expected? Is it missing any features? Does the device even come with drivers? Write down your conclusions and unplug the device.

_____

_____

_____

Step 4   Check the Web site of the manufacturer of the USB device you just installed to see if a driver exists. If there is a driver, download it and install it into your system. Did the installation work? In many cases installation will fail because Windows may have loaded an improper driver when you first installed the device. Does the device work the same as before? You'll probably find that it doesn't, for the same reason.

_____

Step 5   Go to the manufacturer's Web site and see how to remove the device driver properly. Delete the driver and then remove the device.

> ✔ **Hint**
>
> Installing a USB device without first installing the proper driver on a non-HID or mass storage device will almost always require you to uninstall the USB device completely from Device Manager. Even so, you should still check the manufacturer's Web site first!

Step 6 With the previous drivers properly removed, again install the drivers you downloaded earlier. Then insert the USB device. Does the device work as expected? Are there features now that did not appear earlier? What does this tell you about the importance of installing USB device drivers before you install the actual USB device?

_____

_____

_____

_____

Step 7 As time and available hardware allow, practice installing other USB devices and document how they work, both with and without proper drivers.

 30 MINUTES

Lab Exercise 18.02: USBDeview

This next lab is for anyone with a bad case of "peripheralitis," an incurable disease where the sufferer cannot resist buying scads of USB peripherals for their computers. Rather than having to dig through the piles of joysticks, scanners, and USB hubs around your computer, this lab will show you how to view detailed information about everything connected to a USB port on your computer, using a nifty program called USBDeview.

Learning Objectives

At the end of this lab, you'll be able to

- Recognize a system's USB capabilities using Nir Sofer's USBDeview utility

Lab Materials and Setup

The materials you need for this lab are

- A Windows system using USB

- A copy of Nir Sofer's USBDeview utility (www.nirsoft.net/utils/usb_devices_view.html)

- At least one USB hub

- A notepad and pencil

This lab is very flexible in terms of the types of USB (Low-Speed, Full-Speed, Hi-Speed, SuperSpeed) supported on the system, as well as the number and type of USB devices. Add as many USB devices as possible (you can have up to 127 devices per USB controller, so knock yourself out!), and try to get at least one USB hub, either powered or unpowered. The more USB devices and hubs you can get, the more interesting this lab becomes.

Getting Down to Business

Using the USBDeview program, you can view detailed information about your USB controllers and the devices currently running on them.

Step 1 Start the PC with as few USB devices physically installed as possible.

Step 2 Make sure a copy of USBDeview is on the system. USBDeview is a freestanding executable file and does not require installation. Place the file on your Windows desktop for easy access.

Step 3 Open Device Manager and count all the USB controllers (see Figure 18-1). On older systems you should see two types of controllers: a Standard OpenHCD Host Controller and a Standard Enhanced Host Controller. Newer systems will use different names such as "Universal Host Controller" and "Enhanced Controller." Do you see two different types of USB controllers?

Step 4 To get the most out of USBDeview, you need to do some setup. First, go to www.linux-usb.org/ usb.ids and save the Web page as **usb.ids** in the same folder that holds the USBDeview.exe file. Next, start USBDeview and select View | Choose columns. Make sure your first two columns are Vendor Name and Product Name. Then click Options and uncheck Display Disconnected Devices. When you're done, USBDeview should look something like Figure 18-2.

Great! Time to work. Compare what you see in Device Manager to what you see in USBDeview. How do they compare? Do you see any differences? Count the ports reported by USBDeview and compare that to the actual number of ports on your system. Are the numbers the same?

_____

_____

_____

Figure 18-1 Two USB controller types in Device Manager

Figure 18-2 USBDeview in action

> ✔ **Hint**
>
> Sometimes, running USBDeview and Device Manager at the same time will confuse Device Manager. If you're having problems, just close and reopen USBDeview as needed.

Step 5   Insert a USB device, making sure to install the correct drivers first. USBDeview should update as soon as the device is inserted. Document which USB host controller (look under the Device Name column; USBDeview uses the term "hub" when it should say "controller") and port are running the device. Unplug the device and reinsert it into a different USB port. Document the changes. Is it on a different controller (hub)? Is it on a different port?

Step 6   Repeat Step 5 for other USB devices until all of your USB devices are in use.

 30 MINUTES

Lab Exercise 18.03: Paging Dr. Keyboard!

Keyboards are plentiful and common, and a new basic keyboard is very inexpensive. Even with cheap keyboards, users tend to get attached to these devices over time—and in the case of an expensive keyboard with lots of extra buttons and features, the user may have both a financial *and* an emotional attachment! For these reasons, it's important that you learn to play "Dr. Keyboard," fixing these devices when they break.

Learning Objectives

At the end of this lab, you'll be able to

- Repair stuck keyboard keys

- Dismantle and clean a keyboard

Lab Materials and Setup

The materials you need for this lab are

- A Windows system

- As many "throw-away" keyboards as possible (functional keyboards that you won't mind throwing away at the end of this lab; connection type is unimportant as long as they're usable by a Windows system)

- A medium-sized flathead screwdriver

- Compressed air

- A lint-free cloth

✔ **Hint**

Try to avoid using older (pre-2004) laptop keyboards, as many older laptop keyboards used a delicate type of scissors key connector that would shatter if pried off.

Getting Down to Business

In this exercise, you'll dismantle one or more keyboards, cleaning up the keyboard components in the process before reassembling the device(s) and testing for functionality.

Step 1 Disconnect the keyboard from the Windows system. Try prying off two or three keys using the flathead screwdriver (see Figure 18-3). Include more difficult keys such as the SPACEBAR, ENTER/RETURN, and a key from the center of the keyboard such as the letter G. Inspect the bottom of the key and the key post that it sits on—how much dirt is there? Reinsert the keys, making sure they are snapped all the way down.

Step 2 Test the keyboard by plugging it into a Windows system. If any of the keys you removed aren't working, double-check that they're properly snapped in. Shut down the system and remove the keyboard. Repeat this process until all keys are working.

FIGURE 18-3 Removing the CTRL key with a screwdriver

→ **Note**

What should you do if you break a key? Well, nobody sells replacement parts for keyboards—they're just too darn cheap to bother! You might be lucky enough to have a nonworking keyboard that's the exact same model, which you can cannibalize; otherwise, just consign the affected keyboard to the scrap heap after you've used it for this lab.

Step 3   Insert the nozzle of the compressed air under a key and start blasting away. If the keyboard is really old or looks dirty, you may want to do this outside! Did you see any dust or crumbs come out?

Step 4   Completely dismantle the keyboard. Most keyboards have a number of screws underneath that you must first remove to begin this process. Inspect the screws—are they different sizes? Keep track of which screw goes into which hole.

Step 5   The inside of the keyboard will have a number of plastic contact templates (see Figure 18-4). Remove these, keeping track of their relation to each other so you can reassemble them. Wipe down each template with the lint-free cloth dampened with water. If you run into serious dirt, add a bit of mild detergent and repeat until the keyboard is clean.

✔ **Hint**

All keyboards have small circuit boards inside as well. Don't get them wet!

FIGURE 18-4 Inside a keyboard

Step 6 After allowing everything to dry, reassemble the keyboard and test it on a Windows system. If the keyboard is not working properly, dismantle it and try again.

Lab Analysis Test

1. Why is it very important that you always install a USB device's driver before you physically install the USB device?

2. John encounters a system with a Bluetooth USB device installed, and the user is complaining that many of the features that should be included with this device don't seem to exist. What does he need to do to fix this problem?

3. Beth's brand-new USB keyboard has a piece of the packaging stuck under the keyboard in such a way that she simply can't pull it out, even with a pair of needle-nose pliers. What should she do to fix this problem?

4. USBDeview is an interesting tool for observing how USB works. How might this tool come in handy for diagnosing USB problems?

5. Ken has just purchased a fast new 4-GB USB flash drive, complete with the latest U3 "smart drive" technology. He plugs it into his older IBM laptop using the USB 1.0 ports on the system. What should he expect to have happen?

Key Term Quiz

Use the following terms to complete the following sentences. Not all terms will be used.

driver

Full-Speed

Hi-Speed

human interface device

Low-Speed

Standard Enhanced Host Controller

Standard OpenHCD Host Controller

SuperSpeed

USB host controller

USB hub

USB mass storage

USBDeview

1. A USB keyboard or mouse would fall into the _____ category.

2. Every USB device is controlled by a _____.

3. Some USB devices need a special _____ to operate correctly.

4. The four USB speeds from slowest to fastest are _____, _____, _____, and _____.

5. Windows calls the controller for Hi-Speed USB devices a _____.

Chapter 19
Video

Lab Exercises

Few components affect the PC user like the video system, the primary output for the PC. As you know from the textbook, the video system has two main hardware components—monitor and display adapter—that work together to produce the image on your screen. Both components must be installed and configured properly in Windows, or your viewing pleasure will be seriously compromised. Good techs know how to do video right!

In this set of labs, you'll install a display adapter, hook up a monitor, load video drivers, and configure Windows for optimal viewing. You'll then work with the growing practice of using multiple monitors (for example, a projector and a laptop screen) to expand your desktop viewing area. The last lab exercise will run you through some of the typical troubleshooting issues that techs face when dealing with video.

> ✖ **Warning**
>
> It is critical to understand that only *trained* monitor technicians should remove the cover of a video monitor (or a television set, for that matter). The inside of a traditional monitor might look similar to the interior of a PC, with printed circuit boards and related components, but there's a big difference: No PC has voltages up to 50,000 volts or more inside, but most CRT monitors *do*. So be sure to get one thing clear—casually opening a monitor and snooping around has the potential to become harmful to you and the monitor—and in cases of extreme carelessness, it can even be deadly! Even when the power is disconnected, certain components (capacitors) still retain substantial levels of voltage for an extended period of time. Capacitors work like batteries. Yes, they can maintain 50,000 volts! If you inadvertently short one of the capacitors, a large discharge will occur into the monitor circuits, destroying them. If you're touching the metal frame, you could fry yourself—to death. Given this risk, certain aspects of monitor repair fall outside the necessary skill set for a standard PC support person, and definitely outside the CompTIA A+ exam domains. Make sure you understand the problems you can fix safely and the ones you need to hand over to a qualified electronics repair shop.

🕐 30 MINUTES

Lab Exercise 19.01: Installing Video

Your office staff's computers need a serious video upgrade. Some of the PCs have tiny 15-inch LCD monitors that simply have to go, while others have decent 17-inch and 19-inch LCDs that have a year or two of life left in them. Your boss has bought new PCIe video cards and some widescreen LCD monitors. You're tasked with installing the cards, loading drivers, and setting everything up in Windows.

✔ **Cross-Reference**

For the details of CRT versus LCD monitors, refer to the "CRT Monitors" and "LCD Monitors" sections in Chapter 19 of *Mike Meyers' CompTIA A+ Guide to Managing and Troubleshooting PCs.*

Learning Objectives

At the end of this lab, you'll be able to

- Identify the make and model of a video card

- Install a video display adapter card

- Check BIOS for proper video settings

- Adjust the monitor for the proper display

- Optimize the video settings in Windows

Lab Materials and Setup

The materials you need for this lab are

- A working PC with Windows installed

- A working monitor (access to both a CRT and an LCD monitor is recommended)

- A working computer system with access to the Internet

✔ **Hint**

Classrooms that have a variety of different monitor types and video display adapter cards are a plus.

Getting Down to Business

To begin this lab, you'll become familiar with the video components in your system. You'll then step through the proper installation and configuration of a video adapter.

✖ Warning

Some versions of Microsoft Windows have problems when you make changes to the video display adapters, even when you're simply removing and reinstalling the same card into a different slot. If you perform this lab on a test machine, you should have no real problem if things go wrong. If you're using your primary PC to do the lab, however, make certain you have current drivers available for your video card, or a source to get drivers if necessary.

Step 1 Shut down your system properly and unplug the power cable from the system unit and the wall. Remove the cover from the PC to expose the expansion buses.

    a.   Find your video display adapter card (the one to which the monitor is attached). What type of video display adapter is installed: PCIe, AGP, or PCI? _____

✔ Hint

Many laptop computers and some low- to mid-level desktop systems include display adapters integrated right into the electronics of the motherboard. On desktop systems with this configuration, the 15-pin connector will appear in line with the PS/2 and USB ports. If your system uses this type of display adapter, the overall performance of the system may suffer because the display typically "steals" 64 MB or more of system RAM to serve as video RAM. Not only is this a small amount of video RAM for today's PC applications, it also lowers the total amount of system RAM available for the system. Laptops are usually designed around this limitation, but if your desktop system is of this type, you can improve the performance (and usually the video quality) by installing a display adapter card and disabling the onboard video in the BIOS. Typically, you can also balance between video and system performance by selecting how much memory is allocated to the onboard video in BIOS.

---

    b.   Detach the monitor's cable from the video card.

        Using good ESD avoidance procedures, remove the screw that holds the card in place, put it in a secure location, and then remove your video display adapter card (see Figure 19-1). Examine it closely to answer the following questions. Be careful not to touch the expansion slot contacts on the card!

    c.   Look for a name or model number on the adapter's circuit board or chipset.

FIGURE 19-1 This video card has a large cooling fan for the graphics processing unit (GPU) and its onboard RAM chips.

Who is the manufacturer, or what is the model number? Write it down. (Note that for this lab's scenario, you'd actually be looking up the information for the new video cards, not the ones already installed—*those* will most likely be donated to charity!)

_____

Be sure to write down as much information as you can collect from the display adapter for a later assignment.

d. Reinsert the video card into the same slot, and make sure it is properly seated. Reattach the monitor cable and test your system with the case still open to see if it works. This could save you the frustration that results when you close the case, fire up the system, and get a video error. (Not that I've ever done that!)

✔ Hint

AGP and PCIe cards can be a little tricky. They must be seated perfectly or they will not work. Many of these types of cards use slots with locking levers—if you were observant when you removed the card initially, you'll know what you have to do now for proper physical installation.

e. Boot your system and open your favorite browser to search the Web.

Conduct your search using the information you've gathered about the manufacturer and model number of your card.

Can you find the specifications for your display adapter? _____

What is the highest resolution you can achieve with your video adapter according to these specifications? _____

How much memory is available? _____

What type of memory is used? _____

Does the adapter support SLI or CrossFire? _____

Does the adapter have any features that are unusual or unfamiliar to you, such as an HDMI connector? _____

Step 2 Reboot your system and press the proper key sequence to enter the CMOS setup utility. Depending on the BIOS manufacturer and version, there can be as many as five or more video-related settings. My lab system has ten settings directly related to video or the PCIe slot. Complete each of these questions based on your specific BIOS. Some of the names of the sections will undoubtedly differ from the ones presented here. Search around a bit and you'll find video options in your CMOS.

On the Standard CMOS Setup or similar screen, how many choices are there for video, and how is your video set? _____

On the Chipset Features Setup or similar screen, what is the value for your Video RAM Cacheable setting? _____

Are there any PCIe-specific settings? _____

Are there any settings for the amount of RAM the onboard adapter will use? _____

On the Power Management Setup or similar screen, do you have settings to control how the monitor and video adapter will react when not in use for a period of time? What are your settings? _____

On the Integrated Peripherals or similar screen, do you have an Init Display First setting? What are the choices? _____

What does your setting say? _____

Know that when this setting is wrong, the monitor display might not work.

Step 3 You'll now examine a monitor and see what external controls it has. If you're not in a computer lab, you can go to your local computer store and examine a wide variety of monitors.

Figures 19-2 and 19-3 show the control buttons for adjusting the display attributes for an LCD and a CRT monitor, respectively. Both of these have the controls on the front of the monitor, but some have the controls behind a door under the front of the monitor screen, and others may have them on the back.

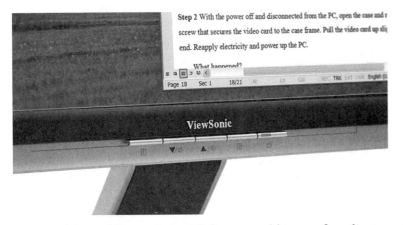

FIGURE 19-2 An LCD monitor with front-panel buttons for adjustments

FIGURE 19-3 Front controls on a CRT monitor

A monitor can have quite a few adjustable features. How many of the following can you adjust on your LCD monitor?

Brightness   _____

Contrast   _____

Clock   _____

H-position   _____

V-position   _____

Color temperature   _____

Auto balance   _____

Sharpness   _____

Gamma   _____

Signal select (for LCDs with both VGA and DVI inputs)   _____

Full screen   _____

Language   _____

How many of these can you adjust on your CRT monitor?

Brightness   _____

Contrast   _____

Color saturation   _____

Vertical size   _____

Vertical position   _____

Horizontal size   _____

Horizontal position   _____

Pincushioning (for adjusting displays that are narrow
in the middle but flare out at the top and bottom)   _____

Keystoning (for adjusting displays that are narrow
at the top but flare out at the bottom)   _____

Degauss (for adjusting displays that have become
fuzzy due to electromagnetic interference)   _____

Play with the controls of your monitor or a test monitor. If the current settings use percentages, write down the settings before doing any adjustments. Then follow these steps:

a.   Change the settings such as color and sizing. Don't be shy!

b.   Put the settings back as close as possible to their original positions.

c.   Optimize the screen for clarity and position.

Step 4   The hardware is set up properly and the BIOS settings should be correct, so now you need to configure and optimize the Windows settings that determine your video display characteristics. To do this, you need to use the Display applet.

✔ **Hint**

This lab simulates a working PC that you upgrade with new hardware and drivers. All the steps can work just as well for installing a video card into a new system, although the pace of that installation would differ. In a new system, you would physically install the video card, let Windows use generic VGA drivers until you make sure you can boot properly, and only then install the drivers for the video card. Finally, you'd go to the Display applet and optimize the video card settings. Windows is fairly good at finding a suitable driver the first time around, but you should still understand how to locate and update drivers for your video card.

In Windows 2000/XP, navigate to the Display applet and click the Settings tab. In Windows Vista, go to Control Panel | Personalization | Display Settings. This displays the monitor settings, such as those shown in Figure 19-4.

✖ **Warning**

You're going to make changes to the look and feel of Windows. Making some of these changes can result in frustrating and time-consuming problems. Use a test machine if you have one available. If you must use your own machine, write down all your display settings before you make any changes.

Each video display adapter manufacturer has different options for its cards. By clicking the Advanced button, you can access more information about the display adapter. You may see a choice for setting the refresh rate, as well as other features. Look through the settings on the Advanced tab, and see what your display adapter manufacturer provides. Remember that the video adapter "pushes" the monitor. If you set the refresh too high, it can cause problems, and in the case of older CRTs may even damage your monitor.

Write down your display's current resolution, color depth, and refresh rate.

FIGURE 19-4 The Display Properties dialog box's Settings tab

Close the Advanced dialog box (if you selected it), but leave the Display Properties dialog box open.

Make some changes to the background and colors on your screen. You'll find these options on the Desktop and Appearance tabs, respectively. Be sure to note the original settings so you can change things back when you're done.

✔ **Hint**

The setting changes suggested in this step are perfectly safe and easy to undo.

Change the desktop background to something you might like better. Then try the following:

- Experiment with color combinations.

- Make some changes to the displayed fonts and menu bars.

- Experiment with changing the colors and resolution of your display.

    Can your machine run in 16-bit color? _____

    How about 24-bit color? _____

    Can you run 800 × 600 resolution? _____

Can you run 1024 × 768 resolution? _____

Can you run 1280 × 960 resolution? _____

Do you have any other options? _____

In Windows 2000/XP, click the Advanced button again. In Windows Vista, click Advanced Settings and open the Monitor tab. Experiment with changing the refresh rate (see Figure 19-5).

✔ **Hint**

Because of the way that LCD monitors work, the refresh rate setting doesn't really apply to them. As a general rule, LCD monitors display a stable, flicker-free image at 60 hertz (Hz). There are no visible differences between 85 Hz and 60 Hz.

Can you make specific numeric changes? _____

Are the Optimal and Adapter Default settings the only choices you have? _____

FIGURE 19-5 A typical refresh setting under Display Properties

✔ **Hint**

The refresh rate is not an option on all video adapters. This setting may be in a different location, or not on your system at all.

Make sure you return all the settings to their original values, and then close the Display Properties dialog box.

Check the drivers for your video card and monitor. Are they "standard" drivers, or are they specific to your hardware? Follow these steps:

a.   Go to the Device Manager, locate your display adapter, right-click, and select Properties.

b.   Locate your driver information.

c.   Can you identify the version number(s) of your video drivers? Write them down.

_____

d.   Go online and find the manufacturer's Web site.

e.   Check to see if newer drivers are available. If so, download and install them. (Do this on a test machine first. Get comfortable with the whole process before you do this on your personal computer.)

How did this affect your machine?

_____

✔ **Hint**

New drivers will sometimes fail to work properly, thereby crippling your PC. Windows XP and higher have the driver rollback feature that enables you to go back to a driver that worked correctly in case this should happen. Refer to Chapter 17 for a refresher on how to do this.

Step 5   One more place to look for video settings is the Power Management Control Panel applet. Take a look at any power management settings you may have.

Go to the Control Panel and double-click the Power Management or Power Options applet, if you have one. Read through the list of available power management schemes.

Which one do you have running? _____

How long is the period of inactivity before your monitor shuts off? _____

Close the applet and the Control Panel.

🕐 30 MINUTES

Lab Exercise 19.02: Configuring Multiple Displays

Your consulting firm has just been awarded a contract to perform complete upgrades on the 12 digital audio workstations at a local recording studio. Among the various considerations for this type of application—large data storage, backups, fast processors, and loads of memory—the application also requires high-performance display adapters with multiple monitors for each station. It is not unusual for a recording engineer to have three or four critical windows open simultaneously during a session, so the studio design has included three widescreen monitors for each station.

You jump on the project and immediately stage one of the systems in the shop to run it through its paces. You decide to use one of the new ASUS motherboards with three PCIe slots and three high-performance NVIDIA display adapters. You finish the video configuration and attach three 30-inch widescreen monitors—this system looks impressive!

✔ **Cross-Reference**

For additional information on configuring your multiple displays, refer to the "Installing and Configuring Video" section in Chapter 19 of *Mike Meyers' CompTIA A+ Guide to Managing and Troubleshooting PCs*.

Learning Objectives

At the end of this lab, you'll be able to

- Install an additional video display adapter card

- Configure a system to use multiple displays

- Expand the desktop across two or more displays

Lab Materials and Setup

The materials you need for this lab are

- A working PC with Windows installed

- At least one additional display adapter or a display adapter that supports multiple monitors

- At least one additional working monitor (CRT or LCD)

✔ **Hint**

This lab exercise does not require any of the high-end equipment discussed in the scenario. You should be able to complete the steps to configure multiple monitors using a few video cards and the monitors in your classroom lab. You can even use the integrated display adapter on many motherboards and install one additional video card to complete the lab steps. If time permits, hop on a system with Internet access and explore some of the components discussed in the scenario. Manufacturers such as ASUS, NVIDIA, and NEC are always adding new technology to their product lines.

Getting Down to Business

To explore the system configuration presented in the opening scenario, you will install at least one additional display adapter and monitor on a working system. You will then use the Display applet in Windows to configure the multiple monitors for use as an expanded desktop.

Step 1   Shut down your system properly and unplug the power cable from the system unit and the wall. Remove the cover from the PC to expose the expansion bus slots.

   a.   Verify the type (PCI, AGP, or PCIe) and location of the current video display adapter. Using proper ESD avoidance procedures and one of the available expansion slots (depending on the additional video card available to you), install a second video display adapter in your system. Remember that AGP and PCIe cards can be a little finicky during installation, so make sure they are in securely.

✔ **Hint**

If you happen to have an AGP adapter installed, your second adapter will need to be PCI, as that's the only type of slot you're likely to have that can handle a video adapter. If you're in a classroom environment, your instructor should be able to provide you with an additional video card and monitor to facilitate this lab. In some cases you can use an integrated display adapter as your primary display, installing the new display as the secondary. Follow your instructor's directions in addition to the directions included in this exercise.

Also, you may have a display adapter that already supports multiple monitors and has two display ports on a single card. If this is the case, you don't need to add a second adapter to set up multiple monitors, but it's good to practice, either way.

b.   Attach the second monitor cable to the new display adapter, and test your system with the case still open to see if it works.

To verify that the second display adapter and monitor have been installed correctly, are recognized by the system, and have drivers available, open the Device Manager and expand the display adapter's icon. View the properties of the newly installed card and select the Drivers tab. Does everything appear to be in order?

c.   If the new display adapter is not working properly, you may need to install specific drivers or updated drivers. Access the Internet to download and install the appropriate drivers for your display adapter.

Step 2   Now that the hardware is set up and functioning properly, you will configure Windows to expand your desktop across two or more displays. To do this, you will again open the Display applet.

In Windows 2000/XP, navigate to the Display Properties dialog box's Settings tab. In Windows Vista, go to Control Panel | Personalization | Display Settings. This shows the monitor settings and should now display two monitor icons, as shown in Figure 19-6.

FIGURE 19-6 The Display Properties dialog box's
Settings tab, showing two monitors available

Now complete the following steps to expand your desktop across the displays you have installed.

a. Click the drop-down arrow next to the Display field. Are both of your display adapters available? _____

b. Click the second monitor icon, check the *Extend my Windows desktop onto this monitor* box, and click the Apply button. Your monitor icons should now look something like Figure 19-7, and the display on your monitors should change accordingly.

c. Click and drag the Display Properties dialog box from one monitor to the other. Notice that the standard setup has the second display as the display to the right, so the expansion should allow you to use the second monitor as the rightmost portion of the desktop. Open a few windows and place them in different locations on the two monitors (see Figure 19-8).

d. Experiment with the "virtual" placement of the monitors by clicking one of the numbered monitors and dragging it around the other monitor(s). Also click and highlight one of the numbered monitors and select it as the primary display.

Can you place the monitors on top of each other (see Figure 19-9)? _____

Can you set the second display as the primary monitor? _____

Right-click one of the displays in the Display Properties window and select Identify. What are the results? _____

FIGURE 19-7 Extending the Windows desktop

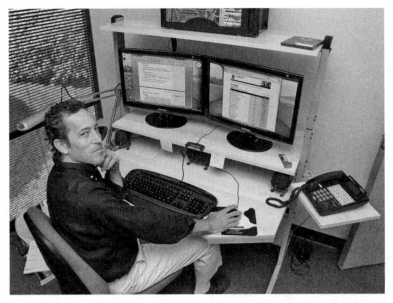

FIGURE 19-8 Dual monitors displaying multiple open windows

FIGURE 19-9 Configuring monitors to be "virtually" on top of each other

30 MINUTES

Lab Exercise 19.03: Troubleshooting Video

Video troubleshooting really boils down to two distinct questions. First, are the physical video components installed and configured properly, as discussed in Lab Exercise 19.01? Second, do the current video display adapter and CPU support the software technologies you're trying to use? (Or have you loaded that killer game and completely overwhelmed your video subsystem?) In this lab exercise, you'll create connectivity problems to simulate real-world installation problems, and use the DirectX Diagnostic Tool to analyze your system.

Learning Objectives

At the end of this lab, you'll be able to

- Recognize and fix typical video installation and connectivity problems

- Use the Microsoft DirectX Diagnostic Tool to analyze and test the graphic display attributes of a PC system

Lab Materials and Setup

The materials you need for this lab are

- A working PC with Windows installed

- Any version of the Microsoft DirectX Diagnostic Tool installed

Getting Down to Business

If you went through Lab Exercise 19.01 and had typical results—video card not seated properly, forgetting to plug things in all the way, and so on—you can probably skip Steps 1 and 2 of this lab. If you had a perfect reinstall, on the other hand, then definitely do all of the steps!

Step 1   Loosen the screws that hold the monitor data cable securely to the video card. With the system fully powered up and in Windows—and being gentle with your hardware—partially disconnect the monitor cable.

What happened to the screen? _____

With many monitors, a loose cable results in a seriously degraded display. Colors fade out or a single color disappears, or the display may appear grainy or snowy, for example. If you run into these symptoms in the field, check your connectivity!

Connect the monitor cable and tighten the restraining screws to resume normal operation.

FIGURE 19-10 Using the DirectX Diagnostic Tool

Step 2 With the power off and disconnected from the PC, open the case and remove the screw that secures the video card to the case frame. Pull the video card up slightly on one end. Reapply electricity and power up the PC.

What happened? _____

You might have to run through this a couple of times to get the desired effect, which is a seemingly dead PC and some beeping from the system speaker. That long-short-short beep code is pretty universally recognizable as the PC's cry for help: "Hey! My video card isn't seated properly!"

With the power off and disconnected, reseat your video card, reinstall the restraining screw, and power up your PC to resume normal operation.

Step 3 Access the Microsoft DirectX Diagnostic Tool. In Windows 2000/XP, select Start | All Programs | Accessories | System Tools | System Information. Select Tools | DirectX Diagnostic Tool (see Figure 19-10). In Windows Vista, type **dxdiag** into the Start Search box and press ENTER.

✔ **Hint**

There is a faster way to get to the DirectX Diagnostic Tool in Windows 2000/XP too! Just go to Start | Run, type **dxdiag**, and click OK.

Figure 19-11 Viewing the DirectX Diagnostic Tool's Display tab

Step 4 Select the Display tab (see Figure 19-11).

What is the name of your display adapter? _____

How much total memory is on the adapter? _____

What is the current display mode? _____

What is the driver name and version? _____

Does it display a driver version date? _____

Should you look for a more current driver? _____

Step 5 Check out the Notes box at the bottom of the Display tab, and read the information provided. This is where you can find out about any conflicts or problem areas.

Do you show any conflicting information? If so, what's the problem?

_____

Step 6 Select and test the DirectDraw feature (Windows 2000/XP only, since the version of DirectX that Vista and 7 use, DirectX 10, got rid of these features), and follow the instructions.

Did the test complete correctly? _____

Step 7 Select and test the Direct3D feature (again, Windows 2000/XP only), and follow the instructions.

Did the test complete correctly? _____

Step 8 Some programs run very slowly or not at all unless Microsoft DirectDraw or Direct3D hardware acceleration is available. On the Display tab, look in the DirectX Features section to see whether DirectDraw, Direct3D, or AGP texture acceleration is set to Not Available.

You may need to enable these items or adjust your graphics acceleration, as described in the following steps. You might also consider upgrading your hardware if necessary to improve performance.

In Windows 2000/XP only, go to the Control Panel, open Display, and select the Settings tab. Click Advanced, and select the Troubleshoot tab. Move the Hardware Acceleration slider to Full.

✔ **Hint**

If you're looking at a Windows 2000 system, the tab under the Advanced options for hardware acceleration is called Performance or Troubleshooting.

Lab Analysis Test

1. If you remove an AGP video display adapter and replace it with a PCIe video display adapter, what must you do to be sure the Windows desktop will display properly?

2. Your nephew Brian visited and used your computer last night, and this morning your monitor is dead. What should you do first, second, and third?

3. What can happen if the refresh rate for a CRT is set too high?

4. Teresa installed a new game, but she is frustrated because it responds too slowly. What might she check?

5. Taylor installed a new video display adapter, but the best setting he can adjust it to is 800 × 600 resolution with 256 colors. What must he do to make it go higher?

Key Term Quiz

Use the following terms to complete the following sentences. Not all terms will be used.

color depth

Direct3D

DirectX Diagnostic Tool

Display applet

Display Settings

hardware acceleration

Init display first

refresh rate

resolution

1. Once software is installed, test your video using Microsoft's _____.

2. Erin's monitor was set to 640 × 480, a very low _____.

3. John complained constantly about getting headaches every day. When you looked at his PC, you noted that the screen flickered. John's monitor had the _____ set too low!

4. The _____ is the one-stop shop in Windows for changing your video settings. In Windows Vista, many of these same settings can be found in _____.

5. _____ can offer excellent visuals in games and not bog down the system.

Chapter 20
Multimedia

Lab Exercises

You have been hired as an entry-level tech for a public school district. Your first day on the job, the technology manager asks how familiar you are with the recording, storing, and playback of audio files on computer systems. It turns out that the history department wants the students to be able to record audio documentaries on historical events, store the files on the network, and produce podcasts of the documentaries. Demonstrating your enthusiasm, you respond that you are somewhat familiar with sound and will tackle the project. You are tasked with researching the sound card, building the prototype system, and providing some basic audio recording and storage training to the history instructors.

As a competent PC tech, you need to understand not just the tasks of installing the physical sound card and associated drivers, but also the applications that take advantage of the PC's sound capabilities. As such, the CompTIA A+ certification exams expect you to know about sound cards and their workings. The following lab exercises introduce you to sound card hardware and drivers, as well as the basic use of some of the popular Windows audio applications.

 30 MINUTES

Lab Exercise 20.01: Installing Sound

The first task on the agenda is to do a little research on sound cards and choose a few that meet the needs of this project. There are a number of different sound chips, and the "card" can be anything from the onboard sound capability of a mid-priced system to professional multichannel (input/output) devices used in recording studios. After you assemble a few candidates, you will select a sound card and then install, configure, and test that card. For the purpose of completing this lab, it is perfectly acceptable to use any working card, or an onboard sound device if that's what you have available.

Learning Objectives

This lab teaches you the basics of installing and configuring a sound card.

At the end of this lab, you'll be able to

- Identify features of sound cards

- Remove and install a sound card and associated devices (speakers and microphone)

- Configure a sound card

Lab Materials and Setup

The materials you need for this lab are

- A working computer system running Windows

- A removable sound card, microphone, and speakers properly installed and functioning (the sound drivers must either be part of the operating system in use or be available on disc or online)

✖ Warning

Different versions of Windows handle drivers differently, to say the least. You should have a current driver for your sound card handy, just in case Windows decides it cannot remember your sound card when you go to reinstall!

Getting Down to Business

This lab will step you through removing, researching specifications for, installing, and configuring a sound card.

✔ Cross-Reference

For more information on sound cards, review the "Getting the Right Sound Hardware" section in Chapter 20 of *Mike Meyers' CompTIA A+ Guide to Managing and Troubleshooting PCs*.

Step 1 Begin by examining the configuration and resources currently being used by the sound card. Turn on your machine and boot to Windows, and then open the Device Manager (see Figure 20-1).

✔ Hint

There are several ways to access the Device Manager. If you need a memory jog, review the discussion of paths in Chapter 4.

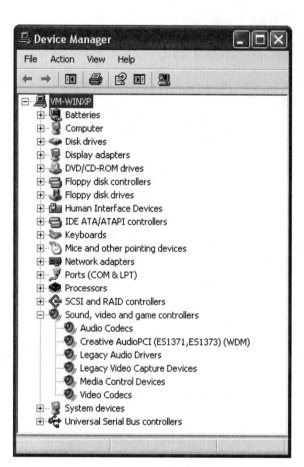

FIGURE 20-1 The Device Manager in Windows XP

Now follow these steps:

a. Click the plus sign (+) next to *Sound, video and game controllers*.

b. Highlight the sound card icon.

✔ Hint

The name of the sound card icon differs according to the type of sound card you have installed. A Creative Labs SoundBlaster Live! card, for example, has the entry listed as "Creative SB Live! Series (WDM)." Try them all if it's not obvious at first glance which is the appropriate icon.

c. Right-click and select Properties.

d. Click the Resources tab.

   Verify which resources the sound device is using, and confirm that there are no conflicts.

   Which interrupt request (IRQ) is listed? _____

   What direct memory access (DMA) channels are listed, if any? _____

   What input/output (I/O) addresses are listed? _____

e. Click the Driver tab, and record all the available information about the driver that is currently installed.

   _____

Step 2   Take a moment and look up the specifications of your current sound card online. Identify the following:

   Resolution _____

   Sampling rate _____

   Dynamic range _____

   Signal-to-noise ratio _____

   Now see if you can find this information online for some other cards—try M-AUDIO Revolution 5.1, Creative SoundBlaster X-Fi, SoundMAX Integrated Digital Audio, and Turtle Beach Montego DDL.

Step 3   Now that you've seen what resources are currently being used, and some of the relevant specifications, the next step is to practice removing and reinstalling the sound card.

✔ **Hint**

This lab assumes that you have a removable sound card, not onboard sound. If all you have to work with is a system with onboard sound, go into the CMOS setup utility and turn off the onboard sound. Make what observations you can and resume the exercise with Step 4. When the time comes in the second half of Step 4 to reinstall the sound card, just go back into CMOS and enable the onboard sound again.

a. Close the Device Manager and shut down your system properly. Unplug the power cord.

b. Remove the case cover from your system and locate the sound card (see Figure 20-2).

   What type of slot does the card use? _____

c. Disconnect any cables that are attached to the sound card (both internal and external), take out the screw that secures the sound card to the case, and then carefully remove the card. Make sure you're properly grounded before you touch the card!

FIGURE 20-2 A typical sound card

What sort of internal connectors does the card have? _____

What sort of external connectors does it have? _____

Does the card have jumpers? What are they used for? Again, look on the Internet for the answers. Find the name of the card manufacturer and search that company's Web site for information on your specific model. This information is also available in the documentation for the card, if you still have it around.

_____

_____

What is the brand name of the sound-processing chip?

_____

Is the name on the chip different from the name of the manufacturer of the card? (For example, the chip might have ESS printed on it, while the board is marked *Creative Labs*.)

_____

Describe the cables you disconnected when you removed the sound card.

_____

Does the card have an IDE interface? If so, you have a really old card. How would the IDE interface be used? _____

✔ **Hint**

In old systems that had only one IDE controller on the motherboard, how were CD-ROM drives connected when you had two hard drives in the system?

Step 4 With the card out of your system, turn on the machine and let it boot to the Windows desktop. Then go to the Device Manager and see if your sound card is still listed.

Did Windows automatically remove the device when the card was removed? _____

If the sound card is still listed, highlight its icon, right-click, and select Uninstall. (Am I sure? Yes, I'm sure!)

Save your changes and shut your system off properly.

The next steps will confirm that the device has been removed:

a. Reboot your system, go to the Device Manager, and confirm that the sound device is no longer listed.

b. Shut down your system and disconnect the power cord. Insert the sound card in the slot where you originally found it, secure the card to the case using the screw you removed, and reconnect all the cables.

c. Reboot the system. When plug and play (PnP) kicks in, your system should recognize that you have added a card.

Windows will now locate the software drivers for the new hardware you installed. In fact, unless you uninstalled them, the drivers should still be on your system.

Step 5 Return to the Device Manager and repeat Step 1 to verify what resources the sound card is now using and confirm that there are no conflicts.

What IRQ is listed now? _____

What DMA channels are listed, if any? _____

What I/O addresses are listed? _____

Are the settings the same as in Step 1 before you removed the card? _____

Go to the Drivers tab and confirm that Windows installed the same drivers in the system. If necessary, use the driver disc to reinstall the correct drivers.

Step 6 To confirm that sound is working properly, start by ensuring that the speakers are powered and connected, and that the volume is set at a comfortable level.

Make sure your speakers are plugged into the proper jack on the sound card.

Is the speaker pair plugged into a working AC outlet, or does it have good batteries?

_____

Is there a volume adjustment knob on your speakers? _____

If you have a volume knob, adjust it to the middle position, and then access the Control Panel.

Now place a Volume icon in the taskbar's system tray/notification area so that volume adjustments will be more convenient. Follow the procedure that matches your operating system.

- In Windows 2000, open the Sounds and Multimedia Control Panel applet, and check the *Show volume control on the taskbar* box.

- In Windows XP, open the Sounds and Audio Devices Control Panel applet, and check the *Place volume icon in the taskbar* box.

- In Windows Vista, right-click the taskbar and select Properties. Then, click the Notification Area tab and make sure Volume is checked under *Select which system icons to always show*.

Once you have the Volume icon in the taskbar, double-click it to open the volume controls and then follow these steps:

a. Check to be sure that the *Mute all* option is not selected (see Figure 20-3).

b. Select Options | Properties.

c. Select the volume controls that you want to control.

d. Click OK to close the Properties window.

e. Now adjust all the sliders to the center position.

You now have a good starting point to play sounds. Once you have ensured that the speakers are successfully putting out sound, you can go back and customize the levels to your liking.

Figure 20-3 Setting the volume controls in Windows XP

Step 7   Test the speakers, and adjust the sound volume to a comfortable level. A good tool to use to test your sound card is the DirectX Diagnostic Tool. This is the same tool you used in Chapter 19 to test video performance. In Windows 2000/XP, click Start | Run and type **dxdiag** to launch the DirectX Diagnostic Tool (see Figure 20-4). In Windows Vista, go to the Start Search box and type **dxdiag**. Press ENTER.

    a.   Click the Sound tab, and examine the information displayed about your sound card and drivers.

    b.   Click the Test DirectSound button (Windows 2000/XP only). This steps you through a series of tests to confirm the operation of your sound system.

    c.   Switch to the Music tab and click the Test DirectMusic button (Windows 2000/XP only). This tests whether your system supports the DirectMusic component of DirectX.

Step 8   You've learned to remove, install, and configure a sound card. You've also learned how to test the various parts of the sound system. Now it's time to talk about troubleshooting.

Your sound system is working, but your speakers sound a little rough. Are they "blown" out because they were overdriven with poor adjustments? You can go to Eminent Technology's Multimedia Speaker Test Web site and test the response of your speakers at different frequencies:

www.eminent-tech.com/music/multimediatest.html

These tests will help you confirm whether your speakers can still handle all the frequencies they are designed to handle.

FIGURE 20-4 Using the DirectX Diagnostic Tool in Windows XP

30 MINUTES

Lab Exercise 20.02: Recording Sound

With the sound card installed, configured, and tested, it's time to get the project really rolling with recorded sound. It is expected that each student's documentary will last from eight to ten minutes and will encompass typical current events. Each student has a microphone, sound card, and speakers. What you want to do is get the speech recorded digitally, maybe add some music, and choose the audio quality based on the expected delivery method.

Learning Objectives

The purpose of this lab exercise is to guide you in the recording of sound.

At the end of this lab, you'll be able to

- Use the microphone to record a WAV file
- Fine-tune the quality of the recording

Lab Materials and Setup

The materials you need for this lab are

- A working computer system running Windows
- A sound card, speakers, and a microphone properly installed

Getting Down to Business

Once you have installed, configured, and tested a sound card, you need to run some applications to see if this is going to work. This lab steps you through recording sound into the computer and saving the recording as a WAV or MP3 sound file.

Step 1 To check your system's ability to capture audio so that you can record the documentaries, you will use Windows Sound Recorder. Make sure your microphone is plugged into the proper connector before you proceed.

Access Sound Recorder in Windows 2000/XP by selecting Start | All Programs | Accessories | Entertainment | Sound Recorder. In Windows Vista, select Start | Accessories | Sound Recorder. What you have now is similar to an audio cassette player. The buttons are the same—Record, Play, Fast Forward, Rewind, and Stop—but they're labeled with icons instead of words (see Figure 20-5).

FIGURE 20-5 Using Windows Sound Recorder

Step 2   You will now explore three different levels of recording. When working with digital audio files, the balance between sound quality and sound file size is driven by the project. If you were recording a project for CD, you would want the highest quality. For streaming audio and podcast audio, the MP3 file format is probably acceptable. Telephone quality, while achieving small file size, is not considered production quality.

   a.   To set the recording quality, select File | Properties and then click the Convert Now button. In the Sound Selection dialog box, click the Name drop-down menu and select CD Quality. Click OK and then OK again to return to the Sound Recorder window.

   b.   Click the red Record button and start talking into the microphone. Watch the graph to see that your voice is being recorded. If nothing seems to be happening, check your microphone connections.

   c.   Record a full 60 seconds of CD-quality audio, and then click Stop (the button with a square icon, next to Record). To hear your recording, click Play (the single right arrow).

   d.   To discover how much space this sound file uses, select File | Properties and observe the file's data size. Record the file size here: _____

   e.   Create a subfolder named **podcast** in your My Music folder (under My Documents) and save the sound file as **CDQUALITY.WAV** in the podcast folder.

✔ **Hint**

As you've probably figured out, our scenario for the history department would require a more sophisticated digital audio recording application. One minute is not going to be a very lengthy documentary! Sound Recorder is a good application to demonstrate the steps required to record audio, and you could use it to set up custom sound files to play during events. An example would be the infamous sound file that announces "You've got mail." If you would like to explore digital audio recording and playback further, you can find and download the open source program called Audacity at http://audacity.sourceforge.net.

Step 3   Telephone quality is very low resolution and frequency response, meaning that it will probably sound muffled and dull. Follow these steps to convert the CD-quality sound file to a telephone-quality sound file:

   a.   Select File | Properties, click Convert Now, and change the Name setting to Telephone Quality. Click OK and then OK again to return to the Sound Recorder window.

   b.   Now check out the data size of the file and record it here: _____. Has the size of the sound file changed? How does it sound? _____

   c.   Save the sound file in the podcast folder as **TELEPHONEQUALITY.WAV**.

Step 4 Finally, you will explore saving a recording as an MPEG Layer-3 (MP3) sound file. This is probably the best balance between audio quality and file size.

    a.   Launch Sound Recorder and open the CDQUALITY.WAV file.

    b.   To set the recording quality to the MP3 format, select File | Properties and then click Convert Now. In the Sound Selection dialog box, click the Format drop-down list and select MPEG Layer-3, then click OK.

    c.   Note the file's data size and record it here: _____. Has the size of the sound file changed? How does it sound? _____

    d.   Open the podcast folder and save the sound file as **MP3QUALITY.MP3**.

✔ **Hint**

In the Sound Selection dialog box, you can also set more specific attributes for an MP3 file; just click the Attributes drop-down list after selecting MPEG Layer-3 and you'll see a number of options to fine-tune the quality of your recording.

---

 30 MINUTES

Lab Exercise 20.03: Exploring Windows Media Player

Now that you have successfully recorded the project, you will have to look at some of the methods used to play the files and create an archive of the documentary on CD. The Windows environment has used Windows Media Player since the introduction of version 6.1 in 1998. You can always download the latest version of Windows Media Player from Microsoft's Web site. In this exercise you will learn some of the basic navigation steps for using Windows Media Player, and burn your recordings to an audio CD.

→ **Note**

The audio standard for the Apple Macintosh environment is QuickTime.

Learning Objectives

In this lab exercise, you'll learn how to navigate and play audio files, and then you'll learn how to burn an audio CD using Windows Media Player.

At the end of this lab, you'll be able to

- Open and play sound files of various formats

- Navigate Windows Media Player

- Burn a CD of your recording

Lab Materials and Setup

The materials you need for this lab are

- A working computer system running Windows

- A sound card, speakers, and a microphone properly installed

- Windows Media Player 9 or newer (WMP11 is used in the lab exercise)

- A commercially produced music CD of your choice

- A blank CD-R or CD-RW

Getting Down to Business

Once you've recorded the sound and saved it as a WAV or MP3 sound file, you need a method to audition the finished product and package the sound file for distribution. You may want to make an MP3 file for portable players or streaming audio over the Internet, or you may want to distribute high-quality audio CDs.

✔ **Hint**

There are a number of paths you could take to accomplish the playback of your recordings and archive them to a CD. This lab exercise steps you through one method that explores some of the features of Windows Media Player 11. Some of the steps, windows, and icons may look different depending on the version of Windows Media Player you use. You can download Windows Media Player 11 from Microsoft to follow along exactly with the steps in the lab.

Step 1 Launch Windows Media Player and then follow these steps:

a. If you have installed Windows Media Player 11, right-click the main menu and select Show Classic Menus. This displays the traditional menu bar with File, View, Play, Tools, and Help (see Figure 20-6).

b. Click the Now Playing tab. To open the three files you created in the previous lab (TELEPHONEQUALITY.WAV, MP3QUALITY.MP3, and CDQUALITY.WAV), select File | Open and then click Look in. Use the drop-down menu to locate the podcast folder and files. Click the first file, and then hold the CTRL key down while you click each of the two remaining two files.

FIGURE 20-6 Windows Media Player

Drag the three selected files to the Now Playing playlist. The first sound file should start to play automatically and display the filename in the right pane.

c. While listening to the podcast, click File | Save Now Playing List As and save the list as **PODCAST.WPL.** This organizes your files into a named list for ease of use.

d. Click the Burn tab, and then click *Burn 'podcast'* in the Burn List pane on the right side of the Windows Media Player window.

e. Insert a blank optical disc into an optical drive on your system with recording capabilities, and then click the Start Burn button.

f. Wait while the podcast audio file is burned to the optical disc, completing the task of archiving your recordings.

Step 2   While you have Windows Media Player open, explore the other options available to you as you work with sound files. One of the most popular uses of the computer when it comes to working with audio is to convert your CDs to MP3 sound files for use on portable MP3 players. Complete the following steps to calculate how many CDs you could fit onto a 2-GB MP3 player:

a. Insert a music CD into the optical media drive.

b. Right-click Rip and select More Options. This opens the Options dialog box for Windows Media Player, with the Rip Music tab selected.

    c.   Under Rip Settings, click the Format drop-down list and select WAV (Lossless). Use the information at the bottom of the dialog box to calculate the number of CDs that would fit onto a 2-GB MP3 player at this resolution. _____

    d.   Click the Format drop-down list again and select MP3. Experiment with the Audio quality slider (which ranges from 128 Kbps to 320 Kbps), and calculate the number of CDs that would fit onto a 2-GB MP3 player at various quality settings.

Lab Analysis Test

1.   Suddenly and for no apparent reason, the speaker icon no longer shows up in the taskbar/notification area. Where would you check to be sure it is enabled?

2.   John replaced his motherboard with one that has built-in sound. He still wants to use his Creative Labs Audigy sound card. What must he do to prevent conflicts?

3.   Theresa has been using her system for a long time to visit with friends in chat rooms. Lately her friends are complaining that her sound quality is getting worse. What should she check first?

4.   Karl is not getting any sound from his speakers. What three things should he check?

5.   John complains about annoying sounds when he opens and closes certain programs and sometimes when he clicks his mouse. He asks you if you can make them go away. Can you?

Key Term Quiz

Use the following terms to complete the following sentences. Not all terms will be used.

aux

compression

line-in

.mid

MP3

sound card

sound file

Sound Recorder

speaker

WAV

1. Joe wants to record himself singing the '50s classic "Hound Dog" to honor the birthday of Elvis Presley. He plugs a microphone into his sound card and opens _____, the recording software that comes with Windows.

2. Joshua is the keyboard player for a local band. He records some of the band's songs into a sequencer using MIDI. When he looks for the files on the computer, he can only find files with the _____ extension.

3. The MP3 format is popular because of the _____ scheme it uses.

4. The most common sound file format for portable sound players today is _____.

5. By default, Windows Sound Recorder saves audio recordings as _____ files.

Chapter 21
Portable Computing

Lab Exercises

The world has gone mobile, and accomplished technicians travel right along with it. General technicians have always worked on the software side of portables, tweaking power management options to optimize battery life for the users. Working on the hardware side of portable computing devices of all stripes, however, used to be the realm of only highly specialized technicians. As portable computing devices become increasingly common and the technology inside becomes more modular, frontline general technicians (think CompTIA A+ certified technicians here) increasingly get the call to upgrade and repair these devices.

Most laptops and netbooks have parts that a user can easily replace. You can swap out a fading battery for a newer one, for example, or add a second battery in place of an optical drive for long airplane trips. Lurking beneath access panels on the underside or below the keyboard on some models are hardware components such as RAM, a hard drive, a network card, and a modem—just like laptop batteries, these parts can be easily accessed and replaced by a technician. Some laptops even have panels for replacing the video card and CPU.

In this series of labs, you'll do four things. First, you'll use the Internet to research the upgrades available for portable computing devices so you can provide proper recommendations to employers and clients. Second, you'll open a laptop and gut it like a rainbow trout—removing and replacing RAM, the most common of all hardware upgrades. Third, you'll perform the traditional task of a portable PC technician, tweaking the power management options to optimize battery life on particular models. Finally, you'll tour a computer store to familiarize yourself with the latest and greatest portable offerings.

✖ Warning

I want to caution you that completely disassembling a laptop can be like trying to wrestle a bear. Even seasoned technicians pause before removing the dozens of screws involved in replacing broken screens or damaged system boards. These types of repairs require patience and finesse as you disassemble and reassemble delicate plastic coverings and connect and disconnect fragile wiring harnesses. Troubleshooting damaged laptops is beyond the scope of this lab manual. The lab exercises here focus on the more accessible upgrades, as outlined in the CompTIA A+ domain objectives.

 30 MINUTES

Lab Exercise 21.01: Researching Laptop Upgrade Paths

Your boss just sent word that one of your most important clients wants to extend the life of their sales force's laptop computers by upgrading rather than replacing. You've been asked to provide an upgrade track for your client. This requires you to research the laptops used by the company to determine which upgrades you can make, and to verify that the laptops themselves are not so old that the cost to upgrade them outweighs the cost of new laptops with new technology. You have to determine whether you can add RAM, replace the hard drives, replace the aging batteries, or add docking stations to provide extra functions when the salespeople are at the home office. Get to work!

Learning Objectives

Given the manufacturer and model number of a notebook computer, you'll figure out how to upgrade your client's computers.

At the end of this lab, you'll be able to

- Determine the replacement price of a battery
- Determine memory upgrades, including the quantity and type of RAM
- Determine hard drive upgrades, including the capacity and price of a hard drive

Lab Materials and Setup

The materials you need for this lab are

- A working PC with Internet access

Getting Down to Business

Limber up your surfing fingers because you're about to spend some time on the Web. Researching information about hardware and software is something technicians do all the time. The better you are at it, the better you are at your job!

When you're searching for replacement and upgrade parts and information, always take a look at the device manufacturer's Web site. Most major PC manufacturers, such as Dell and IBM (Lenovo has purchased IBM's personal computer line, so IBM laptops are now supported by Lenovo), have comprehensive product specification sheets available to the public on their sites. You can even order replacement parts directly from them! A popular tactic for researching upgrades is to grab the upgrade specs from the manufacturer's site and then search the Internet for the best prices. Not only are you doing your job well, but you'll be saving your company money too!

In the following steps, you'll navigate the tumultuous seas of the Internet in a quest to find the Golden Fleece of laptop battery, memory, and hard drive upgrades.

Step 1 Fire up your Web browser, and surf over to the device manufacturer's Web site. Try www.dell.com, or do a Google search for **laptop battery**. Many sites sell every laptop battery imaginable. The goal of this exercise is to become familiar with using the Internet to identify parts, confirm the specifications, and purchase replacement batteries. Once you reach a suitable Web site, answer the following questions:

You need replacement batteries for several Dell Precision M4400 laptops. What's the vendor's part number and price for this battery?

_____

What's the voltage and power capacity of the battery?

_____

✔ **Hint**

Just like any other electrical power source, batteries are rated according to voltage (9.6 V, for instance), current capacity (2600 milliamps per hour, or mAh), and sometimes power capacity (72 watts per hour, or WHr). When purchasing laptop batteries from third-party vendors (that is, vendors other than the laptop manufacturer), make sure to buy a battery that matches the voltage recommended by the manufacturer. Depending on the type of battery (Ni-Cd, NiMH, or Li-Ion), the current or power capacity of replacement batteries may be greater than the original battery. This is not a problem—increased current/power capacity means longer run times for your portable PC.

Step 2   Search the manufacturer's Web site for information on memory. If that isn't available, flip your browser over to www.kahlon.com to check RAM prices and availability. If the site isn't available, perform a Google search to find other Web sites that sell **laptop memory**. Then answer the following questions.

> Your client has a Dell Precision M4400 with 1 GB of RAM. How much RAM can you install? How many sticks of RAM will it take to upgrade this machine to a respectable 4 GB of memory, and how much will it cost?

_____

_____

Step 3   Stay where you landed in your search for memory upgrades. Does the vendor have replacement or additional hard drives available as well? If not, try www.kahlon.com, but now research possible hard drive upgrades for the Dell Precision M4400 the client owns. Answer this question:

> The client's Dell Precision M4400 laptops have 80-GB hard drives plus a currently unused modular media bay that could be housing a second hard drive. How much would it cost to add a second 160-GB hard drive to the Dell?

_____

 30 MINUTES

Lab Exercise 21.02: Replacing and Upgrading RAM

Your client settled on the RAM upgrades as the first step for making their laptops more usable, and you get tagged as the person to remove the old RAM and install the new. Upgrading RAM is the most common technician-performed upgrade on portable PCs and something you're likely to run into in the real world.

Learning Objectives

In this lab, you'll learn essential skills for upgrading portable PCs.

At the end of this lab, you'll be able to

- Access the RAM panel in a laptop

- Remove RAM in a laptop

- Install RAM properly in a laptop

Lab Materials and Setup

The materials you need for this lab are

- A working portable computer (one with modern SO-DIMM or DDR SO-DIMM modules is preferable)
- A very tiny Phillips-head screwdriver
- An anti-static mat

✖ Warning

Opening a portable computer can result in a nonfunctional portable computer. Don't use the instructor's primary work laptop for this exercise!

Getting Down to Business

You're about to open the sensitive inner portions of a portable computer, but before you do, it's a great idea to refresh your memory about avoiding electrostatic discharge (ESD). The inside of a laptop looks different from the inside of a desktop or tower case, but the contents are just as sensitive to static electricity. Watch out!

Step 1   Using your handy screwdriver or other handy tool, open the access panel for the RAM. Every portable PC offers a different way to access the RAM, so I can't give you explicit directions here. Most often, you'll find a removable plate on the bottom of the laptop secured with a tiny Phillips-head screw. Some laptops require you to remove the keyboard, unscrew a heat spreader, and then access the RAM. Figure 21-1 shows a typical panel, accessible from the underside of the laptop.

Figure 21-1 Opening the access panel to find RAM

Step 2 Once you have the panel open, push outward on the restraining clips on the RAM stick(s). This will cause the RAM to pop up partially (see Figure 21-2).

Step 3 Remove the RAM gently, gripping only at the non-contact edges. Place the stick(s) on an anti-static pad or in an anti-static bag.

Step 4 Install the replacement RAM into the laptop, reversing the process of removal. Place the stick(s) at an angle into the RAM slots and push firmly. Once the contacts have disappeared, press the body of the RAM into the restraining clips.

✔ **Hint**

If you don't have new RAM to install, simply install the RAM you removed in Step 3. This gives you the opportunity to practice!

Step 5 Replace the access panel.

Step 6 Power on the laptop to confirm that the new RAM is recognized and functioning properly.

FIGURE 21-2 Releasing the RAM

30 MINUTES

Lab Exercise 21.03: Adjusting Power Management to Optimize Battery Life

Several of your sales staff members have to attend a conference on the other side of the country. The conference came up on short notice, so everyone needs time to prepare, even while on the flight to the conference. You've been tasked with configuring power management on their laptops to optimize battery life so they can work as long as possible while on the plane.

Learning Objectives

In this lab, you'll adjust the power management features for a PC, a task that's vital to proper support of portable PCs.

At the end of this lab, you'll be able to

- Enable and disable power management in the CMOS

- Change power management settings in Windows

Lab Materials and Setup

The materials you need for this lab are

- A working computer with Windows installed

- A BIOS that supports power management

> ### ✔ Hint
>
> Having a notebook computer available is a plus. Performing these steps on a notebook computer will allow you to configure the settings for the Portable/Laptop power scheme and then remove the power cord, running on battery power to experience the actual results. If you're practicing on a regular desktop PC, keep in mind that a notebook will have two options for each adjustment: one for when the notebook is using battery power, and one for when it's connected to the alternating current (AC) source.

Getting Down to Business

Windows PCs have two separate areas for power management: the CMOS setup utility and the Control Panel. You'll start with CMOS and then go to the Control Panel.

Step 1   Boot your system, and enter the CMOS setup utility.

✔ **Cross-Reference**

Refer to the "Power Management" section in Chapter 21 of *Mike Meyers' CompTIA A+ Guide to Managing and Troubleshooting PCs* for more information on power management on portable PCs.

Now follow these steps:

a. Go to the Power Management Setup screen.

b. Enable power management if it's currently disabled.

c. Look at each option for common-sense settings. For example, when operating on battery power, the portable should be configured for maximum energy efficiency, thus increasing run time.

d. Make sure the ACPI setting is enabled if the BIOS supports it.

e. Save your settings, and boot the system to the Windows desktop.

✔ **Hint**

ACPI is short for Advanced Configuration and Power Interface, a power management specification developed by Intel, Microsoft, and Toshiba. ACPI enables the operating system to control the amount of power given to each device attached to the computer. With ACPI, the operating system can turn off peripheral devices, such as optical drives, when they're not in use.

Step 2 Access the Power Options applet in the Control Panel, and make a note of your current power management settings.

Check out the different power schemes available (this will depend on your specific system) and experiment with changing the settings to see how this affects when the monitor and hard drives turn off. Each of these schemes has adjustable times. The tabs and settings will differ depending on which version of Windows you're running. Be sure to look at them all. To see more detailed power scheme settings in Windows Vista, be sure to click *Change power settings* and then *Change advanced power settings*.

✔ **Hint**

The Windows XP Power Options Properties dialog box (on a notebook) has five tabs: Power Schemes, Alarms, Power Meter, Advanced, and Hibernate (see Figure 21-3). You can use the Alarms tab to set the time when the battery alarm is activated. The Power Meter tab shows the percent of charge remaining in the battery.

FIGURE 21-3 Accessing the Windows XP power options on a portable computer

---

✖ Warning

Some PCs and some components don't like standby and suspend modes. They can cause your computer to lock up. Be aware of that, and if your computer locks up, turn those settings off.

Step 3 Once you've finished experimenting, enable or disable power management as you prefer.

⏱ OPEN

Lab Exercise 21.04: Field Trip to Play with the Latest Portable PCs

The best way to understand portable PCs (laptops, netbooks, tablet PCs, and PDAs) is to play with one. If there isn't one available in the classroom, then this exercise is for you.

✔ **Cross-Reference**

Refer to the "Portable Computer Device Types" section in Chapter 21 of *Mike Meyers' CompTIA A+ Guide to Managing and Troubleshooting PCs*. It will give you an excellent shopping list of portable computing devices.

Learning Objectives

This lab will take you into the field for a little computer browsing—for educational purposes, of course!

At the end of this lab, you'll be able to

- Recognize the variations in key features among different portable PCs

Lab Materials and Setup

The materials you need for this lab are

- A local computer store or other retailer with a good selection of portable PCs you can examine

✔ **Hint**

If you don't have a store nearby, use the Web to browse a computer store such as CompUSA (www.compusa.com), or go to a manufacturer's Web site such as Dell's (www.dell.com) and customize a laptop to your heart's content. Be sure to explore all the options and customizations you can add to it. Just make sure you don't click Buy!

Getting Down to Business

Portable PCs are manufactured by a wide variety of companies, and no two notebooks are created equal. Some notebooks feature a slim and lightweight profile and are designed for the busy traveler; others feature a full complement of ports and rival desktop PCs in their power and features. Netbooks are smaller, compact versions of laptops that are ideal as long-term traveling companions. They can fit in a purse or backpack and thus are handy for browsing or doing e-mail on the road. Tablet PCs have pen-based interfaces that allow you to use them like a paper notepad. PDAs are great for portable address books and tasks lists that can be quickly synchronized with desktop programs through infrared or Bluetooth interfaces. Take a look at all the available models and compare their features.

Step 1 Go to your local computer or office supply store and check out the portable PCs on display. Try to find a store with a variety of brands. Bring this lab manual (or a copy of the following chart) with you to record the different specs you find.

Step 2   Pick out three portables, preferably from different manufacturers. For each portable, record the following information.

Feature	Portable 1	Portable 2	Portable 3
Size/weight	_____	_____	_____
Screen type/size	_____	_____	_____
CPU	_____	_____	_____
RAM	_____	_____	_____
Pointing device(s)	_____	_____	_____
I/O ports	_____	_____	_____
PC Card slot(s)	_____	_____	_____
Hard drive	_____	_____	_____
Floppy/optical drive(s)	_____	_____	_____

Lab Analysis Test

1.   Bill wants to upgrade his memory from 2 GB to the maximum amount of RAM his notebook can take. He has a Lenovo ThinkPad T500 notebook. How much RAM does he need to buy?

2.   Teresa complains that her Windows XP notebook turns itself off without any warning. What should she adjust?

3.   Maanit will be traveling from the United States to India. He'll use his laptop to watch DVDs on the way, usually on battery power. Lately, the battery seems to run out of juice well before the battery specifications indicate. What could possibly cause this recent development? Are there any recommendations you would make to Maanit to improve his laptop's performance?

4.   During your research earlier in these exercises, which did you discover to be the most expensive— hard drives, memory, or batteries? Which component was the most inexpensive to replace?

5.   Would the LCD screen or hard drives turn off, for energy conservation, if you set your power scheme to Always On and you walked away for a long period of time? Why or why not?

Key Term Quiz

Use the following terms to complete the following sentences. Not all terms will be used.

ACPI

battery

hard drive

hibernate

memory

netbook

notebook

Power Options

Power Meter

Power Scheme

standby

1.   The amount of time the hard drive will continue to spin once it's no longer being accessed is determined by the _____ setting.

2.   You can use the _____ applet in the Control Panel to set the power conservation options for the notebook computer.

3.   The battery, _____, and _____ are all upgradeable laptop components.

4.   The amount of power remaining in a battery can be determined by looking at the _____.

5.   Software can control power consumption if _____ is turned on in the CMOS setup utility.

Chapter 22
Printers

Lab Exercises

Printers continue to be a major part of the day-to-day working environment, both at home and in the office, despite attempts to create a "paperless office." What this means is that the PC technician will have to understand the operation of several types of printers and be able to keep them in good working order. Many companies have service contracts for their more expensive printers (they're usually leased property anyway!), but there will always be printers that need a good technician's love and care.

This chapter's lab exercises will take you through a scenario in which your boss walks into your office and tells you five printers are being delivered to you—two impact printers using legacy parallel ports, two USB inkjet printers, and an HP LaserJet laser printer using a JetDirect network interface. You need to install them and make sure they work properly so that they're accessible by anyone in the company who needs them. You'll explore different port settings and how to alter them when you need to do so. You'll then learn about some of the key differences between the two most popular types of printers (inkjet and laser printers), and you'll load printer drivers. Finally, you'll look at some of the maintenance issues that are required to keep the printers up and running and some of the techniques to use when they stop.

 30 MINUTES

Lab Exercise 22.01: Exploring Configuration Settings

Printers have used just about every interface available to the computer, from legacy RS-232C serial and IEEE 1284 parallel interfaces to the most recent USB, FireWire, Infrared, and Bluetooth wireless interfaces. The two most common ports used in connecting a printer locally to a PC are the universal serial bus (USB) and parallel ports. It just so happens that the printers you'll be working with use parallel, USB, and network interfaces! In this lab, you'll look at the parallel interface—the oldest of the three—and walk through the process of enabling and configuring the parallel port in the BIOS.

✔ **Cross-Reference**

You have already explored the USB interface in Chapter 18 and will delve into the wonderful world of networking in Chapter 23. The parallel interface is aging, but there is still a large installed base of printers using this interface, and the CompTIA A+ exams expect you to know some of the details of the interface. Refer to the "Printer Connectivity" section in Chapter 22 of *Mike Meyers' CompTIA A+ Guide to Managing and Troubleshooting PCs* for help identifying parallel port modes and their differences and similarities.

Learning Objectives

In this lab, you'll explore the different configuration settings that are available for the parallel interface in your PC's CMOS setup utility.

At the end of this lab, you'll be able to

- Enable and configure parallel ports in the BIOS

- Locate information about the parallel port in Device Manager

Lab Materials and Setup

The materials you need for this lab are

- A working computer running Windows

✔ **Hint**

By now you should be quite familiar with the different paths used by various versions of Windows to get to the things you are looking for.

Getting Down to Business

First, take a look at the ports in your CMOS setup utility. The time is long since past that knowing how to change I/O and IRQ addresses has been useful, but it's really helpful to know, and the CompTIA A+ exams expect you'll be familiar with the information.

Step 1   Boot your PC, and go into the CMOS setup utility. Find the settings for your USB and parallel ports. They'll most likely be under a heading such as Integrated Peripherals (see Figure 22-1).

```
                Phoenix - Award BIOS CMOS Setup Utility
                       Integrated Peripherals

  ▶ OnChip IDE/RAID Function    Press Enter        Item Help
    Init Display First          PCIe
    OnChip USB                  U1.1+2.0       Menu Level    ▶
    - USB Keyboard Support      Enabled
    - USB Mouse Support         Enabled
    OnChip Audio Controller     Auto
    OnChip LAN Controller       Auto
    - Onboard LAN Boot ROM      Disabled
    Onboard FDD Controller      Enabled
    Onboard Serial Port         3F8/IRQ4
    Onboard Parallel Port       Enabled
    - Parallel Port Mode        ECP+EPP
    - EPP Mode Select           EPP1.7
    - Ecp Mode Use DMA          3




▲▼▶◀:Move   Enter:Select    +/-/PU/PD:Value  F10:Save   ESC:Exit  F1:General Help
    F5:Previous Values      F6:Fail-Safe Defaults    F7:Optimized Defaults
```

FIGURE 22-1 The Integrated Peripherals CMOS screen

✖ Warning

When making changes to the system resources in both CMOS and Device Manager, be sure to first write down the current settings. If your changes don't work, you can always return them to the original settings that did work.

How many parallel ports do you have? _____

What resources are the parallel port(s) using? _____

Step 2 Make the following changes in CMOS, and observe any effect on hardware installed on the parallel ports. Make sure you have drivers or parallel devices handy, because making changes at the CMOS level can make Windows unhappy! (You might need to reinstall drivers.)

- Parallel Port = I/O Address 378 and IRQ 7

- DMA = 3

Exit CMOS properly, saving your changes.

Step 3 Reboot your system to the Windows desktop, and access Device Manager in the Control Panel to verify that the resources are assigned.

Confirm the resources allocated to the parallel port by following these steps:

a. Click the plus sign (+) next to Ports (COM & LPT).

b. Highlight the LPT port in the list, and open Properties.

c. Select the Resources tab.

What are the I/O and IRQ settings for this port? _____

d. Click OK to close the Properties dialog box.

Step 4 Verify the resources again by accessing the list of resources used in Device Manager:

a. From the Device Manager, select View | Resources by type.

b. Expand the groups as needed by clicking the plus sign (+) next to the desired resource.

✔ **Hint**

If there's no IRQ listed, it may be by design. In Device Manager, expand the item called Ports (COM & LPT), and display the properties for ECP Printer Port (LPT1). Click the Settings tab—do you see the selection for never using an interrupt? Change the selection to *Use any interrupt assigned to the port*, and verify the resources again as outlined in Step 4.

Verify all of your settings and close the Device Manager, Control Panel, and My Computer to return to the desktop.

30 MINUTES

Lab Exercise 22.02: Examining Types of Printers

There's an enormous amount of information on the Internet about printers. All of the top printer manufacturers—HP, Lexmark, Canon, and so forth—have Web sites that can provide insight about modern printers. As a PC technician, you'll need to visit these sites for information about your new printers, and to download the most current drivers for those printers.

✖ **Warning**

You must have access to the Internet for this exercise. If there's no access or the sites are down, refer to Chapter 22 of *Mike Meyers' CompTIA A+ Guide to Managing and Troubleshooting PCs* for a review.

Learning Objectives

In this lab, you'll compare the features of impact, inkjet, and laser printers using the Internet.

At the end of this lab, you'll be able to

- Recognize the key differences between impact, inkjet, and laser printers
- Identify and visit Web sites on the Internet dedicated to printers and printer troubleshooting

Lab Materials and Setup

The materials you need for this lab are

- A working computer with Windows

- A connection to the Internet

- Access to either an inkjet printer or a laser printer

✔ **Hint**

A trip to your local computer store or other retailer with a good selection of printers would be beneficial for a general knowledge of printers.

Getting Down to Business

Fire up your favorite Web browser and head out on the old Information Superhighway. The Internet is just brimming with helpful information about printers.

✔ **Hint**

Web sites have the annoying tendency to either disappear or drop the information that was once relevant to a particular subject. If any of the links in this exercise are no longer active or don't seem to contain the relevant information, you may need to do a little Web research of your own. As always, practice safe surfing! There are thousands of online forums available, and they can contain questionable hyperlinks, poor-quality information, and in some cases, outright wrong information. Try to stick with legitimate manufacturer and technical Web sites, examine where that hyperlink is going to reroute your computer, and visit multiple sites to verify information you discover in the forums. Consider it excellent practice for real-world tech work!

Step 1　To find information about inkjet printers, access the following Web site to complete this step: http://computer.howstuffworks.com/inkjet-printer.htm/printable. If this link doesn't work, you can also do a Google search and look for information about how printers work.

What's the major difference between impact and non-impact printers?

_____

_____

What part of an inkjet printer moves the print head back and forth across the page?

_____

List the two ways in which the droplets of ink are formed in inkjet printers.

_____

_____

The type of paper used in an inkjet printer greatly influences the quality of the image produced. What are the two main characteristics of inkjet printer paper that affect the image the most?

_____

_____

Step 2   For information about laser printers, access this site to complete this step: www.howstuffworks .com/laser-printer.htm/printable. Do a Google search or refer to the textbook if this site isn't available.

What's the primary principle at work in a laser printer?

_____

_____

What moves the image from the drum to the paper?

_____

Printer Control Language (PCL) and PostScript are both examples of what?

_____

_____

What's toner? Is it an ink, wax, or something else?

_____

Step 3   Put these steps in the printing process of a laser printer in the correct order (don't forget to reference the textbook as well):

Charge _____

Clean _____

Develop _____

Fuse _____

Transfer _____

Write _____

Step 4 If you have access to a laser printer, open it and carefully examine the insides. Also read the printer manual for details on the specifications. Access the manufacturer's Web site for additional information.

If you don't have access to a laser printer, go to your local office supply or computer store and ask a salesperson to show you the differences between various impact, inkjet (black and white as well as color), and laser printers.

Look inside your laser printer.

What parts are easily removable and replaceable?

_____

Practice removing and reinserting the toner (see Figure 22-2) and paper.

✖ Warning

Remember to turn the printer off before removing anything but the toner or paper. Also, be careful not to spill any toner inside the printer.

Look at the manual or the manufacturer's Web site for these specifications. Answer all the following questions you can about your printer:

How much RAM can it hold? _____

How much effect does the amount of RAM have on the cost of a new printer?

_____

Are the drum and toner separate, or are they one replaceable part?

_____

What is the speed of the printer (pages per minute)? _____

What is the quality of the output (resolution)? _____

What are the number and types of ink cartridges? _____

What is the price of a new printer? _____

What is the cost per page? _____

FIGURE 22-2 A toner cartridge with its photosensitive drum exposed

✔ Hint

Most inkjet (and even laser) printers are priced very low, so they're affordable to buy initially. Using them is another question. Calculate the cost of the ink and how many pages it'll print. This calculation will amaze you. They're not so cheap after all.

What can you conclude from your research about the true total cost of printing, including consumables?

 30 MINUTES

Lab Exercise 22.03: Installing a Printer

The key to a successful printer installation is having the correct software drivers and understanding how the printer will interface with the computer. You'll certainly need the drivers when you install those five printers, and you'll also have to configure the printers you are installing to use parallel, USB, and network interfaces. A common practice in multiple-user environments—companies considered to be Small Office/ Home Office (SOHO)—is to use a printer with its own network interface card (NIC), so that computers from anywhere in the network can print directly to the printer through the network interface.

Learning Objectives

In this lab, you'll install a printer, first as a directly connected device, and then as a network device. You will then explore and change its settings.

At the end of this lab, you'll be able to

- Recognize the variations in key features of laser printers

- Install a laser printer in Windows

- Change laser printer settings in Windows

- Configure a TCP/IP port for a network printer

Lab Materials and Setup

The materials you need for this lab are

- A working computer with Windows installed

- An inkjet or laser printer for installation (or you can skip Step 1)

- Optional: A print device with a network interface card

Getting Down to Business

These days, installing a printer is a fairly straightforward task. This is good news, because you'll probably do your fair share of it as a computer technician.

Step 1 If you have an actual print device, start here. (If you don't, skip to Step 2.)

Connect the printer to your system via a parallel or USB port, turn on the printer, and then turn on the PC. As the boot sequence progresses, the plug-and-play feature will locate the printer and install it for you. Follow the instructions on the screen.

✔ Hint

Here's the twist. If your printer is older than your operating system, the OS should install the printer drivers with little interaction on your part. If the printer is newer than your OS, then you'll need to have the driver disc handy because the system will stop and ask you for it. Some printer manufacturers actually require you to start their own printer installation programs even before connecting the printer to a system. As always, consult the manufacturer's instructions first.

Step 2 If you don't have a print device, start here:

a. Access the Printer applet.

b. For Windows 2000, select Start | Settings | Printers. For Windows XP, select Start | Printers and Faxes. For Windows Vista, select Start | Control Panel | Printers.

c. Click the Add Printer icon. A wizard should pop up on the screen. Click Next to proceed.

d. You want to install a printer attached to your PC, so select the option for *Local printer attached to this computer* (see Figure 22-3). Click Next.

e. Follow the steps through the Printer Wizard by selecting LPT1 and then a printer from the list of printers or your driver disc.

✖ Warning

If you weren't able to install an actual print device for this exercise, don't print a test page. You'll receive some interesting messages if you do.

Once you've installed the printer, open the Printers folder in the Control Panel, right-click the new printer's icon, and select Properties.

Figure 22-3 Installing a local printer

You'll see the various tabs and options that are specific to your printer. I used the Epson Stylus PHOTO 870 ESC/P 2 from the built-in drivers list. Check each of your tabs to see the information available and the features you can change:

- **General**   Description, preferences, and print test

- **Sharing**   To share or not to share; that is the question (this is covered in Chapter 23)

- **Ports**   Additional ports to assign the printer

- **Advanced**   Spooling, separator page, and print defaults

- **Color Management**   Automatic or manual

- **Security**   Permissions

- **Utilities**   Nozzle Check, Head Cleaning, and Print Head Alignment

✔ **Hint**

You should know how to navigate all the previous steps for each version of Windows for the CompTIA A+ exams.

Step 3 In the following steps, you will set up a TCP/IP printer interface port for a Hewlett-Packard LaserJet printer with a JetDirect NIC. If you have access to a printer with a network interface, or your classroom is equipped with one, use the IP address or printer name of the printer when configuring the port. This will allow you to actually test the installation.

a. In Windows 2000/XP, open the Printer & Faxes folder by way of Start | Control Panel | Printers & Faxes and launch the Add Printer Wizard by clicking *Add a printer* under Printer Tasks. In Windows Vista, go to Start | Control Panel | Printers. Right-click in the window and select Add Printer. On the welcome screen, click Next.

b. Select *Local printer attached to this computer* in Windows 2000/XP (note the information balloon at the bottom of the dialog box, shown in Figure 22-3) or *Add a local printer* in Windows Vista. In Windows 2000/XP, clear the *Automatically detect and install my Plug and Play printer* box. Click Next.

c. Click the *Create a new port* radio button and select Standard TCP/IP Port from the drop-down menu.

d. This launches the Add Standard TCP/IP Printer Port Wizard (see Figure 22-4). Click Next.

e. In the Add Port dialog box, enter the IP address of the network printer. The Add Standard TCP/IP Printer Port Wizard automatically creates the port name (see Figure 22-5). Click Next.

f. If the IP address is fictitious, for the purpose of completing the lab steps, the Add Standard TCP/IP Printer Port Wizard will be unable to identify the printing device. In the Additional Port Information Required dialog box, click the drop-down menu for Standard and select Hewlett Packard Jet Direct (see Figure 22-6). Click Next.

g. Review the port characteristics and click Finish (see Figure 22-7).

h. You will now follow the steps through the Printer Wizard by selecting a printer from the list of printers or your driver disc as you did when directly connecting to the printer in Step 2.

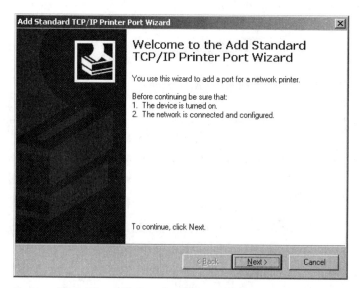

FIGURE 22-4 The Add Standard TCP/IP Printer Port Wizard

FIGURE 22-5 The TCP/IP address and port name of a JetDirect printer

✖ Warning

Again, if you are unable to install an actual print device for this exercise, don't print a test page. You'll receive some interesting messages if you try.

FIGURE 22-6 Selecting the Standard HP JetDirect device type

Add Standard TCP/IP Printer Port Wizard

Completing the Add Standard
TCP/IP Printer Port Wizard

You have selected a port with the following characteristics.

SNMP:	No
Protocol:	RAW, Port 9100
Device:	172.16.1.191
Port Name:	IP_172.16.1.191
Adapter Type:	Hewlett Packard Jet Direct

To complete this wizard, click Finish.

< Back   Finish   Cancel

FIGURE 22-7 Port characteristics

30 MINUTES

Lab Exercise 22.04: Maintaining and Troubleshooting Printers

It is estimated that technicians, especially those working for the help desk or desktop support group for a small to medium-sized organization, spend approximately 30 percent of their time on printer issues. If you think about it, of all the components used in computing technology, printers have the highest percentage of moving parts. Moving parts are more likely to need maintenance than are static components.

Printers also like to be finicky and stop printing, usually resulting in a phone call from the client to the help desk for quick resolution. The following exercises will help you develop some understanding of laser printer and inkjet printer maintenance, and what steps to take when they stop printing.

Learning Objectives

In this lab, you'll research laser printer maintenance kits, clean dirty inkjet nozzles, and troubleshoot a failed print job.

At the end of this lab, you'll be able to

- Select a proper maintenance kit for various laser printers

- Clean and verify operation of inkjet nozzles

- Manage print jobs in Windows

- Restart a stalled print spooler

Lab Materials and Setup

The materials you need for this lab are

- A working computer with Windows installed

- A connection to the Internet

- Access to an inkjet printer

Getting Down to Business

The following exercises will round out your activities as you finish with the rollout of the five new printers in your office. You will want to get your Internet connection fired up again and research the maintenance kit available for your laser printer. Then you'll check the print-head nozzles of the inkjet printers and run the cleaning routine if necessary. Finally, you should prepare for any print errors so that you can correct them quickly and efficiently.

Step 1 Laser printers are, by design, highly precise machines. They typically move thousands of sheets of paper per month through the printing mechanism, placing 1200–1600 dots per inch (DPI) of toner on each page. As such, toner cartridges need to be replaced from time to time and parts that wear out need to be refurbished. Most manufacturers offer a maintenance kit for the printer to assist in the upkeep of the printer when these common parts age or fail. It would be a good idea to have a maintenance kit on hand for each model of laser printer in your organization.

✔ Hint

> Most of the current manufacturers of laser printers—Hewlett-Packard, Lexmark, Kyocera, Canon, and so forth—offer some form of maintenance kit for their printers. You should be able to find via an Internet search the available kits, their contents, and competitive pricing. Don't be surprised to find the maintenance kits somewhat costly, though they should still be only a fraction of the cost of replacing the printer.

Select a laser printer make and model, and perform an Internet search to identify the appropriate maintenance kit, its contents, and the average cost of the kit. Use this information to fill in the following items:

Printer Model _____

Maintenance Kit _____

Contents _____

_____

Price _____

Step 2   Though you have just installed new inkjet printers, if the printer sits idle for an extended period of time (a few weeks or months), or the ink cartridges have been replaced, you may need to check the print quality and clean the nozzles. The following steps were performed on an Epson Stylus PHOTO 890 but are similar to the steps required on HP and Lexmark inkjet printers. Consult the manual for specific instructions.

✖ Warning

The nozzle cleaning process uses a fair amount of the expensive ink. If you are working on a personal inkjet printer, or one in the classroom, after printing the nozzle check page, run the nozzle cleaning process only if required.

---

a.   Open the Printer (& Faxes) folder (Start | Control Panel | Printers & Faxes/Printers) and highlight your inkjet printer.

b.   Right-click the printer and select Properties.

c.   Click the Printing Preferences button (see Figure 22-8).

Figure 22-8 Properties window showing Printing Preferences button

d. Select the Utility tab (see Figure 22-9) and click Nozzle Check. This will print a test pattern using the cyan, yellow, magenta, and black ink nozzles.

e. If the printout is not clear or there are dropouts, click Head Cleaning to clear the nozzles and then return to the Nozzle Check to verify performance.

Step 3 When you are called upon to troubleshoot a failed print job, you should follow a logical step-by-step process to make sure that no obvious, possibly simple failure has occurred. If the power cord has been kicked out or the paper tray is open, troubleshooting the network connectivity or the printer driver would waste valuable time. Once you know the print device is online and ready and there are no paper jams or mechanical errors, then it might be time to open the Print Manager and attempt to restart the document.

The following steps are meant to be a rough guideline to troubleshoot and diagnose a failed print job:

a. First, check the physical print device:

- Is the printer plugged in, and is the power turned on?

- Is the printer out of paper or is there a paper jam?

- Is the toner low or in need of replacement?

- Are there any error messages on the printer's LCD readout or any error indicator lights flashing?

- Is the printer online and ready to print?

FIGURE 22-9 Utility tab under Printing Preferences

If you examine all of these areas and find everything appears to be in working condition, then you may have a problem with the connectivity between the computer and the printer, or there may be problems with the document or drivers.

b.   Make sure that the connections between the computer and the printer are in good condition and securely fastened. These may be USB, IEEE 1284 bidirectional parallel, or UTP using RJ-45 connectors.

✔ Hint

To create a failed print job, disconnect the printer cable, shut the power off on the printer, or open the printer paper tray. If you do not have a physical printer, create a printer, following the steps in Lab Exercise 22.03. Send a print job to the printer; the printer icon should appear in the system tray and indicate that the print job has failed. Then continue with Step 3.

---

c.   After checking all of the physical components, try to resend the document. Open the Print Manager by clicking the icon in the system tray/notification area.

In the Print Manager, select the failed print job by highlighting the job with *Error* in the Status column (see Figure 22-10).

Select Documents | Restart. If you are creating the printer problem, the printer icon in the system tray/notification area indicates that the print job has failed once again.

d.   Highlight the document once again, and then select Documents | Cancel to delete the document.

If this were a real scenario, you would verify that the print drivers were installed and are the correct drivers for the operating system. You would then perform Step 4 to see if the problem is related to the print spooler.

Step 4   If the print device is online and ready, there are no paper jams or mechanical errors, and restarting the document is of no help, you can check to see if the print spooler is stalled. The print spooler is a holding area for print jobs and is especially important for network printers. If the print device runs out of paper while printing a document, you may have to stop and start the print spooler before the print device will receive jobs again.

FIGURE 22-10 Print Manager showing error status on a Word file

FIGURE 22-11 Print Spooler Properties dialog box

In Chapter 15, you accomplished this task using the command line. Now you will use the Services snap-in for the Microsoft Management Console (MMC) to do the same thing, only more quickly and in a GUI.

a. Launch the Services console by opening Administrative Tools in the Control Panel and then double-clicking Services.

b. Scroll down and highlight Print Spooler. Select Action | Properties. You should see that the print spooler is started and running (see Figure 22-11).

c. Click the Stop button. The print spooler indicates that it has stopped.

d. Click the Start button. The print spooler indicates that it has started.

e. Alternatively, you can highlight Print Spooler in the Services console and select Action | Restart. You'll see a message stating that the print spooler is stopping, and then another message indicating that the print spooler is starting.

In the real-world scenario, your print spooler service would be restarted, and you should have a healthy, functioning print server once again.

Lab Analysis Test

1. Patrick and Erik are having a small disagreement. Patrick says that printers can use numerous different interfaces, while Erik says that there are only two: parallel and USB. Who is correct? List the interfaces you are aware of and a typical use of each interface.

2. Theresa is using Windows and just purchased a printer from a friend. When she installs it using the original driver disc that came with the printer, it won't install properly. Why?

3. Danyelle has just joined a large organization as a level II tech and is tasked with the evaluation of all the laser printers in use. The business managers are concerned that all of the units will need to be replaced because of frequent paper jams and poor print quality. Danyelle makes her recommendations, and is actually awarded a bonus for saving the company money. What is her recommendation?

4. Brandon has sent a document to the printer, but the document never actually prints. Where can Brandon check to see the status of the document?

5. Why are laser toner cartridges so expensive?

Key Term Quiz

Use the following terms to complete the following sentences. Not all terms will be used.

DMA

DPI

ECP

IEEE 1284

impact

inkjet

laser

primary corona

TCP/IP port

toner

transfer corona

USB

1. The part of the laser printer that actually causes the toner image to be created on the paper is the _____.

2. To use a printer that's attached to the network with its own NIC, you must configure a(n) _____.

3. The resolution of a printer is measured in _____.

4. The printer that spits ink onto the paper is a(n) _____ printer.

5. Printers with platens are _____ printers.

Chapter 23
Local Area Networking

Lab Exercises

There's no doubt about it—a PC technician *will* have networking issues to work through at some point. Whether it's a three-computer, home-based local area network (LAN), a public Wi-Fi access point, a large company with thousands of connected devices, or the Web itself, networks have become as common as PCs. The main consideration is no longer whether you're going to network your computers—it's now what method you're going to use to network your computers.

A competent PC technician is called upon to be a network guru, answering connectivity questions and making recommendations on the best price/performance considerations for homes and businesses. This happens frequently, especially in smaller companies that can't afford to hire multiple people to support both the network *and* the PCs. The CompTIA A+ certification exams reflect these changing roles of the PC technician and include many questions related to computer networking.

In this chapter's lab exercises, you'll imagine that you've been hired to work for a small company that has made the decision to upgrade the network in their office. You'll need to have a working understanding of network hardware and network operating system issues, as well as some good troubleshooting tools for when things don't work quite right.

 30 MINUTES

Lab Exercise 23.01: Understanding Network Topologies

Networks don't spontaneously come into being—they must be designed and laid out. Choosing the proper layout, or *topology*, is an important decision because each topology has its own advantages and disadvantages. Knowing how a network is put together and organized is an important part of setting one up.

Learning Objectives

In this lab, you'll learn about network topologies.

At the end of this lab, you'll be able to

- Identify different network topologies

- Understand the benefits and drawbacks of each topology

Lab Materials and Setup

The materials you need for this lab are

- A group of four people

- Any small object

Getting Down to Business

This is a group activity that works best in a classroom. If you are working alone or want more practice, you can achieve the same goals with a few more objects—instead of people, use cups or bowls to represent each device and a ball to represent the data going back and forth. For each demonstration, keep in mind the real-world components that would be involved. How many cables would it use? What special devices do you need? What if a component was broken?

Step 1   First, you'll look at the star topology. A star topology has multiple computers connecting to a single, central wiring point (a hub). This is probably the one you are most familiar with, since most home networks are set up this way.

Have your group stand up and form a circle. Designate someone to stand in the middle and be the "hub." Someone else should then begin by taking an object (the data) and passing it to the hub. The hub then passes it to someone else, who must first pass it back to the hub before it can move anywhere else—remember that the object cannot pass directly from one computer to the next. It must first move through the hub.

Write down your observations about this topology, including its advantages and disadvantages.

_____

_____

_____

_____

Step 2   Next, you'll look at the ring topology. In this topology, each device attaches to a central ring of cable to form a network. Have your group stand in a circle again. Begin passing the object clockwise around the circle. Remember that it cannot skip any person in the circle, nor can it cross to the other side.

Now have one person leave the circle, breaking the chain. The object cannot pass to the next person if the circle is broken, so the network becomes nonfunctional.

Write down your observations about this topology, including its advantages and disadvantages.

_____

_____

_____

_____

Step 3   Now you'll look at a bus topology, where each device attaches to a single network cable. Instead of a circle, stand in a line with everyone facing the same direction. Have each person pass the object to the next person in the line, and when the object reaches the last person, pass the object back in the other direction.

Have one person step out of the line. The object cannot skip that person's place, so the object now has to bounce back and forth between the people on one side of the missing person.

Write down your observations about this topology, including its advantages and disadvantages.

_____

_____

_____

_____

Step 4   Finally, you'll look at a mesh topology. This topology connects every computer to every other computer, without the use of a bus or hub. Have everyone in the group stand in a circle again, and now pass the object to whomever you wish. Continue to do so, feeling free to pass it to the person next to you or across from you.

Write down your observations about this topology, including its advantages and disadvantages.

_____

_____

_____

 30 MINUTES

Lab Exercise 23.02: Identifying Local Area Network Hardware

Your boss has decided to upgrade the network in your office, which is about five years old. With the changes in networking technology, he wants your ideas about purchasing the right equipment for the upgrade. Your company is a small one, so the task is quite doable, but you need to make sure you know what you're talking about before you give your report.

Learning Objectives

In this lab, you'll familiarize yourself with networking hardware.

At the end of this lab, you'll be able to

- Identify different kinds of network cabling

- Identify different network interface cards (NICs)

- Identify different types of network hubs

- Identify different wireless networking devices

Lab Materials and Setup

The materials you need for this lab are

- Access to a PC running Windows

- Access to a working LAN and the Internet (you may have demonstration devices provided by your instructor)

Getting Down to Business

One of the best ways to find out what a network is made of is to physically look at all of its pieces. Even then, however, it may be necessary to access a manufacturer's Web site to see, for instance, if the "hub" you're using is really a hub or a switch.

Step 1   If you have access to a LAN (the classroom computer lab network, a friend's home network, or your company's network), spend some time exploring the physical hardware connections and devices. If possible, acquire the diagram of the physical layout of the network, or create a simple diagram of the layout to familiarize yourself with the various devices and connections associated with the network you're analyzing.

> ✖ **Warning**
>
> Don't disconnect anything, and be careful while probing around. One small mistake, like removing a cable or turning off the wrong device, can disrupt the entire network. If you're using the classroom network, ask the instructor what you can and can't remove while you make closer inspections of the cables and devices.

> ✔ **Cross-Reference**
>
> Be sure to check out Chapter 23 of *Mike Meyers' CompTIA A+ Guide to Managing and Troubleshooting PCs* for help identifying network cables and connectors. It's a good idea to have the textbook handy while you progress through this lab.

What sort of cabling does the network use, or is it wireless? Is it twisted-pair cable or older coaxial cable? Are the cable ends RJ-45 connectors? Describe the physical layout of the LAN here.

_____

_____

_____

What sort of NICs do the machines have? Describe the back of the card. Does it have a single connector or a combination of connectors (see Figure 23-1)? Does it have an antenna? Is there a link and/or activity LED? Which of the LEDs is on steady? Which is flashing? Describe the NIC here.

_____

_____

_____

Figure 23-1 A network interface card (NIC)

✔ Hint

It is very important to understand the difference between the link light vs. the activity light. First, these "lights" are really light-emitting diodes (LEDs) and will usually appear in some form of yellow, orange, or green color, depending on the NIC manufacturer. Second, the link light indicates that the NIC and the cable have a valid electrical connection between the PC and the network device, usually a hub or a switch. This does not guarantee connectivity—it just means that the electrical connection is intact. The activity light is a better indicator of whether or not the NIC, cable, and hubs or switches are working. When the activity light blinks, it is indicating that data is being transferred between the networking devices. It does not guarantee that the data is usable—it just means that data is making the trip from the NIC to the hub or switch, or from the hub or switch to the NIC. If you are having trouble connecting to a network or communicating to other machines on the network, the link and activity lights are a good place to start your troubleshooting.

Step 2 Hubs and switches are a part of the majority of networks.

Are the PCs connected with a single cable (crossover cable limited to two PCs), or are they connected to a hub/switch (see Figure 23-2)? Is part of the network wireless? What is the model number of the network hub/switch? Who manufactures the hub/switch? How many devices can be attached? Record your findings here.

_____

_____

_____

FIGURE 23-2 A LAN hub with multiple cables/devices attached

Is the hub or switch a standard single-speed (10BaseT, for instance) device, or can it handle multiple speeds (10/100/1000 Mbps)? Does it have wireless capabilities? Record your findings here. If this information isn't apparent or printed on the cabinet, ask the instructor or the network administrator.

_____

_____

_____

Step 3 Are you going to have a wireless network or wireless devices in your network? Do you plan on installing a wireless network sometime in the near future? In the current world of networking, the terms *hub*, *switch*, and *router* are often used interchangeably, but they really are very different devices with very different functions. Conduct an Internet search on the definition of each device.

Compare and contrast each type of device. How do they achieve their functionality? Where or for what purpose does it makes sense to use each device? Where is each device in the OSI (Open System Interconnection) seven-layer model?

Hub _____

_____

Switch _____

_____

Router _____

_____

30 MINUTES

Lab Exercise 23.03: Exploring Local Area Network Configuration Options

You've made your recommendation, and you've installed the network. The hardware side of installing a basic LAN is really simple these days, so you managed to get that put together in a flash. Now it's time to configure the PCs that connect to the network.

To prepare for the CompTIA A+ exams, and to build your toolbox of skills as a PC technician, you need to be able to set up, configure, and troubleshoot networks that use Windows clients. From a network configuration standpoint, each version of Windows is very similar. The CompTIA A+ exams will test your configuration knowledge for all three versions of Windows, including the paths you use to locate configuration settings.

Learning Objectives

In this lab, you'll explore the network configuration options in a Windows environment.

At the end of this lab, you'll be able to

- Configure network access using the networking applets

Lab Materials and Setup

The materials you need for this lab are

- Access to a PC with Windows installed

- Access to the LAN

✔ Hint

I don't want to sound like a broken record, but if possible, you should repeat the exercises in each edition of Windows. If you only have a single operating system, be sure you understand how to configure networks in the other operating system environments. It's also a good idea to have the drivers for your NICs handy just in case you need to reload any of them. Finally, you'll want to determine the relevant settings (in other words, the proper protocol, the name[s] of the workgroup[s] you'll be using, and so on); write them down, and keep them with you as you go from computer to computer.

Getting Down to Business

For a computer to gain access to or share resources on a network, it must have a NIC installed and configured. Microsoft provides configuration wizards to set up your network with mostly default parameters and a lot of assumptions. In other words, you tell it the computer name, and it does the rest. Using the Microsoft wizards will allow you to set up a default configuration for quick access (good for at home), but this may not always work for a LAN in a business environment.

Whether you use the wizards or manually configure the system, the following steps must be accurately programmed into the software or you won't be able to take full advantage of the LAN. For the CompTIA A+ exams, you need to know *where to locate* and *how to modify* the network configuration. Specifically, each computer that will be connected to the LAN must have the following:

- A NIC with correct drivers installed

- Client software, such as Client for Microsoft Networks

- Protocols (what language[s] you'll use on the network and the settings)

- Services, such as File and Printer Sharing for Microsoft Networks

- A computer name

- A workgroup name

Step 1 Go to Device Manager and verify that the correct NIC drivers are installed. Reinstall the driver if necessary.

In Device Manager, expand *Network adapters*. Right-click your network card and select Properties. Click the Driver tab to see what driver is installed or to update the driver.

Step 2 In this step, you'll verify what network services are installed.

In Windows 2000, go to the Control Panel, double-click Network and Dial-Up Connections, right-click Local Area Connection, and select Properties. In Windows XP, go to Control Panel | Network Connections. Right-click Local Area Connection and select Properties. In Windows Vista, go to the Control Panel and open the Network and Sharing Center. In the Tasks menu on the left, click *Manage network connections*. Right-click Local Area Connection and select Properties.

✔ Hint

Nothing is necessarily wrong if you don't see any or all of the following components listed or if you see more than the ones listed previously. It simply means that the network configuration hasn't been completed on your system, or it's in a network supported by more than one server.

You should find the following components listed in a selection window. Your system may have others as well.

- **Client**   Client for Microsoft Networks (default**)**

- **Protocol**   TCP/IP (default)

- **Service**   File and Printer Sharing for Microsoft Networks

  What client(s), other than the default, are listed in your system? _____

  _____

  What protocol(s), other than the default, are listed? _____

  _____

  What services, other than the default, are listed? _____

  _____

Step 3   Now that you've found the network configuration screen, take a look at the various options:

- **Install**   The Install button enables you to add network components. Clicking the Install button gives you three choices:

  - **Client**   Adds a client to the configuration (must have at least one).

  - **Protocol**   Microsoft TCP/IP is the default (must have a protocol to communicate).

  - **Service**   File and Printer Sharing must be enabled for other computers on the network to access the one on which you're working.

- **Remove/Uninstall**   The Remove or Uninstall button enables you to remove network components.

- **Properties**   The Properties button displays a variety of dialog boxes based on the network component selected.

✔ **Hint**

Each of the preceding options asks questions about what you want to change. If one or more of your required settings are missing, use this screen to add them. When you make changes, you may be asked to reboot the system.

Step 4   Now that your system is configured for networking, you need to have an identity for it and join a workgroup to be recognized by the network and access network resources.

In Windows 2000, go to Control Panel and double-click System. Open the Network Identification tab. In Windows XP, do the same, but select the Computer Name tab. Windows Vista is also the same, but the information should be displayed all on one screen. Record your system settings here:

Computer name _____

Workgroup name _____

Step 5 Now that you've confirmed and recorded the networking components, your computer name, and your workgroup, the next step is to practice reinstalling your network adapter.

✖ Warning

This step is optional and can cause you grief if you aren't prepared. Ask the instructor if it's okay for you to proceed with this step. If not (or if you think this may harm your configuration), skip this step.

Access Device Manager, and uninstall your network adapter. Yes, this will erase all your network settings. Did you take good notes earlier? Expand the *Network adapters* heading, right-click your specific adapter, and choose Remove or Uninstall.

✖ Warning

If your notes are incomplete, ask the instructor to fill in the correct settings you're missing.

Reboot your system, and the adapter will be detected (if it's plug and play) and installed. Access the Network Connections applet, and verify your network configuration using the information you recorded in Steps 1, 2, and 4 previously. If your system doesn't load the drivers for the network card, you'll need the driver disc to complete your settings.

Test your system by accessing the network. Can you browse the network now? Look in My Network Places/Network. _____

 30 MINUTES

Lab Exercise 23.04: Verifying TCP/IP Settings

As you are probably aware, TCP/IP has emerged as the standard transport protocol for network communication. Microsoft operating systems normally use Dynamic Host Configuration Protocol (DHCP), which automatically retrieves and assigns client TCP/IP settings from a DHCP server. This makes it easy to set up a small home or business network of PCs. All systems in the network will communicate with each other using these settings. The problem is that most businesses have their own set of TCP/IP settings (either automatically configured through DHCP or manually configured) that must be used for all new or repaired systems introduced into the network. Your responsibility as a PC technician is to verify the TCP/IP settings.

✔ **Cross-Reference**

To review additional details of TCP/IP, re-read the "Configuring TCP/IP" section in Chapter 23 of *Mike Meyers' CompTIA A+ Guide to Managing and Troubleshooting PCs.*

Learning Objectives

In this exercise, you'll access and verify the TCP/IP settings for a given PC system.

At the end of this lab, you'll be able to

- Define Automatic Private IP Addressing (APIPA)

- Use the IPCONFIG command-line utility

- Manually configure the TCP/IP settings on a PC

Lab Materials and Setup

The materials you need for this lab are

- A PC system that's *properly configured* for LAN access using Windows

- A list of TCP/IP settings provided by the instructor

Getting Down to Business

Typically, in corporate environments, the network protocol configuration scheme has been defined by the senior systems administrators. Unless you've had some experience with the configuration, you would not automatically know all of the TCP/IP settings for a network. For instance, even when you're setting up a small network (one that connects to the Internet), you'll need to contact your Internet service provider (ISP) to set up your router's TCP/IP settings. So don't worry if you have no idea what settings to use. The trick is to learn how to get to them.

TCP/IP requires each system to have two basic settings for accessing a LAN and two additional settings for accessing other LANs or the Internet. You can configure your system to automatically obtain the following settings when you log on (Microsoft's default settings), or you can specify them, depending on the requirements of your network:

- IP address (unique to the PC)

- Subnet mask (identifies network information)

- Gateway (address of the router to the external realm)

- Domain Name Service (DNS)

Step 1   First, you'll locate and verify your current TCP/IP settings.

a. Return to the Local Area Connection Properties dialog box you located in Step 2 of Lab Exercise 23.03. Highlight the Internet Protocol (TCP/IP) entry and click the Properties button. When the Internet Protocol (TCP/IP) Properties screen appears, one of the setting options shown in Figure 23-3 will be selected.

b. If the settings are manually configured, you will be able to verify them in the TCP/IP Properties dialog box. Write the settings down and verify them with the settings given to you by the instructor.

IP address _____

Subnet mask _____

Gateway _____

Preferred DNS server _____

FIGURE 23-3 Viewing manually configured
TCP/IP properties in a Windows XP system

c. If the system is configured to use the Microsoft Automatic Private IP Addressing (APIPA) settings or if the network has a DHCP server (ask the instructor), the *Obtain an IP address automatically* and *Obtain DNS server address automatically* radio buttons will be selected. You will not be able to verify the values of the TCP/IP settings from this window. Close this window by clicking OK. To verify the settings, launch a command-line window and, at the prompt, type the following command:

```
C:\Documents and Settings\%USERNAME%\>IPCONFIG /ALL
```

This produces a listing similar to the one shown in Figure 23-4. Use these values to fill in the following settings and then verify them with your instructor.

IP Address _____

Subnet Mask _____

Default Gateway _____

DNS Server _____

Step 2 You should be familiar with one final configuration: Automatic Private IP Addressing, or APIPA. If Windows is configured to obtain an IP address automatically and no DHCP server is available, Microsoft will automatically configure an address in the 169.254.0.0 network. Follow these steps to explore APIPA:

a. In a classroom lab environment, have the instructor disable the DHCP server if applicable. Alternatively, you can disconnect the DHCP server's UTP cable from the hub or switch.

FIGURE 23-4 Windows IPCONFIG /ALL command results on a system configured to use DHCP

```
C:\WINDOWS\System32\cmd.exe                                    _□×

C:\>ipconfig /all

Windows IP Configuration

        Host Name . . . . . . . . . . . . : test-v93yi93158
        Primary Dns Suffix  . . . . . . . :
        Node Type . . . . . . . . . . . . : Unknown
        IP Routing Enabled. . . . . . . . : No
        WINS Proxy Enabled. . . . . . . . : No

Ethernet adapter Local Area Connection:

        Connection-specific DNS Suffix  . :
        Description . . . . . . . . . . . : VMware Accelerated AMD PCNet Adapter

        Physical Address. . . . . . . . . : 00-0C-29-CC-40-76
        Dhcp Enabled. . . . . . . . . . . : Yes
        Autoconfiguration Enabled . . . . : Yes
        Autoconfiguration IP Address. . . : 169.254.81.77
        Subnet Mask . . . . . . . . . . . : 255.255.0.0
        Default Gateway . . . . . . . . . :

C:\>_
```

FIGURE 23-5 Windows IPCONFIG /ALL command results on a system using APIPA

b.   Verify that your TCP/IP Properties settings are set to *Obtain an IP address automatically* and *Obtain DNS server address automatically*. Close all windows and reboot the system.

c.   Launch a command-line window and, at the prompt, type the following command:

     `C:\Documents and Settings\%USERNAME%\>`**`IPCONFIG /ALL`**

     This produces a listing similar to the one shown in Figure 23-5. Use these values to fill in the following settings and then verify them with your instructor.

     IP Address _____

     Subnet Mask _____

     Default Gateway _____

     DNS Server _____

d.   Exit the command-line window and launch the TCP/IP Properties window again. Return all settings to the normal classroom configuration. Click OK to finish, and close all the windows. Reboot the system, and verify that it's working properly and that you have reestablished network communication to its prior state.

🕐 30 MINUTES

Lab Exercise 23.05: Sharing Resources

With the network all set up properly, the next thing to do is decide how you want to share resources. You can share any folder or other resource. Optical drives, hard drives, and printers can all be shared.

Learning Objectives

In this lab, you'll set up file sharing for others to access information from their system.

At the end of this lab, you'll be able to

- Enable and configure shared directories and other resources

Lab Materials and Setup

The materials you need for this lab are

- A PC system that's *properly configured* for LAN access using Windows

Getting Down to Business

Whew! That last exercise was interesting, but the job is only half done. Now you'll find where to set up sharing for a particular resource.

Step 1 Open My Computer/Computer, double-click the C: drive, and create a new folder on the C: drive. Name it **Shared**. Right-click the Shared folder icon to see the folder options, and select Sharing and Security in Windows XP or Share in Windows Vista. This will open the Shared Properties dialog box with the Sharing tab selected (see Figure 23-6).

Figure 23-6 The Shared Properties dialog box's Sharing tab in Windows XP

✔ **Hint**

If the Sharing tab isn't there, you probably forgot to enable the File and Printer Sharing option in the Networking applet. Go back and do that.

✔ **Hint**

If you're running Windows XP Home Edition or Windows XP Professional Edition in a workgroup environment, the Sharing tab is much simpler. It contains *Do not share this folder/Share this folder* buttons and a space to provide a share name.

Step 2   Try sharing and unsharing the folder. This should be familiar to you since it's exactly the same as what you did in Chapter 16. Note that the share name and permissions are grayed out when you select *Do not share this folder*. Share the folder again, change the share name, and look at the various levels of permissions: Full Control, Change, and Read.

Step 3   When you're done, click OK to close the dialog box.

 30 MINUTES

Lab Exercise 23.06: Testing Your LAN Connections

Various tools are available that will help you test and troubleshoot your new network. The textbook covers using these tools in detail. Some of these tools will be beneficial to you as a CompTIA A+ certified technician and are covered on the CompTIA A+ exams. This lab exercise lets you practice using several key network troubleshooting tools.

Learning Objectives

In this exercise, you'll be introduced to troubleshooting tools for determining proper installation of the network components. These tools are covered in order of importance. First, you'll verify the local settings. Next, you'll try to access other systems on the same LAN. Finally, you'll test the Internet connectivity.

At the end of this lab, you'll be able to

- Use the IPCONFIG command to determine local network settings
- Use the NET CONFIG command to check the local system name and who is logged on as a user
- Use the PING command to test the local TCP/IP software and adapter
- Use the NET VIEW command to check for other computers on the network
- Use the PING command with switches to test connectivity to other computers

- Use the NSLOOKUP command to translate IP addresses and domain names

- Use the TRACERT command to check the path to other computers

Lab Materials and Setup

The materials you need for this lab are

- A PC system that's *properly configured* for network access using Windows

- Access to the Internet

✔ **Hint**

The commands vary slightly, depending on the operating system you use. You should practice with each operating system if possible. Test the LAN first by accessing another computer on the network using My Network Places/Network.

Getting Down to Business

As a PC technician, you should be familiar with several networking tools, both for your own good and because they're covered on the CompTIA A+ exams. You'll begin by looking at IPCONFIG.

✔ **Hint**

Since you have already used the IPCONFIG /ALL command, run through the steps again, either on your own system or on a different lab machine. Ask the instructor if any different networks or system configurations are available to explore.

Step 1 You have already examined IPCONFIG in Lab Exercise 23.04. You'll now use the IPCONFIG command again to determine local network settings. As you have already learned, checking the automatic TCP/IP settings given to you by a DHCP server and verifying your manual settings is easy: just open a command-line window, type **IPCONFIG /ALL**, and press ENTER. The details of your local network connection appear on the screen.

Does the display contain the settings that were automatically assigned by the DHCP server or the ones you entered manually? _____

Record your settings here:

IP Address _____

Subnet Mask _____

Default Gateway _____

DNS Servers _____

✔ **Hint**

If you have a system in a peer-to-peer network (no servers) and there are no routers installed, you won't see information about gateways and DNS. What may appear are Windows Internet Naming Service (WINS) settings. More of this would be covered in the coursework for the CompTIA Network+ certification.

Leave the command-prompt window open; you'll use it throughout the rest of this exercise.

Step 2 You'll now use the NET CONFIG command to check the local system name and to see who is logged on as a user. To confirm the computer name and discover who is currently logged on, you'll again use the command line.

Type **NET CONFIG WORKSTATION** at the command prompt and press ENTER. You'll see how the identification is set up for your local PC. There's a lot of information listed, but you're only interested in a couple of items (see Figure 23-7).

How are these listed?

Computer name _____

User name _____

Workstation domain (workgroup) _____

Software version _____

Step 3 You'll now use the PING command to test the local TCP/IP software and adapter.

```
C:\>NET CONFIG Workstation
Computer name                      \\TEST-U93YI93158
Full Computer name                 test-u93yi93158
User name                          Mike

Workstation active on
        NetbiosSmb (000000000000)
        NetBT_Tcpip_{648CDF58-0028-4B2C-8F28-E82E7A069CA4} (000C29CC4076)

Software version                   Windows 2002

Workstation domain                 WORKGROUP
Workstation Domain DNS Name        <null>
Logon domain                       TEST-U93YI93158

COM Open Timeout (sec)             0
COM Send Count (byte)              16
COM Send Timeout (msec)            250
The command completed successfully.

C:\>_
```

FIGURE 23-7 Using the NET CONFIG WORKSTATION command in Windows XP

```
C:\WINDOWS\system32\cmd.exe

C:\>ping 127.0.0.1

Pinging 127.0.0.1 with 32 bytes of data:

Reply from 127.0.0.1: bytes=32 time=8ms TTL=128
Reply from 127.0.0.1: bytes=32 time<1ms TTL=128
Reply from 127.0.0.1: bytes=32 time<1ms TTL=128
Reply from 127.0.0.1: bytes=32 time<1ms TTL=128

Ping statistics for 127.0.0.1:
    Packets: Sent = 4, Received = 4, Lost = 0 (0% loss),
Approximate round trip times in milli-seconds:
    Minimum = 0ms, Maximum = 8ms, Average = 2ms

C:\>
```

FIGURE 23-8 A successful PING test

At the command-line prompt, type **PING 127.0.0.1** (including the periods) and press ENTER. This is known as the IPv4 LOOPBACK or LOCALHOST address and will test the TCP/IP software and the internal part of the local network card. Look at Figure 23-8 to see a successful test. If you don't see the test results, there are serious problems with the software. Reinstall your network drivers, and reconfigure the TCP/IP settings.

Step 4 You'll now use the NET VIEW command to check for other computers on the network.

You want to establish that other computers are available on the network so that you can test that your network card can transmit and receive data in Step 5.

At the command-line prompt, type **NET VIEW** and press ENTER. You'll see what other computers are on the network by a listing of their computer names (see Figure 23-9).

Step 5 Now you'll use the PING command to test your ability to connect to other computers on the network.

In Step 4 you obtained the names of other systems on the LAN, so now you want to check whether you can actually communicate with them.

```
C:\WINDOWS\system32\cmd.exe

C:\>net view
Server Name            Remark

-----------------------------------------------------------------------------
\\DOUGJ-PC
\\VISTAULTIMATEVM
\\VM-WIN2K
The command completed successfully.

C:\>
```

FIGURE 23-9 Using the NET VIEW command

FIGURE 23-10 Using the PING command

At the command line prompt, type **PING computer name**, where *computer name* is another PC's HOST name on the network you found in Step 4, and press ENTER. The results will look the same as when you used PING to see your own computer, but with the other computer's IP address (see Figure 23-10). Be sure to put a space between the PING command and the computer name. If you get errors, use the NET VIEW command again to be certain of the computer name's spelling. If the DNS is down, you can adjust by pinging the other computer's IP address instead of its name.

➔ Try This: PING Switches

The humble PING command is one of the most frequently used troubleshooting tools for TCP/IP. As you saw in Step 5, you can actually use PING to test whether DNS is working. If you do not receive a response from the computer using its HOST name, but you do receive a response when using the IP address, this points to a problem with DNS.

PING also has a number of switches that add to the functionality of the command. If you need to explore the switches, type the following at the command prompt:

```
C:\>PING /?
```

This will list all of the available switches and their functions. The following combination is typically used for a connection that seems to drop packets intermittently. You would run the command indefinitely and increase the packet size to overload the connection. Type the following command:

```
C:\>PING -t -l 65000 computername
```

To stop the continuous PING, press CTRL-C to break the program.

Step 6   You'll now use the NSLOOKUP command to translate an Internet domain name to an IP address or an IP address to an Internet domain name.

This is a good command for finding out the IP addresses of Web sites. Why do I want this, you ask? Well, when you use a URL in your browser, it has to be translated somewhere to an IP address. This slows down your access time. If you know the IP address and type that into the address of your Internet browser, the site will pop up faster. Follow these steps:

a.   Type **NSLOOKUP microsoft.com**, and then press ENTER.

What's the IP address(es) of http://www.microsoft.com? _____

Try **NSLOOKUP totalsem.com.**

What's the IP address(es) of http://www.totalsem.com? _____

b.   Now enter the IP address you got when you did a lookup for http://www.microsoft.com. If you get a different result, it could be that a Web site is being hosted by someone other than the original domain you looked up.

Step 7   You'll now use the TRACERT command to check the path to other computers or Web sites on the Internet.

This command will show you where the bottlenecks are in the Internet. The TRACERT command will list the time it takes to get from your PC to the Web site or other system you're accessing. Follow these steps:

a.   Type **TRACERT google.com**, and then press ENTER.

Was it successful? _____

How many hops did it take? _____

What's the IP address of the first hop? _____

b.   Use the NSLOOKUP command with the IP address of the first hop to see where your first server is located.

Go ahead—have fun with this! Part of the learning process with PCs is to dive in and tackle a subject that you're not completely familiar with. As long as you remember to write down any information you want to change before you change it, you can enjoy exploring the amazing world of computers and still have a recovery point.

Lab Analysis Test

1.   A user complains that after you installed the new NIC in her system, she can see everyone on the network but can't access the Internet. What did you forget to do? Are there any other configuration problems that could cause this to happen?

2.   What command would you use to test the NIC's internal TCP/IP capabilities? What would the "human readable" address be?

3. Theresa's boss bought a wireless network adapter for her laptop. It works great in the office. What does she need for it to work with her PC at home?

4. How do you access the Local Area Connection Properties dialog box in Windows Vista?

5. Tanner has replaced his old NIC with a new wireless NIC. The office wireless network is set up and works fine for everyone else. Now he can't see anyone on the network or access the Internet. Where should he start checking and in what order?

Key Term Quiz

Use the following terms to complete the following sentences. Not all terms will be used.

Device Manager

hub

NET VIEW

Network Connections applet

NIC

PING

PING –l

PING –t

RJ-45

router

switch

UTP

wireless

1. You use an access point when you network _____ devices.

2. An excellent tool for determining who is currently logged on to the network is the _____ command.

3. A(n) _____ can effectively place a device on its own collision domain, thereby increasing network bandwidth.

4. Twisted-pair network cabling uses a(n) _____ connector.

5. To find out whether a machine can accept a large packet of data, you would use the _____ command.

Chapter 24
Wireless Networking

Lab Exercises

Wireless networks are so common today that most people don't take the time to understand the differences between a hard-wired network and a wireless one. With mobile computing on the rise, it's important for CompTIA A+ certified technicians to know as much about wireless networks as possible so that they are prepared to provide quality service in any situation to the users they support. New technicians may be asked questions like, "When should you set up a network with a server," and, "How do you set up a wireless network?" If you've already read Chapter 24 in *Mike Meyers' CompTIA A+ Guide to Managing and Troubleshooting PCs*, you realize that you need to know not only how to set up a wireless network, but also how to configure and secure that network. In this chapter's lab exercises, you'll set up, configure, and secure a couple of wireless networks so that you are prepared to do the same in a real-world setting.

 30 MINUTES

Lab Exercise 24.01: Setting Up a Wireless Network

Your neighbor is interested in starting a home business and has asked you to help him set up a wireless network. The only equipment he currently has is a desktop computer, a laptop computer, a mobile phone, and a USB printer, all of which he is considering using with his business. His main goal is to be able to communicate with his clients wirelessly from any room in his house. He's asked you to help him decide what additional equipment he needs to purchase.

Learning Objectives

This lab tests basic wireless network setup skills and helps you to think about scenarios you might encounter.

At the end of this lab, you'll be able to

- Recommend proper wireless equipment (for example, wireless cards and routers)
- Identify solutions for proper placement of equipment
- Set up and configure a wireless router

Lab Materials and Setup

The materials you need for this lab are

- A working desktop computer running Windows, with some form of broadband Internet connection
- A laptop with wireless connectivity
- Two Ethernet cables
- A wireless router

Getting Down to Business

First, you will need to tell your friend that he needs to buy a wireless router, and, if his laptop doesn't have a Wi-Fi adapter, he'll need one of those, too. Once he's purchased the necessary equipment, he needs to connect it. It may seem strange, but you have to plug in several cables ("wires") when you set up a wireless network.

Step 1 Figure out how your neighbor's computer is physically connected to the Internet. If you are at home, chances are that he has either a DSL or cable modem that connects to his computer via an Ethernet cable. In order to set up the wireless network, disconnect the Ethernet cable from your computer.

Step 2 Plug the Ethernet cable running from the wall jack or modem into the back of the wireless router. There is often a specific jack labeled "Internet" for you to use. Plug in the router and turn it on, if it doesn't turn on automatically. The router is ready when all the lights remain on and steady. There may be one or two blinking lights—it's okay.

Step 3 Now plug one end of the second Ethernet cable into the wireless router and the other end into the desktop computer's RJ45 Ethernet port. You may be thinking that this wireless network isn't looking very wireless so far, but think of it this way: how often do you pick up your entire desktop setup and move it into another room? Not very often, I'd wager.

Step 4 Now that all the cables are in place, go to the laptop and see if you can find the wireless network. For Windows 2000, you'll need to know the SSID (which you'll learn more about in the next two labs). Once you have the SSID, open the Control Panel, go to Network and Dial-up Connections, and right-click the wireless connection. Under the *Connect using* box, click Advanced. Switch to the Advanced tab and click SSID. Type in the name of your network here. If there is no option to enter an SSID, then you probably chose the wrong network adapter from the Network and Dial-up Connections applet.

In Windows XP and Vista, a pop-up (see Figure 24-1) will alert you when Windows has located a new network connection—so much simpler! It will display the name of the wireless network (something generic at this point) and the signal strength.

FIGURE 24-1 Windows has found a new wireless network.

30 MINUTES

Lab Exercise 24.02: Configuring and Securing a Wireless Network

Now that you've installed a wireless router, you must configure it properly so that it is secure from pesky invaders. Be sure to follow these step-by-step instructions so you can reduce the chances of your data being exposed, stolen, or attacked by hackers.

Learning Objectives

This lab enables you to configure and secure your network.

At the end of this lab, you'll be able to

- Properly configure a wireless router

- Set up security options to keep intruders out

Lab Materials and Setup

The materials you need for this lab are

- A working desktop computer running Windows with some form of Internet connection

- A laptop with wireless connectivity

- A wireless router

Getting Down to Business

Failing to configure and secure a wireless network is like leaving your debit card on the sidewalk outside your house with the PIN written on it—chances are that someone will take advantage of the situation and do something unscrupulous. Configuring and securing your wireless network is a fairly easy task. Just be sure to do it. Many people will simply hook up a wireless router, turn it on, and go about their business, not realizing what they've opened themselves up to. For the sake of your private data and the Internet *you* are paying for, follow the steps in this lab exercise.

Keep in mind that configuring a wireless network depends heavily on the router/wireless access point being used. The following steps lead you through the basics, but for more details, check the manual that came with your device.

Step 1 To secure your wireless network, you will use the configuration tool included with your router/wireless access point. To access it, open a Web browser and type **192.168.1.1** (or sometimes **192.168.0.1**) into the address bar. This is the most common address used for the setup utility. You may get a pop-up dialog box or other screen asking for a user name and password. Again, the defaults for these are often **admin** and **password**. This is true across multiple brands, which is all the more reason to change them as soon as possible!

Step 2   You should now be in the setup utility. Different devices use different names, but look for the Wireless Settings page (see Figure 24-2). If it's not called that, look for a screen with options for network name, security options, or MAC address options. Once you've found it, find the box used to enter a network name, or SSID. Delete the one that is there already and create a new one that is unique but memorable. This is so that when you start picking up other wireless signals, you will be able to know which one is your own and connect to it.

Step 3   Usually on the same page as the network name are wireless network security options. These include choices such as WEP, WPA, WPA2, and None. In this case, None is not acceptable. If it's available, select WPA2; otherwise, select WPA. WEP is an older encryption technology that is far less secure. There should also be an empty box labeled "password" or "passphrase" or "pre-shared key." Enter a unique and memorable password to be used whenever you want to connect to the wireless network. Save these settings.

FIGURE 24-2 The Wireless Settings page for a wireless router

Step 4   Finally, now that you've secured the wireless connection itself by enabling WPA2 or another encryption option, you need to secure the router itself. Remember that 99 percent of routers use "admin" and "password" as the user name and password to access the router's setup utility. Failing to change these is an invitation to intruders. Find the setup utility's administration options, or something similar, and change the user name and password to something unique and memorable.

 30 MINUTES

Lab Exercise 24.03: Setting Up an Ad Hoc Wireless Network

Okay, so you've set up a traditional wireless network and learned how to secure it. But what if all you really want to do is play a game with someone, share some files, or search the Internet without a bunch of wires and a router? In CompTIA A+ terminology, we would call this an ad hoc peer-to-peer network.

Learning Objectives

This lab gives you another option for setting up a network.

At the end of this lab, you'll be able to

- Connect two or more computers together wirelessly

Lab Materials and Setup

The materials you need for this lab are

- Two computers with wireless connectivity and Windows XP or Windows Vista installed

Getting Down to Business

The process for setting up an ad hoc wireless network is even simpler than the process for setting up a normal wireless network. However, due in part to their temporary nature, they're not nearly as common. Still, the next time you've got two laptops, no network, and you desperately need to share some files, you'll be glad you know how to set one up.

Step 1 (XP)   In Windows XP, open the Control Panel and double-click Network Connections. Right-click Wireless Network Connection and click Properties. In the Wireless Network Connection Properties window, select the Wireless Networks tab. Verify that the *Use Windows to configure my wireless network settings* box is selected. If it is not, select it. Click Add.

Step 2 (XP)   The Wireless network properties window opens (see Figure 24-3). In the Network name (SSID) text box, enter the name of the network you want to add. I suggest calling it something simple, like ad hoc. Create a password and confirm it. Uncheck the *The key is provided for me automatically* checkbox

FIGURE 24-3 The Wireless Network Properties

and check the *This is a computer-to-computer (ad hoc) network; wireless access points are not used* checkbox. Click OK. You are returned to the Wireless Network tab, and the new network name appears in the Preferred networks list.

Step 1 (Vista) In Windows Vista, go to the Control Panel and open the Network and Sharing Center. Select *Manage wireless networks* and click Add. From the options given, choose *Create an ad hoc network*. Click Next, and then create a simple network name. Select a security type from the menu provided (WPA2 is preferred) and enter a password. Select Save This Network and click Next. You've now set up an ad hoc wireless network.

Lab Analysis Test

1. What are the primary differences between WEP, WPA, and WPA2?

2. What are two common IP addresses for wireless routers?

3. In what situations would you recommend an ad hoc network to a user?

4. What is the path used to get to TCP/IP properties for a network adapter in Windows XP?

5. How does a wireless router communicate signals?

Key Term Quiz

Use the following terms to complete the following sentences. Not all terms will be used.

49

54

802.11n

cell phone

WAP

WEP

Windows Vista

Windows XP

wireless router

1. Network adapters wirelessly connect your computer to your _____.

2. A(n) _____ router is ideal for multimedia (gaming) applications because of its significant range and speed.

3. An 802.11g router can communicate up to _____ Mbps with a throughput of up to 22 Mbps.

4. _____ was the first operating system to offer ad hoc networking.

5. A Wi-Fi hotspot can be found in most major _____ companies.

Chapter 25
The Internet

Lab Exercises

The Internet is a complex system of communication that allows computers, in-business networks, mobile computers, and home PCs to share information worldwide. Today we even have cell phones, personal digital assistants (PDAs), and other personal devices that we can use to connect to the Internet and access e-mail, download MP3s, and do other tasks.

Because nearly everyone wants access to the Internet, implementing and troubleshooting Internet connectivity is a PC technician's bread and butter. The CompTIA A+ certification exams recognize this and test you on the details of installing and configuring a connection to the Internet. It may be a legacy dial-up analog modem used to connect to an ISP through a phone line, or a broadband cable modem using the local cable company as the provider. This heightened usage brings with it a new task for the PC technician: Internet security! Since most computers are now communicating with the world through the Internet, the exposure to malicious intruders and programs has greatly increased. Two components that go hand-in-hand with the Internet are firewalls and wireless network security. You just finished setting up and configuring the hardware portion of a wireless network in the last chapter, so now you'll look at the software side of network security. This chapter's lab exercises first guide you through the properties of the current wide area network (WAN) connection technologies and then take you through the steps needed to perform the installation and configuration of these technologies. You'll also explore the configuration of Windows Firewall and Windows Internet Connection Sharing and learn how to upgrade to the latest version of the Internet Explorer browser.

✔ **Cross-Reference**

Computer security is such an important component of a PC technician's training that the topic receives its own chapter in both the textbook and the lab manual. Refer to Chapter 26 in *Mike Meyers' CompTIA A+ Guide to Managing and Troubleshooting PCs*. The next chapter in this manual, Chapter 26, covers additional lab exercises to build your security awareness.

 30 MINUTES

Lab Exercise 25.01: Identifying Internet Connectivity Properties

A new client has signed up with your firm, requesting that you evaluate their current Internet connectivity and recommend the best upgrade path for their 12-person office (six desktop PCs and two laptops). Your first job is to assess what method they are currently using to connect to the Internet and what methods are available in their location, and to make a recommendation for upgrades if necessary.

Learning Objectives

This lab exercise tests basic assessment skills. Every technician should be able to go into a situation and quickly understand the state of the technology in question—in this case, an Internet connection. You should also feel comfortable telling your clients about any concerns with aging technology and feel confident recommending upgrade paths to higher-performance technology.

At the end of this lab, you'll be able to

- Verify the Internet connectivity method

- Check the properties of the connection

- Perform an Internet search to learn about the performance of various connectivity methods

Lab Materials and Setup

The materials you need for this lab are

- A working computer running Windows with some form of Internet connection

- Internet connectivity to perform your research

Getting Down to Business

First, you will visually inspect your computer and its surroundings for the method used to connect to the Internet. Then you will run an Internet utility to determine the speed of your connection and appropriate upgrade paths.

Step 1 Look at the back of your computer:

- Is there a phone cable (RJ-11) plugged in? This could indicate that this computer is using an analog modem for the Internet connection.

- Are there any USB or network (RJ-45) cables plugged into the system? Trace the wires. Do they connect to a cable modem or DSL modem? This could be your connectivity method.

- Is there a network patch cable plugged into the NIC? You may be connecting to the Internet through the corporate LAN.

- Are you on a laptop with wireless connectivity? You could have access to the Internet through a wireless access point (WAP) connected to a cable or DSL modem.

These are the possibilities a technician is faced with today, so the more you can explore the various methods of connectivity, the more knowledgeable you will be. Figure 25-1 depicts a typical PC using a wired LAN patch cable to connect to a broadband cable modem.

Examine the physical components that constitute the method your system uses to connect to the Internet and then record the details of the hardware/connectivity type here.

_____

_____

Step 2 Once you have determined the connectivity method, boot your system and launch your Internet browser (popular browsers include Microsoft Internet Explorer, Mozilla Firefox, and Google Chrome). In the address bar, type **http://reviews.cnet.com/internet-speed-test/** and press ENTER. This will take you to CNET's Bandwidth Meter Online Speed Test. Follow the onscreen instructions to test the speed of your connection.

What is the speed of your connection? _____

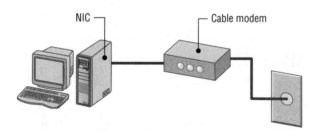

FIGURE 25-1 A PC and cable modem Internet connection

Step 3 Using the Bandwidth Meter Online Speed Test results (where possible), fill in the approximate data transfer speeds of the various Internet connection types:

Dial-up 56 Kbps modem _____

DSL _____

Cable _____

T1 _____

T3 _____

Step 4 Based on the results of the analysis of your client's Internet connection method and performance, are there any recommendations you would make to improve the performance of the connection?

_____

_____

_____

 30 MINUTES

Lab Exercise 25.02: Installing and Configuring an Internet Connection

You determine that the client is currently using dial-up networking through analog modems to access the Internet. Though this is probably acceptable for occasionally connecting to the Internet, these folks have a business to run! You decide to recommend either high-speed DSL or cable. You explain to the client that unlike the analog modem they're currently using, the other methods use a standard network interface card (NIC) and an external device to interface between the DSL or cable lines. Ironically, this device is usually referred to as a DSL or cable *modem*. You will evaluate the current PCs and select one that will act as the interface to the Internet. If required, you'll add a PCI or PCIe NIC, connect the DSL or cable interface, and then configure the interface in Windows.

Learning Objectives

Installing DSL or cable high-speed Internet access requires four steps. First, you should verify whether your system is already equipped with a NIC, either integrated into the motherboard or as a PCI/PCIe card, and if not, physically install such a device. Second, verify that this device is operating properly and has the latest drivers installed. Third, connect the DSL transceiver or the cable modem, and finally, configure the proper settings required by the ISP.

At the end of this lab, you'll be able to

- Install a network interface card (if not already present)
- Verify proper operation, and install or update the drivers
- Install the DSL transceiver or cable modem
- Configure the connection in Windows

✔ **Cross-Reference**

Refer to the "DSL" and "Cable" sections in Chapter 25 and the "Installing Expansion Cards" section in Chapter 8 of *Mike Meyers' CompTIA A+ Guide to Managing and Troubleshooting PCs* for help installing and configuring NICs. It's a good idea to have the textbook handy while you progress through this lab.

Lab Materials and Setup

The materials you need for this lab are

- A PC system with or without a NIC
- A PCI or PCIe NIC
- Access to the proper driver software (either built-in Windows drivers or a separate disc)
- A copy of the Windows installation media (may be needed, depending on the system)
- A Phillips-head screwdriver
- An anti-static wrist strap

Getting Down to Business

Break out your trusty screwdriver and anti-static wrist strap. It's time to install a NIC! The process for physically installing a NIC is functionally identical to the process you've used to install expansion cards in the past, but the software side of things has a few differences that you should pay attention to.

✔ **Hint**

You can omit Steps 1–3 if the system is already equipped with a network interface card, as most systems are today. The steps are included here for completeness. You will be asked to install a second NIC in Lab Exercise 25.04, "Configuring Windows Internet Connection Sharing," so if you have that second NIC handy, go ahead and install it now.

Step 1 Make sure the PC is off and unplugged. While following proper ESD avoidance procedures, remove the cover of the PC. Choose any free PCI or PCIe slot to install the NIC. Remove the back plate if one exists.

Step 2 Plug the NIC into the PCI or PCIe slot (see Figure 25-2). Physically inserting the NIC into the PC is the easiest part of the task. Take care to avoid touching the pins or any of the chips on the NIC. Once the card is inserted, secure it by putting the proper screw through the metal tab of the card and screwing it to the case. Put the cover back on and restart your computer.

Step 3 Now that you have physically installed the NIC, which step you take next depends on your OS. When you restart a Windows 2000 system, the operating system will recognize that you've added new hardware and launch the Found New Hardware Wizard. Windows XP and higher go one step better—when you install a PnP device, the drivers are most likely already part of the operating system, so they'll be installed automatically. This all occurs with no user intervention. The operating system reports success installing the new device with a small balloon from the system tray.

✔ **Hint**

Every Windows operating system has a good selection of network interface drivers built in at the time of release, but your driver may not be one of them. For example, if the NIC you're installing was manufactured after the release of software you're using, the drivers may not be part of the operating system and will need to be manually installed or updated.

FIGURE 25-2 Inserting a PCI NIC

The following is the Found New Hardware Wizard (Windows 2000) driver installation process:

a. As Windows boots, it displays the Found New Hardware Wizard screen (see Figure 25-3). Alternatively, if you're using Windows XP, you can go to Control Panel | Add Hardware to start a similar process.

b. Click Next to continue. If you are using the Add/Remove Hardware Wizard instead of the Found New Hardware Wizard, there is simply the extra step of having Windows find the hardware you installed either automatically or from a list. Then select the option that directs Windows to search for a suitable driver for the new device (see Figure 25-4). If the driver is on a floppy disk or optical disc, select that as the search location, insert the media for the driver before continuing, and then click Next.

✔ Hint

A popular trick is to copy the drivers from the optical disc onto the PC's hard drive and then install them from there. That way, if you ever need the drivers again, you won't need to rummage around for the driver disc. You need to know exactly where you store the drivers, though, because you'll be asked to locate them during the installation process. You could create a Drivers folder at the root of the C: drive to serve as a central repository for drivers. Remember, drivers are constantly being updated by manufacturers. Check the manufacturer's Web site before using the driver disc.

Found New Hardware Wizard

Welcome to the Found New Hardware Wizard

This wizard helps you install a device driver for a hardware device.

To continue, click Next.

< Back   Next >   Cancel

FIGURE 25-3 Using the Found New Hardware Wizard

FIGURE 25-4 Completing installation by locating a suitable device driver

c.   The wizard will search through the drivers built into Windows and then the location you specified for the file(s). It should then report that it found the appropriate driver. Click Next. If prompted, you may also need to insert your Windows installation disc. When the wizard is finished, it'll prompt you a final time. Click the Finish button, and reboot your system. The new NIC and drivers are now properly installed.

If Windows doesn't detect the driver right away, you'll need to do a little extra work. Network interface manufacturers bundle drivers for multiple operating systems on the driver disc, so you often need to navigate to the appropriate folder for your operating system before Windows will find the driver. In other words, look for a Win2k folder when installing modem drivers on a Windows 2000 machine. Other manufacturers package the driver into an installation routine. Check the disc for a SETUP.EXE file, and run it if you find it.

Step 4   Now that the drivers are installed, you should confirm the NIC properties and verify what drivers are installed.

a.   Open the Control Panel. In Windows 2000, open Network and Dial-up Connections. In Windows XP, open Network Connections. In Windows Vista, open the Network and Sharing Center, and then click *Manage network connections*.

b.   Right-click Local Area Connection (note: if this is the second network interface, choose Local Area Connection 2) and click Properties. In the Local Area Connection Properties dialog box, click the Configure button next to the network interface adapter.

c.   In the network interface adapter Properties dialog box, click the Driver tab (see Figure 25-5).

FIGURE 25-5 Network interface adapter driver properties

Record all the information provided about the driver you installed.

_____

_____

Step 5 Now examine the physical device that has been provided by your ISP to connect the computer to the Internet. If the device is a DSL transceiver, it will typically have an RJ-45 Ethernet connection to connect to the NIC of the computer, an RJ-11 connector to connect to the telephone wall jack, and some sort of power adapter. If the device is a cable modem, it will typically have an RJ-45 Ethernet connection to connect to the NIC of the computer, an F-connector to attach to the cable, and some sort of power adapter (refer to Figure 25-1). Both interfaces may provide a USB connection, but for the purposes of the lab exercise, this will not be used.

✔ **Hint**

If you are in a classroom lab environment, you may not have access to the actual DSL transceiver or cable modem. Follow the instructor's directions to connect the computer to the Internet. You should conduct an Internet search or make a trip to the local technology store to explore the specifications of common DSL and cable interfaces. For the most part, going through the full configuration of the actual connection is beyond the scope of this book, but you should at least know where to go to follow instructions from your ISP; that's the purpose of these last steps.

Connect the interface device by following the instructions provided with the device or by your ISP. The layout and configuration of the device may differ somewhat from device to device, but you should be able to confirm that the device is working properly by observing the various indicator lights on the device.

Step 6 To finish this installation and gain high-speed access to the Internet, you will most likely have to follow specific directions from your ISP to configure Windows to communicate through the DSL or cable device. Windows also provides a generic wizard to configure this communication. The following list walks you through this generic configuration by operating system:

- **Windows 2000** Go to Start | Programs | Accessories | Communications | Internet Connection Wizard. Select the option to set up your Internet connection manually or through a LAN. Click Next. Choose *I connect through a local area network (LAN)* and click Next. Select the recommended automatic settings. Click Next and select no when asked if you want to set up a mail account. Click Next, then Finish.

- **Windows XP** Open Network Connections and select *Create a new connection*. Click Next. Choose the Connect to the Internet option and click Next. Select the option to set up your connection manually and click Next. Pick the appropriate option on the next screen, most likely *Connect using a broadband connection that is always on*. Click Next, then Finish.

- **Windows Vista** Open Control Panel. Open the Network and Sharing Center and select *Set up a connection or network*. Select Connect to the Internet and click Next. Choose Broadband as your connection. Type in the relevant information and click Connect. Windows will then attempt to set up your Internet connection. When it is finished, click Close.

If you have followed these steps (and actually have installed a DSL or cable interface), you should now have high-speed access to the Internet.

 30 MINUTES

Lab Exercise 25.03: Enabling Windows Firewall

Your client is very pleased with how the rollout of the office's Internet connection upgrade is progressing. They have been surfing around a little, and are impressed with the speed at which the Web sites are loading. You explain that you must now configure a firewall to protect them from outside intrusion through the high-speed connection. Windows XP (Service Pack 2) and Windows Vista offer very competent built-in firewalls. In this lab you will enable Windows Firewall and explore some of the services (ports) that you can allow or block.

Learning Objectives

Completing the following steps, you will explore Windows Firewall and associated TCP and UDP service ports.

At the end of this lab, you'll be able to

- Enable Windows Firewall

- Identify various protocols and associated service ports

✔ Cross-Reference

To further explore Windows Firewall, refer to "Firewalls" in Chapter 26 of *Mike Meyers' CompTIA A+ Guide to Managing and Troubleshooting PCs.*

Lab Materials and Setup

The materials you need for this lab are

- A working computer running Windows XP or Windows Vista

- Optional: A machine connected to the Internet

Getting Down to Business

Enabling the firewall is as simple as a few clicks of the mouse and verifying that you can communicate with the trusted sites that you prefer. Windows Firewall is practically self-configuring, but if you want to allow access to Web servers or e-mail servers in your organization, you will have to open some TCP ports. The CompTIA A+ certification exams will expect you to know some of these "well-known ports," so you'll explore them in Windows Firewall.

✔ Hint

If you are configuring a single machine for Internet access, you will want to implement Windows Firewall on that machine to protect it from malicious intrusion. However, if you are configuring machines as part of a LAN and using a proxy server or Internet Connection Sharing (as you will in the next lab exercise), you will only want to configure a firewall on the machine that connects directly to the Internet. Assume the computer in this lab is the machine connected to the Internet.

Step 1 In Windows XP, return to Network Connections. Right-click the Local Area Connections icon of the external connection (the one connected to the Internet) and select Properties. Click the Advanced tab, and then click the Settings button in the Windows Firewall box. This opens the Windows Firewall dialog box (see Figure 25-6).

In Windows Vista, open the Control Panel and double-click Windows Firewall. Select *Change settings.*

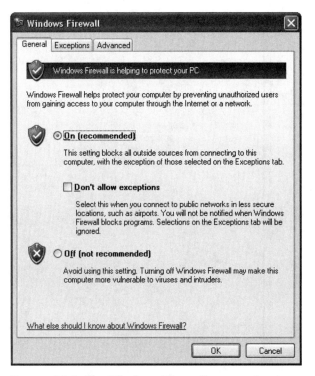

FIGURE 25-6 The Windows Firewall properties screen

Step 2   Select *On (recommended)* to protect the PC from unwanted access through the Internet connection.

Step 3   In Windows XP, select the Advanced tab of the Windows Firewall dialog box and click the Settings button for the Network Connection Settings (see Figure 25-7).

→ **Note**

The following advanced options have been removed from the Windows Firewall Settings in Windows Vista in an attempt to make the OS more secure; thus, the following steps will only work in Windows XP. There are still methods for setting up exceptions (see the Exceptions tab in Windows Firewall dialog box, specifically the Add Port button) but most of the advanced features have been moved to the Administrative Tools.

Step 4   This opens the Advanced Settings dialog box, where you can allow various services to pass through the Internet connection and access dedicated servers on your internal network. For instance, if you have an FTP server that you have technicians update from the field, you will want to enable external communication by allowing TCP service port 21 to pass through the firewall (see Figure 25-8).

FIGURE 25-7 The Windows Firewall Advanced properties screen

FIGURE 25-8 Allowing FTP traffic to pass through the firewall in Windows XP

![Service Settings dialog box]

Figure 25-9 Service Settings showing the TCP port number for the FTP server in Windows XP

Using the Edit button, identify the service ports for the following protocols (I have completed the first one for you, see Figure 25-9):

File Transfer Protocol (FTP Server) _____**TCP Port 21**_____

Internet Mail Access Protocol version 4 (IMAP4) _____

Simple Mail Transfer Protocol (SMTP) _____

Post Office Protocol version 3 (POP3) _____

Secure Sockets Layer (HTTPS) _____

Hypertext Transfer Protocol (HTTP) _____

Step 5 To complete this lab, check with your instructor to obtain the proper configuration of the firewall to allow the completion of further labs. You will probably disable the Windows Firewall for normal classroom use.

 30 MINUTES

Lab Exercise 25.04: Configuring Windows Internet Connection Sharing

Now that the main PC is secure from external threats and attacks, it's time to configure this machine so that all of the PCs can take advantage of the secure Internet connection. Welcome Internet Connection Sharing (ICS)! With ICS, you will be able to set up a small LAN that allows all the client machines to access the Internet through the ICS host computer (this PC).

Learning Objectives

In this lab, you will implement the steps to use ICS. It will take some extra hardware to actually test the configuration, but you can still learn the basic concepts through the configuration exercise.

At the end of this lab, you'll be able to

- Configure Internet Connection Sharing

✔ **Cross-Reference**

To further explore ICS, refer to "Windows Internet Connection Sharing" in Chapter 25 of *Mike Meyers' CompTIA A+ Guide to Managing and Troubleshooting PCs.*

Lab Materials and Setup

The materials you need for this lab are

- A working computer running Windows

- An additional network interface card for the ICS host computer

- A network hub or switch

- A second computer running Windows to be configured as the client

- Optional: A machine connected to the Internet

Getting Down to Business

ICS allows a small workgroup of computers to connect to the Internet through one of the workgroup computers acting as an ICS host computer. There are a few items that need to be configured on both the ICS host computer and the clients. The host will have two communication devices installed (in this case, two NICs). The network will need a hub or a switch to allow multiple computers to communicate. Finally, the client machines will have to be configured to obtain their TCP/IP settings automatically.

➜ **Note**

It may seem convoluted to connect an Ethernet cable coming from your Internet source to your computer just so you can connect another Ethernet cable to a hub or switch—why not just connect the hub to the Internet source? But ICS is perhaps at its most beneficial when dealing with dial-up connections. In that case, you'd use a single NIC and a modem. Since most dial-up modems don't offer an Ethernet output, the only way to share the Internet connection would be with ICS!

Step 1 To use ICS, you will need two communication devices installed in the computer: either a modem connected to the Internet and a NIC connected to the internal network, or a NIC connected to a broadband interface and a NIC connected to the internal network. (If you need to install a second NIC to facilitate this lab exercise, perform Lab Exercise 25.02, Steps 1–3.)

Step 2 In Windows 2000, open the Local Area Connection Properties dialog box for the network device connected to the Internet, as you did in previous lab exercises. Click the Sharing tab. Check the *Enable Internet Connection Sharing for this connection* checkbox. Click OK.

In Windows XP and Windows Vista, open the Local Area Connection Properties dialog box for the network device connected to the Internet, as you did in previous lab exercises. Click the Advanced tab (see Figure 25-10). Under Internet Connection Sharing, check the *Allow other network users to connect through this computer's Internet connection* checkbox. Click OK.

Step 3 Once you've clicked OK, a hand icon (representing sharing) should appear under the Local Area Connection that has just been configured with ICS (see Figure 25-11).

Step 4 Test the ICS feature by following these steps:

a. Verify that the ICS host computer is capable of communicating with the Internet. Connect the external Local Area Connection NIC to the broadband interface (DSL or cable).

b. Power up the hub or switch, and connect the internal interface from the ICS host computer to the hub.

FIGURE 25-10 The Advanced tab of the Local Area Connection Properties dialog box showing Internet Connection Sharing

FIGURE 25-11 A shared Local Area Connection

c. Connect the network interface card of the client PC to the hub or switch.

d. Open the Local Area Connection Properties dialog box, as you did in previous lab exercises. On the General tab, select Internet Protocol (TCP/IP) and click Properties. In the Properties dialog box, verify that *Obtain an IP address automatically* and *Obtain DNS server address automatically* are selected (see Figure 25-12).

FIGURE 25-12 Internet Protocol (TCP/IP)
Properties dialog box

Launch Internet Explorer on the client machine; verify that the connection is set up to use the LAN connection. Type **www.comptia.org** in the address bar and press ENTER. If there are any problems, shut down both machines and check all of the connections. Boot the ICS host computer first (allow all of the services to start), then boot the client machine.

 20 MINUTES

Lab Exercise 25.05: Upgrading and Tweaking Internet Explorer

Now that you have improved and protected your client's Internet connectivity, you will want to make sure that the method they use to interact with the Internet is the most current. Microsoft Internet Explorer (IE) and Mozilla Firefox are currently the two most popular browsers. The following steps will help you upgrade your client to the latest version of IE (version 8 as of this writing) and introduce you to some of the configuration areas that you should be aware of.

Learning Objectives

When it comes to applications—and this includes Internet Explorer—the computer technician is looked to as the Master or Mistress of All Things Computer. For this reason, a knowledge and awareness of applications, in addition to learning and practicing your craft as an IT technician, will enhance your reputation as an expert. In this lab, you'll briefly explore the upkeep of a networking application.

At the end of this lab, you'll be able to

- Evaluate and upgrade the IE application

- Fine-tune IE settings

Lab Materials and Setup

The materials you need for this lab are

- A working computer running Windows XP (at least SP2) or Windows Vista

- Internet access, preferably high-speed to facilitate downloads

Getting Down to Business

Internet Explorer is currently the most popular browser application. You and your client may launch an Internet search engine such as Google or Yahoo! to locate and visit manufacturers' Web sites, to research and, in some cases, purchase new hardware and software. You'll want to make sure that IE is up to date and working efficiently to make your client's browsing more pleasant.

✖ Warning

The following lab steps have you update Internet Explorer and change some of the configuration settings. If you are in an instructor-led class, or performing these operations on machines in your organization, verify you have permission to perform the upgrades.

Step 1   Open your current browser and navigate to the Microsoft Windows Internet Explorer page (www.microsoft.com/windows/internet-explorer/ as of this writing). Examine the new features and requirements (click Support, then System requirements). Does IE8 work with all versions of Windows?

Verify that your system and OS meet the requirements, and then download Internet Explorer 8.

Step 2   When the download has finished, open Internet Explorer. Choose Tools | Internet Options.

On the General tab (see Figure 25-13), you can set the home page (or home pages), set browser history settings, change search defaults, and adjust tab settings. There are also options to set the appearance of Web pages displayed by the browser.

Figure 25-13 The General tab of the Internet Options dialog box in Internet Explorer 8

Step 3 Click the Advanced tab and explore the many settings that can be configured to modify how the browser deals with components and content. Navigate down to the Security heading and locate *Empty Temporary Internet Files Folder when browser is closed*. I like to enable this setting.

Explore some of the other tabs available in Internet Options and experiment with the different items you can configure. Microsoft has done a good job of setting the browser up with default settings that will work in most installations, but as the expert, you will want to be familiar with customizing the browser.

Lab Analysis Test

1. Tanner wants to configure his wireless network so that if Andrew just happens by with a laptop and a wireless card, he will not be able to gain access to the network without Tanner's approval. What component(s) does Tanner need to configure?

2. Brandon is using his school's computer to do some research for a term paper. He attempts to surf to a Web site he has found on Google, only to receive an *Access Denied* message from the browser. What could cause this to happen?

3. Andrew has configured his four-computer network to use Internet Connection Sharing. He has double-checked the ICS host computer, and it can access the Internet. All of the physical connections between the computers and the switch seem to be in good shape. Yet, he still cannot access the Internet from a client machine. What might he have missed?

4. Mary has stated that when she used the CNET Bandwidth Meter Online Speed Test, she achieved Internet transfer speeds around 7.5 Mbps. What type of Internet access do you think Mary has?

5. Cindy is installing a high-speed connection to the Internet. What are the four components she will need to verify and have on hand?

Key Term Quiz

Use the following terms to complete the following sentences. Not all terms will be used.

analog

dial-up

digital

drivers

HTTP

ICS

ISP

PnP

POP3

RJ-11

RJ-45

transceiver

Windows Firewall

1. When connecting to the Internet using a high-speed digital subscriber line, the DSL _____ is often referred to as a DSL modem.

2. The protocol that is synonymous with the World Wide Web is _____.

3. If the NIC isn't detected by _____, run the Add New Hardware Wizard.

4. Every wireless network has a network name that all of the machines accessing it must configure. This network name is known as a(n) _____.

5. The slowest means of accessing the Internet still in use today is _____.

Chapter 26
Securing Computers

Lab Exercises

Obviously, keeping your computer secure is important. Several chapters have already been devoted to securing Windows and networks. But there are still a few more helpful tools you should know about to keep things running smoothly. Local Security Settings lets you set a variety of rules about using the system; Event Viewer shows you information about events you didn't even know were happening; and Microsoft Security Essentials is a free tool that allows you to clean your system of, and protect your system against, viruses and other malicious software. Each of these tools increases the power you have over your own security and the security of your computer.

 15 MINUTES

Lab Exercise 26.01: Local Policies

NTFS permissions are powerful tools to control with great detail what users and groups can do to folders and files. However, NTFS does not cover a number of important security issues that don't directly involve the file system. For example, what if you don't want a particular user group to shut down the computer? What if you want to make sure all accounts use a password of at least eight characters? What if you want to prevent certain users from reformatting the hard drive? These types of security settings are all controlled under the umbrella term of local policies.

✔ **Hint**

There are hundreds of different policies that you may configure for a system. This lab only covers a few of the most basic policies!

Learning Objectives

At the end of this lab, you'll be able to

- Locate and open the Local Security Policy/Settings utility
- Create, modify, and delete local policies with Windows

Lab Materials and Setup

The materials you need for this lab are

- A Windows PC with the C: drive formatted as NTFS

- Access to the local administrator password

Getting Down to Business

Local Security Settings is a very powerful applet that allows you to adjust all sorts of settings and details about your system. Simply put, it is a series of rules you define, ranging from how many attempts to log on a user is allowed, to who can change the time on the clock!

Step 1 Log on using an account with administrator rights. From Control Panel, open Administrative Tools. Double-click Local Security Policy. When opened, it should look something like Figure 26-1.

Double-click the Account Policies icon to expand its contents: Password Policy and Account Lockout Policy. Click Password Policy in the left column, right-click *Password must meet complexity requirements*, and select Properties. Enable this policy, as shown in Figure 26-2, and click OK.

Create a normal user account and call it **Janet**. Try making a simple password like **janet** and see what happens. Keep trying to make a password until you get one that is accepted. What do you need to do to make an acceptable password?

✔ **Hint**

Use the help in the User Accounts Control Panel applet to get some ideas as to what you need to do.

Figure 26-1 Local Security Settings

FIGURE 26-2 Enabling password complexity

→ **Note**

In Windows 2000, right-clicking a policy will give you a context menu with a Security option instead of a Properties option. These are the same tools.

Step 2 Head back to the Password Policy in Local Security Settings and enable Enforce Password History. Open the User Accounts applet from the Control Panel and try to change a password to the same password you already have. What happens?

Step 3 In Local Security Settings, click Account Lockout Policy under Account Policies in the left column. An account lockout is when the operating system no longer allows a certain account the right even to try to log on. Try to change the properties on the *Account lockout duration* setting—it is disabled until you set the *Account lockout threshold* to something other than the default of 0. Try changing the *Account lockout threshold* to 3 attempts. Note that Windows now automatically sets the *Account lockout duration* and the *Reset account lockout counter after* settings to 30 minutes.

Log off the computer. Use the Janet account and intentionally attempt to log on using incorrect passwords. What happens after the third try?

⏱ 20 MINUTES

Lab Exercise 26.02: Event Viewer

With all the pop-ups, dialog boxes, and little message bubbles that Windows throws at you all day long, you would think it's telling you everything that happens every minute of every day—Windows Vista, doubly so. But it isn't. Of course, there are many processes that go on in the background, but even when Windows alerts you of an event, there may be more to the story. Perhaps an application crashes unexpectedly and Windows provides little or no feedback. It's possible that one tool in Administrative Tools took notice and can help—Event Viewer.

Learning Objectives

In this lab, you'll practice using Event Viewer.

At the end of this lab, you'll be able to

- Work with Event Viewer to track events on your system

Lab Materials and Setup

The materials you will need for this lab are

- A PC with Windows

Getting Down to Business

Think about your actions on a computer as a series of events: you log on, you open an application, you close it, you log off, and so forth. This is how Event Viewer sees things, but in a lot more detail. If something goes wrong, Event Viewer usually records it. It also records a lot of things that are perfectly normal—the trick is being able to sort through all the information, which Windows makes fairly simple.

Step 1 Access Event Viewer by going to Control Panel and opening Administrative Tools. Double-click Event Viewer to open it (see Figure 26-3).

Step 2 Windows Vista adds the extra step of expanding the Windows Logs folder in the left column, but otherwise Event Viewer is exactly the same in each version of Windows. Four or five logs should be listed. The important one for now is Application; the events in this log all concern the operation of applications on your system. Click it in the left column and a long list of events should appear on the right.

Step 3 Scroll through the list and look at the different levels used by Windows to describe events (in the Type column, which is usually the leftmost column). Click the Type column label at the top of the list to sort the events by level. You should see a lot of events labeled Information. These are your everyday events—any successful operation, such as proper use of a driver, is marked as Information.

FIGURE 26-3 Event Viewer

Step 4 There might also be a few events labeled Warning or Error. Warnings do not indicate that something bad *is* happening but rather that something bad *will* happen. An example of a Warning event is when Windows is low on resources, such as disk space. Errors are more serious. These events occur when there is a failure or loss of functionality, such as when an application crashes.

Go through the list and see if you can find any Warnings or Errors. Double-click one and look at the Event Properties dialog box that pops up for more information on what happened. A lot of Event Viewer's reports can be very cryptic, which is why Windows Vista now has a handy Event Log Online Help link built into Event Viewer. Clicking the link opens a dialog box asking for permission to send information about the event over the Internet. Your browser will open and take you to the Microsoft TechNet database. There isn't information available on every single event, but it can be very useful in tracking down problems.

If you don't have Windows Vista, you can always record the Event ID number that is listed with the event and search for it on the Internet. For example, if it is Event ID 1002, simply search for **"Event Viewer ID 1002"** and see what comes up. You're likely to find out at least a little more than you knew before.

Step 5 Try searching through the other logs—you can't really hurt anything from Event Viewer, because whatever is included there already happened! Search through the Security and System logs to see what sorts of events they record.

30 MINUTES

Lab Exercise 26.03: Cleaning and Protecting a Client's Computer

Geek Squad, the popular PC repair arm of Best Buy, reports that over 75 percent of their service calls involve cleaning malware off of a computer and then showing customers how to protect their PCs from malware and other attacks.

Windows comes with many programs and features to protect your computer, but these tools are useless if they are not used properly. In this lab exercise, you will check the computer for malware, clean the malware from the computer, and then go through the steps to reduce the likelihood of another attack.

Learning Objectives

At the end of this lab, you'll be able to

- Remove malware from a Windows system

- Configure Internet security software (antivirus/antimalware)

Lab Materials and Setup

The materials you need for this lab are

- A Windows XP (SP2 or later) or Windows Vista PC

- Microsoft Security Essentials (or another Internet security suite)

✔ **Hint**

This is a great lab for students who want to bring a PC from home—or one that belongs to a friend—for testing and cleaning.

Getting Down to Business

A new system brings with it new problems. You've set up user accounts with passwords and activated firewalls, but there is still one more important piece of protection required. Antivirus and antimalware software can actively and passively protect you from unwanted malicious activity. Actively, you can usually scan entire computers for any issues. Passively, many tools are available that will constantly monitor your PC as you use it and watch out for viruses and other problems you may encounter on the Internet.

This lab will walk you through setting up Microsoft Security Essentials software, compatible with Windows XP (SP2 or later) and Windows Vista, available at www.microsoft.com/Security_Essentials/. There are, of course, other software solutions available, some of them free, but Microsoft's tool is fairly complete and multifunctional (and, yes, free).

Step 1 The first step is to download the software (if you haven't already done so). When you open the executable, it will extract itself and begin the installation. Follow the instructions. Then it will run itself, update itself, and scan itself—it's all quite impressive to watch (see Figure 26-4).

Step 2 Microsoft Security Essentials will finish the scan and report its findings. It will give you the option to clean your computer or perform another action, but the defaults are usually correct. The file should then be quarantined or destroyed, and Microsoft Security Essentials will alert you when it has finished.

Step 3 Now that you've completed your initial scan, there are other options available to you. You can pick between running a Quick scan or a Full scan. A Full scan performs the same actions as the Quick scan, but also goes through the Registry. You can also set up a Custom scan to scan only certain directories.

FIGURE 26-4 Microsoft Security Essentials performing a scan

FIGURE 26-5 The Settings tab of Microsoft Security Essentials

The Update tab allows you to update virus and spyware definitions, although Microsoft Security Essentials also does this automatically. The History tab keeps track of all the potentially harmful items the software finds and what actions it performed. The Settings tab allows you to set up the program as you wish, including scheduling regular scans, setting what files and locations to exclude from scans, and adding removable drives to the scan (see Figure 26-5).

To add removable drives to the scan, under the Settings tab, click Advanced in the left column. Check the box for *Scan removable drives*. Microsoft Security Essentials will now scan the contents of each removable drive, such as USB thumb drives.

Lab Analysis Test

1. While browsing the Internet, Maxel has been getting a lot more pop-ups lately. He assumes he has some kind of adware on his system. What should he do to fix this?

2. Jason is working on a document when Word crashes. Which log in Event Viewer will give him more information? Which level would it be most likely identified as?

3. In the Local Security Policy/Settings applet, what does *Account lockout threshold* control?

4. What is the path used in Windows Vista to access the Security log in Event Viewer?

5. What are two methods of learning more about a particular event in Event Viewer?

Key Term Quiz

Use the following terms to complete the following sentences. Not all terms will be used.

adware

antivirus program

definition file

event auditing

Event Viewer

incidence reporting

Local Security Policy/Settings

object access auditing

phishing

polymorph virus

pop-up

spam

spyware

Trojan

virus

worm

1. _____ is a type of unsolicited e-mail that usually contains hoaxes and get-rich-quick schemes.

2. A(n) _____ appears as a new window in front of whatever application you are using.

3. It is necessary to have a(n) _____ to protect your computer from malicious programs and other malware.

4. _____ keeps track of every event that occurs on your system and assigns them a level, such as Information or Warning.

5. A piece of malicious software that gets passed from computer to computer is known most generically as a(n) _____.

Chapter 27
The Complete PC Technician

Lab Exercises

At this point you're well on your path to becoming a CompTIA A+ certified technician. You have an excellent understanding of the major technical aspects of computer systems: hardware, software, networking, and the Internet.

When a client launches an application, that person isn't thinking about what happens behind the scenes: "Hey, look at me! I'm using the keyboard and mouse to input data! The processor is calculating all of the information to produce the desired results and present the output on the screen or in hard copy form on a printer. This is only possible because the operating system, applications, and data were successfully stored on the hard drive." You, as the tech, *do* have to think about all of this, but you also need the user's perspective. When you look at the computer system as a whole—that is, as a practical tool that can create and process everything from your résumé to the latest Hollywood thriller—you'll have a better understanding of how your clients envision the computer.

A PC tech in the real world also has to work with people: customers, clients, supervisors, coworkers, family members, maybe even spouses. You have to develop the skills for calmly gathering information about the state the computer is in and how it arrived there. Usually, your clients won't use the most technical language to explain the situation, and they may be frustrated or even a little on the defensive, so you need to be understanding and patient. You want them to see you as an ally, and to ensure that they do, you'll need to treat them with respect and kindness.

Bear in mind that someone who doesn't understand computers can still be quite intelligent and capable in other areas; talking down to a client is a bad idea! The client also trusts in your integrity to solve the problem in the most efficient and cost-effective manner possible, and to return their machine and data uncompromised.

Finally, and most importantly, you should cultivate a good troubleshooting methodology. It's difficult to give you a specific checklist, but the following guidelines should help:

- Identify the problem.

  - Question the user and identify user changes to the computer and perform backups before making changes.

- Establish a theory of probable cause (question the obvious).

- Test the theory to determine the cause.

  - Once the theory is confirmed, determine the next steps to resolve the problem.

  - If the theory is not confirmed, re-establish a new theory or escalate the problem.

- Establish a plan of action to resolve the problem and implement the solution.

- Verify full system functionality and, if applicable, implement preventative measures.

- Document findings, actions, and outcomes.

→ **Note**

You should be familiar with the six steps of the troubleshooting theory for both real-world application and the CompTIA A+ exams.

Don't forget that often the client will be there with you, hanging on your every word. Explain the steps you are taking to configure a new system, or to repair damage and recover data from hardware failure or malicious software. When backing up data prior to working on a system, err on the side of caution; make your best effort to determine which data is vital to your client and to their business, even if they are vague about what data needs to be protected. Try to give them realistic expectations of what you likely can or cannot do, so that the outcome is a pleasant surprise rather than a bitter disappointment.

✔ Hint

Ideally, for the lab exercises in this chapter, you should have a partner play the role of the client while you play the role of the PC tech. Work through the scenarios in a live, person-to-person role-playing of each situation, just as if it were real. If you are working in a classroom setting, try to work with different classmates through each of the different scenarios, and try to spend time playing the client as well as the tech.

 30 MINUTES

Lab Exercise 27.01: Scenario #1: Computer Obsolescence and Expense of Replacement

An independent salesperson for a multiline musical instrument dealer walks into your shop carrying a weathered laptop case. He lays the case on the counter and asks simply, "Is there anything you can do?" You open the case to find a late-1990s model IBM ThinkPad. You open the lid on the ThinkPad and see a semicircle indentation and spider-web cracks all across the screen. The LCD panel has been completely smashed!

As the expert in this situation, you have to make some decisions about what would ultimately be the most timely and cost-effective solution. You then have to explain your recommendations to the client carefully and respectfully, as either solution will most likely be costly and therefore stressful for him.

✔ Cross-Reference

Before you work through the role-playing scenarios, go back and re-read Chapter 27 in *Mike Meyers' CompTIA A+ Guide to Managing and Troubleshooting PCs*.

Learning Objectives

This exercise will test your ability to stay cool in the face of a concerned client, even as you may have to deliver news that the client doesn't want to hear.

At the end of this lab, you'll be able to

- Assess the damage and back up the client's data

- Convey the options available to the client

- Provide a recommended solution to the client

Lab Materials and Setup

The materials you need for this lab are

- A partner or classmate to play the role of the client (if you don't have a partner, you can still work through the scenario and complete the Lab Analysis Test at the end of the chapter)

- A notepad or computer-generated "trouble ticket" to simulate the practice followed in many computer support organizations

- Optional: A demo machine and/or Internet access, to re-create the scenario and research options on vendor Web sites and tech forums

Getting Down to Business

To begin, have your partner read the Client section that follows. You will then read the PC Tech section and use the specifics to analyze the situation and recommend the best course of action. Sit down and work through the scenario with your partner. If possible, use the Internet or demo machines to make the scenario role-playing more valid.

CLIENT:

You are an independent salesperson for a multiline musical instrument dealer and spend about 20 days a month on the road. You use the laptop to keep all of your customer data and product information up to date. You were finishing up a particularly busy week when you fell asleep with the laptop on your lap. You placed the laptop next to your bed in the hotel only to step on it in the middle of the evening. Your entire business relies on the information contained in the computer, and having it down, even for a short time, is going to create problems.

Along with the time-critical issues, you are also an independent salesperson and self-employed— you pay your own travel and lodging expenses, health benefits, and life insurance. A costly repair or replacement was not in your planned budget. You do know that working with a dial-up connection to the Internet in hotels and using floppies to transfer files between your laptop and your home machine (when you're there) is becoming cumbersome.

PC TECH:

As the technician, you are going to analyze the laptop and quickly recommend that the hard drive be backed up immediately. Using a laptop IDE harness and duplicating the hard drive to a volume on the shop data server, you can alleviate the customer's concern that all his data will be lost.

You know that the machine is over six years old, and that the replacement screen and labor to install it are probably going to cost a fair amount. You use the Internet to research replacement LCD screens and try to estimate the overall cost of the repair. Not only is it expensive, the availability of the screen is backlogged over three weeks. It is also a good bet that other components in the machine will begin to age and fail even if the screen repair is warranted. The laptop does not have wireless access, there is no USB, and the CD-ROM drive is just that, a CD-ROM drive!

Your job is laid out before you. You need to discuss the options of repairing the current machine, warts and all, or having the client upgrade to a more modern laptop.

30 MINUTES

Lab Exercise 27.02: Scenario #2: Hardware Failure, or I Can't See Anything!

One of the marketing analysts in your company calls the help desk and complains that he's unable to get his monitor to work. He arrived this morning and the computer just never booted. There's a mission-critical presentation on this system that is due to be presented today at 2:00 P.M. It's now 1:00 P.M. and nobody has returned his call, even to say that his initial request was received! The analyst storms into the IT department and demands some assistance. You look up from your screen just in time to see your supervisor and the analyst barreling toward your cubicle. Your supervisor asks if you will accompany the analyst to his department and see if you can figure this out.

In cases such as this, the tech's job is not only to troubleshoot the problem and provide a solution, but also to provide customer service and present a good image of the IT department to other employees. As the expert in this situation, you not only have to solve the issue—you must also make your best effort to diffuse the agitation of the anxious analyst.

Learning Objectives

The plan is to have a classmate play the role of the client, and you to play the role of the PC tech. This exercise will give you a great opportunity to display not only your tech skills, but also your professionalism in a tough, time-crunch situation.

At the end of this lab, you'll be able to

- Analyze the problem with input from the client
- Diffuse the frustration of the client
- Provide a complete solution

Lab Materials and Setup

The materials you need for this lab are

- A partner or classmate to play the role of the client (optionally, if you do not have a partner, work through the scenario and complete the Lab Analysis Test at the end of the chapter)
- A notepad or computer-generated "trouble ticket" to simulate the practice followed in many computer support organizations
- Optional: A demo machine or Internet access to re-create the scenario and research options on vendor Web sites and tech forums

Getting Down to Business

To begin, have your partner read the Client section that follows. You will then read the PC Tech section and use the specifics to analyze the situation and recommend the best course of action. Now sit down and work through the scenario with your partner. If possible, use the Internet or demo machines to make the scenario role-playing more valid.

CLIENT:

You arrived this morning and started your normal routine: You dropped your briefcase in the corner of your cube, carefully placed your coffee on the file cabinet (away from the computer), and pressed the power button on the computer. You exchanged a few pleasantries with your fellow workers and sat down to work on the finishing touches for the presentation you will be delivering at 2:00 P.M. today, only to find a completely blank screen. You attempted to reboot the computer, and verified that the power light was lit on the monitor (you do know *that* much about computers). But it was still a no-go!

You placed a call with the help desk and tried not to panic. Some friends invited you to lunch, and you joined them with the hope that the IT department would visit while you were gone so that you could return to a working machine. When you returned, nothing had been done!

You are a little tense, but you know that you are at the mercy of the IT group. You head down to the IT department and visit directly with the support supervisor. He introduces you to one of the techs, who is now traveling to your desk with you. The only thing you can remember doing differently was authorizing an Automatic Windows Update last night as you were leaving.

PC TECH:

Well, you've certainly been here before—a critical situation with severe time constraints, but now it's 1:20 P.M. and the analyst is very tense. You arrive at the analyst's desk and have him run through the routine that he followed when he arrived this morning. You ask if anything has changed since yesterday when the machine worked. You then run a check of the obvious diagnoses and troubleshooting steps.

✔ Hint

It is imperative that you keep detailed records of the diagnosing and troubleshooting steps. If you have set items that you check first (remember: simple to complex), then you will perform a quick check of the power lights, power cord connections, monitor connections, and whether the monitor settings menu is accessible, enabling you to rule out simple items that may have been overlooked in a time of stress.

If none of the simple solutions appear to work, you have two issues on your hands. One is that you need to get the system back up and running, and the other is that your client has a big presentation due in 30 minutes (yes, it took 10 minutes to check the simple items, so it's now 1:30 P.M.). You know that your organization has all of the employees save their documents to Documents, which is mapped to the server to facilitate backups. You have the analyst log on to a coworker's machine, access his Documents folder, and fine-tune his presentation with 10 minutes to spare.

You send a calmer analyst to the meeting, complete the analysis of the system, and perform the required repairs. Record the additional steps you would take to complete this trouble ticket. How would you communicate your findings with the analyst? Share the results with your instructor.

 30 MINUTES

Lab Exercise 27.03: Scenario #3: What Do You Mean, a Virus?

You're just finishing up lunch when one of your neighbors walks into your shop with her family computer under her arm. She knows you from the neighborhood, and has heard that you know a fair amount about computer systems (I hope so, since you are working in a computer shop!). She asks if you can take a look at her system.

You ask what seems to be the problem, to which she responds, "It seems to be running really slow. We can't find some of the documents and pictures we used to have, and every time we try to access the Internet, it kicks us off!"

You recommend that she return to whatever she was doing and leave the machine with you; it just so happens that your schedule is open this afternoon, so you should be able to take a quick look at the system. You ask if there are any passwords you'll need, and the client responds, "No, we don't worry about passwords." You fill out a trouble ticket with the contact information and let her know you'll be in touch with her shortly.

Learning Objectives

Viruses are a simple fact of life in today's computing landscape, and any tech should be able to both remediate existing virus infections as well as take preventative measures against future infections. It's sometimes tempting to treat customers as though their virus infection serves them right, but you have to maintain your professional demeanor in these situations, as you'll come across a lot of them.

At the end of this lab, you'll be able to

- Analyze the machine to determine if it exhibits the symptoms the customer has indicated

- Perform routine maintenance and optimization

- Make recommendations to the client for the upkeep of her machine

Lab Materials and Setup

The materials you need for this lab are

- A partner or classmate to play the role of the client (optionally, if you do not have a partner, work through the scenario and complete the Lab Analysis Test at the end of the chapter)

- A notepad or computer-generated "trouble ticket" to simulate the practice followed in many computer support organizations

- Optional: A demo machine or Internet access to re-create the scenario and research options on vendor Web sites and tech forums

Getting Down to Business

To begin, have your partner read the Client section that follows. You will then read the PC Tech section and use the specifics to analyze the situation and recommend the best course of action. Now sit down and work through the scenario with your partner. If possible, use the Internet or demo machines to make the scenario role-playing more valid.

CLIENT:

The computer you are dropping off to the shop is the family computer and is used by all the family members—two teenagers, you, and your spouse. The machine is constantly online, using a high-speed cable Internet connection, and there are tons of music files, pictures, and games stored on the hard drive.

You are not completely computer savvy, so if asked by the tech, you respond that you do not know if there is any antispyware or antivirus software installed, although it's possible that the kids have installed something. All you know is that the machine is running slowly, you have lost some documents and pictures that you wanted, and the machine will no longer connect to the Internet.

When you drop the machine off at the repair shop, the tech attempts to send you on your way, but you would like to see what he is doing and possibly learn how to make the system run better. You are fairly insistent, and finally work out that the tech will walk you through everything when you return.

PC TECH:

You set the system up on your test bench and boot into Windows XP. The system does take an inappropriate amount of time to boot and load all of the programs (you notice there are a large number of items in the system tray, but it is surprisingly devoid of an antivirus icon). You take a quick note of the version of XP and notice that no service packs are installed, so it's a good bet that Windows Updates has not been running either.

You check Device Manager and Event Viewer to verify that there are no specific hardware issues; everything seems to check out there. You then run Disk Cleanup—which uncovers over 4 GB of temporary Internet files—and then Defrag, which indicates that the disk is fragmented. It is a 40-GB hard drive that is almost filled to capacity, so Defrag is probably not going to run. Finally, you double-check whether any antivirus/antiadware/antispyware programs are installed, and find nothing.

✔ **Cross-Reference**

Refer to Lab Exercise 26.03, "Cleaning and Protecting a Client's Computer," for more information on how to clean up a machine that appears to have no specific hardware problems causing issues, but merely an accumulation of junk files, adware, spyware, and viruses.

You contact the customer and recommend that she return to the shop to discuss your recommendations for the machine. You still do not know if the lost files are recoverable, but you know you'll have to work through the other problems before you get there.

 30 MINUTES

Lab Exercise 27.04: Scenario #4: No Documents, No E-Mail, and I Can't Print!

You arrive at work bright and early at 7:00 A.M. to find several voice mail messages blinking on your phone. You are one of the desktop support specialists at a large financial institution, and you usually make a point of arriving early to catch up on some of the studying you have been doing to pass your next IT certification exam. However, it looks like you will have to put this on the back burner for today. You check the messages, and it appears that the entire proposals department is in already, working on an investment proposal for a prominent client. The messages are frantic requests to fix the computer systems in the proposals department. Apparently, none of the computers are able to access the documents the team has been working with all week; they could not e-mail their concerns and the network printer is down!

You have an idea what might be happening, but you are going to drop by the proposals department and check some of the individual machines before you make a rash decision. You close your textbook, and walk over to the proposals department.

Learning Objectives

Staying cool in high-stakes situations is the hallmark of a true tech, so look at this lab as an opportunity to improve your troubleshooting skills in the face of pressure. At the end of this lab, you'll be able to

- Verify that this is not an isolated problem with one or two machines

- Diagnose and troubleshoot from simple to complex, and record your findings

- Follow proper procedures to escalate the trouble ticket

Lab Materials and Setup

The materials you need for this lab are

- A partner or classmate to play the role of the client (optionally, if you do not have a partner, work through the scenario and complete the Lab Analysis Test at the end of the chapter)

- A notepad or computer-generated "trouble ticket" to simulate the practice followed in many computer support organizations

- Optional: A demo machine or Internet access to re-create the scenario and research options on vendor Web sites and tech forums

Getting Down to Business

To begin, have your partner read the Client section that follows. You will then read the PC Tech section and use the specifics to analyze the situation and recommend the best course of action. Now sit down and work through the scenario with your partner. If possible, use the Internet or demo machines to make the scenario role-playing more valid.

CLIENT:

You are the Chief Financial Officer (CFO) for this large financial institution. You have asked your entire team to come in today at 6:00 A.M. to finish up an investment proposal for a high-profile client. Everybody was on point, but as soon as things began rolling, a number of your staff appear at your door: "The network is down!"

They inform you that they have left numerous messages with the IT department, but you do not expect anybody to be there until 8:30 A.M. or so. Just as you are preparing to call the Chief Information Officer (CIO) at home, one of the desktop support specialists arrives on the scene.

You ask the desktop support specialist if they are up to the challenge of determining the cause of the outage and, if so, whether they have the authority to complete the tasks involved to get the network up and running again. The specialist seems like a sincere individual, so you ask them to perform the initial investigation and report to you as soon as they have a handle on the situation.

PC TECH:

This issue is going to challenge you on a professionalism level more than it will challenge you as a technologist. You should run through some quick checks of the various computers in the proposals department. Check the physical connections and log on to a few of the machines to verify that the network connectivity is down.

As soon as you can verify that the entire department is down, make sure you communicate with the CFO to apprise them of the situation. This is a case of escalation—you need to get your network administrators online and have them troubleshoot the network. You have checked a few machines in other departments to verify that there is network connectivity in the building, and it is only the proposals department that is down.

You assure the CFO that you're on the issue, and will inform them when the network admin is onsite. You then make a call to your friend, who just happens to be one of the network administrators; she is only a few minutes from the office, and tells you to hang tight and plan on joining her in the switch room. You're going to have an opportunity to work the issues through to the resolution. Don't forget to update the CFO!

Lab Analysis Test

1. Write a short essay summarizing the problem, discussion, and solution of the smashed laptop screen from Scenario #1.

2. Write a short essay summarizing the problem, discussion, and solution of the nonfunctioning monitor from Scenario #2. Be sure to include details on handling the analyst's stress level and frustration with the IT department.

3. Write a short essay summarizing the problem, discussion, and solution of the slow machine and Internet connection problems from Scenario #3. Be sure to include details on the steps and updates you would recommend that the client authorize.

4. Write a short essay summarizing the problem, discussion, and solution of the network outage in Scenario #4. Be sure to include details on the steps you would take to escalate the issue to the proper individual, the documentation paper path, and communication with the CFO.

5. Write a short essay describing the six steps included in the troubleshooting theory. List these steps in order and discuss the importance of each.

Key Term Quiz

Use the following terms to complete the following sentences. Not all terms will be used.

CFO

document

FRU

obsolescence

question

theory of probable cause

trouble ticket

troubleshooting theory

verify

1. There are six steps to the _____.

2. You should always _____ the repair after you verify full system functionality.

3. A(n) _____ is any spare part you bring with you to help you complete the repair.

4. After you establish a(n) _____, you should always test.

5. A(n) _____ is a computer-generated report that usually includes contact information, the problem description, and the problem solution.

Index